OLD HOUSES

GEORGE NASH is currently teaching shelter design at Vermont Institute of Community Involvement and lives with his family on a run-down hill farm that he is slowly rehabilitating. Several years after he graduated from Wesleyan University with a degree in English, he found himself restoring to useful life a derelict old house in northern Vermont and since then he has worked as a carpenter, contractor, housing consultant, and homesteader.

OLD HOUSES

PRENTICE-HALL, INC., Englewood Cliffs, New Jersey 07632

A SPECTRUM BOOK

A REBUILDER'S MANUAL by

GEORGE NASH

Illustrations by
Jill Lindenmeyer
Photography by
Joe English

Library of Congress Cataloging in Publication Data

NASH, GEORGE (date).
  Old houses, a rebuilder's manual.

  (A Spectrum Book)
  Bibliography: p.
  Includes index.
  1. Dwellings—Remodeling.   I. Title.
TH4816.N36 1980   690'8.   79–12986
ISBN 0–13–633883–6
ISBN 0–13–633875–5 pbk.

Old Houses: A Rebuilder's Manual by George Nash © 1980 by George Nash

A SPECTRUM BOOK

10 9 8 7 6 5 4 3 2

Printed in the United States of America
Editorial/production supervision
  by Norma Miller Karlin
Interior design by Peter Bender
Page layout by Martin Behan
Cover design by Jack Bratman
Cover photo by Donna Elberg
Manufacturing buyer: Cathie Lenard

PRENTICE-HALL INTERNATIONAL, INC., *London*
PRENTICE-HALL OF AUSTRALIA PTY. LIMITED, *Sydney*
PRENTICE-HALL OF CANADA, LTD., *Toronto*
PRENTICE-HALL OF INDIA PRIVATE LIMITED, *New Delhi*
PRENTICE-HALL OF JAPAN, INC., *Tokyo*
PRENTICE-HALL OF SOUTHEAST ASIA PTE., *Singapore*
WHITEHALL BOOKS LIMITED, *Wellington, New Zealand*

To Russell,

who taught me to slow down and enjoy

CONTENTS

PHOTO CREDITS

All photographs by Joe English, except as noted below:

Elaine Conklin: Pages 66, 67
Jon Gregg: Pages 123, 126, 129, 130
Richard Mahoney: Pages 13, 69, 87, 215
George Nash: Pages 1, 24, 51, 58
Jane Nash: Page 204
Dennis Scannell: Pages 171, 287
Gregory Slocum: Pages 70, 329, 334
Diana Smith: Frontispiece; Pages 8, 337, 339
A. Van Swearington: Pages 27, 29

ACKNOWLEDGMENTS

I would like to thank the following, as well as many other friends and neighbors, for the help, ideas, learning, patience, and inspiration without which this book could never have been written:

To my wife, who kept the fires burning and the household together during a long winter; to Dai, whose old place was the beginning; to Susan for a late-night phone call; to Bill Coley for the connection; to Gloria Stern for the encouragement; to Dennis for his example as well as his photographs; to Sue and Van, Trim and Elaine, Bill and Lisa, Dick Mahoney, Jon Gregg, and the many others who supplied not only photographs but good advice.

Acknowledgment is also gratefully made for permission to reprint excerpts from the following:

Allen R. Foley, *What the Old Timer Said* (Brattleboro, Vt.: Stephen Green Press, 1971), pp. 18, 27, 39. Reprinted by permission of the publisher. Copyright ©1971 by Allen R. Foley.

Kahlil Gibran, *The Prophet*, pp. 31–34. Reprinted with permission of the publisher, Alfred A. Knopf, Inc. Copyright 1923 by Kahlil Gibran; renewal copyright 1951 by Administrators C.T.A. of Kahlil Gibran Estate and Mary G. Gibran.

J. Frederick Kelly, *The Early Domestic Architecture of Connecticut* (New York: Dover Publications, 1963), pp. 1–2. Reprinted by permission of the publisher.

"Woodworker Ching." Reprinted from B. Watson, trans.: *Chuang Tzu: Basic Writings* (New York: Columbia University Press, 1964), by permission of the publisher.

OLD HOUSES

> . . . this square home, as it stands in unshadowed earth between the winding years of heaven, is, not to me but of itself, one among the serene and final, uncapturable beauties of existence: that this beauty is made between hurt but unvincible nature and the plainest cruelties and needs of human existence.
>
> [James Agee, *Let Us Now Praise Famous Men*]

At the Threshold:
Why buy an old house?

What is it about old houses? What strange spells do they cast, so that an otherwise perfectly rational human being is compelled against all sanity and sense to commit large amounts of money, time, and ultimately, himself to its rebuilding? Surely it cannot be a matter of mere economics. Even with low purchase price, an old house, when all the costs of remodeling are finally tallied, will cost as much as, and possibly more than, a comparable new house. Is it then a matter of aesthetics, the charm of a bygone style? The contrasts between the developer-assembled "product" of today and a house built by individuals in an era when things were still done by hand is obvious. But it is possible to build a copy of a traditional house, complete down to the last details of the woodwork, without the inadequacies of plumbing and wiring that plague their prototypes.

The root of the aesthetic is in the perception of beauty, and this perception, in turn, touches upon a spiritual dimension. Like woodsmoke from the cooking fire that has worked into the plaster and fiber, the very walls of an old house have absorbed something of the spirit of its inhabitants, so much so that it seems to live a life of its own, breathing in slow and subtle rhythms of shifting lines and weathering wood. Like all living things, a house represents the attainment of a delicate equilibrium, a precariously maintained and constantly changing relationship to time, the seasons, and its people. It responds to the care its families give it; growing, changing, adding windows, doors, porches, sprouting sheds and dormers in season. And when its people leave, it begins to die. Up here in the North Country a house does not remain vacant very many winters before it begins to sag, slip, and ease itself back into the soil from which it was so laboriously raised. The process occurs with a grace, beauty, and terrible simplicity. The tilt and sag of the walls, the weathered shades of clapboard and peeling paint, the tired angles of the roof seem to give mute expression to the ebb and flow of the lives once harbored within. Sitting quietly, listening, you can hear and feel their reverberations.

There is something deeply satisfying about bringing back to useful life an old abandoned house, rekindling the fires, and immersing yourself in the grain and texture of an earlier way of building and living. Such a house is a testimony to a time when form and function complemented each other, attaining fulfillment in a humble austerity of appearance which yet reveals a depth and beauty of spirit that has been left behind in our heedless rush into the future.

Rebuilding is an act of resurrection, of both the house and its owner. It is a profoundly spiritual as well as physical undertaking. Thus you, the would-be rebuilder, survey your ramshackle empire with a mixture of pride, anxiety, and not a little awe. If you are truly lucky or perspicacious indeed and have purchased a structurally sound house, the repairs and the drain on your financial and moral reserves will be minor and the results immediately gratifying. There is no faster or simpler way to lift the spirits than a new coat of paint or cheerful wallpaper applied over a dingy wall, a window added to bring light into a gloomy corner,

or old floorboards refinished to a glowing and time-warmed luster. You can go as far as your imagination and budget allow in this direction. Essentially the work is free from the pressures of structural necessity. The house may not be everything you always wanted, but at least it is livable.

Very few people who buy old houses, particularly those with limited means searching for that ''handyman's special'' (real estate agent's euphemism for crumbling disaster), have such good fortune. Obviously one of the ostensible reasons for buying an old place is low purchase price.

It should be equally obvious that the price is a function of either the neighborhood or the condition of the place. How *much* work it may need is the crux of the matter. You hope the repairs can keep pace with the cash flow. No matter how astutely you examine the structure for salient defects, others will be found. It is quite likely that you will discover not only rotting beams but also window sills eaten away clear down through the sheathing boards, a roof as watertight as the old pail used for target practice out back, and a torrent deep enough to float a river raft pouring through the foundation wall every time it rains. You will soon discover that, as bad as you thought the place might be, it's actually much worse. Your original estimate of time and money needed to restore it to bare livability will increase by a factor of three. This money will disappear into largely invisible, and therefore very ungratifying, structural repairs. And winter will be coming on early this year.

Of course you probably knew all this at the outset, knew of course that the place really was in terrible shape even as you were poking your finger through the dry-rotted beams and telling yourself, yes, there will have to be some minor repairs here and, yes, perhaps the cracks in the foundation wall need some patching, or is it pointing? And of course that ghastly linoleum on the walls will have to go, but the plaster seems sound enough, just a coat of spackle ought to fix it up fine. So strong is the spell of the old place that you simply ignore the obvious, locking your reservations and sense into a closet in the back of your mind even as the real estate agent is crossing his fingers and thanking his stars for city slickers. And so you proceed to sign not only a mortgage but body and soul, wife and children, over to an idea that will soon become a joy and a burden, a monster that devours every molecule of your time, money, energy, and spirit. Yet even when you discover that the only things keeping the place from blowing away are the holes in the walls and the weight of the mouse droppings in the attic, you wouldn't have it any other way. If you haven't decided to cash in your fire-insurance policy and move to a grass hut in Tahiti by now, then you might be the person for whom this book is written: a rebuilder—a person who is one part ability, one part inventiveness, two parts determination, and nine parts damn foolishness.

This book is a manual for the rebuilder. There is a difference between rebuilding and restoration. The aim of restoration is to simply put a house back into its original condition, to re-create the trappings and furnishings of an earlier form and style. This strikes me a little like collecting antiques or old bottles, which, whatever can be said for its merits, can be carried to ludicrous extremes. It is a question of personality I suppose, whether one wishes to live in a museum piece. In restoration, little consideration is given to the elements of antique design that may be impractical or totally unsuited to modern living. It is like donning the whalebone corset and bustle of yesteryear. Instead of a house that is a tool for living, and that reflects the priorities of a given lifestyle, some people force themselves to fit into the constraints imposed upon them by their houses. Like specimens in a glass case, they are fixed in total bondage to what may be a dead image. Eric Sloan may be thinking of such people when he cautions us in *An Age of Barns* that "the only thing about age is that it affords time for learning and for good deeds. If you do not learn or do good works, old age will do for you what it does for a dead fish, but slower."

The design of a house, in order to be successful (if success is the felicitous marriage of form and function), must derive from the needs of its occupants. Our lifestyle is not usually that of eighteenth-century pioneers or early nineteenth-century gentry. We do not consider it necessary to exchange our blue jeans for waistcoats and garters as we cross the threshold of our antique houses. It seems to me that antiques have real value only if they are useful as well as beautiful. Indeed a problem of our culture today is, so very little is produced that is beautiful as well as useful or durable. Where is the equivalent of Shaker furniture, designed for use, refined to a simplicity that elevated it beyond the merely useful? There was once a time when all tools were magical objects, when creation was itself magic, and the gulf between the spiritual and the profane less profound. It is in the sense of the first words of Goethe's Faust, as he rewrites the Book of Genesis: "In the beginning was the Word and the Word was the Deed," in that thought and deed are one and the same act, that old houses have achieved this ideal. They are spare and simple structures, born of necessity, that invoke and recapitulate the spirit.

This hierophany is a rare occurrence. Like the Gothic cathedrals of the late Middle Ages—which degenerated in design from a symphony of light and stone to the mere pursuit of elaboration and which collapsed as style surmounted the limits of engineering—an old house can often be a creature of architectural whimsey, a confection of style. The Victorian gingerbread house is an example of the enervation of a formerly robust style. An old house can also be prohibitively expensive to heat and afflicted with high ceilings and cramped rooms that reflect the age of collar and corset. Restoration is limited to working within the framework of these conceits.

As rebuilder, however, you are free to adapt the old to the new, to preserve or uncover the spirit while changing the form to suit your needs. This is a delicate process. You must take care not to do violence to the spirit, not to render it all but unrecognizable in the rush to remodel. You should instead try to divine the spirit of the place before you disturb its bones. Listen to its heartbeat and then try as best as you can to match yours to it. Only then begin to rebuild, to add your new wing, tear off an old porch, open new windows, walls, whatever you must do to adapt the house to the way you live. A house is never a monument. But, like a block of raw wood, it can be shaped by your creative energies, its grain released and polished to a flowing grace by imagination and care.

This book is designed as a reference manual and road map that will enable you to successfully tackle problems usually left to professionals. It should help you decide what to do, when to do it, how to finance it, and lastly, when to seek outside help if the task is too overwhelming. But beyond the technical it attempts to chart the psychic waters of the house as a personal resurrection, waters that are seldom clear or calm. Many a marriage, many a self-image, have run aground on the rocks of rebuilding. All too often the rebuilder is caught in a whirlpool of obsession, the work at hand becomes more important than the reason it is being done. You will have to keep a firm hand on the tiller of self as you navigate this passage.

You don't have to be an accomplished carpenter to rebuild your house. Because the project dilates over time, you can learn as you go, matching your skills to the job, stretching your abilities to the task. But this book does presuppose a basic familiarity with tools and an ability to use them. It also presupposes that you have the determination to tackle some godawful, difficult, and tedious jobs for the simple satisfaction of their completion. Rebuilding requires inordinate amounts of will power and perseverance for what may seem to be nebulous rewards. Fortunately we seldom realize how difficult the job can be; otherwise we might prudently turn aside and thereby miss the opportunity to test our mettle.

Because I live in rural, northern New England, my experiences are based on the problems of building in a rigorous and cold climate. A house that can survive in Vermont should prosper anywhere. Adapted to local climates, the information in this book should be of use in any part of the country. Those who are involved with rebuilding houses in the cities or suburbs may have to contend with problems of a bureaucratic nature that we rustics are not yet plagued with. In fact, local codes may prohibit you from doing much of your own work at all. In that case, the information in this book will at least let you know what to

expect when undertaking the renovation of an old house and also help you keep tabs on your contractor.

In reading through any number of carpentry or remodeling books in print today, it soon becomes apparent that although there are instructions on how to do most anything a person might ever conceivably wish to do to a house, almost without exception these instructions are predicated upon an ideal situation, where wood is uniform in thickness, walls are square, doors plumb, and foundations firm. Certainly one of the main advantages of new construction is that a building can be started right and kept with fairly close tolerances of the ideal. This may not seem all that important until you try to fit a rectangular sheet of plywood into a trapezoidal corner. In new construction the builder can proceed in logical and rectilinear fashion. The actual nature of the work is relatively simple and closely resembles the clear line drawings in the textbook. An already existing structure is not that simple or coherent. Not only do you have to deal with someone else's mistakes, but with an old house you confront large imponderables and profound dilemmas. An old house has settled and shifted through years of use, and often abuse, into a totally idiosyncratic entity. Walls lean, floors sag, major supporting beams are rotten or missing entirely. Utility systems, if they exist, are woefully inadequate, insulation is unheard of. You may as well take that framing text, with its precise drawings of modular systems, and its lucid prose, and use it to kindle the rubbish pile for all the use it will be as you ponder where to start unraveling this carpenter's nightmare of crumbling walls and patchwork roofing.

The typical house in need of rebuilding is often a century or more old and built with a heavy-timber post-and-beam framework that is as individual and arbitrary as its builders. You certainly won't find the answers to your questions in books. Fortunately, there is a large body of knowledge that is part of an oral and manual tradition, learned by, and passed on through, generations of carpenters. A goodly part of it is totally contradictory, being based on the personal experiences of whomever you might be talking to at the moment. Each situation requires a different approach and yields unique results. That is particularly so in a rural area where old houses are constantly being propped up and patched together by their inhabitants, who are often making do with the place their great grandfather's father hewed the beams for. Almost every old country carpenter has had direct experience either with his own place or a neighbor's, with the problems of preserving houses and barns from the ravages of difficult weather and hard years. Before the boom of the urban exodus brought the prosperity of new work to the backwoods, that was really all the work there was to do. That this pool of knowledge has remained largely inaccessible to the novice builder is no surprise. It is also unknown to more than a few modern trade-school carpenters as well. As building has progressed from what can be seen as a community art form, based on unarticulated but innately understood principles and designs, to a systematic ''industry,'' based on the greatest possible consumption of ''products,'' there has been a corresponding movement away from the use of native, minimally processed materials, such as wood and stone, to almost total reliance on mass-manufactured, imported high-technology substances such as plastics, artifical wallboard panelings, and sheetrock.

The old houses were a product of the constraints of the available materials and the limitations of the tools used to work them. Builders united form and function and thereby achieved the balance we find so resonant today. New houses are the products of almost unlimited choice. It seems as if imagination is always the victim when surface appearance becomes the goal. This is a false economy. As time and fashion have left the old houses to molder away in the back lots of raised-ranch developments, those who built and understood them have also been cast aside as relics of no importance.

A few of these relics are still very much alive today. Their knowledge is purely empirical, the direct result of an intuitively derived, common-sense approach to the problems of experience. Enough of these people are still working back in the hills, where time shambles along like a tired horse on a dusty summer road, so that by asking around you might find someone who's done it before, or has a fair idea of how to go about doing whatever it is needs must be done. With enough listening and asking and a good bit of thinking, you can generally manage to cobble up an answer for any problem, be it fixing a foundation, raising a pig, or straightening out your life.

I know a fellow who is a bridge between two cultures, a dairy farmer starved out of farming turned carpenter, father of eight children, who in his own words was "born too late for a big family and too early for birth control." He is old enough to be my father, and when he was my age he owned five-hundred acres of prime farmland. Now he owns six. The rest he sold off to a succession of wealthy newcomers from downcountry whose houses he built. What makes him so special is his keen awareness of what he has lost. It is a thing you can almost touch, an aura that creates an eerie counterpoint to the humor with which he customarily faces the world about him. We were wondering once how things had come to such a state, and he told me how in his father's time people got by. They didn't have much, but they didn't need much either. They always seemed to have enough. There was one tractor on the hill when he started farming, the other places all used horses. But when they came back from the wars they brought with them the itch to have some of those things they had seen out there. It was easy to sell a few cows and make a payment on the new pickup truck, a television set. The things his father had valued didn't seem as important. One by one they left the farm; the big money was in construction, and once they got a taste of it, by God, they were bound and determined to spend it. What they couldn't see was that they were spending their heritage, their spiritual

capital, as well. Once the cycle started it just seemed to run in one direction only. More and more, the old ways were tossed aside and simply forgotten, like the rubbish heap at the edge of the sugar woods.

Old houses are like my old friend, tossed aside and forgotten, gone by. They are a bridge between the ways of a slower and more harmonious time and our own shallow frenzy. In some ways, too, I hope this book is a bridge between these cultures. There is a new appreciation and respect emerging for the knowledge and experience of our forebears. When they die, a great treasure will die with them, a way of life that may have increasing relevance to our coming age of scarcity will be forever lost. The resurrection of old houses and the rediscovery of old ways may show us that there is more to the experiences of life than using them up and throwing them out.

> Consciously or unconsciously, man looks with satisfaction upon that which is substantially and enduringly built. It is primarily, or at least largely, this sense of sheer structural value which makes us admire the Pyramids, the temples of Greece, the mighty cathedrals of the thirteenth century. The same instinct infallibly communicates to every observer, even the most casual, the bluff and rugged strength of our old houses; and he who knows these ancient dwellings more intimately, perhaps through having been fortunate enough to live in one of them, is keenly and sensitively responsive to the security, the abundance of strength, which they embody. Their mighty frames of oaken timbers—which measure sixteen and even eighteen inches—have stood unshaken for two centuries or more. By comparison the frame house of today, built as it is of 2-by-4 studs which must be sheathed with inch boards to impart to the framework the practicable modicum of rigidity, seems pathetically, not to say ludicrously, frail. He who warms as he ought to the spirit of these old houses must revel in the well-nigh barbaric massiveness of their framing.

> The Colonists, hewing their homes out of the primeval forest, were never free from the menace of wolf, famine, or lurking Indian, there was neither time for anything non-essential nor place for anything flimsy and impermanent. The staunch houses which they built unconsciously expressed these circumstances in every timber of their tremendous frames. . . .

> [J. Frederick Kelly, *The Early Domestic Architecture of Connecticut*]

CHAPTER I

STRUCTURAL EVALUATION

"Do you see, Pooh? Do you see, Piglet? Brains first and then Hard Work. Look at it! *That's* the way to build a house," said Eeyore proudly.

[A.A. Milne, *The House at Pooh Corner*]

Most authors writing on the subject of buying old houses advise you to examine the property carefully for structural defects that would necessitate difficult and expensive repairs. They propose a checklist of some sort by which a prospective owner can evaluate the structure and compare it to others. The quite sensible advice is that if enough items appear on the wrong side of the list, you should look for another place. This approach assumes that there are other properties in the area for sale (which is not always the case) or that you have unlimited time to look around. It also ignores the possibility that the property you are considering is the only one you can afford to buy. The rational approach is certainly the most prudent way to buy an old house but is not always the road taken.

I remember quite well that leaden April morning, the front end of our ancient van clanking in protest as we climbed the steep washboard road through the forest where stale snow still clung to the dark places, climbed to where the woods shrank back from the dull, matted fields to reveal the ridges rolling away to the mountains at the end of the valley, like some rusty purple blanket that had lain out by the garden all winter. And there it sat, at the end of a sparsely graveled drive, dwarfed by a pair of towering cottonwoods. The clapboards had weathered to a delicate filligree of grain and fissure, which to us seemed the purest distillation of poetry. The front of the house leaned opposite of the back, the dormer slouched, the chimney crumbled even at a distance. The floorboards of the porch were rotted through. We walked into the kitchen, where plaster hung from the ceiling in leprous patches of decay. The floors tilted in so many planes, we were seasick looking at them. There were at least two feet of water in the basement, where the front wall of loose stones had collapsed inward. We bought the house that very day, for what to us seemed quite a bargain price— the very first place we saw, the very first day we went looking. And three years and many thousands of dollars later, I'm quite sure it could have happened again. The only difference would be that I'd know better what price to offer the real estate agent.

Some places are just *there*. In all of the universe, at that moment this is your particular place. No amount of rational consideration or temporizing will change the destiny that has already begun to manifest itself. There is some deep congruence between your innermost self and the molecules of the old house. You have no choice but to buy the place. You were meant for each other. This description is not in the least facetious. The experience is very real. With the surface of your mind you are telling yourself the obvious, that the place is in terrible shape, only a fool would buy it, and within, you are already setting the window boxes out on the sills, the tea kettle singing on the stove.

I do not wish to denigrate the usefulness of the checklist approach. You should at least know what you are getting involved with. The checklist may act as a filtering device, which weeds out all but the strongest vibrations. All houses are resonant with perturbations of the spirit, but not always on our personal frequency. The rational mind should be the cutting edge of the intuitive.

What should you look for? What are the symptoms of an unsound structure? Anything can be fixed if you are willing to spend time and money enough, but unless you are one of those people who have more dollars than sense, there are several major caveats.

First, disregard absolutely the external appearances. A coat of paint is a notoriously popular technique for raising the selling price while avoiding basic repairs. It's something like the undertaker's cosmetic act. I know of just such a place: Viewed from the roadside its neat white clapboards and trim black shutters give the impression of a perfectly quaint old farmhouse. Underneath that new paint, the foundation wall and the sills are suffused with rot.

Instead, take a close look at the actual shape of the house. Sight along the ridge of the roof. Does it sag noticeably in the middle? And look at the front and rear walls. Do they bow out or in? Do the end walls likewise tilt? These are sure indications of structural failure.

Figure 1–1 schematically indicates how the forces operating on a house can cause its collapse. A house is essentially a triangle. The stability of the structure depends on maintaining the integrity of each corner. This translates into proper bracing and uniform transfer of internal stresses within the building. Walls can be pulled in at the cost of great labor on your part. The tilt of a house can be a result of a settled or a collapsed foundation. Consider another property unless the place must be yours at all costs.

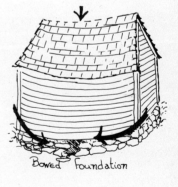

Bowed Foundation

1–1   How a house falls in

—Dead Load

While you are looking at the outside of the house, examine the roof. First determine what kind of roofing material was used and its condition. Moss-covered, crumbling cedar shingles that remain damp will have to be replaced. Asphalt shingles that have become swollen and brittle will also have to be removed and replaced. Try to ascertain how many layers of old roofing the deck is carrying. If there is only one existing layer, you may be able to lay the new shingles directly over the old. But if two or three layers are already in place, another layer would severely tax the rafters, which must carry not only the weight of the shingles and decking (dead load) but also the weight of the snow and the force of the wind (live load). If steel roofing covers your house, examine the seams for tightness. Over the years a metal roof will work itself loose by repeated contraction and expansion against the nails. The nail heads may have to be driven tight and sealed with a daub of roofing cement. Likewise, the vertical seams themselves may need renailing and cement. If the metal is rusted but still sound, the roof can be restored for years of useful life by painting with any of various metallic or asphalt-base roof coatings. Slate roofing lasts a very long time. Replacement of individual slates is possible. When the slate wears thin, the entire roof will have to be replaced. Re-roofing is a job that can easily be done by the owner-builder. The materials themselves are relatively inexpensive (between $25 and $30 per 100 square feet of coverage for asphalt or steel). Unless the previous owner has done so within the last ten years, plan to replace an asphalt roof within a few years. Asphalt roofing material has a short life, particularly under severe climatic conditions. Fifteen to twenty years is considered a reasonable life span.

While you are still poking about the outside of the house, look closely at the windows. The glass more than likely is in need of reglazing, which is time consuming but quite inexpensive. The putty between the glass and the wooden frame (sash) will probably have dried out and cracked, allowing water and wind to infiltrate around the glass. Examine the sash itself for rot, particularly at the bottom corners and the edge that rests on the windowsill. A rotten sash will fall apart when you attempt to raise the window. Check the windowsill also. Its top surface will frequently be rotten, particularly where it abuts the trim boards and the sash. If the rot is not too severe, it can be dug out and the holes filled with patching putty or cement and painted. It often happens that water has worked down behind the sill and into the boards that sheathe the wall. Water can also work behind the drip cap (at the top of the window) if it is improperly flashed (sealed by a layer of metal and caulking). The accumulated effect of this water, over the years, can cause considerable damage to the sheathing and even rot the framing and sills behind the walls. Extensive reframing and the rebuilding of the windows will be necessary, or you may find that it makes more sense to replace the old windows with new factory-built, double-glazed units. At around $150 to $250 each in 1978, that could add up to a considerable expense.

The sills are the part of the house frame that rests directly upon the foundation wall (or piers) and carries the weight of the house. Following the path of water down the wall, check the sills for external rot. A danger sign is extensive rot in the exterior sheathing boards that cover the sills. Poke the rotten areas or any suspicious places with an ice pick or jackknife to determine how deeply any rot has penetrated. If there is enough sound wood left to support the framing above (when less than half the thickness of a timber has rotted), the rot can be dug out and filled in. But where the rot has been so extensive that sections of the sill have actually collapsed or crumbled away causing the house above to settle, they will have to be replaced.

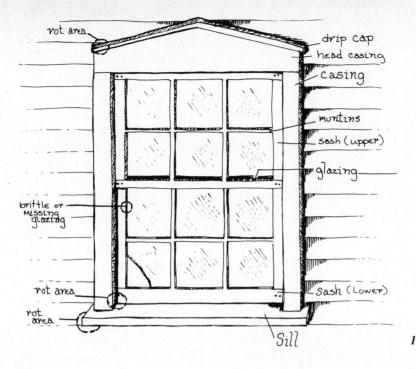

Labels on diagram: rot area, drip cap, head casing, casing, muntins, sash (upper), glazing, brittle or missing glazing, rot area, rot area, sash (lower), Sill

1–2   *Anatomy of window troubles*

Now is a good time to check the exposed part of the foundation wall for cracks and other signs of obvious settling. Notice how the ground slopes away from the wall. Ground water and water from the eaves should not run back against the foundation wall. Minor regrading can be done with a hand shovel. A major job will require a bulldozer. If you live in the far North or the far West, termites are not a problem, but in most other areas of the country they are a definite threat. Examine the sills of the house carefully for evidence of either a termite shield (a metal collar between wall and wood) or signs of infestation. Look for the characteristic tubes that these insects build from the soil up the foundation walls to edible wood. A termite-infested house is worthless. Unless the infestation is small enough to be eradicated by a professional exterminator, the foundation beams will soon be beyond repair. Northerners are not entirely secure from the threat of wood-chewing insects. Carpenter ants belie their name. They don't build anything but bore through wood instead. Be prepared to spend time with toxic chemicals tracking down their nests and tunnels, which can be anywhere in the structure of the house.

Any attached sheds or porches should also be evaluated. Often these were tacked onto the main structure at a later date in a lackadaisical manner or framed with inferior lumber. It may be best to remove them entirely. In any case they are likely to be rotten or resting on makeshift foundations, which are subject to heaving from frost penetration. The entire structure will frequently be thrown out of alignment. Notice in particular the junction between the addition and the main house. Improper caulking or sheathing may have allowed water to work into the walls, causing hidden rot.

If you can do it without having to clamber onto the roof, try to determine the condition of the chimneys. Look for obvious signs of decay, large cracks, or missing bricks. If you can get out onto the roof, examine the chimney more closely. Often the portion exposed to the weather will have to be rebuilt, as the mortar has crumbled away, leaving only a loose pile of bricks. Look for a tile flue liner. You should be able to see it projecting an inch or two above the top of the chimney from the ground. A flue-less chimney is a fire hazard and will have to be torn down and rebuilt. The size of the chimney itself is a good indication of the presence of a liner. A four- or six-brick chimney generally is unlined. More than six bricks per course indicates multiple flues or a very large single flue. As a rule, most older chimneys are unlined, so be prepared to replace them. An exception to the necessity for a flue can sometimes be made for a very massive fieldstone chimney.

If the external examination of the house has failed to daunt your spirits or reveal any gross defects, proceed to an internal. Sagging floors may well be the first thing you notice. These are not usually very serious and can be straightened with jacks and timbers with relatively little effort. For some people a certain amount of tilt contributes to the charm of the house. You should be able to keep your coffee on the table, though. Ignore the floors and proceed to the basement where the true state of the house will be revealed. As you descend the stairwell, note its condition: are the treads rotten, is it steep and narrow, does it tremble with each queasy step? Can it be negotiated without striking your head on a beam? It may well have to be rebuilt.

The cellar of an old house is the place of childhood terrors—of damp, nameless dread, of vermin and mold. Remember to bring a flashlight, as often there will be no subterranean lighting in working order. You will need it to examine the beams in any case. First, can you find the floor, or is it underwater? If it is, go no further. Look for another place unless you are prepared to sink a great deal of time or money into a new foundation. Try to do your house hunting in the spring of the year, as the water table will be highest then and any seasonal infiltration problems will be obvious. After a spell of dry weather, you may not discover a serious leakage until too late. Water in the basement is not always a guaranteed sign of foundation trouble. It can be caused by run-off from a heavy rainstorm saturating the ground outside the foundation wall and working through it. Run-off can be a problem with unmortared rock walls. External drainage and proper grading can help. Small amounts of water can be removed with a cellar pump. But in most cases water in the basement indicates the need for difficult and tedious foundation repairs.

An earth-floored cellar is likely to be damp in the spring, and there is not much you will be able to do about it short of covering it with a layer of crushed stone and a concrete slab. Look for high-water marks on the walls and cellar posts or signs of rot at the bottoms of these posts if the cellar seems otherwise dry. Rotten posts must be replaced. Now examine the foundation walls themselves. Do they appear sound and whole? If masonry or concrete, are they free from extensive cracks, which might indicate settlement? If there are cracks, have sections of wall bowed in or tilted? If the walls are loose stone, are they sound, or have they collapsed in part? Look for evidence of earth having been washed through the wall and into the cellar. Examine mortared stone walls for the same structural cracks that typify masonry walls. Sometimes an attempt may have already been made to shore up a collapsed section of wall by pouring a thin tapered wall of new concrete against it. This is rarely successful if nothing has been done about the exterior drainage of the foundation wall. If the outside problem is corrected, the shored-up wall will not have to be removed unless it, too, has settled and cracked. Any settlement or heaving of the foundation will likely mean replacement of the foundation wall in whole or part.

Here is where the demon must be squarely faced. How badly do you want this house? Can you find or afford another? Will you have the time and funds for the necessary repairs? A bad foundation must be fixed before any other work can be done on the house. If you replace a wall yourself, it is hard, dirty work, consuming a great deal of time with very little visible reward for your labors. If you hire outside help it will be expensive. No one will be able to give you an accurate estimate of the cost because the variables are too great.

If you think you can talk the agent down fifteen hundred or two thousand dollars because of the foundations, continue with your examination of the sills themselves. Check the major timbers for soundness and freedom from rot or insect damage. Dry rot, which is actually caused by a fungus nourished by exposure of the wood to moisture, results in soft, dark streaks in the wood, resembling seams of reddish charcoal. Powdery deposits with the appearance of sawdust are the work of carpenter ants or various species of bark beetles. They are a problem where logs have been used for floor joists and the bark left intact. If the sills are rotten, it is likely that the damage will not be confined to one area alone. Once again, use an ice pick to determine the extent of the rot. Replacing a sill is not as expensive or difficult as replacing a foundation, but it is nothing you would want to do for a hobby either.

As you grope about the murk, remember to look for a waste drain. This will be a cast iron or fiber pipe with at least a four-inch diameter that leads from a thicket of drain connections out through the foundation wall, preferably to a septic tank. Absence of a drain line indicates absence of indoor plumbing as well. Installation of a septic tank can add anywhere from $500 to $2,500 to the cost of your home. Sometimes the toilet drain is separate from the sink drain, which may be connected to a dry well or simply run out to a convenient ditch.

Other important items to look for include the furnace and hot-water heater and pump (if there is no municipal hookup). Turn on the furnace (if there is one) to see if it works. Likewise, open a hot- and a cold-water tap and note the flow for amount, pressure, and color. Taste the water. Is it drinkable? You should consider obtaining a sample bottle from a local health officer and having the water tested for bacterial contamination if you have any doubts about the source. What type of supply system delivers the water—spring, well, gravity feed, or pumped? What is the condition of the spring and of the pump itself? These and several other hard questions should be put to the real-estate agent. Before you leave the cellar look about for the service panel. This gray steel box is the heart of the electrical system. Is it an old fuse-type panel or a modern circuit-breaker kind? Unless the house has been recently rewired, it will most likely not have adequate capacity. The size of the box itself is a fair indication. The larger the box the greater its electrical capacity. Open it and find the main fuse or cut-off switch, which will be imprinted with its rating. One hundred amps is a bare minimum for today's electrical needs. Finally, find a bulkhead or other passage to the outside and note its condition.

At this point you will have gathered enough information to make a structural assessment. The foundations, sills, walls, and roof are major trouble areas. If any of them are in need of serious repair you should probably forget about the house. It is probably not worth the trouble and price. If, however, the house has passed this basic perusal, there are additional considerations before you sign the papers. If the spell of the place has already captured you, at least try to talk the price down.

You should also look around the upstairs rooms, noting the condition of the wall finishes and evidence of water stains. Determine if the walls will have to be replaced, the kind and number of bathroom fixtures, the condition of the floors. Are they the original or have they been layered over? What is underneath them? As you work your way up into the attic, check the stairwells for ease of access. Can you move a chest of drawers or grandma's old bed frame up those narrow, winding stairs? Can the attic be easily remodeled into living space? Look for evidence of insulation under the attic floorboards. Chances are there won't be any. Beware of loose, blown-in insulation in the walls. For reasons that will be made clear later, this material is susceptible to moisture and rot as well as settling. It may have to be removed and the house reinsulated.

Now go outside and ask the real-estate agent those hard questions. Ask him or her to show you the spring or other water source. Is the line buried below frost depth? If it is galvanized pipe, it will most likely be corroded and in need of replacement with plastic pipe, particularly in hard-water regions. Ask the neighbors if the spring ever runs dry. Drilling a well is a form of legalized gambling not for the weak of heart. You should inquire as to the use of the land above the water source. A septic field or outhouse above your spring or cattle pasturing in the stream that feeds your spring box will contaminate your water. Ask about the sewage disposal. Does the place have an existing septic tank? What is its size? A large family can overload a 500-gallon tank. If you need a septic system, consider a soil-percolation test. Many local zoning codes require one before any property can change hands or a new system be installed. Examine the soil. If it is a heavy clay, you will be faced with a very expensive leach field. Sandy soil will spare you the importation of gravel fill.

Before you contact a lawyer to negotiate the closing, find out if that lovely winding drive that leads to the house is a town road or not. There are several categories of roads in rural areas and this one may have been "thrown up." That means it is no longer an official town road, and the town therefore has no responsibility for its maintenance. Town policy toward these roads varies with locality and the condition of the road and is sometimes a matter of politics. Quite frequently the town will agree to put a road back into service if you will be living there full time. Sometimes you will have to shoulder part of the expense of fixing it up. You may even discover that although the town may be legally required to maintain your road, you will have to take the matter to court to enforce that requirement. Unfortunately, in some areas, road service can depend upon the length of your hair or the weight of your wallet. Contact the road commissioner or the selectmen to find out the status of your road; and get their assurances—in writing—that they will indeed maintain it.

If your road must be privately maintained, you will have to hire a snow-plowing service or buy a plowing vehicle yourself. In areas of no snow but heavy rains, you will have to regrade or culvert the road as necessary. Examine the existing road. Is it well-graveled and graded so as to drain water? Are there signs of washouts and ruts that may require a culvert to repair them? (The cheapest steel culvert is upwards of five dollars a foot.) Building a new road is about as expensive per foot as drilling a well. And what seems to be solid earth in August can be a car-swallowing morass in April.

Does the property have electricity and telephone service? Generally only the first 100 feet of power and the first three-tenths of a mile of phone service are free. Local regulations affect the cost greatly. If power must be brought in, are you willing to pay for it, live without it, or develop an alternative source? I had a chance to buy 100 acres and an excellent old house once for about $16,000. The hitches were a four-wheel-drive road over a mile long and a power-hookup cost estimated at $8,000. Any alternative energy system capable of supplying the needs of an average household is going to be very expensive.

That says something about either the wants and needs of the average household or the state of the art of home-power generation.

If power must be brought in, try to pin down the electric company to a realistic estimate. These figures are slippery and estimates are often higher than the actual cost. In any case, the wire will cost so much per foot and the poles so much each. You will also have to provide the hardware and the hookup from the weatherhead to the meter socket. The utility company generously provides the meter. Since the policy of each company varies, you may be able to save a significant part of the cost by doing or contracting some of the work yourself. Brushing out the right of way is a possibility; setting your own poles is another. If any misunderstanding does occur and you feel taken advantage of, you should take your complaint to the state regulatory agency.

If you have school-age children, you should also contact the local school board to find out how far you are from the school-bus route. While calling officials, find out about any restrictive zoning regulations, building codes, and the like. Inquire as to the regulations concerning the acceptability of alternative sewage-disposal systems, such as the Clivus Multrum or outdoor privies. Try to find out what kind of work you can and cannot do on your own place without a licensed contractor or inspection, a permit, or fees. Building codes are not in themselves an evil or a deliberately oppressive attempt to keep people at the mercy of the building industry. The original intent of building codes was to protect unwary purchasers from victimization by unscrupulous contractors using substandard materials. Unfortunately the codes enshrined the existing practice at the time they were written and very few administrators seem to have escaped embalmment along with them. The zoning administrator is not a fiend. If you approach her or him as a human being, the compliment will most likely be returned. In the rare case when you must deal with a bona fide cretin, there are several strategies to adopt. Ken Kern, author of the *Owner-Built Home,* has recently published a book outlining these strategies: *The Owner-Builder and the Code.*

Make one more phone call to set up an appointment with a local lawyer. Then go and visit the place again. Walk around and look at it. Sit under a tall tree and try to feel it as your place. Is it comfortable? Visit with the house. Sit in the front room and listen, try to hear its quiet talk of groans and rumbles, let the emptiness fill you, the dust of the world dancing before your eyes in the clear light of the afternoon.

That night read through a copy of Les Scher's *Finding and Buying Your Place in the Country,* to prime yourself for the appointment with the lawyer. Your lawyer should make sure that there is a clear title to the place—no undischarged mortgages, liens or attachments, or right-of-ways that could in any way hinder the sale or your enjoyment of the property. A policy of title insurance, or an abstract, should be furnished. Find out if the land is surveyed, or if not, who is to bear the cost? Even though it is not cheap, don't make the mistake of thinking that a survey is not all that necessary. A deed generally specifies x acres "more or less," to cover any margin of error. The land I own had remained an undivided parcel for over 100 years, during which time its owners were taxed on 100 acres. Before I acquired it, the parcel was surveyed. The results showed 68½ acres "more or less." As its former owner pointed out, "There warn't no rebate on taxes either."

The final consideration, the most pertinent perhaps, is, can you afford

it? What terms are available? What will be the monthly payments on the mortgage? Will the owner finance, or will you need bank financing? Will you have
a source of income to make the payments while you are working on the house?
The condition of an old house seems to vary in inverse proportion to the financial
liquidity of its prospective buyers. Even though it may categorically fail every
structural requirement mentioned above, it may also be all you can afford to
buy. Whatever the disadvantages, at least you can move in and begin acquiring

TABLE 1–1 Checklist For Rebuilding

CONDITION—COMMENTS

Item	Good (does not require any work)	Passable (needs work, but can wait)	Poor (needs major repairs, immediately)
1. Walls, roofing (check for bow or sag)			
2. Sills (rot or insect damage)			
3. Structural timbers, joists, framing			
4. Foundation (cracks, settlement, leaks)			
5. Cellar floor (type, water in basement)			
6. Roof (condition and material type)			
7. Windows, doors (rot, glazing, replace)			
8. Exterior sheathing			
9. Exterior trim, paint			
10. Attached structures (porches, sheds, etc.)			
11. Chimney and flue			
12. Landscaping, grading, rubbish removal			
13. Interior walls (type finish)			
14. Plaster			
15. Paneling and woodwork			
16. Stairs			
17. Insulation, type			
18. Kitchen, appliances			
19. Bathroom fixtures			
20. Water supply (source supply lines, pump)			
21. Plumbing system, waste lines, distribution lines, hot-water heater			
22. Electrical system (capacity and type, type wiring, number outlets, lighting fixtures)			
23. Heating system (type)			
24. Electricity and telephone hookups			
25. Outbuildings			
26. Land (number of acres, type, features)			
27. Access, private or town.			
28. Legal, title, survey			
29. Zoning regulations			
30. DOES IT FEEL RIGHT? (scale of 1–10)			

equity rather than paying rent. Don't delude yourself into thinking that rebuilding a house is cheap or easy. It will be a bigger job than you can imagine. Before you buy, make up a checklist (see Table 1–1) and use it not only to compare prospective properties but to organize your rebuilding priorities once you start.

Hiring a Contractor

Should you hire a contractor? Those of you who are not inclined either by temperament or pressures of economic necessity toward performing the actual physical labors of rebuilding your old house will probably consider hiring out all or part of the dirty work to a local contractor. You might feel that some jobs are best left to someone else with more experience; determination is not always the better part of valor. Time and money exist in a rough equilibrium. Your outside income may be great enough to pay for work that you would lose money on by staying home to do yourself. More on this subject later.

One of the perils of moving to a new area is that you have no base to compare the merits of a particular contractor against another. You won't know whose opinion to respect and whose to disregard. The longer you can live and work in a community, the less you will be on the defensive. You begin to build up a network of friends and neighbors whose advice can help you navigate the tricky currents of settlement. This is a powerful argument for renting a while before you buy in the area where you'd like to live. You will develop a sense of what houses are selling for and get a line on the range of properties for sale as well. You might even save several thousand dollars by buying directly from an owner rather than through a real-estate agent.

Begin by asking at the local lumberyards for the names of contractors and good independent builders in your neighborhood. But remember, the lumberyard will tend to recommend those with whom it deals in large volume, and the larger the outfit, the more you pay to support its overhead. Ask your neighbors who they think does reliable work. If you hear the same name mentioned by several sources, it's a fair bet you can trust that builder's work.

You may be able to get estimates from several bidders, but chances are that you'll have to decide on faith and what you've been able to glean from your advisors. Like anywhere else, there are honest people and knaves in the country, but the pressures of city life seem to select in favor of the knaves and even good folk must waver a bit. People work differently in the country. A man's* word is still good enough security for most business, and written contracts are rare and tend to be avoided. A man who gets work on his reputation may seem reluctant to give a bid. He'll say, "Oh, I guess that might cost you five or six thousand, depending on the weather and what we might run into behind that wall." If he's the right man, that is exactly what it will cost you. Typical of this is a fellow I know who in seventeen years of carpentering has never once been asked to bid a job. People hire the person, not the price.

---

*The use of "man" or any of the male pronouns is not intended to exclude women—even the relatively tradition-bound building trade is beginning to feel the influence of the women's movement. Today there are many women carpenters and contractors. Unfortunately, our language has yet to reflect felicitously this cultural change. The author merely wishes to avoid the inevitable awkwardness of "him and/or her" or the contrivances of the various nonsexist pronouns.

This system is changing of course. As more and more people move to the rural regions from the cities, the tight fabric of community and kinship that made it possible for this system of handshake and nod to work is wearing thin, in some places, unraveling. There are people who don't understand, or simply ignore, the unspoken rules. Lawyers and contracts assume an ever-increasing prominence, like shingle fungi on the trunk of a dying tree. The relationship between neighbors becomes codified into a legal document between client and contractor.

If you feel uncomfortable with this culture of easy understanding, if you are not at home in your judgments, by all means ask for competing bids and sign contracts. Remember though that a builder is apt to bid higher than he or she thinks the job should run in order to cover the unknowables of the occupation. Also, remodeling an old house contains so many variables that it is almost impossible to give an accurate bid. Any contractor forced to bid a firm price will make that a high one.

Be sure, however, that you discuss quite specifically with your contractor exactly what it is that you want him to do, signed contract or not. Make sure you understand each other completely. Most problems over bills are a result of a lack of communication. Explain whether your priority is saving money or doing it right. Discuss how right for how much money; then *trust* him. There is nothing an honest builder resents more than a client who is constantly checking on him, inspecting the job in progress, worrying out loud how much every step is costing. Do your inspection of the work after he's gone home for the day. Speak to him when his helpers aren't around or within earshot. Unless you have good reason, don't put him on the spot. A good contractor will save you money; he operates from a strong moral base and will give you every break he can if he feels that you trust and respect him. On the other hand he will feel no remorse about sticking it to you for every penny if he decides you are riding him too closely. This is particularly true of the old-timers who work by themselves with a helper or two; they are a fiercely independent and proud people with a soul as hard as hornbeam: they do not suffer fools gladly.

The worst situation to put yourself into is that of absentee owner. You will have little opportunity to check your sources, to locate that ideal honest person. There is something about being perceived as one of those ''rich bastards from downcountry'' that strikes a deep-seated chord of resentment, the same xenophobia that natives of the Third World might feel towards their former colonial masters. Because you are not his neighbor you set yourself up for exploitation. The process is seldom conscious; it springs from an innate class antagonism that arises whenever one individual works for another. It is different when a person works for someone he sees as struggling on the same level as himself. That's just trading favors. Most of us realize that life is not necessarily just and keep this rancor within formalized bounds. It is the well of humor and irony. But an attitude that may manifest itself as an occasional charging to your account of a hammer that broke or a sawblade that needed replacement can become much more serious as the perception of distance between contractor and client increases, both spiritually and geographically. This does not mean that you will get taken automatically. It's just a distinct possibility. The temptation to ''Yankee'' the city slicker often becomes too strong to resist. Anyone who works for another person feels entitled to certain bonuses as a fair due—the extra three or four 2×4s that he'll use to build himself a sawhorse for the next job are charged to your account without remorse. This percentage added to the operating costs is rationalized by the notion that "he can afford it." Where this attitude ends and outright dishonesty begins is a function of the moral consciousness of your contractor and his feelings about you as a fellow human being. Hours can be padded and accounts stretched. There are those who will do it if given a chance. If you must place yourself in the position of absentee inspector, avoid being your contractor's gravy ticket. Unless you trust him absolutely, do have a specific contract signed, sealed, and delivered. Ask for itemized weekly invoices and check through them carefully, set up your own account at the lumberyard you wish to use, and have him charge the job materials to it. You should receive the cash discount he would on his own account if the charges are paid by the tenth of the month. But if you use his account (which is much safer, as you cannot be left holding the bag) it is only fair that he receive the discount.

By reading through this book you should acquire a solid base for keeping up with the progress of whatever work you hire out. You should understand its logic and direction. Don't be afraid to ask your contractor the reasons for a particular operation. Avoid putting him on the defensive when you do, though; it is the tone that makes the difference between the interrogative voice and an interrogation. If you do think that he is doing something very wrong or otherwise taking advantage of you, discuss your feelings with him promptly. There may be an honest misunderstanding. He may not always know what he is doing either. If you feel that you have been absolutely fair and yet you have been given short shrift do not hesitate to inform him of your dissatisfaction and settle up with him then and there. A lot of ill will can be avoided by trying to stress the common humanity of each side. You both have to work for a living. And remember, it was you who were fool enough to hire him in the first place.

> The Old Professor tells a story of a Vermonter who was less than pleased with the work done for him by a local contractor, who enclosed the following note along with his check:*
>
> July 1, 1950
>
> *Mr. Nelson:*
>
> > *Inclosed find check as per your bill.*
> > *Your charge and services were both very unsatisfactory.*
> >
> > Very truly, etc.

Organizing Priorities

> A New York lawyer busy with the many chores in closing his place for the winter, interrupted his work to say goodbye to his neighbor at a time he thought appropriate for the farmer's schedule. It turned out, as it sometimes does with supposedly taciturn denizens of the hill country, that his neighbor wanted to talk, and after some exchange the lawyer said, "I'm sorry but I've got to go along. Have a hundred things to do."
>
> "You've got a *hundred* things to do?"
>
> "Well, perhaps not quite," the New Yorker replied, "but it seems that many."
>
> "Let me give you a piece of advice," said the Vermonter, "Do 'em *one at a time*." [Allen R. Foley, *What the Old Timer Said*]

---

*From Allen R. Foley, *What the Old Timer Said*.

A house is a physics equation writ large in a script of stone and wood. It proceeds in an orderly fashion, one link leading to the next. But sometimes, as with a knotted ball of string, we can easily find the free end and not work the tangle loose. In its simplest terms, a house overcomes gravity. The triangle of the roof is supported above the earth by walls that are anchored to it through the foundation. But because the framing of a house is never seamless, being broken by joints and nails, while the forces that operate upon its members are, stresses can concentrate at any number of the weak points. These places act as hinges, causing failure; the house sags and leans. As the static equilibrium of the ideal structure decays, the house inexorably moves from the vertical toward the horizontal until the triumph of gravity is complete. Your house is likely to be somewhere along this curve of accelerating decay. Reversing the direction of the curve is a question of knowing at which end to push.

A sound house needs a firm foundation, a good roof, and tight walls. No amount of renovation will compensate for a crumbling foundation. It makes absolutely no sense to remodel the interior of a house without first making sure that the house stands on solid ground. The lesson of the idol with the feet of clay would seem to be obvious, yet I know of more than one case in which this principle was completely ignored. I remember a house where the entire wall was reframed from sill to plate, but the foundation wall under it was left intact. The loose stone did not even extend below the frost line. The owners now enjoy the novelty of a constantly changing floor height, and cabinets and doors that open or close depending on the season of the year.

A foundation as solid as Gibraltar will not support a house with a leaking roof for very long. Water works its way into the timbers, leaving rot to pave the way for gravity. The skeletal remains of old barns collapsed into their cellar holes give mute confirmation of this activity. Finally, a house without tight walls is little better than an open shed. You may as well insulate the walls with dollar bills to save on heat.

As you make a list of the work to be done rebuilding your house, you will notice that that work tends to arrange itself into two major categories; *structural* work, which must be done immediately, without which the house is not safely inhabitable, and *cosmetic* work, which can be done as time and money allow. Which work fits which category is frequently self-evident.

I remember a day in June . . . the grass now deep and golden green, parts to let our van up the drive. Like an ark wallowing in the waves, we roll to a stop. Tired motor hissing, we stretch our cramped arms and legs in the warm sunlight. The cicada song fills the silence shimmering around us. In this strong light, the weathered grey clapboards show their subtle depths, the feathers of some huge dull bird. Key in hand, I remove the rusted padlock from the back door; no need, it wasn't hitched to the latch. We are home.

Later, while cooking dinner on the Coleman stove perched on an orange crate in the middle of a bare linoleum floor, we try to make up a list of our priorities, where and how to begin the metamorphosis of house into home. That night, as the rain pours through the ceiling, overflowing our meager supply of pots and pans, we move our sleeping bags to the highest corner of the floor and begin to get a fairly good idea . . . it is obvious that fixing the roof is in the first category. So is the hole in the foundation wall. The plaster dripping from the ceiling is only a cosmetic defect at this point.

Structural work is the starting point of a logical chain. For example, changing the foundation will affect any work done inside the house. Wall finishes will crack, doors and windows will stick or skew open, partitions and floors will go out of level and plumb. Also, structural work frequently results in the exposure of the vitals of the house to the elements. Thus your work schedule should be arranged to perform this kind of work during warm weather. Nothing is more conducive to an ulcer and frostbitten fingers than a house standing barelegged, jacked up on timbers in November in Vermont. Always allow plenty of time for structural work. It always seems to take longer than you figure since the links in the chain are never as clear as the metaphor; one muddy timber doesn't always connect to another. If you can only work part time, you will be lucky to rebuild a foundation in a summer. Plan to do the work of finishing off interiors during winter months after the house is footed and roofed. With the exception of replacing the exterior finish of a house, most cosmetic work is indoor work. Of course the realities of your life will not always fit very neatly into your schedules. Neither will the scheme of structural and cosmetic work always be so clear. It helps to visualize the range on a sliding scale. A chart can be drawn that will correlate the work with the seasons, time available, and estimated costs (see Table 1–2).

Table 1–2 suggests another loose correspondence: the ratio between input to output, or effort to satisfaction, is generally greater at the cosmetic end of the scale. That is a psychological factor that must never be underestimated. An unwholesome amount of simple drudge labor and great sums of money can be poured into a mud-filled foundation hole. When the job is finished and the hole backfilled after weeks of hard work, nothing has visibly changed. Of course you have the satisfaction of knowing that at least your house will stand safely and that whatever else you do rests on a firm footing. But it simply isn't *dramatic* enough.

TABLE 1–2   Planning the Work—Structural and Cosmetic

Time	Scheme	Item	Estimated Cost	Estimated Time	Climactic Scheme
N O W	S T R U C T U R A L C O S M E T I C	1. Foundation repair 2. Rotten framing repair, sills 3. Roof repair 4. Chimney repair			S P R I N G
S O O N		5. Sheathing, (only when rotten, otherwise leave for next year) 6. Windows and doors 7. Attached structures 8. Interior walls—gutting			S U M M E R
L A T E R		9. Rewiring 10. Replumbing 11. Insulation			F A L L
		12. Interior partitions 13. Refinishing interior surfaces 14. Cabinet work, fixture replacement 15. Refinishing floors			W I N T E R

The reward of hard labor comes in the satisfaction of being able to stand back and look at its results. There is a revitalization of the spirit that allows you to tackle the next job with renewed energy. As you spend increasing amounts of energy on these largely invisible repairs, you will feel a mounting exhaustion and gnawing despair. It will seem as if nothing has been accomplished. It is then that you need to stop a while and perhaps plant a flower garden, build a hen house, or tear down a rotten porch. Take a few days to clean up the rubbish pile festering out back. Changing the subject can give you needed psychic refreshment. Skirting the abyss of gloom and self-pity will take a great deal of support and understanding from your helpmate, right up to the threshold of total burnout. Focus on that day to come when the grass lifts its tentative length from the newly graded backfill and you can stand back, looking at the clapboards, newly stained, the enamel gleaming on the reglazed window trim and say to yourself, "Now, at last, it looks as if something has been done around here."

Rebuilding a house is a lot like giving birth. However it started, either quite by accident or like a divine spark of inspiration, you must then carry the increasing weight for a long and uneasy time; you wonder if this burden will ever be released. But in a moment, it all falls together: you are lost in an eternity of pushing, then there comes a great spasm of peace. The baby is born.

How to Rebuild and Stay Sane

A house cannot be experienced separate from its householders. Even if you contract out the entire renovation it becomes impossible to maintain any distance between yourself and it. Unless you hire an architect, approve the plans and leave for South America for the next six months (some people do this and are thereby diminished by the emptiness they build into their lives), you will find yourself inexorably eaten up by the idea of the house. It becomes all-encompassing, your womb. As we shall see, it can also become a tomb. At first the house is a welcome thing. You are full of energy, enthusiastic, and blissfully unaware of how much work actually lies ahead. You embrace the work, constantly measuring in your mind's eye where the curtains are to hang, where the bookshelves should go, the woodbox behind the big old iron cookstove. As the days wane and the nights grow sharp and clear, your horizons shrink. Getting the place closed in for winter becomes a consuming passion, a cancer that is rapidly occupying every waking thought. You sit down at the breakfast table and eat insulation. A rainy day is a personal insult from a malevolent god. You begin to understand how Sisyphus might have felt. You wonder why he just didn't let that rock roll right over himself. At night, lying in bed, your head is in the cellar jacking up a rotten beam, your spouse wondering where you are and why you never sent a postcard.

This obsession has a tendency to destroy family or interpersonal relationships. Whatever tensions already exist become exacerbated, like the scab on your knuckle that is constantly sluffed off every time you pick up a tool. Life becomes an incubator for a host of new and increasingly virulent strains of discord between you and your loved ones. The day comes when the woman turns on the man and accuses him of trapping her in a role. The charge is undeniable. The usual pattern is for the woman to take care of cooking meals, raising children, and household chores so that her mate is free to pursue the "all-important" work of rebuilding the house. She becomes his support system. He takes this for granted and explodes in frustrated rage the one night she asks him to cook dinner, to allow her a break from her routine. He forgets that it is her work that enables him to devote himself to his singleness of purpose.

Although cultural patterns are changing, most of us are the victims and products of our upbringing and tend to fall into role stereotypes. Girls were raised with dolls, boys with blocks. Women are conditioned to expect the man to know all about the hardware. Men assume that women are tailored for the household manager role. The man fixes a leaky faucet, the woman fixes dinner. Even couples who consider themselves "liberated" fall into this pattern. They

begin by invoking EFFICIENCY as an unfortunate evil. Because the male is often the stronger and more agile with tools and because there is so much to be done, he is the one who runs the chain saw while she stacks the firewood. He measures and cuts the boards and nails them into place. She pulls nails out of old boards, picks up the rubbish, and moves piles of building materials. He does the skilled labor and she is left to the menial tasks. After a while expediency becomes expectation. It is assumed that she will do those tasks in addition to her domestic duties, which are viewed as inconsequential. And hardly is there time taken to say thank you.

As the work increases and the days shorten, so do the resentments and tempers. The couple who can start off equally unskilled are at an advantage. A woman can learn to use a hammer as well as a man. A man can actually cook a dinner. Both can learn to use tools with equal skill. Flexibility is possible as brute strength is not the main component of intelligent carpentry. I know of one woman who wired and plumbed the entire house while her husband worked out to pay for the materials.

Most couples are not that well balanced. The care of children tends to complicate the equation. In most cases the man is definitely the one with the skills and the woman the one with the children. The time factor is an inescapable reality. It *really* is more efficient for him to do the work while she does the dinner. Ask yourself, what is more important, efficiency or your marriage?

For those living on the lower end of the economic ladder, time becomes of critical importance. If the male partner has to work at a full-time job to support the rebuilding as well as the household, he will be under a great pressure to accomplish as much as possible on weekends and the long weeknights of summer. As winter comes on, time telescopes like the days of a death-row inmate. The pressure tightens. Far less anguished is the man who is independently wealthy or the couple who have prudently saved enough to allow them to work on the house and nothing else. They can afford to be relaxed about their work roles.

The conflict between the need to make a living and the necessity of rebuilding soon acquires an interpersonal polarization. He has no time for his mate; her needs are an annoying interference with the important work that must be done. If she speaks to him about it or acts upset she is immature or emotional. She becomes an additional weight on his already overburdened back. The same is true for his family. The conflict accelerates, the fights grow in frequency and intensity, a snappish remark touches off a flood of anger and invective.

The argument degenerates into a vicious circle—a damned if I do, damned if I don't, bind. She accuses him of ignoring her needs, he says he is working off his butt for her needs. She says she doesn't need it that bad, and he says he certainly doesn't need any more of this. More than one relationship has been the casualty of a remodeling project. How do you avoid getting caught in this vise? The advice is easy enough to give but damn hard to implement. You can read the writing on the wall but not always know what it says.

To begin: You should sit down with your mate and try to state clearly what you expect of each other. Try to define the areas of responsibility and who will do what. My wife and I both started out with the idea that we could share the building and the housework. This seemed reasonable enough. I could be up on the scaffold nailing on the siding. She would be on the ground, cutting it to length. After a half dozen attempts at forcing that board to fit the measurement, I found my patience wearing thin and she was deciding that carpentry really wasn't all that interesting. We were both frustrated by our impatience. We knew that she would eventually learn how to use a saw, I only had a seven-year head start on her, but on-the-job training doesn't work when dark is coming on. She went and cooked supper. I cut the boards and nailed them myself.

That evening after I had done the dinner dishes we talked about it and decided that liberation is a matter of situation rather than role. You don't have to be a carpenter in order to be liberated. It is a question of reciprocity. A house is not built in a vacuum of time and space. The needs of daily life are not suspended during its construction. The labors required to support a household are every bit as important and as critical as those necessary to move walls or nail boards. A house is a vehicle for a higher purpose. We should build the house around our lives, to shelter and contain us, to aid us in achieving the things we have been living for, not to live for the building of the house. A liberated person tries to see how he or she can best utilize the resources and givens of personality and skills to harmoniously achieve the agreed-upon goal. They realize that they have a contract, between equals and with all aspects of the work given intrinsically equal value. The goal can be renegotiated if the contract proves unworkable.

It is a good place to start. But it won't carry you all that far. Constant vigilance will be required to keep from slipping back into those old roles, those comfortable habits, into self-righteousness, the feeling that one person's needs are less important than his or her partner's. You will know you are succeeding when your complacency is disturbed, when you feel tongue-bound and uncomfortable. You will have to keep the communications lines open; talk about things before they come to a head. Don't bottle up frustrations or let too much slide. Knowing when to let up or when to lean a little harder is a delicate balancing act. How successful you are at it is a measure of the strength and viability of your relationship. Ultimately and simply, you have to TRUST each other.

Touch home base. Remember why you are doing this. You are building the house as a means towards an ongoing end. It is not the end in itself. There are times when you should put your hammer down, say "to hell with it" and go out to dinner. Buy a bottle of wine, get drunk, go upstairs and make love

to each other. Learn to recognize the danger signs. Listen to your partner. Keep your sense of humor well oiled. Listen to your self, know when you need to stop. And stop. If you don't stop yourself, your body will. Do not ignore this advice. There is nothing sadder than a house that has devoured the souls of its people, or than the emptiness of waking up at night and looking at a stranger lying beside you.

> Better is a handful of quietness than two hands full of toil and a striving after wind.   [Eccles.:4:6]

> By letting go it all gets done
> The world is won by those who let it go.
> But when you try and try
> The world is beyond the winning.
>> [Lao Tzu–Tao Te Ching]

The Blitzkrieg or the Caterpillar:
Approaches to rebuilding

Short of tearing the place down to the ground and starting from scratch, what are some of the alternatives to untangling this Gordian knot masquerading as a would-be house? What is always the most efficient is not always the most practical. Rebuilding an old house can be a form of economic strangulation, even suicide; it can also be the only way you will ever get to own a house. If you are bled all at once you will likely die, but if the bleeding occurs at sufficient intervals you can continue bleeding for a long time.

For purposes of illustration, let us discuss the ideal: you purchase a worn-down, but not quite moribund, old place at a price you couldn't refuse, and you have just enough money left in the bank to be able to devote the next six months wholeheartedly to its resurrection. Building up a financial reservoir large enough to capitalize such a venture is definitely a wise way to begin. If you live in the city and work at a well-paying job, but are thinking of moving to the country, start by cutting expenses and suffer whatever austerities you can to accumulate this cash reserve. Aim to provide a surplus fund that will cover living expenses for at least six months, above and beyond the mortgage and building materials cost. At a 10 percent rate, mortgage money will cost you $13.22 a month per $1,000 borrowed over ten years. Over fifteen years the cost is $10.75 monthly. Over twenty years the cost drops to $9.66. But the cost of the interest increases greatly the longer the term of the mortgage. For example: $10,000 borrowed over ten years will cost $132.20 a month, or a total of $15,864. Over fifteen years ($107.50 a month), it will cost $19,350, and that same amount financed for twenty years ($96.60 per month) will cost you $23,184! Can you afford the $35.60 extra each month to save $7,320 over ten years? Your living expenses in the country will be considerably lower than in the city. Trade in the car for a pickup truck. Convert all convertible assets into cash or tools. The last variable is the amount you can budget toward repairs, which even if you do all the work yourself, can run as high as $500 averaged monthly over the entire year. ($15,000 to $25,000 over a three-year period should restore all but the worst or largest house to usable but spartan condition.) Do not forget the down payment (usually 25 percent of total) and closing costs. The building fund is really impossible to estimate. You can spend as much as you want to for as long as it takes. Ten thousand dollars, spread thinly over three years, is what it took me, and it seems to be a reasonable mean for a 24′ × 32′ typical five-room farmhouse. The labor would have been worth more than half that amount. On your weekend visits to your country estate try to get a few rough estimates from local builders as to the cost of restoring the place. If the place is at all habitable, you might consider renting it out for a period of time to help defray taxes and/or a portion of the mortgage expenses while you remain in the city accumulating your capital fund. Take your estimate and double it before you make the move. This figure may actually cover half your final expenses. Performing your own labor nowadays does not save as much as you might imagine since the cost of materials is so high. On new construction, labor is roughly figured at 40 percent of material cost. On remodeling it often equals and can even exceed the cost of materials. But remember, you will be working for nothing and with far less efficiency than a professional. Figure your time into the equation at coolie wages. You still will have to pay real prices for materials with real money. You can often exchange rent for labor by tenants. This is not always a good idea because you have no real quality control. It sometimes seems that every eager hippie who has built a bookshelf bills himself as master carpenter when it comes to this exchange. Ask for references and check them out. Beware of open-accounts in your name and buy all materials yourself. A written understanding is helpful.

If your capital fund is large enough, consider the option of living in a tent, trailer, or outbuilding. Perhaps fix up the garage into temporary quarters. Sometimes you can purchase an old house trailer quite inexpensively to live in while the house is rebuilt, and then you can sell the trailer when the house is ready. I know of a couple who converted a shed into a small but quite serviceable house, enabling them to remodel their charming but unliveable farmhouse as time and money allowed. Freed from the pressure of having to get it all done, they can rebuild it when they have the time and energy. When the house is finished—and they have been working for five years now—they will have a rental income from the toolhouse. This approach is by far the most sensible for utilizing time and money. Living in a temporary shelter while rebuilding your dream house will go a long way toward relieving the tensions that arise amidst the dust and rubble of remodeling. The entire house can be torn down to the sheathing and framework to facilitate replacement of walls and structure. Remove interior walls, expose wiring and plumbing, and repair structural weak points as necessary. Dormers are framed in or sections removed. Whatever is rotten and in need of replacement is done while the house is exposed. Excavation and foundation work can be done at any time during the stripping process. The framework of the house can be straightened much more easily when the interior or exterior walls have been removed—assuming, of course, that the walls are rotten enough to require replacement. Each additional layer of board or finish, every partition, has a bracing effect that must be overcome if the frame is to be moved. Exposing the skeleton of the house simplifies the task of deciding where to begin. It also lightens the load that will have to be lifted if foundations or sills are to be replaced. Drafty old sheathing boards can then be replaced with new, tighter materials, and the house can be reroofed without worry that a sudden downpour will damage finished ceilings. You will in effect hang a new house on the framework of the old. You can gain great freedom in adding or removing windows and walls, particularly with post-and-beam framed houses. In many cases the framework is the only part of the house worth saving. Hand-hewn beams could not be duplicated at today's costs in any case.

Of course, the blitzkrieg approach to rebuilding has the advantage of quick results. Most important, the work can proceed in a logical order. You will be unhampered by having to live around your work or work around your life, by having to redo work you did the month or season before as a temporary expedient. Instead, you can do it right the first time. First, draw up a clear master plan. Spend the winter before you start drawing up this plan. Gather your family around and discuss your wants and needs. Each member of the family should start by writing down (or telling about) his or her idea of what the house should be. Note changes, sketch rough designs, and generally give your imaginations free rein.

A house organizes space into three basic units, which are defined by the activities that take place within them. These are the *endospace*, which encompasses private activity, such as sleeping, love making, and bodily care; the *ectospace*, which contains family and social life, such as food preparation, eating, and entertaining; and the *mesospace*, which serves as a transition zone between these functions and between the house and outside and includes laundry rooms, mudrooms, porches, hallways, playrooms, and the like. (An excellent discussion of house design concepts can be found in chapter 3 of *From the Ground Up* by Cole and Wing, and in volume 4, chapter 1 of *The Owner-Built Home* by Kern.) These architectural categories can also relate to the inner space of the inhabitants and the larger cycles of the seasons. As we move through the year we move through space as well. In winter the family draws together; it moves within, gathering around the hearth or stove, thinking deep thoughts, sleeping late. In summer it expands outward onto the porch and into the gardens, into activity. We continually move from the inner (bedroom) to the outer (kitchen) within the sphere of the house itself. The house should be designed to facilitate these transitions with grace. The feelings of each individual as to what is private and public can vary within a given household. By analyzing these feelings, it is possible to arrive at a flow chart that gives a rough idea of how your house should be laid out.

Working within the confines of an already existing structure places some limitations on your design freedom. It can be a creative challenge to reshape the house to suit your needs without doing violence to the integrity of the structure itself. Much of this reshaping can be an opening up of the often cramped and highly compartmentalized spaces that typify old homes. Do your drawing with a scale ruler. It helps to make scaled cutouts of cook stoves, large appliances, and furniture, which can be placed in various trial combinations on your scale floor plan. Use tracing-paper overlays to project changes in the original plan.

This exercise will help you to better understand the needs of your lifestyle and how they relate to the house. With this rough master plan, you can complete the chart shown in Table 1–2, adding details concerning the type and kinds of finish materials, the amounts needed, and cost estimates. You should catalog your energy requirements and the means of meeting them, particularly if you plan to use wood heat. This completed rough plan together with a set of drawings that detail proposed wiring and plumbing changes will give you a good guide to work from. At this point it might be a good idea if you have a friend in the building business, to ask him or her to look at your drawings some night over dinner. There are likely to be things you have overlooked or problems you are unaware of. It is much easier to correct your mistakes with an eraser than to have to live with them.

The disadvantage of the blitzkrieg attack is the converse of its strength: You are not allowed much time for reflection. Your idea of what you require for living spaces will change and evolve as you live in the house. What seemed like a good idea at the time may prove to be unworkable. A kitchen that seemed large to an ex-apartment dweller might be far too small to handle the harvest of the neo-rustic. The arrival of children will require a complete reorganization of a house. After the former urbanites have lived in the country a few seasons, they will discover a whole new crop of needs rising to replace those they had plowed under. Previously important functions and their attendant spaces may well languish unused: The study and TV room may be collecting dust as they look in vain for a place to store the growing stock of tools or hang wet laundry in winter.

Living in the house and changing it to conform to your changing needs over a period of years is the solution to this dilemma. For example you may have planned to panel the bedroom walls with plasterboard when you got around to it next winter only to have come across a great deal on pine boards that fall. Or you might decide to add an attached woodshed after a winter spent chipping frozen logs out of a snowbank.

Unfortunately, most purchasers of old houses are a good deal less flexible in their options than those who have provided for their economic needs before they start. Fewer and fewer people have the initial liquidity that it takes to build or buy a new house. An older home will suffer you to live within it even if it is barely habitable. There is enough slack in most places to allow you a grace period before you must absolutely do something about whatever needs fixing:

"Why haven't you fixed that roof yet?"

"Well, I can't fix it when it's raining. When it's not raining, it doesn't leak."

The purchase price and mortgage terms might be all a family can afford. They will have a roof of sorts over their heads until they can become well-enough established to fix it piecemeal or purchase a few more buckets. It pays to buy the best house you can afford. Fixing up as you go is sometimes the only choice. It is unfortunately the most expensive way to rebuild. The efficiency that derives from being able to do a job rapidly and right the first time will not be possible. Like a forty-year mortgage, you pay the cash several times over as the interest accumulates. Slow as the process will be, as wearing on the spirit, there are some compensations. You will be able to reflect on the process and progress, so long as your vision is not clouded by squabbling, and to adapt to circumstances as they arise. Most important of all, you will be able to establish a foothold in the community, to become increasingly privy to the resources as well as the gossip of the neighborhood. You will hear about the fellow down the road selling old beams. You'll know whom to see for a good used refrigerator. You'll learn whose opinions to value and where to get advice when you need it. Yard sales and barn sales, auctions and rummages will be good sources of needed items. You will build the credit necessary to finance your remodeling venture.

Finding steady employment within the community will generate the capital you need but will force you to become a weekend builder. That stretches the span of your rebuilding project and, once again, increases the likelihood of tensions. You will always be burdened, busy for the forseeable future, with no time of your own. Whether the monkey sits heavy on your back for a month or light for a year is a matter of personal preference. If you can find self-employment at a craft or skilled trade, you will have the freedom to organize your time somewhat. You can leave blocks of time open to do major jobs on the place. The work becomes organized in stages. For example, you can arrange a three-week break during the early fall and then not touch the place until the following spring.

The temptation is to spread yourself too thin. You commit yourself to a large project and then spend all of your time working to pay for it and trying to sandwich the actual work into the weekends and nights. You can easily get caught on a dizzying seesaw of working on the place until the bills are too large to ignore and then working out until you have enough to go back into debt. In the meantime you never get a chance to live in the house. Striking the proper balance requires iron self-discipline and the patience of a saint. You must be able to immerse yourself in the here and now, to enjoy the process in and of itself rather than as a means toward a goal. No matter how fast and how hard you work, there always will be more to do. If getting it done becomes your highest motivation, you will soon be done in. Work methodically, let your plan guide you, not ride you. The result will be far healthier.

When the project is completed, it can always be sold. If you have financed it as you went along, you will have built up a good deal of equity in a property that has increased substantially in value. If you figure in the cost of all your time, you will be lucky to break even. But the money has been spent over a long period of time in small increments—in retrospect, almost painlessly, like an automatic savings account. If you decide to sell you should realize a good return on your investment. Suppose you bought the place for $18,000 with $6,000 down, the balance at 9 percent over seven years, and you put $12,000 cash in materials into it over a period of three years. Then you sell the place for $35,000. After the agent has taken his cut and mortgage interest is paid off, you net a profit of about $5,000, which is a return on your money of about 16 percent. This figure, of course, does not include your labor (which is worth at least $5,000), but you must remember that it was done in your spare time (unless, of course, you saved up, quit your job and spent six full-time months blitzing the house, in which case the economics are not as attractive). Think of it as a somewhat demanding hobby. The $35,000 is used to pay off the remaining principle of the original mortgage. That leaves you with $25,000 to put down on your next place, buy a farm, or leave for the South Seas.

If you have the initial capital to finance a blitz approach, you can actually build up a decent bankroll fixing up old houses and selling them, reinvesting the returns in the next place, constantly pyramiding your capital. You must be able to afford to live in it until it is sold, and that may take a good deal of time. This life isn't for everyone. It certainly doesn't appeal to me. I need a place to grow roots. But there are those who would find it a good way to make a living, capital gains taxes notwithstanding.

If you do not have enough money to purchase a house by yourself, you might consider a joint partnership. By pooling resources, you can often buy a larger multifamily dwelling. If you take that route, draw up a contract with your prospective partners carefully and specify responsibilities and duties as well as the means of its dissolution. A partnership of this nature is no different from a marriage and should be undertaken with equal caution. A clear understanding of the business arrangements is a good place to begin. ''That's not what I said,'' ''Oh yes it is,'' is a poor substitute for a good contract. The pressures of group living can sometimes be offset by its advantage as a safety valve for marital tensions. Sometimes your lover is not always your best friend and it helps to have other close friends as mediators and conciliators. But group living is not for everyone. If zoning codes allow, consider converting a large house into a duplex or a single dwelling with rentable apartments.

> What you receive depends upon what you give. The workman gives the toil of his arm, his energy, his movement; for this the craft gives him a notion of the resistance of the material and its manner of reaction. The artisan gives the craft his love; and to him the craft responds by making him one with his work. But the craftsman gives the craft his passionate research into the laws of Nature which govern it. The craft teaches him Wisdom.
>
> [Isha Schwaller de Lubicz, *Her-Bak: Chick-Pea, Egyptian Initiate*]

CHAPTER II

FOUNDATIONS

A Vermonter had bought an old, run-down farm and had worked very hard getting it back in good operating condition. When it was back in pretty good working shape, the local minister happened to stop by for a call. He congratulated the farmer on the result of his labors, remarking that it was wonderful what God and man could do when working together.

"Ayeh," allowed the farmer, "p'raps it is. But you should have seen this place when God was running it alone." [Allen R. Foley, *What the Old Timer Said*]

Drainage

Left to follow the path of its own nature, wood returns to the ground from which it has sprung. A foundation seeks to delay this reunion. It supports the building beyond the moist embrace of the earth. It is also a link: The building is joined to its mass by the downward thrust of gravity and, through it, anchored to the earth itself.

All things return to earth and the earth washes to the sea. As the rain wears down the mountains, water is the enemy of foundations. Water seeping against poorly drained walls exerts a force called *hydrostatic pressure*. Water weighs 62.4 pounds per cubic foot; for every foot of height of the water table against that wall, 62.4 pounds of pressure are exerted. Suppose in a wet spring the water table is high, almost to the ground surface. At a height of 5 feet, the water will exert 312 pounds of pressure. If that wall is 8 feet high and 128 feet around its perimeter, a total lifting force of 319,488 pounds ($5 \times 62.4 = 312 \times 8 \times 128 = 319,488$) is exerted. That is considerably greater than the weight of the entire building. A good drainage system will lower the water table against the wall to the level of the drain and effectively reduce that pressure to zero. Installation of such a system is standard practice in new construction, but many old houses have no drainage provision at all, relying solely on the nature of the soil and hope of a low water table. They are often subjected to the full brunt of hydrostatic pressure. The heaving action of frost, especially in heavy clay soils, adds additional momentum. Small wonder that between the crushing weight from above and the irresistible forces from below, it is only a matter of time before the foundation begins to buckle, settle, and shift.

Water in the basement is a good indication of a high water table. The level of water will fluctuate with the seasons, being high in the spring, after the rains and the snow melt, dropping as dry weather lowers the table. At certain times of the year your cellar will be a swimming pool, at others, a mudhole. There are instances where a house has been deliberately built over a spring or seep to tap the water for household usage. The overflow should drain under the foundation and away from the house. Sometimes it doesn't. Water in the basement also means expensive repairs. This is the first crossroad. Either look for another house or be prepared to commit yourself to exhausting and tedious labors.

There is a difference between infiltration of water caused by ground water run-off and that caused by seepage from the water table. Surface water will flow toward the house if the ground outside has not been properly graded. The run-off from the roof will work along the foundation wall and through any cracks into the cellar itself. This is particularly a problem with so-called dry walls of unmortared stones. The walls will appear damp, and after a heavy rain, a trickle may actually flow through the wall itself. A solid concrete wall or mortared

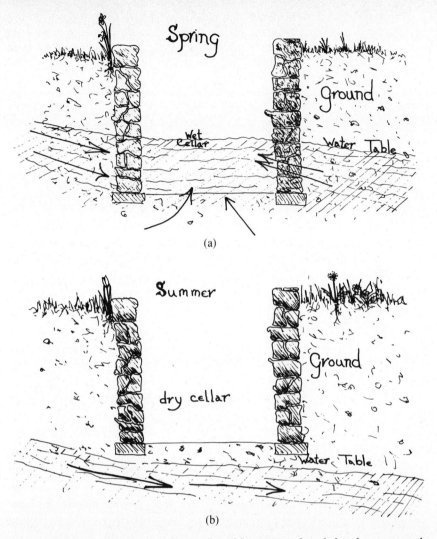

(a)

(b)

2–1a, b Effects on cellar moisture of seasonal variations in water table

stone or block wall is no barrier against this water unless it has been properly waterproofed on its exterior surface. Puddles will appear on the cellar floor when water has worked up between the footings and the floor itself or through a dirt floor.

Figure 2–2a shows how surface water can work into the foundation when the ground alongside the foundation is not properly graded. If you were to walk around the perimeter of the foundation, sunken areas and what appear as small tunnels will often indicate where the water has found its way into the wall, taking the soil with it. A few wheelbarrow loads of clay soil should be spread over these places and the grade built up to slope away from the house. If the ground pitches toward the house, a grass-filled trough called a *swale* should be cut into the slope to divert the water away from the house. This is generally bulldozer work except in the lightest of soils.

Although correcting the grade will cure the immediate symptoms of subterranean water, it will only forestall the emergence of long-range troubles if it is not coupled with good subsurface drainage. Water in the soil itself is still free to push against the foundation wall. Differential pressures are created by frost penetration into wet earth. The heavier the soil, the greater its capacity to hold water and frost. A clay or silty soil will hold the most moisture. As the water freezes, it exerts tremendous pressure on the walls, like thousands of tiny jackscrews. A gravel soil will allow the water to drain away, if there is someplace

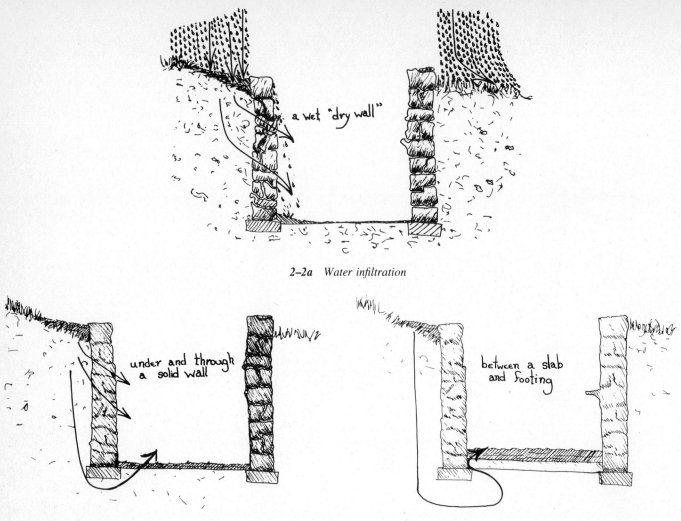

2–2a Water infiltration

2–2b Infiltration through a "dry" foundation wall

2–2c Infiltration caused by improper grading

for it to drain to. If the foundation wall is to be replaced, you should make provisions for adequate foundation drains when the new foundation is built. When the foundation itself appears to be solid but there is a water seepage problem, excavation of the exterior perimeter and installation of drains is the answer.

Figure 2–3 indicates the elements of a good foundation drain system. Concrete or masonry is actually very permeable to moisture, and water can move easily through the wall, which results in a damp cellar. This dampness is prevented by coating the outside of the wall with an asphalt waterproofing compound. Coating an old rock wall may prove difficult or impossible as the dirt will prevent adherence. Special waterproofing paints or hydraulic cement coatings (Thoroseal®) designed to withstand the pressure of water trying to move through the wall, can be applied to the inside wall instead. These compounds will stop water infiltration but will not alleviate the problems of wall buckling caused by hydrostatic pressure unless coupled with adequate foundation drainage systems. If there are no existing foundation drains, the outside perimeter of the wall should be excavated and footing drains installed. At this point it makes more sense to pour a thin (3 or 4 inches) "buttress" wall against the existing rough stone wall. This concrete surface can be waterproofed with a standard asphalt (far less expensive) foundation coating. One caution: Since the new wall will now extend beyond the face of the sills and house-wall sheathing, the joint

Foundation Drainage

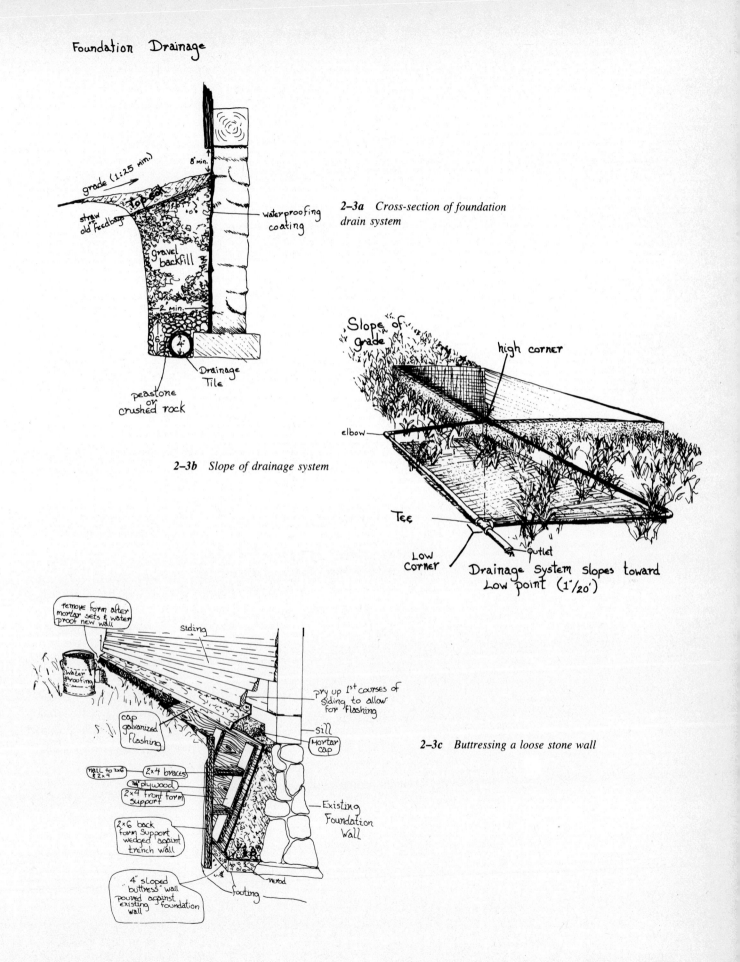

grade (1:25 min.)

8" min.

straw or old feedbag

waterproofing coating

gravel backfill

2" min.

Drainage Tile

peastone or crushed rock

2–3a *Cross-section of foundation drain system*

Slope of grade

high corner

elbow

Tee

Low Corner

outlet

Drainage system slopes toward Low point (1"/20')

2–3b *Slope of drainage system*

remove form after mortar sets & water proof new wall

siding

Water proofing

cap galvanized flashing

pry up 1st courses of siding to allow for flashing

sill

Mortar cap

nail to 2x6 & 2x4

2x4 braces

¾" plywood

2x4 front form support

2x6 back form support wedged against trench wall

Existing Foundation Wall

4" sloped "buttress" wall poured against existing foundation wall

rerod

footing

2–3c *Buttressing a loose stone wall*

must be protected from the weather by a strip of metal flashing inserted under the first course of wall sheathing and over the outside of the concrete. Otherwise water will sit on top of the joint and cause the sills to rot (see Figure 2–3).

Proper drainage is obtained by laying a continuous length of perforated 4 inch drain pipe around the perimeter of the footings. The perforations allow water to enter the pipe whence it can be carried away. ADS pipe is flexible and available in 250-foot-coils. Rigid plastic and asphalt fiber pipe (Orangeburg) are available in 10-foot lengths as well. Fittings are available for these systems, for splices and bends, tees, or wyes. Odd lengths of Orangeburg pipe are coupled with a few turns of a tarpaper strip. Whatever pipe system you use, it should be laid at a slope of 1 inch per 20 feet, relative to the foundation. On sloping ground the pipe is extended to where it surfaces above the grade. On level ground the discharge feeds into a dry well, which is simply a gravel-filled pit that holds water until it permeates into the surrounding soil.

The foundation drain lowers the water table around the foundation to the level of the drain itself, thereby reducing the hydrostatic pressure on the wall to nothing. The tile is covered with a layer of crushed stone or (''chestnut'' stone) about six inches deep. The trench is then backfilled with gravel to within a few inches of the surface grade. A layer of hay or old feed bags is used to prevent soil particles from washing down through the gravel and plugging the pores in the pipe. The topsoil is then spread and graded for seeding. Eaves troughs and downspouts are used to divert the roof water away from the foundation in areas of heavy rainfall and mild winters. In the far north, these tend to fill with ice, which split the seams or back up under the shingles. Assuming the original foundation is in good condition or has been recently replaced, an exterior drainage system should prevent water from seeping into the cellar. Even an earth floor will remain fairly dry unless there are springs in the cellar itself.

Cellar Floors: *Earth and concrete*

A good earth floor has several desirable features. Chiefly, it acts as an effective temperature regulator. The heat capacity of any object is directly related to its mass. Since for all practical purposes, the mass of the earth is infinite, it has an extremely large heat-storage capacity. All summer long it is absorbing heat, slowly warming up. It remains cooler than the surface temperature (this is why cellars seem cool in the summer). During the cold months, the process is reversed and the earth gives off that stored heat as it slowly cools throughout the winter. This same thermal-lag principle is behind passive solar-heating systems, which utilize the heat-storage capabilities of massive materials to condition the heating environment. The temperature of the earth follows a curve that corresponds to the ambient air temperature but in a slower and larger cycle.

Figure 2–4 shows how an earth floor will cool the house in summer and keep it relatively warm in winter. Because the temperature fluctuations are moderate, the cellar lends itself to storage of root vegetables, potatoes, apples, smoked meats, and canned items, as well as such staples as dandelion wine and hard cider. Unfortunately, this moist, cool, even temperature is also an ideal environment for mold, and that accounts for the musty odors associated with these cellars. Insufficient ventilation coupled with moisture rising from the earth will lead to rotting timbers. Any wooden objects or benches in direct contact with the floor will take up water and soon rot. Metal objects will rust. Concrete

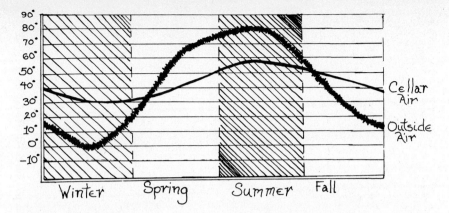

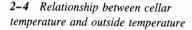

2–4 Relationship between cellar temperature and outside temperature

pads are generally poured in order to prevent direct contact with the earth when installing furnaces and water systems. Anything you might wish to store in such a cellar must also be kept from contact with the floor. Use boards set upon concrete blocks. An alternative is to spread a 4″ layer of crushed stone over the entire floor. Moisture will not then work into stored objects.

Pouring a Concrete-Slab Floor

Earth floors are also just plain dirty; crushed stone, however, is even worse than dirt if you wish to use a portion of the cellar as a workshop. Heavy tools will be difficult to slide around, cleaning impossible, finding a small screw that falls off the workbench frustrating. All of these are good reasons for pouring a concrete slab floor. Figure 2–5 shows the components of a first-class concrete slab.

Prepare the cellar for the slab by first removing whatever you can move. Store those boxes and barrels in the garage or outside on skids of old boards. Cover them with a poly sheet for protection from rain. Large objects like the furnace or hot-water tank are most likely already resting on concrete pads. If they are set on bare earth or flat stones, you may need to raise them up to the level of the finished floor. Use a crowbar or a good 2 × 4 edgewise to lever them up and slip as many bricks or cement blocks under them as are needed to

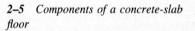

2–5 Components of a concrete-slab floor

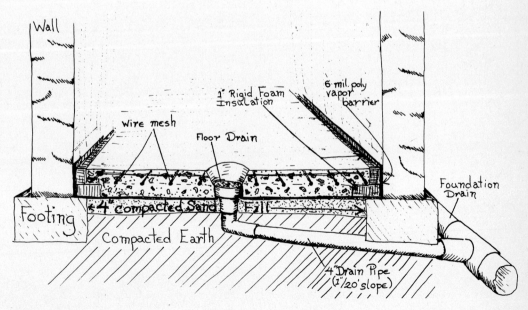

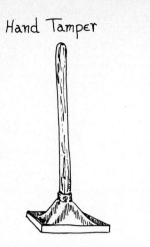

Hand Tamper

2–6 *Tamper for compacting earth floors*

hold them at the desired height. Do the same for the water pump and pressure tank. If you keep a freezer in the cellar, you might consider emptying it, carrying it outside, and refilling it temporarily. The more you can clear from the cellar, the easier the job will be. Supporting posts for the floor should already be resting upon flat rocks or cement pads of their own. Coat the portion that will be in contact with the new concrete with tar or wood preservative. Do the same with the bottom edges of the stair stringers unless you plan to remove them entirely. Posts in need of pads will have to be raised.

Next, using a rake or coarse broom, pick up all loose material, stones, pieces of bark, and whatever other debris may be lying about. Chances are good that the floor itself will be compacted from years of use. There may be some unsettled and loose areas, though, and you should rent a hand tamper to compact them. A hand tamper is nothing more than a heavy, flat, iron plate mounted on a stout wood handle (see Figure 2–6). You use it like a toilet plunger. Gas-powered compactors are more effective and faster, but the fumes will poison you unless the cellar itself is wide open. The weight of the concrete will cause the slab to settle and crack if laid upon uncompacted ground. With a shovel and a wheelbarrow, lower any noticeable high spots and use the fill to raise low areas. Tamp any fill especially well. The object is to save on concrete by making a uniform base for the slab.

You will notice that Figure 2–5 indicates a floor drain. Pouring a slab turns your cellar into a large bathtub. Any water that might enter from plumbing leaks or through the outside walls has to go somewhere. A drain also allows the option of washing down the floors. Ideally you will have provided a connection under the footing so that the floor drain can connect with the exterior foundation drainage system. As mentioned earlier, a foundation without proper drainage is no proper foundation at all. You should dig alongside the outside wall until you locate the drain and then dig a tunnel under the footing into the cellar to make this connection if it hasn't already been provided for. Digging under the wall is easier than breaking through it. If there is no foundation drainage system, consider putting one in at this time. If, however, the soil is so sandy as not to hold water or the water table is always well below the cellar floor, you won't have a drainage problem and don't need any special installation, as long as the surface water drains away from the building. A thick sod planted over a layer of clay soil will keep water away from percolating into the ground near the foundation.

An alternative to tunneling under the foundations and all the attendant excavation is to dig a *sump pit*. That is simply a concrete-lined box, twelve to eighteen inches deep and square, in which water collects until it can be pumped somewhere else. A length of plastic pipe extends from it to the outside so that the water can be removed when necessary. A wood cover is set over the pit when it is not in use. Sump pumps are readily available at any hardware store. The floor should slope toward the sump and the pump inserted in it. If you decide to make a sump pit, pour the concrete for it before you pour the slab. If the earth can be cut cleanly, it alone will form the back wall of the sump. Then construct a wood box of scrap board or plywood with the outside dimensions the size of the sump. Dig the pit 3-to-4 inches wider and longer than the box. The box will have to be as high as the pit is deep. Anchor it on the inside with small stakes driven into the corners. Mix enough concrete in the wheelbarrow to fill the space between the form and its earth wall. After it sets, remove the form. Pour an additional 3-to-4 inches of concrete in the bottom, and the

Sump Pit

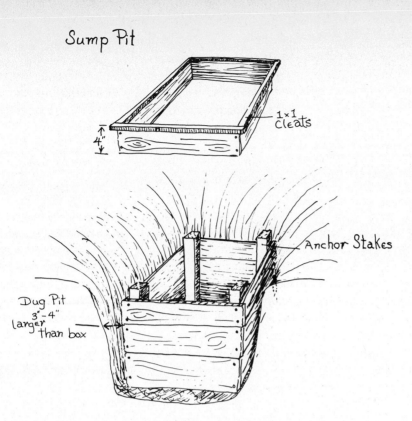

1 × 1 Cleats

4"

Anchor Stakes

Dug Pit 3"–4" larger than box

2–7   Forms for a sump pit

sump is finished (see Figure 2–7). An additional frame equal to the thickness of the slab floor is set on the top edges of the sump when the concrete is poured for the floor. A lip that will carry the cover is made from 1 × 1 stock.

A layer of clean, washed sand or fine gravel is now spread over the earth floor and graded to approximately eyeball level. It is then compacted. Sometimes there will be a spring or seepage within the cellar itself, causing water to ooze from the floor, particularly during periods of high water table. The hydrostatic pressure under the slab will act like water under a boat and lift the entire building or at least the slab itself. You should dig a shallow trench along the footings and lay drainage pipe exactly as with an exterior wall. The pipe is likewise covered with crushed stone. The pipe is sloped toward the sump or the outlet to the exterior drain line. Crushed stone or gravel is spread over the entire floor. This layer will allow the water to filter harmlessly into the drainage system to be carried away from the house (see Figure 2–8).

2–8   Drain along inside perimeter to remove excess water

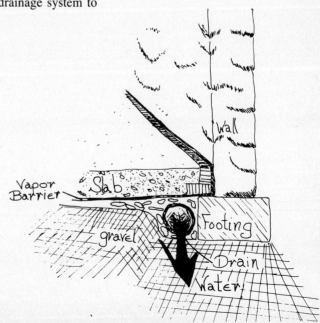

Wall

Vapor Barrier

Slab

gravel

Footing

Drain Water

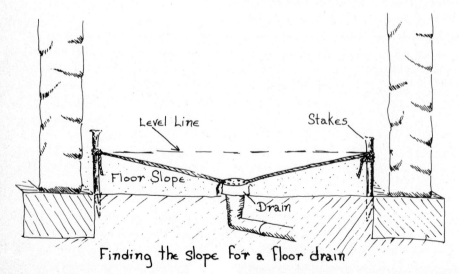

Finished
Floor level
Marked on
Wall

Eyeball
Level

High Spot

Ideal
grade

Low Spot

Finding the grade for a slab Floor

2–9 *Finding the grade for a slab floor*

Next, guidelines must be set to the height of the finished floor. With a chalk or felt marker pen, mark a point on the wall 4 inches above the surface of the tamped fill. Using a 4-foot level, a line level and string, or a transit level, extend that line around the perimeter of the walls. If there is a poured footing under the wall (there won't be with a rock wall) you can assume that it is level and simply measure up the wall the same height in each corner. Using a chalk line, snap a line between these points. You can also stretch a string from stakes set in front of an uneven wall to find the approximate height. With a helper, you can stretch a string across the cellar from wall to wall on the level line. As you move it up or down the length of the walls, you will see any high or low spots that might need leveling. Perfection is not necessary. These lines will help you find the grade when working around any furnace slabs, pillars, or other spots where the eyeball level is hard to use. The same technique is used to establish the grade for the slope toward the drainage outlet (Figure 2–10). Set the top of the drain an inch or two below the level line. Tie strings from stakes driven along the foundation level line to the drain outlet. This will give you the line to which the floor is laid. You may wish to slope only a portion of the floor. You can dispense with a floor drain entirely if you want. It is a convenience rather than a necessity. Save time and simply lay the slab level.

2–10 *Finding the slope for a floor drain*

Level Line

Stakes

Floor Slope

Drain

Finding the slope for a floor drain

Lay a vapor barrier of 6-mil polyethylene over the entire floor. Carefully cut around existing pads or blocks if you cannot slip it under them. Avoid puncturing the plastic. The vapor barrier prevents moisture from slowly being absorbed through the slab, which is the cause of damp floors. Wire reenforcing mesh is then laid over the poly. It should be propped up on small stones. Use a bolt cutter to fit it around posts and pads. Bend the cut edges down to help support the mesh above the floor, but again, be careful to avoid puncturing the vapor barrier. Any serious rips should be taped with gaffers tape, an aluminized heavy-duty masking tape that sticks to just about anything. If you haven't already done so, estimate the amount of concrete you will need and call the ready-mix company. I usually try to order in advance, leaving enough time to finish my last sandwich before the truck arrives.

Ready-mix concrete is sold by the cubic yard. To figure how many yards you need, multiply the perimeter by the depth in feet and divide by 27. For example, if the inside dimensions of the house are $24' \times 30'$ and the slab is to be 4 inches thick, you will require 8 yards of concrete. ($24 \times 30 = 720 \times .3$ [$4''$ is $\frac{1}{3}$ or about .3 of 12] $= 216 \div 27 = 8$ yards. [$3 \times 3 \times 3 = 27$ cu. ft. per cu. yd.]) I strongly recommend ready-mix concrete for all concrete projects of a yard or more. It is possible to mix concrete in a power mixer by the batch, but each batch takes time to mix and the mixer must be kept clean between batches. Concrete gives better results if it sets as a unit. Mixing by the batch will materially affect the strength of the concrete as each batch must bond to the next. The setting time becomes critical when pouring a slab floor and leveling the pour.

Only one problem remains, how to get the concrete into the cellar. Cellar windows and ventilation openings can sometimes be used. An outside hatchway is often the best place to start the pour. If you are lucky you will be able to pour from several locations. More likely, the driver will not be able to reach more than one or two openings. Cement trucks carry additional sections of chute, but there is no way they can reach into the farther corners of a cellar. A temporary chute can be built from plywood or boards, which will extend the reach of the truck chute. This chute can be set on blocks or sawhorses and removed as the farther reaches are poured (Figure 2–11).

Gather your help and equip them with rakes and shovels. You will have to pull the cement from the chute to the back corners first. Ask the driver to

2–11 Pouring a cellar floor

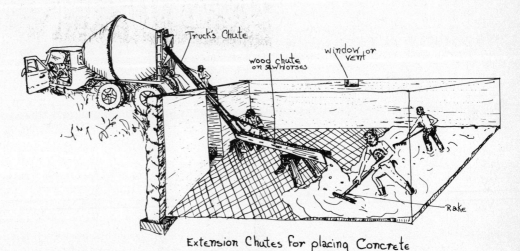

Extension Chutes for placing Concrete

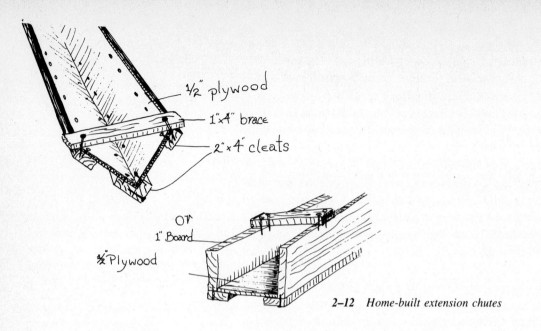

½" plywood

1"x4" brace

2"x4" cleats

OT

1" Board

½" Plywood

2-12 Home-built extension chutes

make the mix on the wet side. Additional water will make the concrete easier to spread and slow down the setting time. Work quickly, trying to distribute the cement evenly, working from the farthest point back toward the truck. As the concrete is placed, lift the wire mesh so that it floats in the middle of the slab. Wear rubber boots. Treading concrete offers none of the joys of stamping grapes. Concrete contains enough lime to eat away leather soles as well as bare feet. The truck driver usually can give you good advice on how to place the concrete. Don't be afraid to ask for it.

An alternative to this frantic shoveling and spreading is to have the concrete pumped from a special boom truck. Pumping raises the cost per yard considerably, but it may well be worth the expense. If you cannot get a truck across the yard to the hatchway, pumping may be the only way you will get the concrete into the cellar. Once the truck leaves curbside, you are responsible for damages. Beware of backing over septic tanks and dry wells. If the ground is too soft to support the truck, the cost of extricating it will come out of your pocket. It takes a mighty big tow truck.

Once the floor is poured, it must be finished. Move a straight length of 2 × 4 back and forth over the surface while slowly drawing it toward you. This is called *screeding*. Ideally a screed board reaches completely across the width of the area to be leveled, but in a cellar a smaller one is more practical because you have to work around posts and furnaces, and the like. Before beginning the pour, drive stakes around the perimeter of the slab and additional stakes down the middle of the floor. Straight 2 × 4s are nailed to these stakes at floor level. The top edge of the boards will provide a bearing for the screed board. Once the area is screeded, the stakes are pulled and the holes smoothed in before the concrete sets. If you are not particularly concered with getting a perfectly level floor you can dispense with the screed guides and eyeball the floor as best you can. Screeding leaves a slightly ridged finish, which is suitable for any rough storage area but difficult to keep clean. To further smooth the floor and remove the ridges where the screeding lines overlapped, a "bull float" is necessary. This is nothing more than a flat board attached to the end of a long pole—a kind of mop. You can make one or rent one. It skims along on the surface waters, smoothing the flow of water, sand, and cement. When the concrete has set enough to bear your weight but is still soft enough to take an imprint, it should be finished with a wood float (a slab of wood with a handle). The surface will appear frosted when it is ready for wood floating. You will easily develop a feel for the float so that you manage to keep the edges from digging in and raising ridges. Work from 1 × 1 plywood kneeling boards to reach the far ends of the slab. The boards should not sink into the surface more than a quarter inch. When the concrete has set hard enough to bear your weight without imprinting it, it can be steel troweled for a polished, hard finish. Troweling by hand is tedious work, but power trowels, like power compactors, run on gasoline and make fumes. A steel finish is very smooth and can be dangerously slippery if wet but it is necessary as a base for floor tiles or carpeting. A masonry sealer should be used to keep the concrete from dusting. Remember that concrete gives off heat while setting, enough to turn the cellar into a veritable sauna. It isn't a job for the weak of heart.

I remember the day we poured our own cellar floor. By noon the temperature was already in the low 90s and the humidity was a dripping towel. A scene from Dante's *Inferno,* three near-naked bodies, clad in rubber boots and cut-off shorts, sweating and grunting, tugging at the sluggish puddle with shovels and hoes. The cellar was a Turkish bath, the cement was setting fast, exhaling a heavy breath of moist heat. My glasses fogged in, the light bulbs glimmered dully in an aura of dew. But we could not stop, not yet. The concrete was stiffening, setting almost as fast as we could place it. In broad, rough strokes, I smoothed the pour with a piece of board. "Good enough for a cellar hole, this ain't the Taj Mahal!" And we left it just like that—no screed, no float—and escaped blinking into the shimmering daylight.

Foundation Walls:
Repair, and replacement, HOUSE JACKING

"Funny, I don't remember those cracks being so deep back in October." Back then the real estate agent had assured you, all they needed was a little patching.

Cracks in the foundation wall *can* be patched. This assumes that they are not currently active faults, that their cause is no longer present, and that you have provided the good drainage previously mentioned. A wall that cracked from settling or frost heaving or from hydrostatic pressure, can be repaired and remain perfectly stable so long as there is no additional water working against the wall. Filling in a crack in a mortared or solid wall is called *pointing*. A narrow trowel, called appropriately enough, a pointing trowel, is used to force new mortar into the cracks. You can use a special hydraulic-patching cement to form a watertight bond. Sometimes fingers seem to work better than a trowel, especially for the inexperienced mason. If you use a "finger" trowel, be sure to wear gloves. The lime in the mortar will otherwise eat away your fingertips. Use pressure to force the mortar as deeply into a fissure as possible. Any crack to be patched should first be moistened in order to prevent the water in the mortar from being absorbed too rapidly by the dry masonry. That would weaken the bond. Follow this rule whenever you bond any old masonry materials, especially brick or fieldstone.

The terms *cement, mortar,* and *concrete* are often confused and misapplied. Willis Wagner in *Modern Carpentry* defines cement, or Portland cement mix, as "a pulverized mixture of limestone and clay or marl which has been heated to, and maintained at, a temperature of about 2700 degrees F. in a kiln.

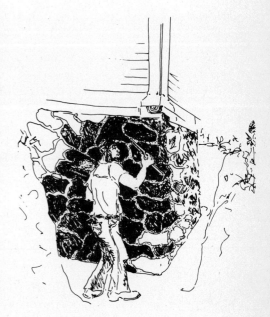

2–13   Pointing a stone wall

The resultant clinker is then ground into powder.'' When this cement is mixed with sand (or fines), crushed stone or gravel (coarse aggregate), and water in the proper proportions, a chemical reaction called *hydration* takes place. The result is concrete. When the reaction is complete, the concrete is said to have ''set.'' When cement is added to a mixture of sand, fire clay, and water alone, it is called *mortar*. Mortar does not have the strength of concrete and should never be substituted for it. Cement is sold as Portland cement mix for making concrete and as mortar mix for making brick mortar. For mortar, one part mortar mix is added to three parts sand. Enough water is added to give the proper consistency. Too much, and the weight of the brick or block causes it to ooze out. Too little, and the mortar will dry crumbly and have little strength. For general-use concrete, one part cement is mixed with two parts fine and three parts coarse aggregate.

When only a small amount of concrete or mortar is required, it can be bought already mixed with the sand and gravel, in 40- or 80-pound bags, under

2–14   *Cellar vents*

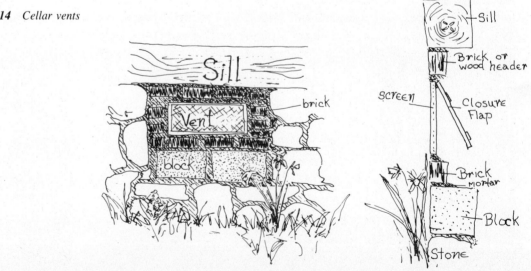

the trade name Sakrete. It is an expensive way to buy sand and a bag does not go very far, but where only a bucketful of mortar is needed for a patching job or if the sand pile is frozen solid, it saves the trouble of finding and mixing sand.

Back to the walls. Many old foundations were laid up without any mortar at all to bind the stones. This type of construction is often called a dry wall. If the ground water is kept outside, it generally lives up to its name. These walls were laid with remarkable skill, and there is no reason why they should not provide a sound foundation. Often that portion of the wall extending above the ground to the sills was plastered to keep out the wind. The plaster may have dried out and crumbled away and should be repointed.

Another common foundation repair is around fixed cellar windows. In the days before electricity these units were often installed to provide light. Rare is the wood frame that has not rotted away, leaving an entrance for water and rodents and other pests. Cellar windows are always potential trouble spots, especially if they are below grade. Windows that are below grade are best blocked in completely. The remains of the wood frame are removed with a hammer and pry bar and the stonework cleaned with a wire brush and moistened. Using bricks and/or concrete blocks, mortar in the opening. Do not close in the opening completely, but instead add a ventilating louver. These louvers are inexpensive screened vents manufactured in a size that will fit the space of a standard cement block. In summer they can be opened. Where possible, provide at least two vents along each long wall, to allow cross ventilation of the cellar hole. Ventilation will help remove the moisture and prevent condensation, which furthers rot and causes odors. In winter the vents are closed and a piece of fiberglass insulation stuffed behind them.

Where windows are sufficiently above grade (a minimum of 8 inches), they can be replaced with a modern thermopane unit designed specifically for cellars. These units will open and can be used with screens for ventilation. I do not recommend the use of cellar-window wells unless they are set into a well-drained gravel base that connects to the foundation drain. A block louver is cheaper. There is no real need for natural light in a cellar.

Before a wall can be replaced, the work area must be cleared. A trench is dug on the exterior side of the old wall. If all the walls need work, the trench must follow the entire perimeter. It should extend to the depth of the footing (the base of the foundation). If the foundation wall does not extend below frost line, the excavation definitely should. The trench should be about three feet wide at the bottom to allow room to work. Trenches *can* be dug by hand if you have sufficient determination, lots of time, light soil, and a very strong back. Most of Vermont is blessed with a stoney ground that eats shovels. Where boulders are lacking, there is "hardpan" instead, a dense clay that laughs at a pickax. I recommend a backhoe. A good operator can do more for that $20 per hour than you can do in a day. Digging against a foundation wall is a ticklish affair, and you will want the best operator you can find. It's not a job to cut your teeth on. You will discover that the excavator will not guarantee the wall against cave-in. Instead, he will probably ask you to sign a paper releasing him from liability if the wall does give. But take heart, a backhoe is an extension of an experienced operator's hands and mind. He can make it do tricks that would amaze a circus elephant and will have a pretty good idea of how far to go.

But ultimately, it will be you calling the shots. If you say go, he goes, and if the wall goes with him, well he just works here, mister. If you don't

have confidence in your judgment, consider hiring a contractor who specializes in this kind of work. Whether he will guarantee the job against failure while in progress is open to negotiation, but at least it won't be you who did it. While failures occur often enough for you to need to be aware of the possibility, they generally result from foolhardiness and rushing the job. If you proceed with the excavation slowly and cautiously, you will have no trouble detecting a potentially serious problem before it occurs. Trust the advice of your operator. Nothing really happens without warning. You learn to listen and feel for the signs, to become sensitive to the vibrations of the earth and the stress of the wood. In time you will feel the timbers strain just as you feel the muscles in your own arms.

Dig as close to the wall as you can. With a poured-concrete wall, this is generally right up against it, unless the wall splays out at the bottom so far as to appear unstable. Leave enough earth to shore it up. Losing a small section of wall is no cause for alarm. If the sill above is solid, it will span the opening and carry the weight: Simply remove the collapsed section of the wall along with the rest of the rubble. More caution is necessary when digging against a dry stone wall. Often the only thing holding it up is the fill you are in the process of removing. These walls are built like a pyramid, with wider, larger stones at the bottom. As you dig down, you cannot remove the base without weakening the support for the entire wall.

Another precaution: Determine where water and sewer lines and phone and electric cables pass through the wall before you dig. Examine the walls from the inside and measure down from the sill and over from a corner to the location of each particular pipe. Drive stakes in the ground to mark each location. You might write the depth on each stake with an indelible marker. When the backhoe is within a foot or so of the expected pipe or line, dig with a hand shovel until you locate and expose that pipe. Remember where your septic tank or dry well is when the backhoe starts wheeling about the yard. It's more than heavy enough to put a dent in a steel tank or crush the lines in the leach field if the sod is soft.

2–15   A working trench along the foundation

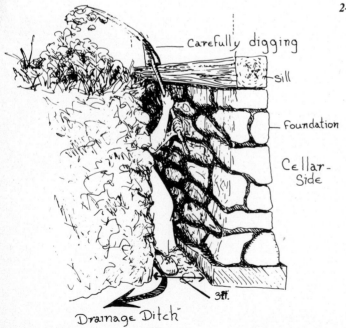

Carefully digging

sill

Foundation

Cellar-Side

3 ft.

Drainage Ditch

One last precaution: Dig an outlet ditch for your trench. Otherwise the first rainfall will create a moat. Not only will that hamper your work but there is a good chance of losing the wall because of softening of its earth supports. It will be muddy enough down there without complicating matters. Dig the ditch carefully as it will later be used for the foundation-drain outlet line.

House Jacking

Once the trench is finished and the wall exposed in all its sad glory, you will have to decide the best method for raising the house up and keeping it there while you take the wall out from under it. The weight of a house is transferred to the foundation through a heavy timber called a sill. Most old houses will have an 8″ × 8″ sill, which spans the length and breadth in one or two pieces. Joists are the timbers that span the cellar and support the floor. A girder (girt or carrying beam) often supports the joists themselves, either running under them or notched into one. Sometimes logs hewed flat on the top edge are used for joists. If the bark has been left on, it should be stripped with a drawknife or flat chisel. Insects and rot are harbored under the old bark. Figure 2–16 shows variations on typical floor-framing systems that may confront the would-be house raiser.

A stud-frame house uses essentially the same framing techniques as a heavy-timber frame house, substituting lighter framing members. Joists are nailed rather than notched into the sills (see Figure 2–16d).

2–16a–d Typical foundation-framing systems

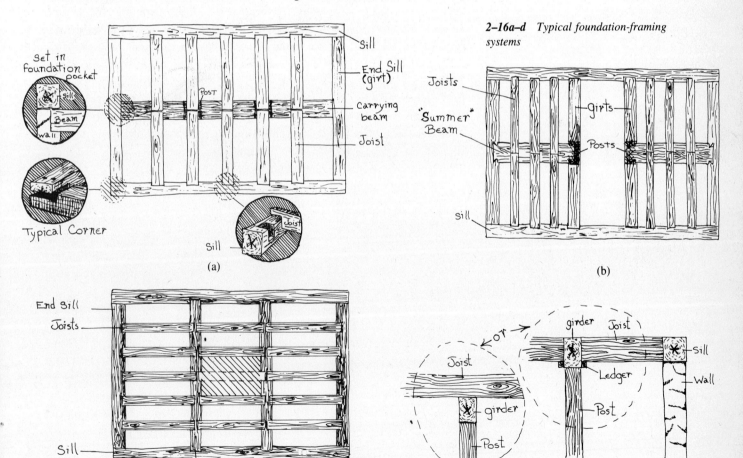

A house is lifted with house jacks, or screw jacks. These jacks are simple machines—a large screw threaded into a sleeve, which widens into a base. There is a flat collar that rotates on top of the screw to provide a lifting surface. The top of the screw is fitted with a hole through which a steel turning rod is inserted. The base is often stamped with a number that indicates the weight it can safely lift. Screw jacks lift hard. They turn slowly, and as the height of the lift increases, the force required to turn the screw itself also increases. I prefer to use them to support a timber once it has been lifted to height. I use a hydraulic jack to do the actual lifting whenever possible. Hydraulic jacks are oil-filled pistons, miniature hand-operated pumps. They can hold more weight and lift it faster with less effort. A small valve at the base of the jack is turned to release the pressure, allowing the jack to lower. It must be shut before the jack will raise. I always keep a screw jack turned up alongside the hydraulic jack in case the seal should fail and the jack lose pressure. The weight can then be carried by the screw jack. You will need a flat steel plate about 6 inches square and ¾ inch thick as a lifting plate because the head of a hydraulic jack is quite small and will act as a wedge, splitting the wood it is to lift when force is applied.

Jacks can be rented by the day or week from hardware or rental stores. Often a neighboring farmer will have a pair of two of house jacks lying around the barn or shed. You may be able to borrow these. You can sometimes find them at junkyards, barn sales, and auctions if you think you'd like to own a few. Unless you plan on doing a lot of jacking, there is really no reason why you'd ever need to own one. They make terrible lamp bases. Ask around, perhaps a foundation contractor would consider renting his to you, if he's not using them. Hydraulic jacks of the size you will require are harder to come by. They should be in the 8- to 12-ton range. Jacks of this capacity are expensive, both to buy and to rent. Plan to do all your lifting with the hydraulic jack in one day if possible, and use screw jacks to hold the timbers in place.

Other necessities are cribbing and jacking timbers. Cribbing, or cobbing, as it is sometimes called, is any short length of timber used to build a platform on which to place your jacks. You will need a truckload of it. Jacking an entire foundation may require a dump-truck load.

Finding the odd pieces of 6 × 6, 8 × 8, 2 × 8, 4 × 12, and so on, can be a challenge. Quite often contractors keep piles of it around which you may be able to borrow. Check with your neighbors too. Carpenters who specialize in building timber-frame houses will sometimes keep odds and ends of beams around. If you have an old building or barn to tear down, you can find all you need. Check around construction yards. Steel fabricators often have such timbers. You may be able to strike a deal.

I knew of an old fallen-in barn down a back road. It's downcountry owners hadn't been around in years. The place was probably a tax shelter. One fine summer day a chain saw could be heard above the buzz of crickets. I had a van load of cribbing and that old barn had fallen in just a bit more. I confess this crime by way of illustrating the desperate lengths to which a man can be driven. I certainly wouldn't recommend anyone's doing such a terrible thing.

Jacking timbers are another scarce item. I was lucky enough to borrow a few from a friend who had a barn full of old 8 × 8s. You may know someone like that yourself. Or you may own a barn in need of tearing down. Be cautious with used timbers as they will have mortises cut out of them, which can seriously weaken their effectiveness as jacking timbers. These timbers will carry the entire weight of the building. You might consider having some sawn out at the local

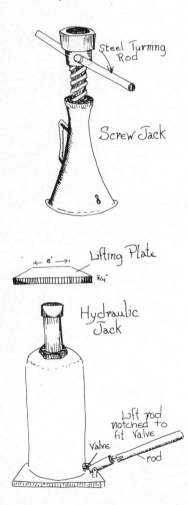

2–17 *House jacks*

Steel Turning Rod

Screw Jack

Lifting Plate

Hydraulic Jack

Lift rod notched to fit Valve

Valve

rod

mill. They should be 8 × 8s (6 × 6s are suitable for light stud-framed buildings over short spans) of the greatest length you will need to span—a minimum of 16 feet. Since it will be green wood and quite heavy, specify *spruce* timbers. Hemlock isn't any stronger and weighs twice as much. Pine and balsam aren't strong enough to be trusted. Timbers should be free from any serious splits or bad knots, which could weaken them. At over a dollar a running foot, this may seem a hefty investment. When the house is back on its new foundation, the timbers can always be reused as sills for a barn, porch, shed, or other addition. An entire structure can be framed with timbers if you want. I know of several people who left the jacking timbers protruding out of the front wall and built a porch deck over them. You can always sell them at a slight loss. An advertisement in the local trading paper should bring quick results.

By this time your yard resembles a World War I fortification. Huge mounds of earth all but obscure the house. Trenches encircle it like a moat. Piles of heavy timbers are strewn about like Paul Bunyan's match sticks. You should be studying that maze of beams in the cellar, which doesn't look at all like the drawings, trying to puzzle the key to lifting it and at the same time keeping it all in one piece. It doesn't seem possible that such a mass will ever go anywhere. Perhaps you should have hired old Archie . . . Old Archie . . . when he was a young fellow they say he could lift a horse, now he can hardly lift his own elbow. But his eyes are still clear ice blue and alive with light. In between the splat of tobacco juice he'll be able to tell you what to move and how fast and where to lift. He'll probably do it just for the pleasure of being

useful. The few dollars you pay him are just an excuse to make it legal. In his quiet way, he'll tell you more than you ever thought there was to know.

To lift a house, you must determine where the weight is concentrated and provide for its support as you lift. Removing only one wall is pretty simple. Four walls means four times as many jacks and cribbings and a lot more lifting. There are at least eight basic principles to bear in mind as you lift:

1. HAVE A SOLID BEARING. Keep your cribbing as level as you can and distribute the weight over as large an area as feasible. A crib is a pyramid. Use lifting blocks to distribute the force of the jack.

2. LIFT STRAIGHT. If the jack begins to tilt, lower it and straighten or shim the jack so that it lifts plumb. A weighted jack that slips sideways can kill you.

3. BLOCK UP AS YOU GO. A safety precaution. You can't get hurt if nothing can fall.

4. LISTEN AND LOOK. The house will creak and groan as it is raised. Watch for cracks to open. See if the joists move with the sills or stay in place.

5. DON'T LIFT TOO MUCH. You only need to relieve the weight on the foundation wall. In most cases that requires an inch or less of lift. Even if the entire house is to be raised several feet to provide for a deeper cellar or higher wall, do it in small increments. Give the timbers time to settle and adjust to their new positions.

6. LIFT SLOWLY. Lift evenly. Move from lift point to lift point in succession, raising each jack an equal amount. Don't hurry. Rapid lifting can stress the timbers past the breaking point.

7. BALANCE THE LOAD. Keep your cribbing as close as possible to the lifting points. Avoid lifting from the ends of a beam and leaving the middle unsupported. An 8 × 8 is not a lever.

8. THINK. Lifting a house out of a hole is a whole lot harder than putting it in there, especially if you happen to be under it when it falls. If faith can move mountains, you can move your house.

Let us assume for purposes of discussion that the sills and beams of the house are sound enough to be lifted. That is more likely the exception rather than the rule, and any rotten sills will have to be replaced before the house can be moved. Reduced to its simplest elements, to lift a wall you slide a long jacking timber under the sill. Crib it on both ends and begin lifting with your jacks until that portion of the sill lifts from the foundation. Repeat this process at intervals along the wall. Girts or carrying beams must also be raised to keep the floor from sagging and stressing the joints. Know what is above you when you begin to lift. You should slide your jacking timbers under any weak points, e.g., where a girt or carrying timber may be mortised into a sill or spliced over a post. It is quite common for a major load-bearing post to rest above these posts carrying the weight of the upper stories (see Figures 2–29 and 2–30 for timber-framing diagrams). If you cannot support a splice directly, you must lift both sides of it, jacking each side a little at a time to avoid twisting the joint.

But how is the jacking timber to slide under the sill when the sill itself is resting firmly on the wall? Hammer away at the rock or concrete with a sledge until you have a hole large enough to admit the timber. If the wall will not break easily, use a rented heavy-duty impact hammer. After all the timbers are in place and the weight lifted off the foundation wall, you can push the wall itself out into the trench where it is removed by hand or backhoe. Consider saving those flat stones used in the wall. They can be the start of a beautiful garden or patio wall or a fieldstone fireplace. I used one huge flat stone as an outdoor bench. They have cost you too much simply to bury.

To save on jacks and cribbing, you can span the entire width of the work trench with your jacking timber (see Figure 2–18). Set up cribbing in the trench for lifting if you cannot fit a jack under the end that rests on the undisturbed soil of the original grade. After the lift has been completed, you can crib up the far end. Let it settle the blocking, which will sink into the earth before it stabilizes. Raise your jack enough to slip more blocking under the settled end until you reach level. Then remove the cribbing from the trench. A way to accomplish the same thing without the cribbing in the trench is simply to dig a platform into the earth alongside the trench deep enough to admit both jack and blocking. Make sure the backhoe operator has placed his spoils far enough back from the edge of the trench where you plan to jack. You must lift upon the relatively compacted, undisturbed grade, not fill. While you can use the hydraulic jack to do all your lifting and then block up to the desired height and remove the jack entirely, I prefer to leave a screw jack in place under every lift point. I have enough of them, and this method facilitates fine adjustments, making it

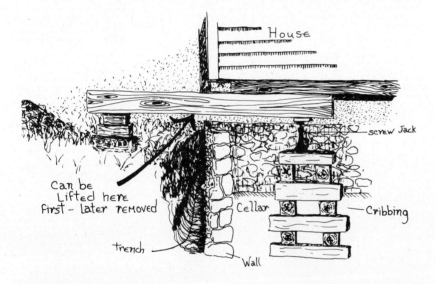

2–18a   Using a single jack to lift a sill

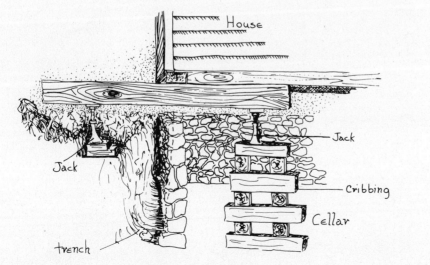

2–18b   Using two jacks to lift a sill

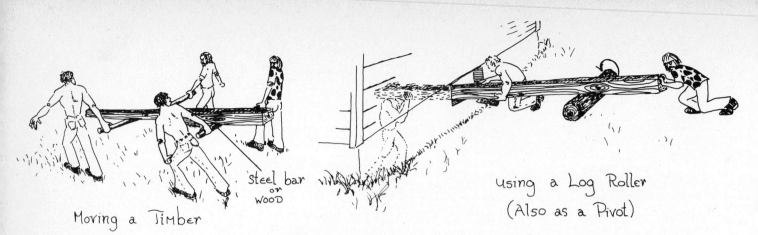

Moving a Timber

steel bar
or
WOOD

Using a Log Roller
(Also as a Pivot)

2–19   Moving heavy timbers

easier to level the entire house once it is raised. The house is kept as level as possible, making it easier to work the new wall in under the sills. You can also insert your jacking timbers diagonally across the corners of a house to lift two walls with one timber, but if the corner joint is not strong enough to carry the corner post above, you will have to jack directly under the corner with your timber. Ideally, a jacking timber should span the entire width of the foundation. If your house is 16 feet wide, you can do this with a 20- or 24-foot timber and jack from the cribs on the inside. Most houses, unfortunately are at least 24-foot-wide. A 26-foot-long 8 × 8 of green spruce is a heavy stick of wood. You will have to lever it into position. That may be a moot consideration, however, as most sawmills only saw timbers to 24-foot maximum length. It is easier to use a shorter timber and jack from the inside and outside of the wall.

If the carrying timber is set below the level of the joists and sills, you will not be able to lift across the cellar unless you slip a block that equals the girder in thickness under each outside sill and lift all three members simultaneously (Figure 2–20c).

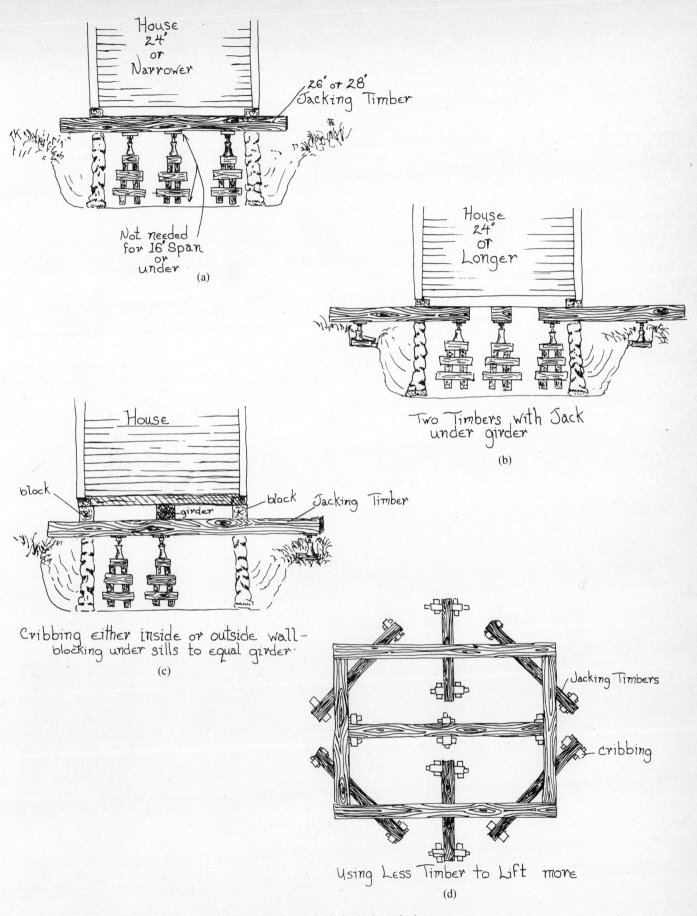

House
24'
or
Narrower

26' or 28'
Jacking Timber

Not needed
for 16' Span
or
under

(a)

House
24'
or
Longer

Two Timbers with Jack
under girder

(b)

House

block   block   Jacking Timber
girder

Cribbing either inside or outside wall-
blocking under sills to equal girder.

(c)

Jacking Timbers

cribbing

Using Less Timber to Lift more

(d)

2–20a–d   *Methods for jacking the house*

The New Foundation

Clear the rubble from under the house, piling it against the back wall of the trench. Save whatever stones you like. A backhoe may be necessary, as some of the foundation stones will be too large for hands or lever to move. The new foundation must now be laid out. A foundation wall is supported on a footing—a wide, continuous concrete beam. A rule of thumb is to make it twice as wide as the width of the wall it supports and as deep as the wall is wide. An 8-inch wall is considered standard. The footing is then 16 inches wide by 8 inches deep. If the soil is soft clay, the footing should be 2 feet wide by 12 inches deep. Although the actual depth of the footing is not critical and may vary a few inches, the top must always be level. Footings are set below the depth of

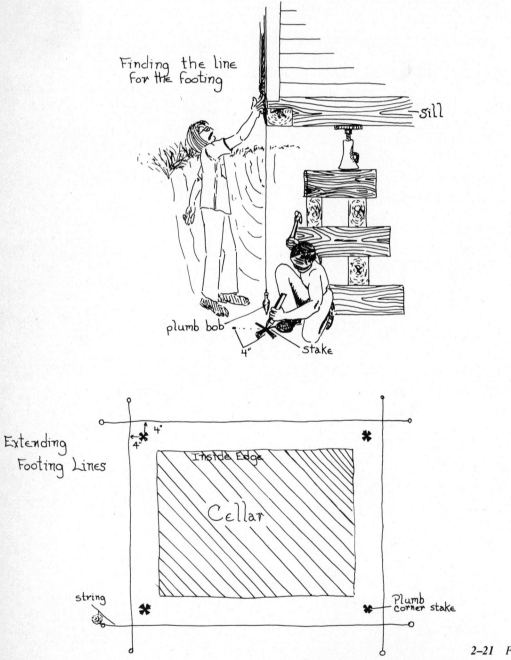

2–21 *Footing layout*

maximum frost penetration. Four feet is considered standard for the north. Frost has been known to penetrate deeper than that on bare ground but seldom goes very deep when there is a snow cover. Clean all loose debris and soil from the trench where the footing is to be placed. Then, with a plumb bob, drop a line from the outside corners of the sill above. Drive a stake at these points. Now measure an additional 4 inches beyond these stakes and drive another set. Stretch lines between them. This gives you the line for the outside of your footing. The inside will be set 16 inches toward the cellar.

Remember that although the string marks the *outside* of the footing, it also marks the *inside* edge of the form board for that footing. Using 2 × 8 boards and stakes cut from short lengths of 2 × 4s, and pointed, lay out the boards along the line. Secure one end of a board, and nail the stake to its outside (nail the form to the stake so the nails will not set in the concrete). Drive another stake at the end of the board. Adjust the board until it reads level. Mark the level line on the stake with a pencil, and then nail the form board to the stake at the mark. Repeat this procedure for each board around the entire perimeter, and then drive additional stakes every six feet or so between the end stakes or wherever the board may bow off the line. Then cut a 16-inch length of block for a spreader. Using this spreader will enable you to lay the inside form board without stringing additional lines. Repeat the entire process. Check for level across both form boards. When all the forms are laid out, bank the outside with loose dirt to anchor the forms and fill in the spaces under them to prevent the concrete from pushing them off the line.

Trim the tops of the stakes below the top of the forms. That makes it easier to screed the concrete. If you wish, reenforcing steel can be added to the forms, although it is rarely necessary for residential buildings. Check for level one final time and make any adjustments with a sledgehammer before calling for the cement truck. Don't forget to provide a collar under the foundation for your drain outlet. Now is also the time to plan for any future water or electrical lines that you may wish to run to outbuildings. Plastic pipe is used as a sleeve to facilitate removal at a later date if necessary. Figure 2–22 shows footing forms with earth banking.

2–22   Forms for footings

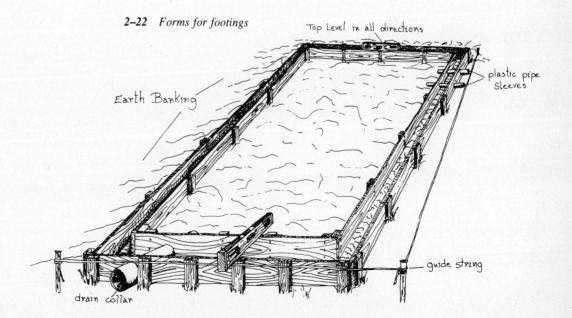

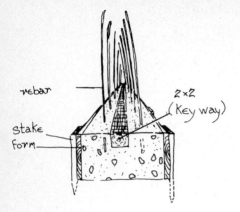

2–23 *Footing with keyway*

Before the concrete sets hard, a 2 × 2 strip of wood is pressed into the center of the footing flush with its surface. This leaves an indentation called a *keyway,* which will anchor the wall to the footing. Also four-foot lengths of reenforcing steel or old scrap steel, auto springs, and the like, are stuck upright along the center as additional anchors. Leave the forms in place the next day as you begin to lay out the wall. They will protect the soft concrete from damage. After three days they can be removed.

At this point you have a choice. You can:

1. Hire a concrete contractor to pour your wall. You may also consider hiring him to do the footings as well. He has all the necessary forms and equipment and is good at it.
2. Rent the forms yourself, which is not always possible and is never cheap.
3. Build the forms you need, which takes time. Unless you can reuse cement-stained plywood and odd lengths of 2 × 4s for another project, it is also expensive.
4. Build a block wall. This alternative is the cheapest as far as material costs go, but it is tedious and difficult for an amateur. The quality of the wall may not be as good as a poured wall.

Your choice will be based on a time/money equation. Which do you have more of and which do you value the most? Personally, I subcontract out concrete work if I can. I don't much care for it. I don't much care for laying block either. But this is purely a matter of personal preference. Don't let lack of experience prevent you from attempting what may be a rewarding project. The concentration with which a novice belabors his task often bears first-quality fruit. Under the right circumstances, a well-laid block and a perfect mortar bead may be a source of delight that far surpasses a view of the Parthenon.

Whatever method you do opt for, that original plumb line dropped from the outside corners of the sills is now marked on the footing. A chalk line is snapped between these points, giving you the outside edge of the foundation wall. The forms are set to this line. Because the sill of the house may bow out or in, check along the length of its run with a plumb bob or level. If the sill projects over the wall an inch or so, it is no great problem. Leave it. Under no circumstances should the sill sit inside of the wall, as water will collect on the wall and rot the sill. If the offset is not more than an inch or so, tilt the wall or, better still, adjust the line of the wall to match the run of the sill. An alternative is to insert metal flashing from under the sheathing down over the joint. There is also the possibility of using a turnbuckle, or come-along, to pull the sills together after they are resting on the new wall, but that is a lot of trouble to go through. Rectilinear perfection is not generally an attribute of the rebuilt house. For the same reason the footing is run from the actual corners of the house rather than squared to itself. The house will seldom be square, and the wall might miss the footing entirely if it is laid to the house and the footing laid square. Unless you plan to jack the house up several feet higher than the height of the foundation wall, plan the height of a poured wall to come within 17 inches of the bottom of the lowest point along the sills. Since forms generally come in standard modules of 4, 5, 6, and 8 feet, you may not be able to do this. Come as close as you can. It is not practical to pour the wall right up under the sill. The chute will not fit, and even if it could, the concrete must be tamped with a shovel and a vibrator or long stick while it is being placed to ensure even settling and avoid honeycombing. Sixteen inches is the space required by two courses of concrete block. If need be, jack it a few inches higher to allow finger room. Some space is needed to stuff insulation into the cavities in the block. Half blocks 4 inches in height are available to fill in the last space. Block walls are laid right up to the sill if possible. The cavities should be filled with vermiculite or fiberglass wool, since the block itself has very little insulating properties. A layer of rigid foam can be bonded to the outside wall with construction adhesive. This layer is waterproofed with asphalt below ground and stuccoed above with a thin plaster of mortar. The expense of rigid foam is offset by the warmth of the cellar. The very top of the wall is capped with an 8-inch-wide strip of homosote or asphalt-impregnated sheathing board and/or a layer of sill seal (a thin fiberglass roll 8-inches wide). When the wall is lowered, these materials compress to form an air-tight seal between the sill and the masonry. Any small imperfections will be filled in. In areas of termite infestation an aluminum termite shield should be installed first. After the wall is finished and the forms stripped, the concrete and mortar should be allowed to set at least three days before the house is lowered down onto it. Concrete actually continues to cure over a period of weeks but reaches most of its strength within the first week. Setting the weight of an entire house onto a "green" foundation wall (new concrete actually does have a greenish hue to it, which changes to the familiar grey as it cures) could cause it to crumble like a stale cookie.

When the block filler wall is laid, a block is left out wherever a jacking timber runs across the wall. It is sometimes necessary to leave out more than one block. After the wall has set, the house is lowered onto it and the jacking timbers removed. At that point the missing blocks are mortared into place. Ventilation windows or louvers may be added at this time. They can also be added anywhere else along the block wall. Do not forget to provide sleeves for water or electrical lines that may pass through the wall, before the pour takes place.

Building your own forms from ¾" plywood or one-inch tongue-and-groove board is a lot of work. If the forms are coated with a mixture of kerosene and crankcase oil, they will be easier to strip from the concrete. I strongly recommend

2–24b Sill offset from wall

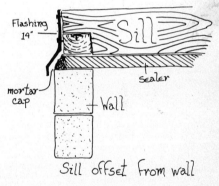

Sill offset from wall

2–24a Rebuilding the wall

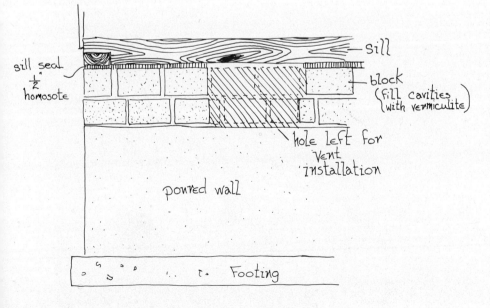

2–24c Termite shield

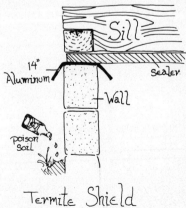

Termite Shield

that you read a good carpentry manual on the subject of forms and concrete work before you undertake such a project. Willis Wagner's *Modern Carpentry* or the Audel *Carpenter's and Builder's Library* are both excellent in this regard. Figure 2–25 shows a design for home-built forms.

Before pouring footings and walls, you should decide if you want to add an outside entrance, or bulkhead. This is the familiar cellar hatchway, with its sloping double door, which can be made from wood or prefabricated steel. Doors of this type work well where the grade is more or less level. A set of rough stairs is framed inside the wall. Pouring the wall against a strip of 2 × 4 (coated with a wood preservative) set in its ends provides a nailer for fastening the door jambs. An alternative is to slope the grade away from the cellar wall and frame a bulkhead with an open end and a gable roof, like the entrance to an igloo.

The key to laying up block walls is to start at the corners (see Figure 2–27).

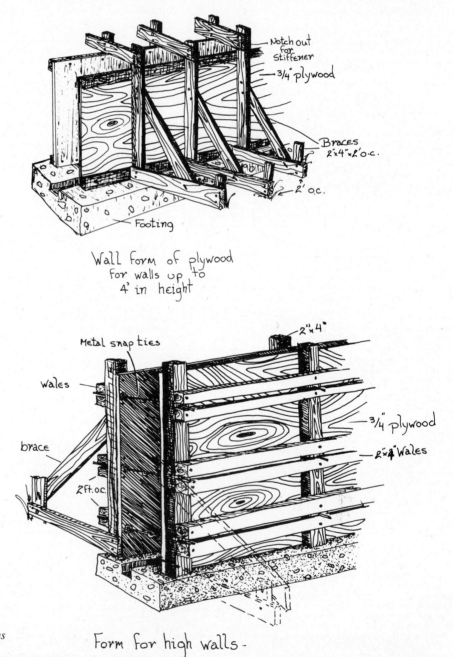

Wall form of plywood
for walls up to
4' in height

2–25   *Home-built forms*

Form for high walls.

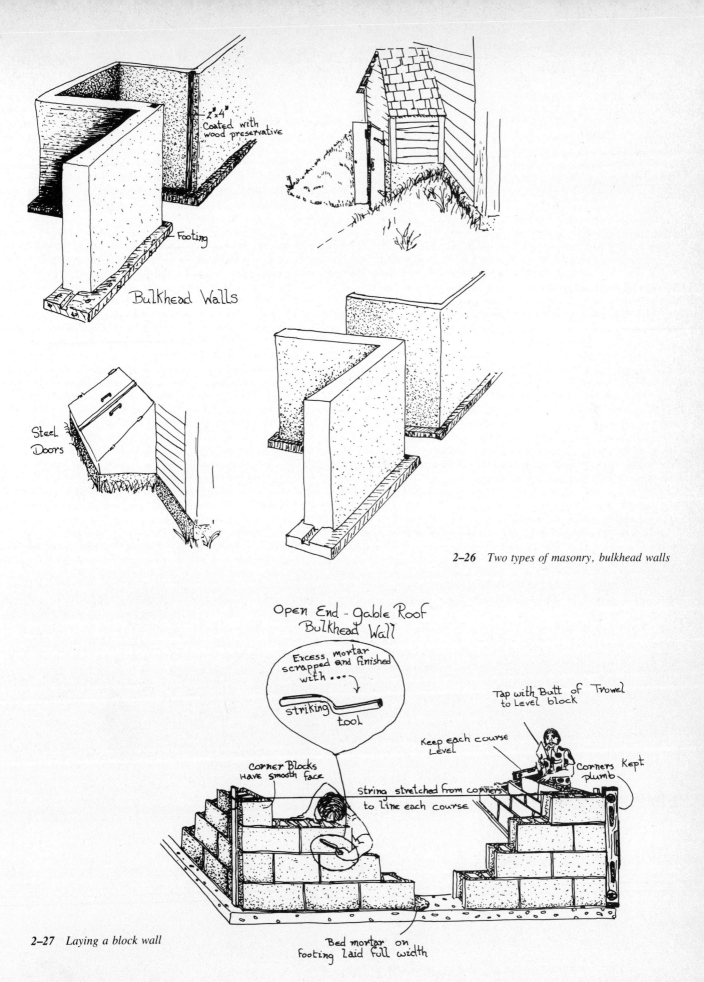

2″x4″ Coated with wood preservative

Footing

Bulkhead Walls

Steel Doors

2–26 *Two types of masonry, bulkhead walls*

Open End - Gable Roof Bulkhead Wall

Excess mortar scrapped and finished with...

striking tool

Corner Blocks have smooth face

String stretched from corners to line each course

Tap with Butt of Trowel to Level block

Keep each course Level

Corners Kept plumb

Bed mortar on footing laid full width

2–27 *Laying a block wall*

When whatever wall you build is complete, and the house is sitting solid and square on its new foundation, you should coat the outside of the wall below grade level with a foundation coating. This is a heavy asphalt compound, which is applied with a stiff brush on the end of a long handle. It spreads best when hot. Build a fire of scrap boards under the bucket, and leaving the cover loosely in place, heat it to a gentle boil. Take care to avoid getting hot tar on your skin. Besides burning, it doesn't wipe off easily. Periodic reheating is necessary in cold weather. A foundation coating prevents the absorption of soil moisture through the wall and its passage, by osmosis, into the cellar. Refer back to the section on drainage systems and lay the pipe. Avoid dips and high spots if using

Just Because It's There Doesn't Mean It Has To Stay There

The logical extreme of foundation repair—perhaps it may be the simplest and least expensive solution—is to move an otherwise sound house off a bad foundation onto a new one, rather than build a new one in place.

(a) The crane moves into position and the house is braced for the lift.

(b) The cable slings are in place on the lifting timbers, which run under the sills of the house.

(c) Slowly, the house is lifted and swung toward the waiting new foundation.

(d) Contact. The house is carefully aligned by corner ropes before being set down. The lifting timbers are to be left in place as a frame for a porch deck. They can also be dropped into pockets in the wall.

flexible pipe. Temporary shims can be made from boulders or wood scraps. Hand filling the trench with gravel and stone is tedious work. It takes a lot of wheelbarrow loads of stone. So consider hiring the backhoe. The bucket of the hoe can dump the stone into the trench while you level and shovel it around the pipe. The backhoe operator can start backfilling as soon as the stone or gravel is in place. Use great care in backfilling. If too much earth is pushed too quicky against the wall, it can collapse inward. As the trench fills, you will be able to work faster.

While the backhoe can fill a trench quickly and efficiently, it is not very useful for finish grading. You will probably need to hire a bulldozer to spread the topsoil around. (You should always try to save the topsoil during the original excavation. The deeper layers of soil will not support new grass growth very well. Pile the topsoil separately from the rest.) A bulldozer can backdrag the ground with its blade, leaving a surprisingly smooth finish, ready for a hand rake and some grass seed. Seed should be covered with a scattering of old hay to protect it from birds, rain, and wind. While the bulldozer operator is on the property, have him attend to any odd jobs that need doing. Unsightly stumps or large boulders can be quickly pushed up and buried somewhere else. You can even clear a small field of alders or brush, excavate a bank for a future root cellar or garden cold frame, or crush and bury a junk pile. Every time you hire a piece of heavy equipment, you pay a moving charge, which is equal to at least an hour's work. So use that bulldozer every minute it is on your property and keep it for a few extra hours if you need it and can afford it. Save having to call it back for a small job at a future date when you would have to pay another moving charge. Jobs that might take you hours or even days may be just a few minutes work for the dozer. Use the engines of heavy technology sparingly and intelligently. A bulldozer is nothing more than a big shovel. Your back will thank you in years to come. Digging a very big ditch with a small shovel is not the best path to heaven.

If you can serve a cup of tea right, you can do anything.
[George Gurdjieff, *All and Everything–Beelzebub's Tales to his Grandson*]

Replacing Rotten Structural Timbers

I have a vision of rotting sills—rich and crumbly red, like dried blood, compost, growing mushrooms, close cousin to that lurid pudding of mold, last year's pumpkin . . . "And the dust returns to the earth as it was, and the Spirit returns to God who gave it" (Eccles. 12:7).

A sill is a sermon on paradox. It is the bridge between heaven and earth. It raises the house up from the ground and yet is the path of return. It is the strongest and the weakest link in that intricate chain of force and counterforce that is the frame of a house. Because they are the bottom of the house, sills are closest to the earth. Water is the breath of earth and the seduction of wood. Water brings to life spores that lie dormant in the fibers of the wood. Like seeds in the spring earth, the fungi unfold, their tendrils devouring the muscle of the wood, replacing its strength with the damp softness of decay. Snow banks season after season against wood. From this cold embrace, the melt quickens. The rains ricochet against the skirts of the house, leaving tiny capsules of moldy earth to colonize the timbers. Water from above works its way through conduits between walls, along the borders of windows. The wind drives rain under door jambs. Water kindles the slow fire of decay as it works downward. Myriad reservoirs collect on the interface of wood and stone, spores swell and are nourished. The cycle completes itself—wood and earth will be one.

Meditations on the mortality of wood are better suited to forest glades. Whatever poetic sentiments they arouse are small comfort when you are crawling under the house, poking at beams with an ice pick, sounding the rot for its bottom. Sills rot because water can work at them from both ends. It enters the walls through the eaves and above windows, alongside and under windows and thresholds. Often the foundation wall is laid too close to the ground. Although a minimum of eight inches is the standard specification, a house should really stand a good two feet above grade to be safe from damage caused by water dripping from the eaves and splashing back against the walls. Snow melts into low sills each spring. The bottom boards of the wall sheathing will rot first. They act as sponges, holding moisture against the sills. Wood cannot rot unless it is kept moist and unventilated. The space between the sill and the masonry wall or between the sill and its sheathing boards will trap moisture very well. Condensation is another cause of rot and can occur inside poorly insulated walls. Water drips down the wall and collects on the sills. If kept constantly exposed to moisture, new wood will rot in about seven years. Older timbers rot sooner because age has dried the natural oils that preserve the wood. Wood preservatives such as creosote oil or pentachlorophenol will prolong the life of wood in contact with moisture. Unfortunately these products were unknown when the sills were first laid. If wood is kept dry it will last a very long time. John Cole, in *From the Ground Up,* observes that "wooden doors, frames, and furniture, buried with the ancient Egyptians several thousand years ago, are still as strong, functional, and lovely as the day the tombs were closed."

A few pages back we suspended our disbelief and raised a house. If we had lifted a rotten sill beam, the jack timber would have cut through it like soft cheese. You can't lift a bucketful of water without a bucket. If a rotten sill is not replaced, over the years the weight of the house will tend to compress it, like a brick supported on a loaf of white bread. As one side of the house frame is lowered relative to the others, the house is thrown out of balance and begins to tilt. When the frame loses its equilibrium, all the forces and moments that once worked in concert now seek the path of least resistance, and the tendency toward the horizontal accelerates. Often the rot can be discovered in its initial stage and this cancer excised before it spreads.

A clue to rotten sills is the condition of the sheathing boards that cover them. Very often, clapboards or shingles will have rotted at the bottom of the wall. The sheathing boards beneath them will also have rotted. All these boards should be cut back to the nearest sound stud and removed. Expose the sill. Clean out all the rotten wood with a chisel or hatchet until good, solid wood is showing. The rotten portions will be crumbly and stained a dark reddish or brown color. Sound wood is pale and resists the chisel. Coat the exposed area with a wood preservative such as creosote or Cuprinol. Small pockets of rot in an otherwise sound timber are best filled with mortar. Mix up a batch of patching cement on the stiff side and force it into the cavity. Tack a piece of board across the face of the sill to hold the mortar until it sets. The mortar helps the sill bear whatever is above it. Another method of patching rot is to saw and chisel a rectangular

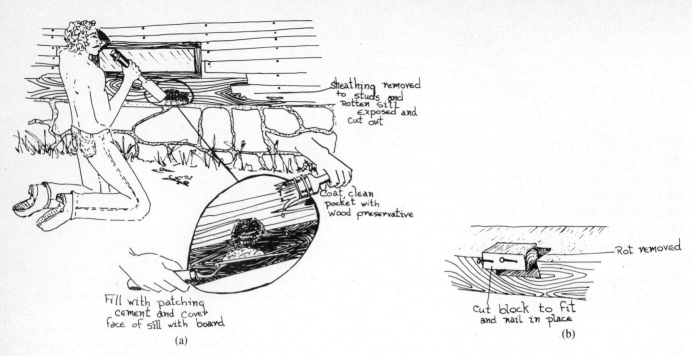

Sheathing removed to studs and Rotten sill exposed and cut out

Coat clean pocket with wood preservative

Fill with patching cement and cover face of sill with board

(a)

Rot removed

Cut block to fit and nail in place

(b)

2–28a, b   *Patching small pockets of rot*

area of sound wood around the rot and fill it with a block of new wood, cut to fit. Pound it into place and nail it securely.

In a post-and-beam-framed house, the major portion of the sill beams are not actually bearing any great weight. They act more as a continuous anchor to hold the upright bearing posts in alignment and transfer the great weights they support to the horizontal. They are more bracing than bearing.

Although the sills do carry the weight of the floor joists (which is considerable), portions of the sill between major upright posts can be removed and replaced so long as the joists themselves are supported. A new sill can be spliced into the sound portions remaining.

Elements of the House Frame

Before decisions can be made intelligently, you must have an understanding of the basic elements of house framing. Knowing where weight is concentrated and how it is carried across a span makes repair work a matter of logic instead of luck.

For hundreds—even thousands—of years men had framed their wooden buildings of heavy timbers, often more than a foot square, that were mortised, tenoned, and pegged together and then raised into position by group labor. In the middle years of the (nineteenth) century, a radical new method called "balloon framing" was evolved, a method of construction using light two-by-four studs nailed rather than joined together in close basket-like manner, the studs rising continuously from foundation to rafters. Uninjured by mortise or tenon, with every strain coming in the direction of the fiber of some portion of wood, the numerous light sticks of the structure formed a fragile-looking skeleton that was actually exceptionally strong. As one contemporary observed, since no mysteries of carpentry were involved in such construction, houses could be thrown up by relatively inexperienced labor in quick time. The method had had to wait until cheap, machine-made nails were available in quantity, which they generally were as early as the 1830's.   [American Heritage, *History of Notable American Houses* quoted in *Shelter* (Random House, 1973), p. 29]

It was only a matter of time when the thinning-down process began to make itself evident in the traditions of colonial carpentry. . . . The difficulty of securing good labor in the West, and also the increasing use of the power sawmill, made it possible and necessary to standardize a quick and easy method of building which would meet the great demand for houses in rapidly growing communities.

[H. V. Walsh, *The Construction of Small Houses*, ibid., p. 29]

In the rural backwaters of northern New England, the old methods persisted well into the latter half of the nineteenth century. Heavy timbers more than sixteen feet in length were still hewn by hand. They were used with sawmill timbers and heavy, dimensioned studding in a hybrid framing system that was common through the early years of the present century. Massive timber frames were used as "insurance," just in case the new-fangled sticks didn't work. Chances are good that if your house was built before 1860 it will have a timber frame. The innovations of mass production did not filter from the cities to the rural areas until after that. Out on the Great Plains, in fact, building lumber was scarce and it was not until the advent of the railroads that light framing materials were available. After machinery and hardware could be moved West by steam engine it became possible to saw the vast forests of that region into the stick lumber needed by the mushrooming towns, and the sawn-up lumber could then be transported to the Great Plains.

The popular image of the farmer and his sons hewing and notching up their timber-frame house themselves is a misconception. A settler newly arrived in the vast wilderness of northern New England had enough to do with the business of mere survival without taking the time to hew and, with an adze, painstakingly turn trees into beams and cut the difficult mortise and tenon joints required to fasten them. Joinery was an art and science, the secrets of which had been jealously guarded since the guilds of the Middle Ages. The settler

2–29   A traditional timber frame house

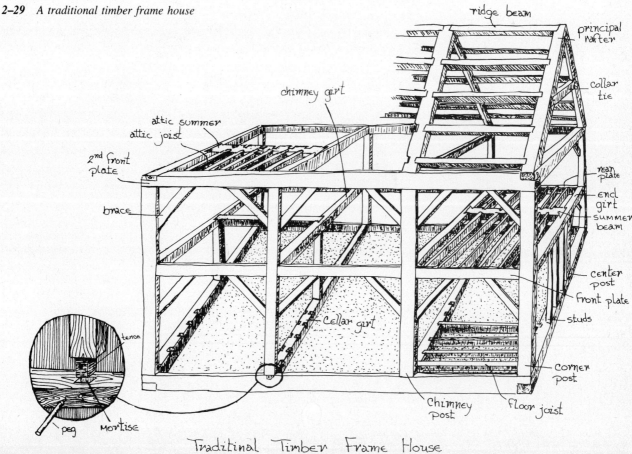

Traditinal Timber Frame House

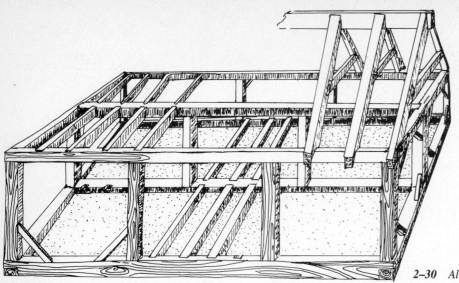

2-30 *Alternate timber frame*

quickly cut down logs and notched up a rude cabin and got on with the work of clearing the land. As his farm prospered and the settlement grew, he could afford to hire a master carpenter and his crew of framers to hew timbers and cut the intricate joints. After all the beams for the house had been cut and assembled on the ground by the hired specialists, the farmer gathered his neighbors for the traditional house- or barn-raising. The carpenters were paid and they departed. The farmer and his sons finished the work of roofing and sheathing the building.

The frames of a heavy-timber house tend to follow a set pattern. They are centered around a massive central fireplace—the focal point of life in the house. The chimney is an integral part of the frame, limiting the freedom of the design and yet making it possible. The need for a central fireplace explains the remarkable similarity of the framing systems of the early house. Figure 2–29 shows the importance of the chimney in the frame and is a fairly accurate guide to a traditional framing system.

With the advent of the heating stove, it became possible to eliminate the large central fireplace and chimney and its corresponding girts and summer beams. A variation of the traditional framing, which is a direct ancestor of modern framing layouts, developed. Figure 2–30 shows this system employed with a single-story house. Note also the use of smaller rafters.

In these drawings it is evident that the weight of the roof and the second floor is transferred to the foundation by the upright posts, at very specific points. The sills tie the bottom of the posts together and anchor the braces that keep them plumb. Obviously then, the entire length of sill between the uprights can be replaced without any jacking other than what is necessary to carry the floor joists.

2-31 *Supporting a floor joist when replacing a rotten sill*

2nd Jack (of course)

Jacking Timber supporting joist for replacement of rotten sill

2-32 *Fastening a joist to a new sill*

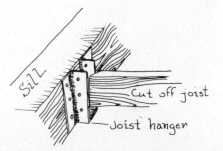

Sill

Cut off joist

Joist hanger

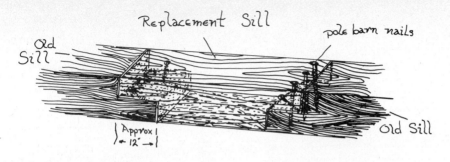

2–33   *Replacing a section of sill*

Rather than mortising out the new sill to accept the ends of the joists, which may themselves be rotten, simply trim the joists to fit flush against the sill and use steel joist hangers to fasten them.

The old sill should be cut to accept a half-lap joint where it abuts the new. The old sill should carry the new. Spike the ends together with 40d spikes driven at an angle or pole-barn nails (long, ring-shanked, heavy spikes) driven through the top surface of the splice. That allows you to lift the entire beam as a unit if the foundation wall must be replaced. It also ties the sill together much more securely than a simple butted joint.

The situation is a little more complicated where a sill has rotted directly under an upright. A method of lifting the post must be devised. If the weight carried by that post can be supported, then only the weight of the post itself is left to manoeuver. The sill may be sound somewhere near the post. The plate beam carried by the post is jacked from both sides, leaving the post standing free, which is then levered to one side with a crow bar. The interior or exterior wall sheathing should be removed to allow working space and room for the jack to fit into the wall cavity. If the sill is so rotted along its length that no solid spot is available, you will have to support the entire weight of the plate beam. See Figures 2–35 and 2–36. When replacing the post, saw off the tenon if you do not wish to cut a new mortise. Since the old post was most likely pegged

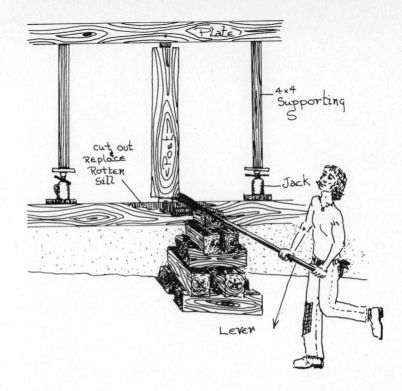

Plate

4×4
Supporting
S

cut out
Replace
Rotten
Sill

Post

Jack

Lever

2–34 *Replacing the sill under a post*

into place, you will probably have to cut it free anyway. The old pegs seldom
drive out easily. Toenail the post to the new sill with spikes (Figure 2–34).
Cribbing is not necessary to jack the plates. Use a length of 4 × 4 as a jacking
post. Be sure to block the jack itself with a large pad of wood. Any angle braces
will have to be loosened before the post can be lifted or moved. Saw through
a stubborn brace if necessary and replace when the post is repaired.

If you have removed the wall sheathing, you can jack the plate at several
points along its length directly from a pad placed over the rotted sill. When the
weight of the roof is supported, you can use lengths of 4 × 4 or 6 × 6 or old
rafter poles to build a cradle under the beam. These are firmly braced against
a bearing block outside the house and against a block nailed to the floor boards
over a joist on the inside. Be sure the floor joists themselves have been cribbed
up with a jacking timber, as in Figure 2–35, to support the additional weight.
An alternative is to insert a lifting timber under the plate, and using 6 × 6 lifting
posts braced to the jack timber, jack up the plate from cribbing. Cribbing can
be stacked quite high as long as it is kept level. Use as much cribbing and as
little post as possible. The jacking timber can be inserted diagonally under an
end girt and front plate to lift a rotten corner post or sill. Relieved of their load,
the posts should remain securely hung from the top plate joint unless the post
itself is rotten and in need of replacement. The rotten sills are then completely
removed and replaced. Saw off the butt ends of the joists flush with the sill as
before and fasten with hangers. Any studding will likewise need to be trimmed
and simply toenailed into the new sill.

If the rot has worked up into the post and weakened it enough to require
replacement, several methods are possible. A horizontal sill can suffer a good
deal of rot without its function being seriously impaired. A vertical post cannot.
The uprights carry a tremendous load. While the compressive strength of wood
is very great, damage to a post under the stress of the weight it carries is
potentially dangerous. The cardboard tube of a toilet-paper roll stood on end

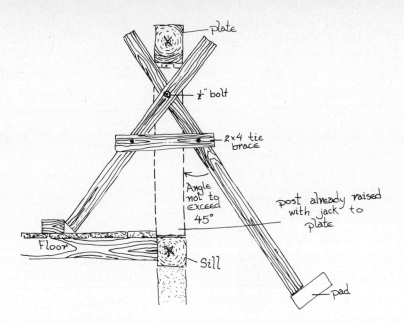

2–35 Replacing a post

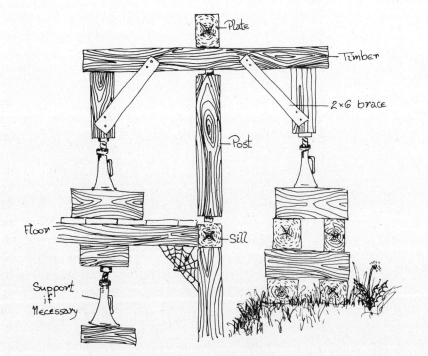

2–36 Another way to replace a post

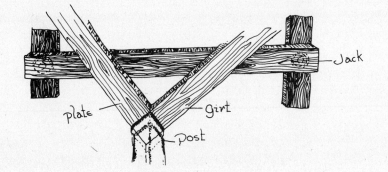

2–37 Supporting a corner to remove a post

will support your weight if you balance yourself carefully. But should the balance shift or the end of the tube suffer a dent, the tube will immediately collapse. A rotten post is similar.

The plate must be lifted to replace the post as described above. A jack post is used. Once the weight is supported, any braces are cut and the tenons are sawed through at top and bottom. Sheathing boards will still be nailed through into the post and will have to be pried free before the post can be removed. In most cases, complete removal of the post will not be necessary. Instead, a new post can be "scabbed" alongside of the old one, on one side or both, depending on the extent of the rot. The new posts can be of 4 × 4 stock, which will remain hidden behind the wall if the beam itself is to be exposed. Cut the scab posts to fit around any angle braces if you do not remove them first. These cuts should fit as tightly as possible as only those surfaces in direct contact with each other bear the weight.

Figure 2–39 outlines the elements of a typical stud-frame house. The principal difference between stud and timber framing is anatomical. The timber frame is modeled on the human skeleton. The bones are large, heavy members upon which the skin is hung. They bear all the weight, and the very weight itself makes the frame stable. It won't blow away. The sheathing only fills in the spaces between the beams, tacked to whatever odd lumber was available for studding, contributing very little to the stability of the frame. In a stud building, the skin and bones are of equal importance, in fact, they must function as a unit. The entire frame would collapse were it not for the bracing effect of the diagonal sheathing boards or let-in corner bracing. This system is analogous to the hard shell of an insect, which is at once skin and bone.

2–38 Stiffening a post

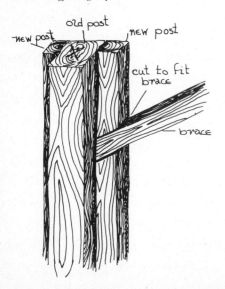

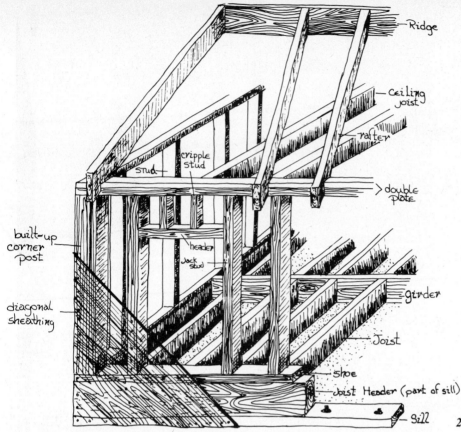

2–39 *Elements of a stud-frame house*

Although the sills carry weight continuously along their length, the actual weight at any given point is considerably less than the concentrated loads that characterize a timber-frame structure. A piecemeal replacement of small sections of sill is usually possible without the use of any jacks. The top plate possesses sufficient rigidity to carry the wall studs from above. The wholesale removal of large sections of sill along the length of a wall is simple. A jack timber is placed under the floor joists, which carries their weight and stiffens the floor

2–40 *Replacing the sill of a stud-frame building*

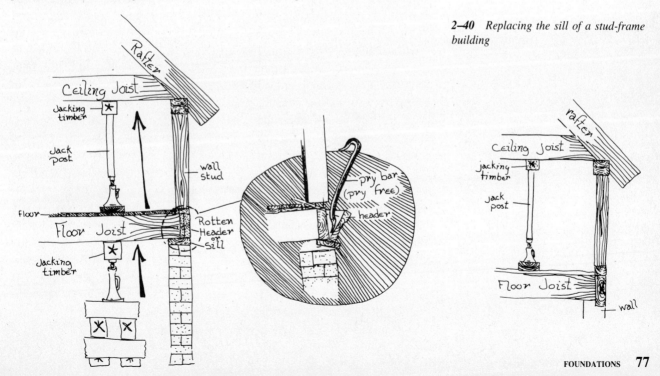

to support a jack used to raise the ceiling joists. The latter should carry the weight of the rafters where they attach to the plate. If the ends of the floor joists rest on the foundation wall itself, the jacking timber in the basement can be eliminated. A plank is placed under the jack to distribute the weight over the floor joists. A pry bar will be necessary to pull the sill free from the joists to which it will be nailed. The wall itself may not lift appreciably from the sill and header because it will be nailed through the shoe. The prybar will force them apart. After the sill is removed, the protruding nails can be cut with a hacksaw. Cut halfway through each nail and then strike it with a hammer. The shank will snap cleanly, saving you time and effort. The new sills are then nailed in place. Be sure to coat all surfaces and edges of the sills with wood preservative. Replacing the sill on the gable end of the house should not require any jacking because the end wall does not support any of the roof weight other than the end rafter pair. Pry bars and sledgehammers should be all the muscle needed.

Sagging Floors

With new sills and foundation walls under it, your house should not fall down before the next winter. You can attend, at this point, to the sagging floors and leaning walls. Trusty jack in hand, it's back into the cellar. You have probably come to know every beam and post in that dark hole by name. Some by all kinds of names, more than once.

Floors sag because whatever is supposed to be holding them up, isn't. Refer back to Figures 2–29, 2–30, and 2–39. Joists are the main floor supports. These are in turn supported by carrying timbers, or girders. These girders are held up by posts which should rest on rocks or cement pads on the cellar floor. Joists seldom span the entire width of the building because the weight they are required to carry would necessitate a huge timber for a single span. Often a post has rotted away at the bottom or twisted out from under its girder, causing the floor above to settle. Sometimes the earth under a post will have been washed out by the subterranean waters of an undrained cellar.

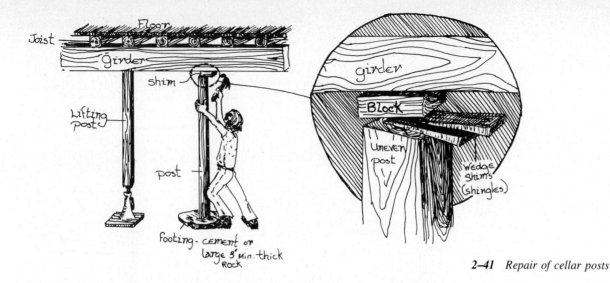

2–41   Repair of cellar posts

If the post is on solid footing, all you need do is jack the girder higher. Lift directly alongside the post if possible. When the girder has been raised to the desired height plus a hair more to allow for settling, simply insert a shim of the appropriate thickness on top of the post and lower the girder back down. Before releasing the full weight, check the post for plumb with a level. Use a sledgehammer to tap it true, then release the jack completely. Shims can be blocks of 2 × 8 or 4 × 8, whatever is necessary to obtain the desired height. They should be wide enough to cover the top of the post and span the width of the beam itself. Tapered shims cut from cedar shingles are used to compensate for a sloping post or a canted girder.

An insufficient number of posts will also cause floors to settle. Often the load on a girder is too heavy for the number of posts (the span between them is longer than the girder can bridge without sagging). Additional posts are inserted under the girder where needed. Once again, the post is cut slightly longer than the desired length to allow for settling. Shims may be necessary as well. For a footing use a large, flat stone at least 3 inches thick or pour a 16-inch-square 4-inch-deep plop of cement into a hole dug in the cellar floor. A concrete slab will support a post without additional footings unless the post is carrying an unusually heavy load, which might be the case in a multistory dwelling or commercial warehouse. Break through the slab and excavate a 2′ × 2′ or 3′ × 3′ square and pour a foot of cement in the hole.

To figure the amount of lift needed to bring a girder back to level, stretch a string from one to the other along its face. The distance that the girder bows below the line is the amount of compensation required. Occasionally, particularly if the house has been haphazardly remodeled, a joist has been cut through for a stairwell or chimney passage. Extra posts are required under the dangling ends of the joists if they are not otherwise supported.

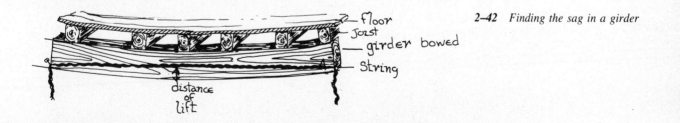

2–42   Finding the sag in a girder

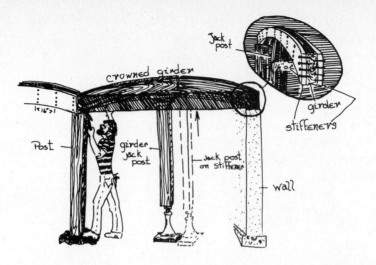

2–43   *Stiffening a sagging girder*

If a forest of posts seems to be growing in your cellar, an alternative is to stiffen the girders themselves. Jack the girder from its middle. Lift it past the level line so that it is "crowned." A plank that corresponds in width to the girder is cut to length and nailed to the joist flush with the top of the girder. This stiffener is only nailed at each end. An additional jack is used to raise the middle of the plank flush with the crowned edge. The stiffener is then nailed along the entire length of the girder using 16d or 20d spikes, 4 in a line every 16 inches apart. Repeat this process on the other side of the girder if additional stiffness is required. The jacks are then released. The girder should settle to near level. It will be prestressed by the jacking and will therefore resist bowing down. Split or cracked joists and girders can be rebuilt using this technique and dry-rotted timbers strengthened.

Several floor joists may have been damaged by dry rot, as often happens when plumbing fixtures above have been leaking unrepaired for years. Carpenter ants or termites can often weaken these timbers. New joists must be scabbed alongside the old ones and tensioned by jacks in the middle of their spans after the ends have been nailed. The new joists may need joist hangers to fasten them to a girder. If they must slip over a girder, they will have to be pushed between the flooring and the girder at a slant and then pounded plumb. When joists that run perpendicular to other joists must be replaced, they should also be fastened

2–44a   *Stiffening a joist*

2–44b   *Replacing a joist*

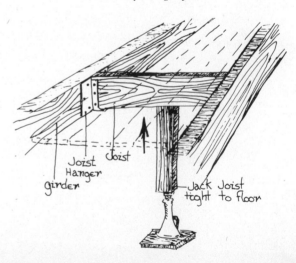

with metal hangers. These units are inexpensive (even if custom made at a welding shop) and strong and help tie the floor together. Custom hangers of ¼-inch steel, finished flat black, can be a handsome solution to the problem of repairing exposed ceiling joists.

If the joist has rotted completely, leaving the joints of the floorboards above nailed to empty space, pry the remains of that joist free and break off any protruding nails. Insert a new joist and jack it up tightly under the floor from both ends. Attach joist hangers and nail it in place.

This scabbing technique can be used to repair sagging ceiling joists as well as cracked rafters and porch roofs, with or without jacking. A good substitute for a jack where a great deal of weight is not present is a 2 × 4 jammed at an angle to the timber to be lifted. The lift occurs as the brace is hammered tight. A lever can be substituted for the hammer to give a compound lift.

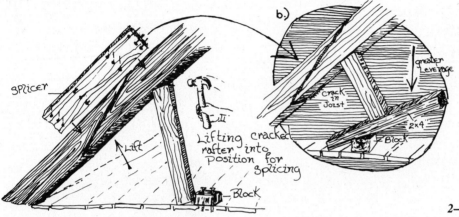

2–45 *Repairing split or sagging rafters*

After the plaster and lath are stripped from the ceilings and walls of a house, it is not unusual to discover deep cracks running through the exposed beams. These cracks, called *checks* or *shakes,* are caused by uneven drying out of the wood and in most cases are not too serious. As the outside dries first, it draws away from the green inside. This happens especially when a house built with green timber is heated soon after it is finished. Most checks are part of a natural process and nothing to worry about. Practically speaking, there is nothing you can do to stop them. A heavy timber has no choice but to dry unevenly. The timbers soon reach equilibrium and check no further.

Occasionally the timber will be stressed where a check has occurred, especially where a portion of a beam has been removed in order to notch it into another. A serious crack can open along the entire length of the timber. A tenon weighted from above tends to split open at the point where it is unsupported. Although, as in Figure 2–46, the joist itself is 8 inches thick, its effective

2–46 *Relationship between load-bearing portion of joist and mortise size*

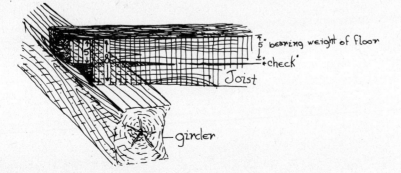

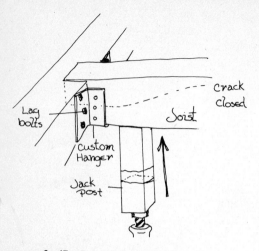

2–47 *Repairing a split joist*

thickness is only that portion actually supported by the girder. The rest of the beam is dead weight and will only add to the stress already on the beam. Thus for an 8-inch beam, only 5 inches are actually bearing the floors. The crack opens along the line of the joint.

I am of two minds about such cracks. If a 5-inch joist has held up the floor for so many years already, it will most likely continue to do so. I would simply leave it alone. Heavy-timber houses were often built with much larger timbers than an engineering analysis would require. On the other hand, the floor above may be loaded by its new occupants with greater weight than it can carry.

A piano and several heavy dressers could cause failure of beams meant to carry only a few bushels of onions or old trunks. If there is a sag in the ceiling directly attributable to a cracked joist, it should be repaired. The cure is not difficult. Jack the split up tight and install a custom joist hanger. Use ¼-inch lag screws to fasten the joist together. Predrill ³⁄₁₆-inch holes and use a socket wrench to turn in the lags. Avoid turning them too tightly as the heads can twist off. Lag bolts can also be used to draw together checks in other structural beams if they are likewise jacked closed. In many cases the beam will not draw in appreciably because it has set so long in its present position. Leave stable beams alone. Lag screws may prevent further cracking by relieving any strains.

When a timber has actually cracked and the danger of failure is obvious, it should be jacked from both sides of the crack back into line. A steel splicing plate cut from ¼-inch steel is lagged across the split. A major supporting beam, such as a top plate or girt, should be fastened through with carriage bolts and steel plates on both sides of the failure. Timbers will sometimes fail where the grain twists around the timber or at large knots. A U-shaped collar support can be used to stiffen a large span or a cracked upright. Steel angle braces can be fabricated for strengthening weak joints between girts and uprights or to add a beam across a span. Steel plates will stiffen a beam that has been cut out for a chimney or stovepipe. Using jacks and common sense, it should be possible

2–48–d *Reenforcing timbers with steel plates*

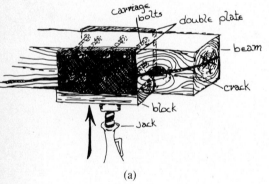

(a)

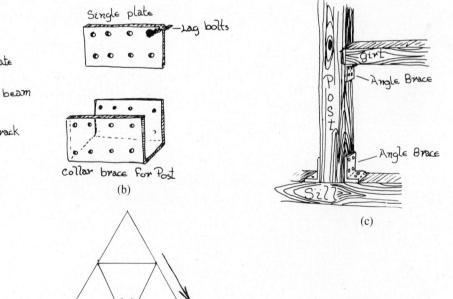

to make even the worst old place structurally sound. This may seem like a lot of labor and expense. It is. Unless there is a compelling reason or an overwhelming compulsion, houses in need of major foundation and timber work are better passed by. This information is offered for those who discover undreamed-of horrors lurking beneath the gloss of fresh paint or who had no other choice but to buy the only place they could afford. Jacking up a house from its foundation is an excellent way to increase the property value of a structure set on posts or a crawl space. A full basement can be excavated under a cellar-less house for not much more than the cost of excavating and pouring a cellar for a new house. And unlike new construction, you can live in the old place while building the cellar under yourself.

Leaning Walls

The foundation is firm, the sills solid, and the floors more or less level. The walls still can bow out. The rafters may have failed or the ceiling joists themselves broken. A sag or hump in the roof indicates additional trouble. Figure 2–49 shows how the house can lean if the integrity of the triangulation principle is violated.

Most of the leanings and saggings of a house can be corrected when the foundation is realigned. If, however, the house was not properly built in the first place and insufficient corner and roof bracing used, the walls can still tend to the horizontal. Careless remodeling may have resulted in the weakening of major structural ties. In some cases a chimney girt may have been cut through for a later stairwell. The weight of the roof can then spread the walls. Joists or rafters insufficiently nailed to the plate can spread over time (although flooring makes that difficult). As a house spreads, the roof is pulled down with it. Where the top plate of a timber-frame house is not continuous, spreading or twisting

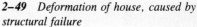

2–49 Deformation of house, caused by structural failure

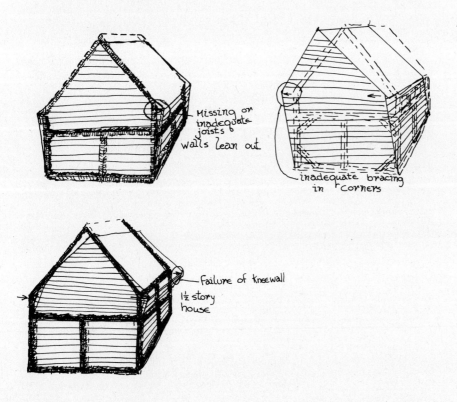

Missing or inadequate joists — walls lean out

inadequate bracing in corners

Failure of kneewall 1½ story house

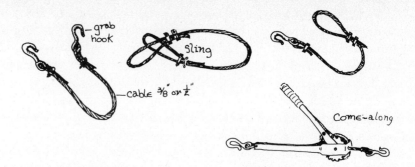

grab
hook

sling

cable ⅜" or ½"

Come-along

2–50 *House-straightening tools*

can occur at a weak splice. Like a pair of dividers, the angle increases with the spread, and from the outside we see the tell-tale swaybacked ridge. However charming this may seem, it indicates a serious defect. A heavy snow, a freezing rain, more snow, and the entire house may collapse, crushed by its own weight.

Skewed walls can be pulled back together. A heavy-duty come-along is the tool you will need. The kind that are sold in hardware stores generally are rated for a one-half or a one-ton pull. While this size would suffice to straighten a bare frame, it will not be a great enough pull for an entire house, with its bracing of sheathings and floorings, roof weight, and so on. By sniffing around a construction yard, especially a structural-steel fabricator's, you should be able to locate the mother of all come-alongs. A two-ton pull is the minimum size. By this time, your negotiating skills should be sharp enough to allow you a weekend's use. With the come-along you will need lengths of ⅜-inch or ½-inch steel cable and various grab hooks or slings. Ask advice about the best way to "rig" your cables and pullers.

The cable is hooked around the plate. Sheathing boards will have to be removed to allow the cable to go through the wall. The other end is hooked to a come-along, which is in turn fastened to the sill, opposite the wall to be pulled. Begin pulling, watching closely to see which moves first, the wall plate or the sill. If the sill moves first, you will have to obtain a more stable purchase. Perhaps the cable can be passed through the wall to a large tree outside the house. Slip a length of 8 × 8 or 8 × 12 between the sill and the foundation wall to help anchor the fixed end. As the tension increases, the house should pull together with a great groaning and creaking. The roof will rise with a heavy shrug. It will generally be necessary to cut and/or remove angle braces on the posts of the frame before the house will move any great amount. These braces must be renailed when the frame is pulled into position, *before* the tension of the come-along is released—otherwise the frame will ease back into its original repose.

2–51 *Pulling crooked walls together*

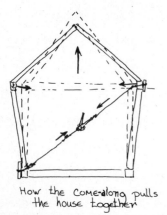

How the come-along pulls
the house together

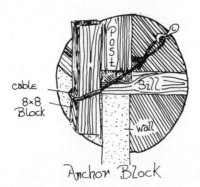

cable

8×8
Block

post

sill

wall

Anchor Block

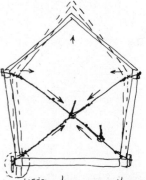

using two come-alongs

If it is at all possible to find a suitable purchase point, a jack from the first floor to the ridge pole will help shoulder the load on the come-alongs. If there is no ridge beam, a jacking timber can be used under the rafter peaks. This technique will work particularly well with a cathedral ceiling. Houses that were gutted inside to open up such a space will sag unless the plates were properly tied together when the floor joists were removed. Jacking from the second floor to the ridge will only work against the lifting force of pulling in the walls.

After the first wall is pulled in, another set of cables and come-along is rigged up from the opposite wall. The entire operation may proceed more smoothly if both come-alongs are operated simultaneously, with the force applied slowly and evenly. Sometimes only one wall will be in need of straightening. After the wall is plumbed, temporary 2 × 4 braces can be nailed to upright posts to help maintain the alignment until the permanent braces are reinstalled. It is always a good idea to pull the walls farther in than their desired position, to compensate for their tendency to return to their repose after the tension is released. The cables can be hitched along the wall wherever there is a serious bow. Before the come-alongs are released, clamber up into the attic and fasten *collar ties* across the rafter pairs. Those are simply 2 × 6 or 2 × 4's nailed at a point one-third of the distance from the peak to the plate. These braces should be solidly spiked. They prevent the rafters from spreading and thereby help hold the building together. A lack of collar ties and undersized rafters is often the cause of a sagging roof. Jack from the attic floor to the peak, as in Figure 2–52, and add the collar ties to straighten the roof. Be sure the joists under the jack are also supported from below.

This is a great deal of trouble to go through. My advice is, if the walls only lean a few inches, learn to live with it. By all means, add collar ties to the rafters to keep them from further spreading. Add strong braces to the gable end walls. Make sure the walls are braced wherever possible. Braces can be let into a partition that falls under a chimney girt.

A popular device for preventing spread of walls, which will also pull the house together, is a turnbuckle—two long steel rods threaded at both ends, which together span the house from plate to plate. Turnbuckles are generally made of ½-inch steel and can be cut to length at a local welding shop. A hole is bored directly through the plate and a flat bar of steel at least six inches square is used as a washer. Nuts are threaded on a projecting rod. The threads where the rods meet at the center of the building are opposite to each other. The ends are screwed into a specially forged bracket—the turnbuckle proper. As it turns, the turnbuckle draws the rods together and pulls in the walls. Additional slack can be taken up outside the plates. The extra ends are then sawed off with a hacksaw. The turnbuckle is turned with a wrench, once the tension increases.

The advantages of turnbuckles over a come-along are several. They accomplish the same job with a minimum of effort and dislocation of sheathing. They can add an interesting design element to an exposed cathedral-ceiling space. They are not terribly expensive to make up. They can be hidden in a ceiling if their appearance is objectionable. Or they may be used as a temporary support until a girt can be added across the walls and lagged in place with angle irons. They are sometimes used in conjunction with dummy beams, where they are partially hidden by a cosmetic timber.

Pulling in walls that lean in the same direction must be done from the outside of the building. A large tree is the most convenient anchor. You can

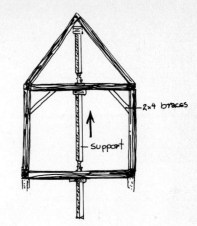

2–52 Raising a sagging roof

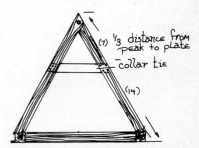
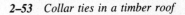

2–53 Collar ties in a timber roof

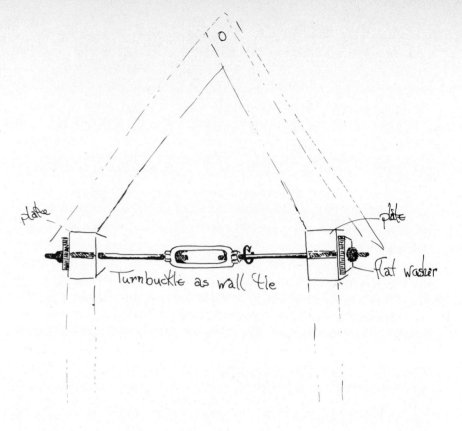

2–54 *Steel turnbuckle used to pull walls in*

Turnbuckle as wall tie

plate

plate

Flat washer

pull the house over before the tree will move. As one wall is pulled into place, its opposite should follow. If you are lacking suitable trees, a tractor may do the job. There is a good possibility, however, that a tractor will tip over, too. A bulldozer will provide the necessary weight and horsepower. This type of work is easiest when the house has been stripped to the bare frame. A hardware-store come-along would then suffice. If the inside walls are left intact, you will crack every bit of plaster as soon as they begin to move. Be careful to pull slowly, as chimneys and fireplaces can crack and windows can rupture with explosive force if they are bowed or twisted. Jacking the house will often necessitate refitting doors and windows, as will any operation that disturbs the structural repose.

Gable end walls can be pulled from either the inside of a gutted house or from the outside. A cable should be fastened onto the end girt at the point of maximum bow. Because they carry relatively little weight, these walls should straighten without difficulty. All these methods involve time and expense. Success is not guaranteed. When a timber has been in place for a long time, it has taken on whatever shape it needed to stay there. Like old bones, old timbers

2–55 *Straightening the side walls*

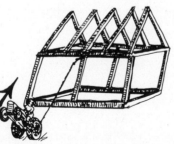

2–56 *Straightening the end walls*

don't spring back very well. They can break before they will bend. Sometimes, no matter how much lifting or pulling force is exerted, a beam will not budge. You may move the entire wall in a foot or more and not materially affect the shape of a warped beam. Big timbers are not like 2 × 4s, which can be straightened with a nail or two. A beam will stay the way it wants to.

I am not particularly bothered by a house that leans in odd directions. As long as the foundation is firm and the roof well braced, it isn't going to go anywhere. There is something to be said for the delight of skewed walls and corners that meet in another dimension. It's like living in an M. C. Escher print. Once a house has settled into a comfortable shape, it requires unnatural energy to change it. Those who feel that the music of the spheres is played on symmetrical strings can pursue the perfection of form and the correction of corners. For such readers, I outline the repair procedures. For myself, I remember that the Chinese believed only demons traveled in straight lines.

> The house itself is only a detail forming a part of the surrounding country, like a jewel in its setting and harmonizing with it. For this reason, all signs of artificiality must be hidden as much as possible and the rectilinear lines of the walls must be hidden or broken by overhanging branches. A perfectly square house, shaped like a magnified piece of brick, is justifiable in a factory building, because it is a factory building where efficiency is the first consideration. But a perfectly square house for a home to live in is an atrocity of the first order.
>
> [Lin Yutang, *The Importance of Living*]

CHAPTER III

THE ROOF

"No roof—no building."

"A roof over our heads . . ." From the day the first man crawled under an overhanging ledge, shelter has entailed the attempt to keep a roof over our heads. Foundation and wall, post and beam, are only the handle of the umbrella.

> In Japan, the roof of a house is called *yane*. Now yane literally means *house-root;* . . . the name might have been applied through association; a tree without a root dies, and a house without a roof decays. . . . the Chinese character *ne* meant origin. . . .   [Edward S. Morse, *Japanese Homes and Their Surroundings*]

As the root is the tree it is also the leaves. A roof grows out of the frame just as the foliage grows from the branches of the tree. The leaves are the life and sustenance of the tree. Like the leaves, the roof is in intimate and existential contact with the weather. As the leaves are renewed each spring, roofs too, have their seasons.

Materials and Types

Because water flows downhill, a roof works like the scales of a fish or the feathers of a bird—in one direction only. If the integrity of the lattice is broken, as with damaged or missing shingles, water can wander inward under the roofing and through the sheathing, into the house, where rot begins to grow.

A flat roof is nothing more than a bathtub on top of a house. The drain plug must always be pulled because the framing will not support the weight of a full tub. Likewise, the tub will not work if it can drain through places other than the plug hole.

The asphalt-mineral-surfaced shingle is one of the truly significant contributions of modern technology to the art of building. Cheap, simple to install, and relatively long-lasting, it provides a tight seal against the vagaries of wind and rain. Asphalt shingles come in a wide variety of colors, textures, and patterns and can contribute significantly to the overall appearance of the house.

Until asphalt roofing became widely available, the only roofing materials in general use in this country were made of wood, metal, clay, or slate. Thatch

3–1 How a roof leaks

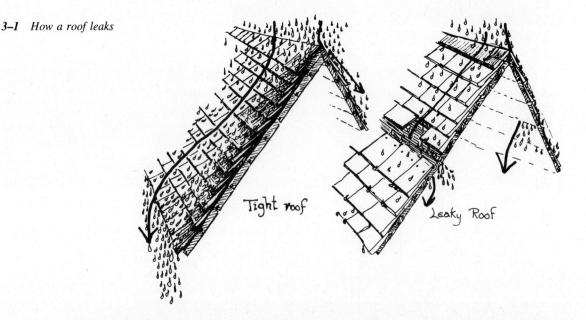

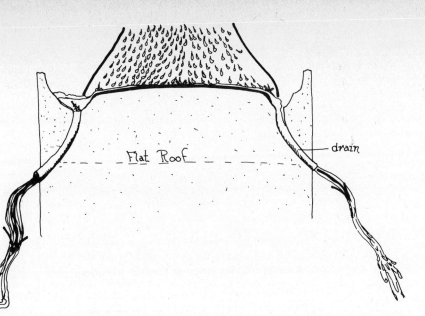

3–2 How a flat roof drains

was quickly found to be unsuitable to the rigors of the North-American climate, with its severe storms and heavy snows. Slate was expensive and required steep and heavy roof framing. Although metal is one of the oldest and most durable roofing materials in use (the copper and lead roofs of Europe are still sound after 800 years), its expense confines it to public buildings and the homes of the wealthy. Cheap sheet-steel roofing was not readily available until the advent of the industrial economy and its distribution system. The invention of galvanizing made it possible to protect the steel from rust without using expensive alloys, overcoming its major disadvantage. Galvanized steel roofing found wide use in commercial structures and in rural housing because of its low cost. Formerly, wood shingles were easily manufactured from local materials and used extensively. Today the cost of labor both in their production and installation has considerably diminished their use.

Asphalt roofing is available either as individual overlapping shingles or in roll roofing, either mineral-surfaced or unsurfaced, which is cemented and nailed to the deck. The pitch of the roof determines which type of roofing is best (Figure 3–3). Mineral-surfaced roll roofing is used with saturated-felt underlayment for roof pitches under 4 inches per foot to within 1 inch of horizontal.

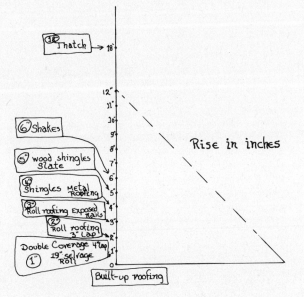

3–3 Roof pitch and choice of roofing materials

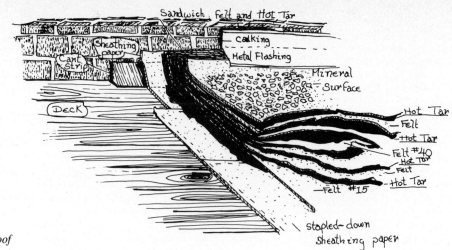

Sandwich Felt and Hot Tar
Caulking
Metal Flashing
Sheathing paper
Cant Strip
Mineral Surface
Deck
Hot Tar
Felt
Hot Tar
Felt #40
Hot Tar
Felt
Hot Tar
Felt #15
stapled-down Sheathing paper

3–4   Construction of a built-up roof

There is no reason why it cannot be used for steeper pitches other than its appearance, which some find unacceptable. The broad seams with their exposed nails or ribbons of tar are better suited to industrial buildings and sheds where economy rather than aesthetics are the prime consideration.

Flat roofs involve the construction of a continuous watertight membrane built of layers of saturated felt and hot tar. The resurfacing of such a roof is best left to professionals who have the equipment to boil the tar and pump or lift the molten material to the roof. Sometimes it is possible to rent the necessary outfit. The tar comes in solid blocks weighing about sixty pounds each. Figure 3–4 shows the construction of a built-up roof deck. The most frequent trouble spot is where the deck meets the side wall. Punctures can be repaired with flashing cement and felt paper.

As you walk down a city street, look at the roofs of the buildings. You will observe a bewildering variety of shingle types and patterns. Most of those are older roofs; today, only three basic types of shingles are available outside of the larger urban areas, where distributors may still stock some of the older patterns. In most areas, the choice is actually limited to two basic kinds of shingles. The most common type is generally what comes to mind when people think "shingle,"—the three-tab strip shingle. It is available in a variety of weights. A variation on the strip shingle, which is fast replacing its use in new construction because of the speed with which it can be applied, is the random-embossed, self-aligning strip shingle, also known as a *jet* shingle. A variation on the jet is the *architect* shingle, which is designed to recreate the random patterns and overlapping effect of wood shakes. Both of these types are available in a *wind-seal,*® thermoplastic-cement coating, which seals courses to each other. The third major type of shingle is the lock-tab shingles. It once enjoyed large usage, particularly for reroofing, because it can be laid directly over old shingles without revealing the pattern underneath. This type is becoming harder to find, which is unfortunate, because it is easily applied. Older patterns of shingles, generally no longer available, are the individual tab and hex shingles.

On a given roof slope, which shingle style you use is a matter of preference. All will give roughly similar results. The heavier-weight shingles will last longer. Their extra weight is attributable to the thicker mineral surface on the weather exposure. This is also an advantage of the jet shingle, which because it has no cutouts, allows less wear on the shingles below. Some people object

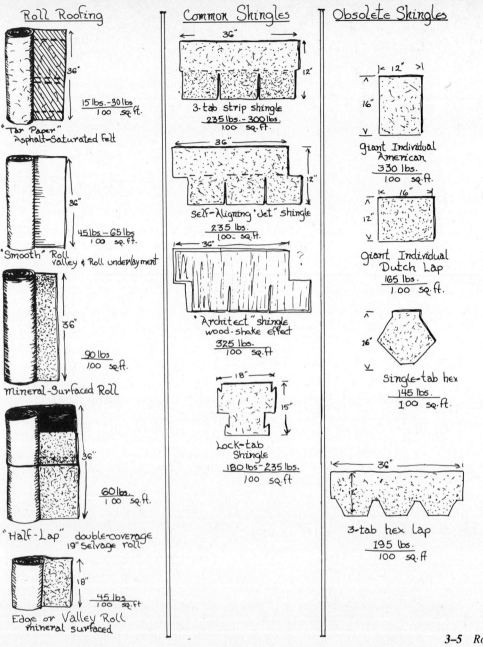

Roll Roofing

15 lbs.–30 lbs.
100 sq. ft.

"Tar Paper"
Asphalt-Saturated Felt

36"

45 lbs.–65 lbs.
100 sq. ft.

"Smooth" Roll
valley & Roll underlayment

36"

90 lbs
100 sq. ft.

Mineral-Surfaced Roll

36"

60 lbs.
100 sq. ft.

"Half-Lap" double-coverage
19" selvage roll

36"

18"

45 lbs
100 sq. ft.

Edge or Valley Roll
mineral surfaced

Common Shingles

36"   12"

3-tab strip shingle
235 lbs.–300 lbs.
100 sq. ft.

36"   12"

Self-Aligning "Jet" shingle
235 lbs.
100 sq. ft.

36"

"Architect" shingle
wood-shake effect
325 lbs.
100 sq. ft.

18"   15"

Lock-tab
Shingle
180 lbs–235 lbs.
100 sq. ft

Obsolete Shingles

12"   16"

giant Individual
American
330 lbs.
100 sq. ft.

16"   12"

giant Individual
Dutch Lap
165 lbs.
100 sq. ft.

16"

single-tab hex
145 lbs.
100 sq. ft.

36"   12"

3-tab hex Lap
195 lbs.
100 sq. ft

3–5 Roofing materials

to the strong horizontal line that these shingles give the roof and prefer the alternating "shadow lines" of the standard three-tab cutout shingle. Architect shingles look best on a steeply pitched roof where the pattern is most clearly readable. Because they are actually two layers of shingles bonded together, they wear very well and will last longer than other types of asphalt roofing. They also cost almost as much as real wood shingles but this factor is mitigated somewhat by their faster application time.

Wood shingles are one of the most widely used alternatives to asphalt roofing. Shingles are commonly cut from cedar, although redwood and cypress are used in some localities. All these woods have a natural resistance to rot because of their high resin content. When properly applied, they will furnish a very durable and extremely handsome roof. The wood mellows with age to a soft silver, and as the years pass, moss and lichens begin to create a living tapestry (which does not affect the tightness of the roofing). Their wide use is limited by cost (the material is expensive and the labor intensive) and by the fire hazard they present. Zoning codes in some areas actually prohibit their use. Fire-insurance premiums will be higher where they are allowed.

For durability and rugged beauty of texture, the ultimate in wood roofing is achieved with wood shakes. These are the direct descendant of the roofing used by the pioneers, and the techniques of their manufacture and use have changed little since our forefathers split great white-oak bolts with a mallet and froe. Except for clay tiles, shakes are the only type of roofing you could manufacture by yourself if you had the inclination.

Metal roofing today falls into two major categories: individual sheet roofing of galvanized steel or aluminum and the standing seam roof of *terne* metal, which is a copper-bearing steel coated with a lead-tin alloy. Galvanized steel-sheet roofing is manufactured in a wide variety of corrugation and ribbing patterns and in stock lengths up to twenty-four feet. A coating of two ounces of zinc per square foot is the accepted minimum standard. Steel roofing is popular because of its low initial cost, rapid application, and light weight. It is common in heavy-snow regions because it will shed snow easily. Because it does not require solid decking for support, sheet roofing is economical for large structures such as barns as well as for houses. On slopes of less than 4 in 12, it has a tendency to leak along the vertical seams, especially when accumulated snow begins to melt. The seams can be sealed with a bead of flashing cement or silicone caulking. When used over a heated building special precautions must be taken to avoid condensation which will occur when water vapor strikes the cold undersurface of the metal. A layer of plywood or Aspenite® sheathing between the top of the rafters and the underside of the metal roofing will alleviate this difficulty. Corrugated aluminum roofing is similar to galvanized steel except that it is available in wider sheets. A solid deck or more-closely spaced nailers are required to furnish extra support for this weaker metal. Also, it is prone to corrosion in salt-water areas and is much more expensive than steel roofing.

Terne-metal roofing provides an absolutely watertight and extremely durable roof deck. As with galvanized roofing, it can be repainted, which continually extends its useful life. The roofing itself comes in sheets or seamless rolls, which must be applied over a solid deck. The joints between the sheets are crimped and/or soldered to make them watertight. The usefulness of terne-metal roofing is limited by its extremely high cost and its general unavailability. Roofers with the necessary experience or tools to handle it are likewise scarce.

Slate shingles are all but unavailable today. They are a relic of an age when labor and materials were far less expensive. Even then, they were an indication of a householder's prosperity. Few could afford them. Although there may be several quarries that will produce them on a special order basis, almost the only practical source for slate roofing is salvage from torn-down buildings.

Slate shingles are installed in the same way as American individual shingles, using copper nails. Iron nails would rust out before the slate even began to wear. It may prove difficult to locate a roofer who is familiar with the methods for repairing slate roofs. They are a dying breed. Far less expensive and more readily available are asbestos-cement composition shingles. Like slate, they are immune to rot, decay, fire, and weather. They should also be installed with copper-clad nails and likewise require substantial framing to support their great weight. The heavier the material, the steeper the pitch.

Reroofing:
Stripping the shingles and other techniques

Reroofing a house can be done in two ways: complete removal of the existing shingles or laying new shingles over old. If the original shingles are not badly warped or humped and the roof deck underneath is sound, the new roofing can be laid over the old. Be sure the framing is of adequate strength to carry the additional weight along with the snow and wind loads. I would never add a new layer if there were more than two existing layers of roofing, and even with two layers, it is a question of their condition and the framing. Most roofs will accept a third layer if the pitch is steeper than 6 in 12 and the rafters are 2 × 8 or larger. If in doubt, calculate the dead and live loads from a framing table in your carpentry handbook.

To lay a roof over an existing roof, all loose shingles are first renailed. Protruding nails should be pulled. All broken shingles are replaced with pieces of new shingles to fill in the gaps. Warped shingles are flattened and nailed. The object is to smooth the bumps and wrinkles in the old roof as much as possible, since they will show through the new layer. This process can be carried to the extreme of using *feathering* strips (tapered pieces of wood similar to clapboards), which are nailed parallel to the butt edges of the old shingles, although with the extra labor involved, it may make more sense to strip the entire deck instead. Where cornice moldings are used along the edge of a roof, there will be a gap between the edge shingles and the roof decking. The old shingles are broken back at least six inches along the edge of the rakes and eaves (those portions of the roof deck that overhang the side and bottom edge of the roof respectively), and 1 × 6 wood strips are nailed over the gap to provide solid nailing for the shingles. A metal *drip edge* is run around the perimeter of the roof. Where the decking is sound, the old shingles are broken back flush with the edge of the deck and the drip edge laid to the edge as above.

Drip edge is manufactured from galvanized steel or aluminum in 10-foot lengths and 5- and 8-inch widths. The wider piece is used at the bottom edge of the roof. Overlap all joints by at least 1 inch. The narrower strip is applied along the rakes from the bottom up, overlapping each successive piece by at

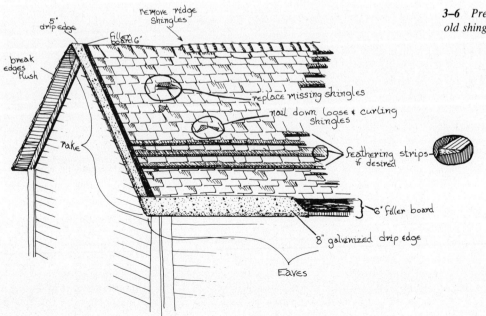

3–6 Preparation for reshingling over old shingles

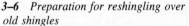

least 2 inches. If eavestroughs or gutters are to be added or replaced, the work is done before the new roofing is laid. Finally, strip the ridge-cap shingles from the peak of the roof.

New shingles are laid exactly as if a new roof deck were being covered. The only exceptions are, first, the starter course along the eave is made from a shingle cut in half lengthwise instead of from a full-width shingle—this provides the necessary double coverage and avoids an unsightly hump at the bottom of the roof—and, second, longer nails must be used for old work. Use 1¾-inch nails for reroofing and 1¼-inch nails for new work.

Pull the nails from the chimney and vent-pipe flashings and lay the shingles under them, as with new work. If it is not possible to pry up the old flashings, apply a liberal bead of flashing cement under and above all shingles that abut the chimney or pipe, running the flashing cement well up the surface of that projection. When you are flashing against the side of a building, the old shingles can often be broken back and the step flashings refitted to the new shingles. That may be more trouble than it is worth and can cause a leak-prone hollow if more than one layer of old shingles is to be covered. Nail an 8-inch width of smooth-surfaced roll roofing along the entire length of the sidewall and coat it with flashing cement. Embed the new shingles in this cement. Run an additional bead of cement along the junction of this sheet and the wall siding, either with a caulking gun or a trowel fashioned from a 1-inch width of cedar shingle. Cedar shingles make excellent flashing trowels, as they are flexible and can be manipulated much more easily than a metal trowel, providing greater control and a neater appearance. If the old flashing around a chimney has rusted or corroded away, it should be replaced with new metal.

Television antennas are another problem area. Lead-in insulators should be pulled and replaced with new ones after the shingles are laid. Seal them with a daub of cement. Guy wires for the antenna mast are attached by screw anchors to the roof. They are unscrewed one at a time and started in a new hole after the shingles are applied and sealed with cement. It is not often practical to remove the antenna-mast anchor. Cut the shingles to fit closely to it and tar the hell out of the whole mess.

The guiding principle for the use of flashing cement is to imagine yourself a raindrop looking for a way under the shingles, between a crack, and into the roof. Cement any of the places a raindrop can work into, a step that is especially necessary where a chimney does not straddle the ridge of the roof. Snow can collect against the high side and work up under the shingles. A layer of cement under the first few courses above the crotch will prevent this infiltration. Keep a jug of kerosene or waterless hand cleaner handy; flashing cement has an uncanny knack of smearing itself on everything. Check your elbows and the seat of your pants, your cuffs, and your knees before leaning or sitting on anything.

If the old shingles are badly buckled and split or if the roof deck will not support the weight of additional shingles, the old roof should be removed. That is particularly important if the old roofing consists of badly rotted wood shingles. The thick butt ends will show through the new roofing unless feathering strips are used. Schedule this operation to coincide with a predicted run of good weather, as once the deck is exposed, a rainstorm can thoroughly soak attic insulation and ruin plaster, ceilings, and furniture. In Vermont the saying is, if you don't like the weather, wait ten minutes; long-range forecasts are not given much credibility. Strip as much roofing as you think you will be able to

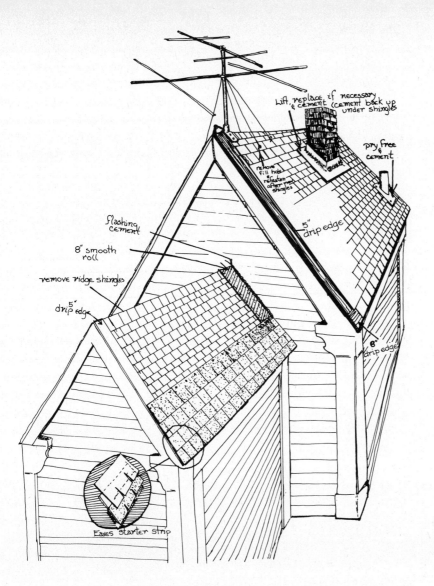

Lift, replace if necessary
& cement (cement back up
under shingles

remove
Fill hole
& refasten
after new
shingles

pry free
& cement

flashing
cement

8" smooth
roll

5"
drip edge

remove ridge shingles

5"
drip edge

8"
drip edge

Eaves starter strip

3–7 *Flashing-cement application in reroofing*

replace in a day unless you can provide cover for the exposed deck with a tarpaulin of sorts. Do not strip more than one side of the roof at a time.

There are various theories as to the best direction in which to strip shingles—down from the top, up from under the butts, or even sideways. My experience indicates that all these methods work to some extent, depending upon the layers of roofing and the holding power of the nails themselves. A common practice before self-sealing shingles were invented was to nail each side of the tab to increase wind resistance. If that was done on your roof, stripping will be considerably harder. You will have to experiment with different techniques to see which one will work best for you.

Exactly how does one get up onto a roof and, more important, stay there? Although it is theoretically possible for the human body, by clever and careful attention to balance and the center of gravity, to scale almost any surface, working comfortably on that surface is another matter entirely. The upper limit of slope that can safely be worked without aid falls somewhere between 5″ in 12″ and 6″ in 12″. Roofers have solved the problem through the use of a clever invention—the roof bracket. A bracket is made of steel or wood and can be adjusted to various pitches. It fastens to the roof deck and supports a staging plank that provides a horizontal surface from which to work. Brackets can be rented or borrowed from a carpenter neighbor. They are not expensive to buy. You can also build a nonadjustable bracket from a length of 2 × 4 and a scrap of sheetmetal.

Starting is always the slowest part of roofing. There are two options. You can begin with a ladder, stripping away as many shingles as you can reach, moving along the eave until the entire bottom portion has been stripped clean. Aluminum ladders are dangerously unsuited to this kind of work. They are too light to resist any sideways impetus and will slide as you lean out from dead center. They also blow over in a strong breeze. Metal slides easily along a metal-edged roof. Wood ladders are heavy enough to resist blowing over, and in addition, they tend to cut into a metal edge, thus stabilizing themselves. They resist sideways motion because of the friction of the wood fibers.

A more efficient approach is to rent pipe scaffolding. It comes in panels of several heights, which are easily assembled with braces to create a simple and very stable working platform as high or higher than you would like to climb. They can be rented quite economically by the week or month. On soft earth, use blocks of wood under the pipe ends to prevent the staging from sinking in. These blocks will also compensate for differences in the level of the terrain. The panels should be close to eyeball level, otherwise they will tend to bind during assembly. Scaffolds over 10 or 12 feet high, should be roped to the building for safety. Once the platform is built to the desired height, which should be between knee and waist level relative to the edge of the roof, 2 × 10 or 2

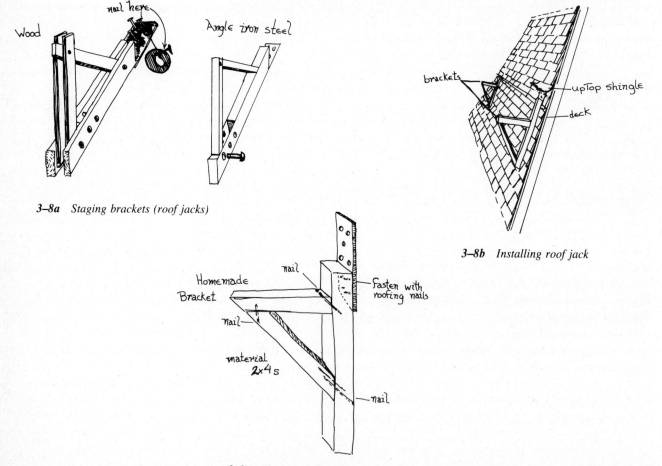

3–8a *Staging brackets (roof jacks)*

3–8b *Installing roof jack*

3–8c *Homemade bracket*

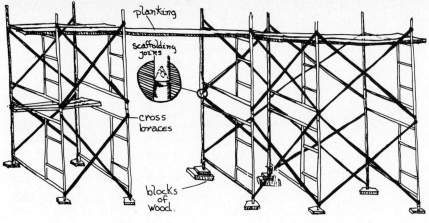

3-9 *Scaffolding*

× 12 staging planks are laid across them, and 4 × 8 sheets of plywood laid across these planks will make the Cadillac of staging platforms.

While the ideal staging would run the entire length of the building, you can cut down on the number of panels needed and, consequently, the rental cost, by erecting individual towers. These are easily moved as a unit. Several towers can be set along the length of the building and the gaps spanned with 2 × 10 planks. Two men can pick up a twelve-foot tower and carry it to where it is needed. Greater stability for taller towers is gained by adding a third panel section.

Pump jacks are another method for building a staging platform. They work on the same principle as bumper jacks. A sleeve can be moved along the length of a 4 × 4 post, the top of which is braced to the roof deck. When the jack handle is raised, the entire staging is inched up the post. The possibility of failure in the rachet mechanism, while remote, is enough to deter many people from using them. Although a pump jack must also be moved to allow new shingles to be laid under the brace, using one is a lot faster than working from a ladder.

3-10 *Pump jack*

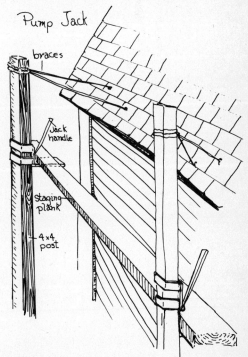

Working from the ladder or scaffolding, strip the shingles as high as you can reach along the entire length of the roof. A bracket is then nailed directly to the bare deck no higher than you can reach comfortably from the ladder or scaffolding. Another bracket is nailed to the deck to support the other end of the staging plank. The plank is laid across these two brackets and a third bracket added to the middle of the span. The middle is always added last, after the plank is in place. This method allows the plank to sit well and compensates for any bows in the plank or differences in height that would otherwise make the ends rest unevenly. Use 8d common nails, three nails per bracket. If your nails do not catch solid decking, move the bracket. Use 16-foot lengths of 2 × 10, free from any knots or splints that might weaken the wood. Use dry wood for planks, as green wood will be too heavy to move around the roof. Three brackets will support a 16-foot plank. Figure a pair of brackets to every 8 feet of staging length.

On long roofs, the entire length should be spanned with a course of staging, if possible. As the shingles are stripped, successive courses of brackets are added until the peak is reached. Space courses of staging as far as you can reach. If you do not have enough brackets and plank to run the entire length, divide the roof in half and clean each side to the peak first.

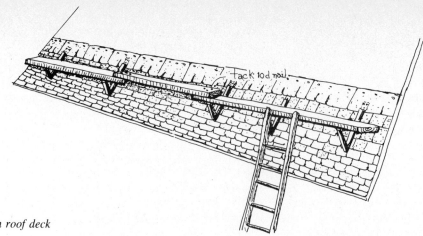

3–11   Staging layout on roof deck

There are several tools that will prove invaluable in stripping shingles. A long-handled, flat-bladed shovel is perhaps the most useful. Drive it under the butts of the shingles and pry up while pushing. Often great sections of roofing will tear free, nails and all. The flat edge of the shovel will pry most of the nails out. You will make only a small dent at first, but once you have cleared an area, the shingles will begin to come off quickly. Another tool that works almost as well is an ice chopper. Keep a flat file handy to periodically touch up the edges as they curl over. A flat steel bar, often called a *Wonderbar,*® is the second most useful item in a reroofers tool kit. It can be used to pry up ridge shingles, which will resist the shovel, and to work loose flashings. Hammer in any nails that may still protrude from the deck.

Keep a wary eye over your shoulder for the weather. A sudden shower can sweep full blown over the ridges on even the clearest summer day. If rain appears imminent and a great portion of the deck is bare and defenseless, a poly sheet can save the ceilings. The nails under the top course of shingles are removed and the sheet slipped up as far as it will go. This prevents water from flowing down under the top of the sheet. Secure the poly with battens and staples to keep it on the roof.

Tarpaper can be used instead of poly to cover the exposed roof. Some people make the mistake of papering as they go, which results in the scraps of shingles falling down behind the paper where they cannot be removed. It is far better to work until your weather eye warns you of the approaching storm and then, beginning at highest point, lay the tarpaper to the roof, slipping each course under the one above it. You will have to remove the brackets and staging as you work your way down the roof. Secure the paper with batten strips along the overlaps and edges to prevent the wind from tearing it away. If the paper extends to the ridge, it can be left in place when the new shingles are applied. Otherwise remove it and try to salvage it for reuse.

3–12   Protecting the exposed deck

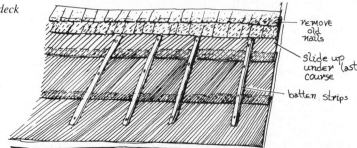

remove old nails

slide up under last course

batten strips

One person working alone will not find it easy to cover a roof with paper or plastic, especially in a breeze. Before he can slip the top edge up under the old shingles, they will crack and the paper will slip. Consider hiring a young neighbor to supply the extra hands and feet. Or you may be able to exchange labor with a friend—a day in the wood lot for a day on the roof. I know of one fellow who provided the beer for a dozen or so friends and got a new roof on in record time. Granted, it wasn't the neatest roof in the world, but it did shed water. Try to hold off on the beer until the bulk of the work is done.

Spread a sheet of poly on the ground below the eaves before you set up the scaffolding. It will not only protect flower beds and shrubs from damage by roofing debris but also facilitate cleanup. If you neglect the cleanup, nails will be sprouting up with grass each year. And although shingles eventually rot, they do not make a very attractive mulch.

As you strip the accumulated layers of shingles and dust from the decking, it may become apparent that the decking itself is in need of replacement. If your shovel pushes clear through the roof boards, you can count on it. Open roofing that once supported wood shingles will not carry asphalt. Frequently, large sections of decking will have rotted away, especially near the edges of the roof. If the roof lathing was nailed down in relatively straight courses of even width, you may be able to fill in the gaps with sheathing boards. Individual rotten boards are cut back to the middle of a rafter, removed and replaced with new boards. If the top of the rafter itself is too rotten to hold nails, "scab" a piece of 2 × 4 alongside the rafter's edge.

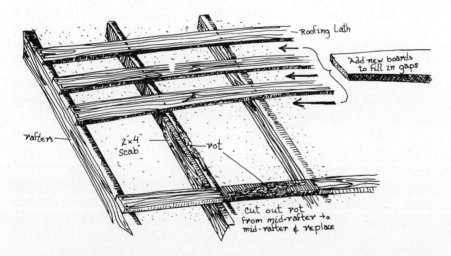

3–13   Repair of roof deck

Condensation is the culprit in cases of rot under the shingles. It is a result of poor insulation and insufficient attic ventilation. Warm moist air will rise through an uninsulated attic and condense on the cold underside of the shingles, which are fairly impervious to water vapor. Condensation occurs to some extent in all houses and is impossible to prevent entirely. The underside of a roof deck will show frost crystallized on the points of the nails sticking through the decking, even in a well-insulated attic. Most of this frost evaporates without becoming liquid and does no harm. But if the attic is unventilated, the problem is much more serious. Ventilating louvers are installed in the gable ends of the attic, under the peak, to allow air to escape. Often these louvers are too small or even nonexistent. As the moisture condenses between the shingles and the decking, the water rots the boards.

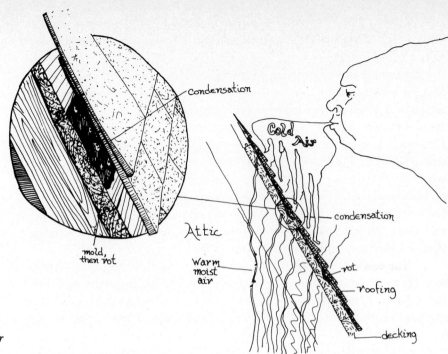

3–14 *Condensation caused by improper ventilation and insulation*

When a large portion of the original deck has decayed or there are too many irregular spaces between lathing boards to give good nailing, the deck should be rebuilt. Apply ½-inch CDX sheathing plywood directly over the old decking. Cut the starting sheet to the proper length so that the joints of successive sheets will fall over a rafter. You may have to trim additional sheets to compensate for variations in the spacing of the rafters. Use 8d common nails spaced 8 inches apart on the rafters and 4 inches apart on the joints. Measure up from the bottom of the roof and mark the 4-foot points. Snap a chalk line across the roof. Tack the first course of plywood temporarily in place to the line. You may have to adjust the height of the line to compensate for gross irregularities in the roof edge. Trim off any resulting overhang. Any small gap will be covered by the drip edge. Plywood must be laid so that the joints match closely along both horizontal and vertical edges.

The roof deck is now ready for drip edge, felt underlayment, and shingles. Shingles are made from asphalt and asbestos fiber. Unfortunately, asphalt melts at relatively low temperatures. On a hot day, shingles can become almost liquid. If you stand on them, your footprints will leave a permanent record. The life of the roof is shortened by too many of these smears; the shingle flattens out,

3–15 *Laying plywood over rotten deck*

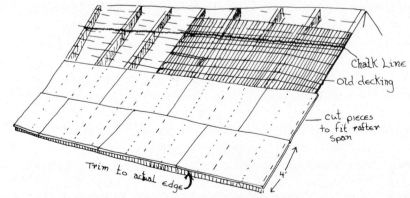

and the protective slate granules are pushed into the asphalt base, making the roof vulnerable to the weather.

Consider the temperature when you schedule your reroofing operation. Shingles absorb heat; the darker the color, the more heat they absorb. While the air temperature may only be 70°F., up on the shadowless oven of the roof deck the temperature can soar high enough to make the shingles too hot to touch. The reflective properties of a light-colored shingle must be measured against its greater susceptibility to marring and staining. Footprints that may be hardly noticeable against a black shingle will stand out with striking clarity against a white background. You should be careful about what you wear on your feet. Smooth-soled leather shoes are the best. Sneakers are gentler on your feet but will wear out against the abrasive surface and tend to mark more. Never wear vibram-soled boots.

The best weather for shingling is a cloudy, cool day, but if you have to do it on a sunny day the pleasure of being outdoors on a fine day may compensate for having to spend it up on the roof. If it is sunny and warm, start early in the morning, on the sunny side, and try to plan your work to finish before the sun heats up the deck. This plan works only if the area is very small or if you have an entire crew of shinglers slapping on shingles as fast as they can be carried up the ladder. In any case, try to avoid doing the major part of the work under the blazing afternoon sky. You should not overcompensate, however, by laying shingles when the temperature is too low. Asphalt becomes very brittle as the thermometer moves toward freezing. The shingles will snap rather than bend.

Life seldom flows within the channels we arrange for it. I found myself one January day, banging shingles on a roof, one man with a push broom struggling to keep the deck clear of the swirling snow, while I fumbled in my frozen nail apron with leaden fingers. A cold shingle can skin a knuckle as effectively as a block of rough granite. The ridge shingles were brought up in small batches from the cellar where they had been cut and placed the night before and were quickly bent over the roof before they could cool and crack.

Or there was an August day when I started shingling at 5:30 in the morning. By 8 A.M. I had taken off my shoes, working in stocking feet to avoid marking the shingles. At noon I stumbled down the scaffolding, blinded by sweat, my pants hanging wet and limp from their belt. The rest of the afternoon was spent in an old innertube in the middle of the pond.

Shingles are applied like bricks. The joints between one course and the next should never break over each other. Standard three-tab shingles can be started either from one end or in the middle of a roof. The batten strips holding the tarpaper in place make a good temporary ladder upon which you can climb to the peak. The tarpaper itself protects the deck from rain until the shingles are laid and also prevents the resins in the wood decking from eating away at the undersurface of the shingles. Metal drip edge is laid under the tarpaper at the eaves and over it, along the rake. Any water that blows under the shingles will then run over the tarpaper.

If the roof is over 30 feet long, you should start from the middle. This allows you to work towards both ends, which is faster and results in less chance of having shingles run crooked. To start in the middle of a roof, measure the top and bottom of the roof and mark the center. Mark another line 6 inches to the right or left of center and snap a chalk line for both these lines. The second line gives you the required 6-inch offset between courses. The end of one course is laid to the first line, the end of the succeeding course, to the second line. This

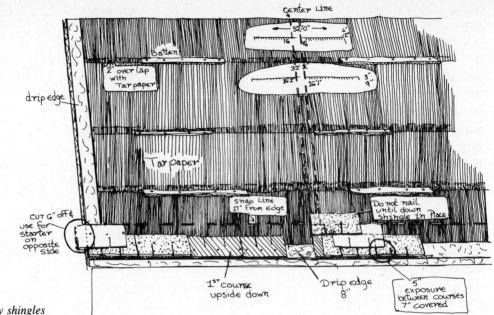

Center line

32'0"
6"
16'
16"

Batten

2" over lap
with
Tar paper

32' 3"
3"
16' 2"
16'
9"

drip edge

Tar paper

Snap Line
17" from edge

Do not nail
until down
Shingle in place

CUT 6" off &
use for
starter
on
opposite
side

1ST course
upside down

Drip edge
8"

5"
exposure
between courses
7" covered

3–16   *Layout of new shingles*

is called a shadow line. You should calculate how the shingles will end up at the edge of the roof. Individual shingle tabs are a 12-inch module. On a 32-foot roof, they will break evenly at the rake. On a 32-foot 1-inch roof, the last piece will either be 7 inches or 1 inch. You should avoid filling in with pieces under 2 inches, as they will be difficult to nail and look poor from the ground. To compensate, the starting line should be offset from center by 2 inches to give a 3-inch and 9-inch end piece, respectively (Figure 3–16).

When beginning at the end of the roof, special starting shingles are cut from a full shingle. Use a plywood scrap for a backing board, a utility knife and metal straight edge to make the cut. Always cut through the under surface of the shingle, as the mineral surface will soon dull the blade. You need only score the shingle once and snap it on the line. Do this in the morning or in a shady place where the shingles will not become warm and soft. Measure 6 inches in from the edge of the shingle and square down a perpendicular line. Save the first piece as a pattern for marking the rest. Most shingles are manufactured with a mark at the middle of each tab along the top edge, to help in aligning them on the roof as well as to indicate where to cut the starters. Alternate starter shingles with full shingles and carry up this mixed stack onto the staging.

The eaves starter course is a full shingle laid upside down. That gives the double coverage that insures that the cutouts will have mineral surface under them. Be sure to stagger the joints between the starter course and the first course, which is laid directly on top of it. Snap a chalkline 17 inches up from the drip edge, across the roof. The top edge of the second course is laid to this line, compensating for irregularities in the bottom edge of the roof and allowing the succeeding courses to be laid straight. (Standard shingles have a 5-inch exposure, and a shingle is 12 inches wide—5 + 5 + 7 = 17.) Although experienced roofers can and often do lay the rest of the roof without any other additional lines, it is helpful to snap a series of lines spaced every 20 inches (four courses) apart measured up from the 17-inch line. The top edge of every fourth course will then align itself to the line making up for any inaccuracies in your application. Where there is a very noticeable dip in the roof deck, measure up from the drip edge and snap the line to that point rather than snapping the line in one length across the entire roof. The shingles are designed so that the 5-inch exposure falls just above the cutouts. The nails should be driven within an inch above the cutout, so as to be covered by the next layer. If the nail does not hold, drive another slightly higher. Be careful not to nail the end of the shingle that overlaps the course below it until a shingle has been slipped into place. Do not nail shingles within 4 inches of the rakes. When the entire roof is finished, snap a line along the edge. Using sheet-metal shears, cut the shingles back along this line starting at the top of the roof and working down. Then, starting from the bottom and working up, nail each end into place. Do not attempt to cut shingles with shears when they are soft. The blade will gum up, and the shingles will tear unevenly. Leave it until morning. You should scrape the cutting edges clean from time to time during the course of normal use. You can also cut each shingle as each course is laid. Mark it to length and use a knife and steel square to trim it evenly. A knife will cut hot shingles when shears won't. The last course of shingles is also trimmed if it will not fold over the ridge.

A *valley* is the intersection between two different roofs. It is made of mineral-surfaced roll roofing or sheet metal and should be installed before the shingles. First, determine if the original valley is still usable. When the shingles are stripped, the valley can be left in place if it is under all the layers of roofing. If it is between successive layers, the nails are pulled and the valley removed. A copper sheet valley without tears or gashes is perfectly reusable. Galvanized liners that have rusted should be torn up and replaced. If the rust is only slight, the metal can be painted with a rust-resistant paint and reused. When you are laying new shingles directly over old, the valley should be resurfaced with a new mineral or metal roll. Aluminum is a frequently used valley material. Use aluminum nails with aluminum to avoid electrogalvanitic corrosion. (The more active metals replace the less-electrochemically active ones; aluminum is a very active metal.)

To lay a new valley, first run a layer of 36-inch-wide roofing felt from peak to eaves, down the middle of the valley. Cut the metal or mineral valley roll to length, leaving several feet extra to fold over the top and trim at the bottom edge. Metal is preferred for snowy regions, as less snow will stick to it. If possible, use a single length of material. Otherwise an 8-inch lap is necessary. The seam should be sealed with a layer of flashing cement. A single

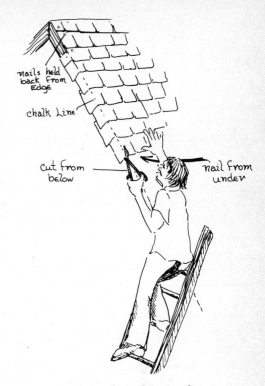

3–17   Trimming edges of new roofing

3–18   Installing top of valley

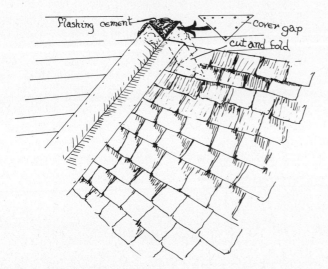

3–19   Trimming shingles in valley

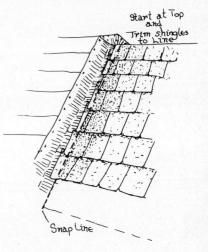

nail is used to hold the top edge and the valley roll aligned with the center of the valley. One side is then nailed completely from top to bottom. Use your knee to form the material into the valley and then nail the other side. Avoid crimping or twisting it. The top is cut to fold over the ridge. The same process is repeated if another valley meets the ridge on the other side. The gap at the top of the valley is filled with flashing cement and a triangular piece of flashing material nailed over it. The new valley material should extend at least 10 inches under the shingles. If you are using mineral-surfaced roll roofing, be sure to roll it out into the sun to soften first. As the shingles are laid to the valley, they are roughly trimmed to the center. A line is snapped down each edge of the valley. The valley should increase in width about 1 inch for every 8 feet of run. A 6-inch width is the minimum top width. Measure and mark a point half the desired width from the middle with your chalk line. The shingles are cut from the top down and nailed from bottom up, exactly like trimming a rake. Nails are also held back from the edge when the shingles are first laid. If a nail is exposed in the valley, it should be sealed with flashing cement. You can squat quite comfortably in the valley of even a steeply pitched roof so long as you avoid marking shingles.

When cutting and trimming shingles to fit up against the side of a building, the proper measurement is obtained by butting the shingle smooth side up against the wall and marking the point where it overlaps the side of the shingle already laid.

As you work your way up the roof, you will need to nail brackets to carry the staging planks. Be sure to nail them so that the nails will be covered by a shingle and not exposed through the cutouts. A bracket has holes for the nails that allow it to be removed by sliding the bracket upward. Strike the butt of the bracket with a hammer to move it. Drive the nail heads firmly into the roof decking after the bracket is removed to prevent them from working through the shingle (see Figure 3–21).

Ridge caps are pieces of shingle that cover the gap at the peak of the roof and whenever two roofs meet to form a "hip." These shingles are cut from a three-tab shingle. The shingle is laid out smooth surface up. Lines are scored from just above the cutout back to the edge of the shingle, at a slight angle. If the cut were not angled, portions of the unsurfaced part of the shingle could show when the caps were folded over the ridge. A line is chalked along the ridge so that the cap can be centered over it. It should completely cover any nails in the last course of full shingles. An extra course is added if necessary. The ridge shingles are laid away from the prevailing winds. One nail is driven on each side of the ridge so that the nails in the next shingle will also penetrate it. The last shingle is cut to size and the exposed nails are tarred. Use 1½-inch nails for nailing these shingles.

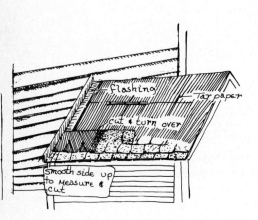

3–20   Shingling against a side wall

3–21   Removing brackets

3–22   Cutting ridge cap

3–23   Laying ridge opposite prevailing wind

Roofing material is estimated by the *square,* which is equal to 100 square feet of coverage. Measure the roof and multiply length by width to find its area. Divide the total by 100 to find the number of squares needed. Allow 10 percent extra for waste and allow extra shingles for the ridge caps. A general rule is to add one square for every 100 feet of ridge and valleys. You can multiply the length of the ridge in feet by 12 and then divide by 10. Multiply the result by 2 to determine the actual number of ridge caps needed. Divide that number by 3 to find out how many shingles are required, and figure 27 shingles to the bundle (one-third of a square) for three-tab shingles.

Jet shingles are applied exactly like tab shingles except that the starter is made by cutting a full-length shingle in half, giving an 18-inch lap. The nailing pattern is roughly the same as a strip shingle, 6 inches up from the bottom every 12 inches across by eyeball measure. Jet shingles can be started only at the end of a roof. Use tab shingles for ridge caps. Otherwise make a pattern piece, and take care that the mineral surface faces the same direction with each shingle, as there will be no tabs to orient the shingle by. Lock shingles are applied according to the same general principles as strip shingles. Half shingles are used for rake starters. Bottom-course starters are made from cut-out pieces of the lock shingle laid over standard strip shingles or roll roofing. Figure 3–34 shows how ridge caps and bottom and end starters are cut from a single shingle.

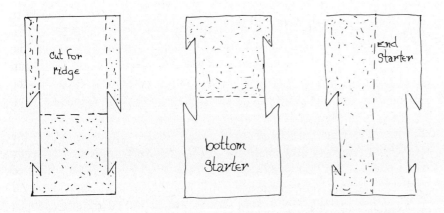

3–24 *Layout of lock-tab shingles*

Complete instructions for application are generally printed on the wrapper by the manufacturer. What is not printed is how to maneuver an eighty-pound bundle safely up a ladder and onto the roof. There is an art to carrying shingles; it is a matter of balance more than brute strength. Unless you have access to a mechanical lift or hoist, your shoulder must be the vehicle. You can manage a half-bundle at a time and make twice as many trips. Split bundles actually handle harder than packaged bundles. The individual shingles flop around and fold over your shoulder, throwing you off balance. When starting a roof from the ladder, drive a 16d spike into the deck as high up as you can reach. The nail will keep your half bundle of shingles from sliding around as you work. To lift a full bundle of shingles, stand it upright, facing you but slightly to your side. Assuming you are right-handed, squat and place your right hand under the bottom left corner of the bundle and tilt it so that its center will fall across your right shoulder. Then straighten your legs and hoist the bundle onto your shoulder, keeping your back straight. The bundle will balance surprisingly well. Your hand prevents it from tilting back as you climb the ladder, using the left hand to grip the side, not tne rungs. Always keep one hand in contact with the side of a ladder at all times. Climb with a steady pace. At the top of the ladder, roll your shoulder forward, flopping the entire bundle onto the roof. You will feel the weight in your calves, long before your back begins to bother you. After the first square, they will feel like a sponge. You should carry up a square at a stretch. Your staging will safely hold that plus your weight. A square will occupy a good roofer for an hour. As a novice, you will have plenty of time to recover your breath for the next trip down the ladder. Remember to fill up your nail apron each trip. My father told me never to come up a ladder empty-handed. He was used to working piecework and every step saved was a penny earned. He was also the fellow who would carry up all twelve squares of the shingles onto the roof deck without a pause, collapse for an hour, eat his lunch, and then begin work. I guess he liked to work uninterrupted.

Wood Shingles

There are several principles to bear in mind when laying wood shingles on a solid deck. The pitch of the roof determines the exposure of the shingle. The lower the pitch, the smaller the exposure and the greater the number of shingle courses covering the surface.

Wood shingles are spaced about ¼″ apart. This spacing allows the shingles to swell when wet. If laid tightly, they would buckle as they expanded. Joints on alternate courses should not align. Maintain a minimum offset of 1½ inches between the edge of one shingle and that of the course above it. Use two nails in each shingle, 1½ inches above the butt line of the following course and 1 inch in from the edge. Tarpaper underlayment is not recommended over

3-25 Layout of wood shingle roofing

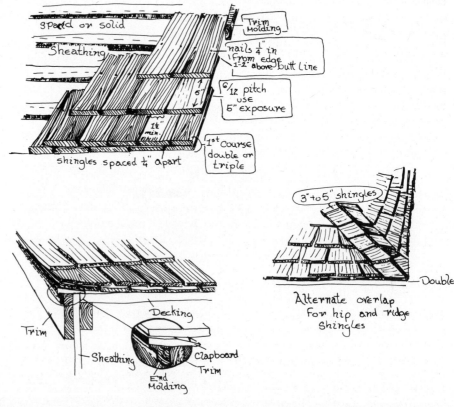

open-nailing laths because moisture will condense under them. Valleys should be 4 inches wide at the top. Use a straight-edged board to align each course of shingles. Tack it in place so that the butts rest against it until they are nailed. On steeply pitched roofs the alignment strips can be used as cleats for maintaining your footing. Figure 3–25 shows the details of roofing with cedar shingles.

A ridge cap can be fashioned from two boards nailed together and caulked at the joint. The angle of the cut will vary with the roof pitch. Use a protractor to convert the pitch of the roof to degrees of cut for your saw. Clear cedar is best for ridge boards. All butt joints between sections should be caulked and covered with a band of flashing metal.

Wood shakes are laid much the same way as cedar shingles. They are longer in length with greater exposure and thicker in cross section, requiring longer nails. An 18-inch layer of 30-pound roofing felt must be laid between each course of shingles. The felt, which is laid twice the width of the exposure under each course, is actually the sole waterproof layer, so care must be used not to tear or puncture it.

Eaves Protection

In areas of heavy snowfall it is quite common to find a 2-to-3-foot-wide strip of galvanized steel or copper metal along the eaves. Ice dams are a problem in the North, and the metal prevents water from backing up under the bottom courses of shingles and into the house. The snow does not adhere well to the metal, and the surface is seamless. If the metal is in good shape, it can be repainted and left undisturbed. The new shingles are applied over its top edge with a 6-inch overlap. If the old metal is to be removed or new metal installed for the first time, gutters should be in place first. Drip edge is nailed to the eaves. A line equal to the width of the metal sheet less a ¾-inch allowance for the overhang is marked and chalk-lined onto the roof. Cut the metal to the length of the roof, tack the top corner to the line, and unroll. It can be raised or lowered as necessary to compensate for unevenness in the edge of the roof, so long as the lap approximates the required ¾ inch. Nail the top edge of the sheet with galvanized roofing nails spaced 6 inches apart. It is best to work from the middle to the outside edges to avoid buckling. Sheet-metal crimpers rented from the

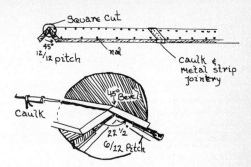

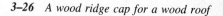

3–26 A wood ridge cap for a wood roof

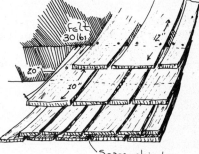

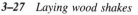

3–27 Laying wood shakes

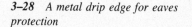

3–28 A metal drip edge for eaves protection

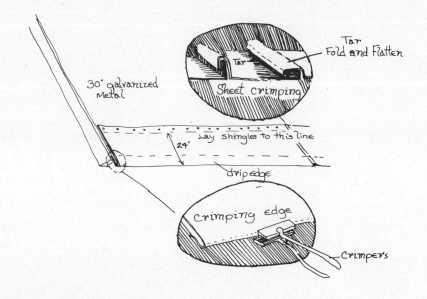

hardware store are used to fold the overlap around the bottom of the drip edge, locking the sheet firmly to the roof. Measure down from the top edge of the sheet the distance to the bottom of the first course of shingles and snap another line. Lay the tarpaper to this line and begin shingling. If the metal sheet is not long enough to span the entire length of the roof, splice the pieces together by crimping the edges and flattening the seam to the roof. Nail it tightly and seal it with flashing cement.

Steel Roofing

Steel roofing can be applied directly over old asphalt roofing—a very convenient solution to the problem of repairing a rotten roof deck or worn-out shingles. "Strapping" of roughsawn $1\frac{1}{2} \times 4$ or 1×6 is nailed to the roof, spaced 16 inches on center to carry steel. Roughsawn lumber can be used because the steel will mask any irregularities in thickness, and width is not a consideration. A roughsawn $1\frac{1}{2} \times 4$ represents a 25 percent savings over the cost of 2×4, yet gives as much strength as a milled 2×4. A 1×6 contains the same volume of wood as a $1\frac{1}{2} \times 4$ but is not as strong, since strength of a timber is related to thickness rather than width.*

Any overhanging old shingles are broken back flush to the edge of the roof. The first nailer is fastened flush to the edge of the trim board. A 12-inch spacer block will align the subsequent courses on the necessary 16-inch centers. Likewise, blocking is used to fill in the spaces between the courses along the rakes. Block around chimneys and vent pipes and run nailers down the center of the valleys. Fill the valley out with an 18-inch-wide strip of $\frac{1}{2}$-inch CDX plywood. New 1×4 trim boards are applied over the nailers and the edge of the roof fascia board. The steel roofing is laid to the nailers, allowing a $\frac{1}{2}$-inch overhang on the bottom edge.

Steel roofing is applied with the seams opposite to the direction of the prevailing winds. If possible, use roofing sheets long enough to cover the length of the roof in one piece. Otherwise, overlap any seams at least 6 inches. The bottom of the overlapping seam must be fastened to a nailer. Cut and fold the sheets against the chimney, allowing the fold to run 6 inches up the side of the masonry. The metal is secured by driving nails into the mortar joints and sealed with flashing cement. Cut out around pipes and seal all edges liberally with tar. The flashing can be nailed to the blocking. If no blocking is under the seam, fasten it with self-tapping sheet-metal screws. A line is chalk marked across the ridge to guide application of the ridge roll, which is generally available in ten-foot lengths.

Metal roofing is extremely slippery. A 4-in-12 pitch is about the upper limit that can be worked without a ladder. Use rubber-soled shoes or sneakers

---

*Lumber is roughsawn to a "nominal" size, which is more or less the full size. E.g., a 2×4 is actually 2 inches by 4 inches. Green lumber that is thickness planned will be milled to an actual size of $1\frac{5}{8}$ inches by $3\frac{5}{8}$ inches for the same timber. Kiln-dried lumber is milled to a module of $1\frac{1}{2}$ inches $\times 3\frac{1}{2}$ inches. Lumber is sold by the board-foot measure. One board foot is equal to a piece of lumber $1'' \times 12'' \times 12''$ or 144 cubic inches. Milled lumber is sold by the nominal size measure. There are tables that show the accepted milled sizes for each nominal size. Unless otherwise specified in this book, size nomenclature will be taken to refer to milled lumber. I.e., a 1×6 board will actually be $\frac{3}{4}$ inches by $5\frac{1}{2}$ inches. Remember to allow for the finished thickness of the lumber in all your calculations.

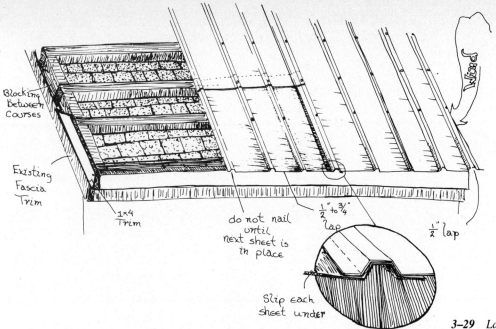

Blocking
Between
Courses

Existing
Fascia
Trim

1×4
Trim

do not nail
until
next sheet is
in place

½" to ¾"
lap

½" lap

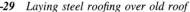

Slip each
sheet under

3–29 Laying steel roofing over old roof

on steel, as leather shoes give much less traction. The roof strapping serves as
the ladder. You reach back over each sheet to nail it until the end of the roof
is reached. A ladder with an attached hook is used to fasten the last sheet and
allow you to climb off the roof. If the last sheet must be trimmed to fit, measure
from the edge of the lap to the edge of the roof and allow an extra ½ inch.
Cutting steel with tin shears is slow and often results in gashed knuckles. Wear
gloves or, better, use a skilsaw. Find that old blade you ruined slicing through
nail-filled lumber and install it in the saw backwards, to make an excellent
sheet-metal saw. Snap a chalk line to guide your cut and wear safety glasses
to guard against shrapnel. Earmuffs might be helpful too, to protect your ears
from the banshee scream of metal on metal. The edge of the last piece is folded
over the top of the trim board by pounding with a block of wood and hammer.

There are two types of nails for fastening steel roofing: the lead-head
type and the neoprene-gasket type. Lead-head nails have a washer of that metal
under the head, which compresses when hammered to form a watertight seal.
Unfortunately, the lead gasket is easy to snap off, which is what will happen
if you must shovel off the roof in winter. The lead can sluff off every time you
move a ladder across the roof. Neoprene-gasket nails use a washer with a seal
made from neoprene—a very durable synthetic-rubber compound. They will not
snap off. Although they cost twice as much per pound as lead nails, they are
half the weight of the lead nails, so in the long run they are a better buy.

Whatever type nails you use, drive them into the top of the corrugations
only. A nail driven into the flat of the roof will leak. Prime rib roofing is nailed
only on each rib. Corrugated roofing is nailed on every third or fourth corrugation. Each brand of steel roofing has its particular pattern of ribbing, which
is seldom interchangeable with others. That is of particular importance when
selecting ridge-cap and special end-wall flashing pieces. Start the roofing from
the same end of the roof on each side to help keep the ridge cap in alignment.
Some patterns have a top and bottom, and the distinction must be observed to
avoid leaking along the vertical seams. Ask the dealer for a specification sheet
for the roofing you select. When laying roofing in more than one length to the
peak, be sure to run from the eave to peak before running across the roof. The

horizontal seams must be interlocked so that no top sheet is ever under a bottom sheet.

New galvanized roofing will not accept paint until the coating has weathered for at least a season. Use a special metal primer as a base coat. Old roofing should first be brushed clean of any loose scale. All loose nails are driven tight. Any split seams or holes are patched with flashing cement and left to dry. There are several grades of roof paint; asphalt-roof coatings are more or less the same as foundation waterproofing but thinner and easier spreading. Apply them with a mop. They are the least expensive coating. The aluminized emulsion is very tough and long lasting and about four times as expensive as the asphalt base. These paints are sometimes called trailer-roof paint. There are also a large number of rust-resistant metal paints in a variety of colors as well as an aluminum-pigmented type. They are all fairly durable and inexpensive. These coverings are applied with a brush or roller. After a few years, the rust will bleed through the paint, and the roof will have to be recoated. If kept regularly painted, a steel roof will last a very long time.

One of the best salvage bargains is used steel roofing, which sells for a fraction of its new cost, and which, with proper care, will perform every bit as well as the new. After the roofing is nailed in place, all nail holes, splits, and punctures are filled with flashing cement. Holes too large to support the flashing

3–30a *Valley treatment for a steel roof*
3–30b *Fitting steel around chimneys*
3–30c *Vent flashing*
3–30d *Using a ladder hook*

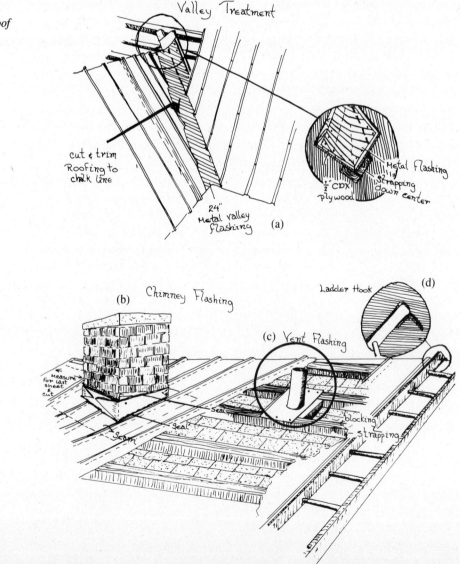

cement are patched with fiberglass cloth embedded in asphalt. The Tremco Company markets a fiberglass asphalt-patching emulsion, which works very well for this purpose so long as the material can cure for twelve rain-free hours. As soon as the cement dries, the roof can be painted. Painting is done from a ladder and ladder hook. Two lengths of light aluminum ladder are tied together and used on long roofs where a single ladder will not do. Before you plan to use steel roofing, check your local zoning ordinances. Steel roofing is actually prohibited by some codes on the theory that its appearance lowers property values.

Roofing, Ventilation, Insulation: *The "cold roof"*

A reroofing option that has gained increasing popularity in the North is the "cold roof." The steel roof laid over the existing shingle deck is a kind of poor man's cold roof. A true roof of this sort is a passive air-conditioning system that allows cold, dry air to circulate freely under the entire roof deck, thereby removing any moisture-laden warm air, which escapes through the attic. Not only is condensation prevented but, because the air under the roof is never warm relative to the outside air, the snow cover does not melt. There are no ice dams formed above the eaves, and the snow cover helps insulate the house. In summer the house is cooled by the flow of air under the deck, which removes heat from above and below.

The old shingles are removed, if necessary, and 1 × 4s are nailed parallel with the existing rafters, 2 feet on center. They should project 2 inches beyond the eaves trim. Nail ⅝-inch CDX plywood over these for a shingling deck. Alternatively, roughsawn 1 × 4 strapping can be nailed perpendicular to these false rafters to support metal roofing instead of the plywood deck. Steel roofing will not hold much snow if steeper than a 4-in-12 pitch and will tend to leak along the seams if under that pitch. The pitch may be an advantage if the roof

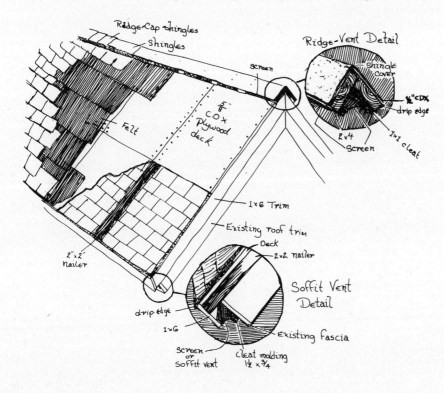

3–31 *A cold roof over an existing roof*

framing is not heavy enough to support a greatly increased snow load. Seal all horizontal seams with a bead of clear silicone caulking or asphalt cement. The decking is held back 2 inches from the center of the ridge on each side. Nail 1 × 6 trim boards across the eaves and rakes. The shingles are laid as with a new roof. The last course is likewise held back at the ridge. Cleats are nailed over the rafter nailers, and a screened and vented ridge is constructed, sheathed with plywood, and shingled (see Figure 3–31).

As Figure 3–32 shows, outside air is drawn in a constant flow from under the soffit vent along the roof deck and out the ridge vent. This moving air carries with it any moisture-laden attic air. The attic can be heated and insulated under the first roof deck or unheated and insulated between the attic floor joists. Ice dams are caused when heat escaping through the roof deck melts the snow cover.

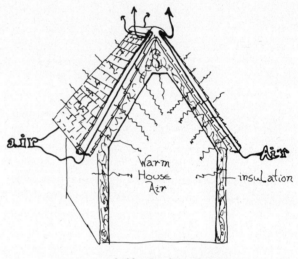

3–32   Roof ventilation

The water flows down the roof until it reaches the projecting eave, which because of its unheated underside, is cold and causes the water to freeze. As this layer of ice builds up, it acts as a dam to further melt waters. The water continues to back up along the roof, seeping under the shingles and entering the house. This is one of the obvious reasons why ranch houses with their wide, projecting eaves and low-pitched roofs are a very unsuitable design for northern climates.

3–33   Ice dam formation over eaves

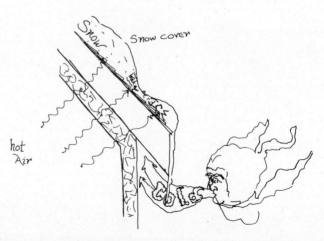

Keeping the snow off a roof designed to shield the walls of a house from a desert sun requires energy, either as an electric heating cable or as body energy running a snow shovel. The shingles soon become tattered from the ax blows that will be necessary to break up the ice dam.

When the roof is cold under its entire surface, no snow is melted. The resulting snow cover adds insulation to the existing attic insulation. (The rafters must be able to carry this heavy load.) In warm weather this same air flow removes hot air that is generated by life inside the house and by the heat of the sun when it strikes the deck and is absorbed by the shingles.

You may not care to install a cold roof, but you must plan proper attic ventilation. It is of the utmost importance. Air should be free to circulate between the back of the insulation and the decking. New houses are built with screened louvers under the soffits and in the peak of the gable ends of the house wall. Where it is impractical to remove existing cornice trim to add such soffit ventilation, small circular louvers can be inserted in holes drilled into the fascia or soffit board between the rafters. If the insulation runs completely to the peak of the roof rather than across the ceiling ties or the attic floor joists, a gable louver will not be of any use. A vented ridge is necessary.

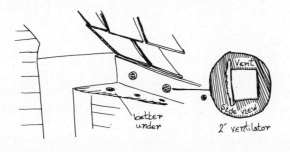

3–34   Soffit ventilation

Several types of prefabricated, aluminum ridge vents are marketed. They will work quite satisfactorily in regions of mild winters, but it has been my experience that the heavy snow loads of the North soon flatten these ridge caps, seriously impairing their effectiveness. A custom-built unit similar to the one detailed in Figure 3–31 will take more time to build but will last as long as the roof.

3–35   Methods for ventilating attic

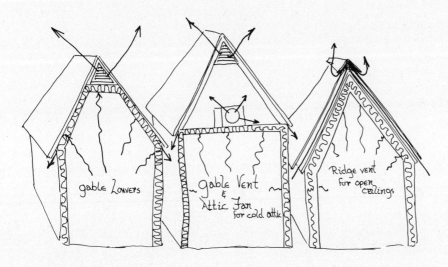

Water and Roofs – Eavestroughs and Downspouts

Water falling from the eaves can collect along the foundation wall and find its way into the cellar, especially if the drainage system is inadequate. Even good drainage can be overloaded by a heavy downpour or long periods of spring rain. Eavestroughs, or gutters, catch this water and channel it through a downspout, or leader, away from the foundation. In areas of heavy seasonal rainfall and mild winters, they are a sensible addition to any roofing system. In northern Vermont and similar climates, they are not only unnecessary but often dangerous. Gutters fill up with snow and ice and split apart or form ice dams. Water freezing behind them often works its way into the cornice and under the roof or sheathing boards, eventually causing rot and decay. Downspouts can become plugged or freeze solid, splitting apart at the seams. There is simply no reasonable way to build a house that will make it secure from every conceivable weather condition. In Vermont, we have every conceivable type of weather. It is something a person learns to live with. If a gutter must be under an eave at all, the only sensible location is a short length over an entrance.

A good entrance has a gabled *stoop* above the door. All too often, design triumphs over common sense and an unprotected door is placed directly under an eave, so that when people leave the house, they may be immediately greeted with a chilling downpour or a lethal ice avalanche. A short length of gutter will at least prevent the shower. It should be hung so that it can be removed once freezing weather settles in.

In southern New England, it is quite common to find a type of built-in gutter called a *yankee gutter* on old buildings. The name probably originates from the economy and simplicity of its construction, being little more than a sloped trough framed into the roofing itself. My memories of them recall an equally traditional aspect of the Yankee character: cantankerousness. Because yankee gutters project from the very bottom edge of the roof, roofers find them a quite convenient substitute for the first course of staging brackets. Unfortunately, like the fellow who stopped at a fork to ask the old farmer if it mattered which road he took to get to Montpelier and was told, "not to me, it don't,"

3–36   Gutter over unprotected door

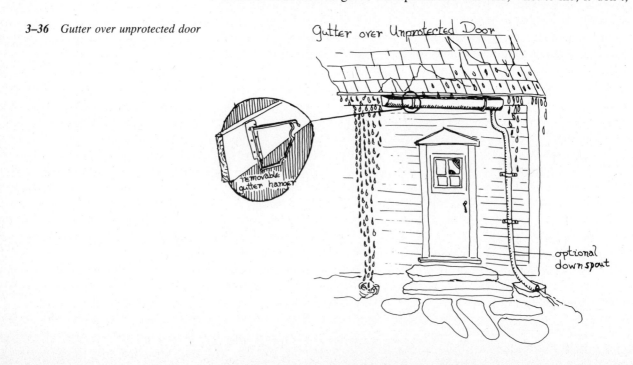

you can't always know where you stand. You could never quite trust a yankee gutter not to rip clean off the roof when you put your weight on a hidden rotten place.

I would imagine that coastal New England is the natural northern limit of their practicality. Because snow will not slide easily over such an obstruction, ice dams are a real possibility in them. However, if the gutter flashing is extended well up onto the roof (30-inch exposure and 6-inch overlap) and the attic is well insulated and properly vented, such a gutter can be an excellent way to help utilize the snow cover for insulation. With proper care and maintenance, it should last as long as the house itself. Overflow water can't work its way behind the cornice as with a standard gutter.

Most people tend to let their gutters and roofs go unmaintained until a leak becomes too troublesome to ignore. By then, damage has been done to the roof deck and the house itself. An inspection each spring and fall would help extend the life of gutter systems and prevent expensive repairs at a later date. Gutters should be periodically cleared to remove all debris that has washed down the roof. Clotted leaves and twigs should also be removed. Frequently the entrance to the downspout becomes plugged up. The leaves themselves act as sponges, holding moisture that tends to rot the gutter.

All small tears or punctures in a lined gutter should be patched with flashing cement and fiberglass webbing. Bubbles in the old asphalt coating should be broken and patched over. Recoat the entire length of the gutter with a layer of cold asphalt cement, clear to the line of the shingles. If the gutter is badly split or worn, it should be relined. First clean the surface thoroughly with a coarse broom or brush. There will be time for wet spots to dry out while you remove the nails from the first few courses of shingles. Remove as many courses as necessary to allow you to slip the entire width of the roll roofing up under the shingles, with a minimum overlap of 6 inches. Fold a narrow scrap of roll roofing in place to determine how high onto the shingles it will extend. A narrow gutter will require a roll 18-inches wide and the removal of only one shingle course. Save the old shingles for reuse if possible. To avoid breakage, remove the nails only after the shingles have softened. Old shingles are very brittle.

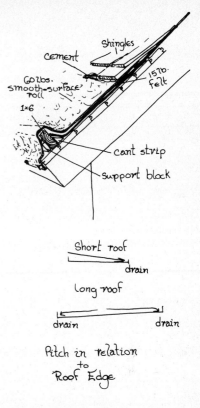

3-37   A yankee gutter

3-38   Relining a built-up gutter

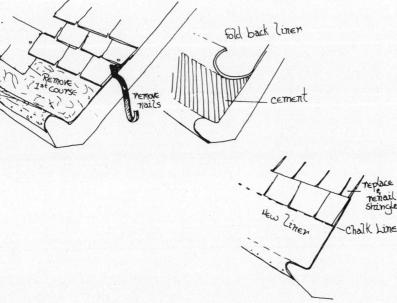

Slip the roll roofing (use an unsurfaced roll, which has softened in the sun) up under the shingles and nail the top edge of the roll to the roof deck. All seams are lapped 6 inches and sealed with flashing cement. Fold the roll back over itself onto the roof and coat the entire sheet with cold cement. Form the sheet into the gutter. Use your knee to smooth out wrinkles, working from the middle to the ends and from the top edge to the outside. Nail the outside to the fascia or top of the cornice with galvanized roofing nails spaced 3 inches apart. Measure down from the butt of the last course of shingles and snap a line across the roof to start relaying the old shingles. Use new shingles of matching color if necessary. A bead of flashing cement under the first course will help seal them to the gutter and give added protection against ice dams. Cut out the drain and reline with a standard copper fitting if necessary. Apply a liberal amount of flashing cement above and below the opening.

If a yankee gutter has been allowed to deteriorate to the point where the wood framing is rotten, it should be torn off and any rot in the deck itself repaired with new boards. A replacement can be built, although it is probably much easier to hang a standard gutter from the eaves instead. In such a case, the shingles are nailed from the top courses down, slipping each course up under the one above it. Use a chalk line to align each course. If the distance to the bottom edge of the roof will not divide evenly by 5, either crowd or spread the courses to compensate for the difference, so that the spacing will work out evenly at the edge and you will not have a 2-inch strip or uncovered cutouts showing.

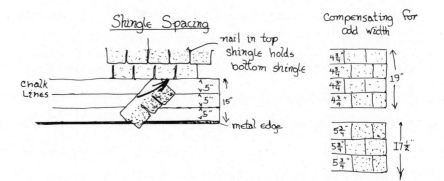

3-39 *Shingle spacing for reroofing*

The repair of wood gutters is similar to the relining procedures outlined above. If the gutter is solid and the wood has not rotted, often a cleaning and a recoating with asphalt emulsion is all that is necessary to restore it to useful life. Wood gutters are best relined with a special synthetic roll manufactured for that purpose, which is available in 12-inch widths. It is far more flexible than roll roofing, which would never form into the narrow angle of the gutter. The roll is embedded and formed to the gutter. A less expensive alternative is to coat the gutter with a water-soluble asphalt emulsion paint and form an asphalt-impregnated fiberglass cloth into the coating. When dry, the paint is waterproof, and the webbing adds structural strength. A final coat is applied over the material after it has set.

Remove all wood gutters that have rotted. Frequently the boards behind them will also need replacement. The bed molding under the gutter should be pulled first. Pry the gutter free of the cornice with a crowbar. Often the gutter will have to be split with a chisel to ease its removal. Work a pry bar behind the back edge. Take care to save the wood end blocks that trim the gutter, or they will have to be replaced; they split easily and are often rotted. Pry gently until the nails can be pulled. Wood putty is used to patch any holes. Wood gutters are heavy. Pry very carefully along the length of the gutter until it is barely hanging from its nails. It's a good idea to use two ladders and rope one end of the gutter to the roof while you work to free the other end and carefully lower it to the ground. Be aware of the weight as you pry the gutter loose. Gutters pull hard and tend to go, when they do, quite suddenly—the shift can easily throw you off balance and off the ladder as well. The free end of a falling gutter is a very good battering ram and can scar the side of a house before it smashes through the first-floor picture window.

If the old gutter is not replaced with a new one, its removal leaves a gap against the wall of the house. The gap should be covered by a shim and a trim board of sufficient width to fasten over the fascia as well. Because of the expense and the frequent unavailability of wood gutters, an aluminum gutter is generally used for a replacement.

Although metal gutters are available in both galvanized steel and aluminum, the steel type is rarely used any more. Because it rusts easily, it suffers from a relatively short life, and also it is somewhat difficult to install; all joints must be soldered. Prefinished aluminum gutters have a baked-on enamel finish that makes them virtually immune to corrosion, even in salt-water regions. These

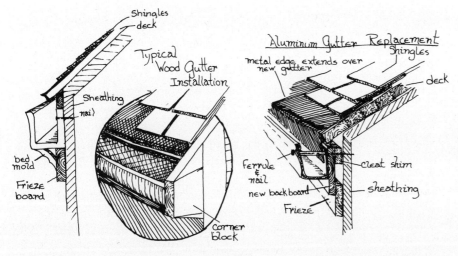

3–40 Typical wood-gutter installation and aluminum-gutter replacemment

systems are manufactured in a wide variety of styles, with corresponding fasteners, hangers, downspouting, and fittings. Individual stock pieces are available up to 24 feet in length. Some roofing contractors own metal-forming machines, which make seamless gutters to any length out of a roll of stock metal carried on the truck. Since these gutters are made on site and are seamless, greater accuracy is possible than from joining smaller pieces. The higher initial cost of aluminum over steel is soon amortized by the durability and ease of installation that characterize aluminum systems. A riveting plier and a tube of special sealant are all that is required for installation.

Gutters can be attached directly to the cornice fascia board or hung from the roof. Hangers are available for either. The straps must be installed under the first course of shingles and over the drip edge when hung from the roof. In order to drain properly, the gutter must pitch; 1″ over 16′ is considered more than adequate. On spans over 30′, the high point of the gutter is at the center of the roof. The gutter thus drains to downspouts at both ends. On shorter spans, it can be drained to the most convenient end.

Hang the gutter from a strap nailed to the roof at the high end. Check first with a strap temporarily nailed to the low end—a pail of water is dumped onto the roof and the pitch of the gutter adjusted so that the gutter drains evenly without high or low spots. The hangers are driven home along the length of the gutter. When a gutter is hung from the roof or fascia, the complete length of the gutter is assembled and hung at once. Long spans will require a helping hand to keep them from buckling as they are carried up the ladders and positioned. The ladder itself should rest against the wall of the house below the gutter. Wrap rags around the top of the ladder, or use a special support bracket that holds the ladder away from the edge of the roof, allowing you to work at a comfortable height. A support bracket is a necessity if the roof is to be reshingled after the gutters are installed. If the roof is reshingled first, the bottom course of shingles is left unnailed to allow for insertion of the strap hangers. Climbing up a ladder resting against a new gutter with a bundle of shingles is like kissing a guardrail with the fender of your car.

You can avoid the bother of having to climb over the gutter or lift up old shingles for straps by hanging the gutter directly from the fascia board. A chalk line is used to set the pitch. All the hangers can then be nailed in place before the gutter is installed if strap-type mounts are used. The edge of the roof itself must extend over the back of the gutter. If not already in place, a metal drip edge is necessary. A special aluminum flashing, which extends from the ridge over the lip of the gutter, can be used instead to provide a leak-proof seal. You can custom make it from a length of enameled 6″ aluminum roll.

The easiest way to hang a gutter from the fascia is with large aluminum spikes driven through the top edge of the gutter, through a tube called a *ferrule*, which supports the gutter and keeps it rigid while nailing, into the back of the gutter and fascia. A gutter hung from a ferrule will easily support your weight. It will be held much tighter to the building than with a strap hanger, which creates less opportunity for overflow damage. A ladder can also be placed against the gutter over the ferrule without buckling the gutter. Temporary nails are driven under the gutter to hold it in proper alignment until the ferrules are nailed, using a 3- or 4-foot spacing, with one on each side of a joint.

The width of a gutter is determined by the area of the roof surface to be drained; 4-inch gutters will serve an area up to 750 square feet, 5-inch, up to

3–41 Protecting the gutter

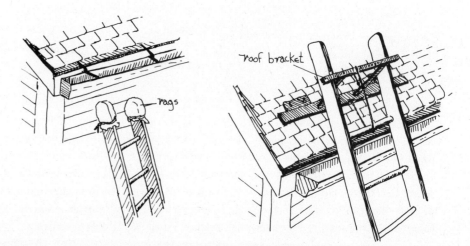

Ferrule & Spike

Fascia Strap hanger

Roof-Hook

3–42 *Fasteners for gutters*

1,400 square feet, and a 6-inch gutter, larger areas. For roofs over 1,000 square feet, use 4-inch downspouts; otherwise use standard 3-inch pipes. A downspout should always drain the water away from the foundation. A stone or concrete slab under the outlet will prevent the escaping water from washing away the soil.

Vinyl-plastic gutter and leader systems are gaining popularity. But for several reasons, it would seem to me, its use should be ruled out. For one thing, vinyl is manufactured from scarce and expensive petrochemicals. For another, all plastics tend to break down after exposure to sunlight, manufacturer's promotional literature notwithstanding. Also, vinyl becomes brittle at low temperatures.

If you are removing old gutters, notice the kind of metal they are made of. Copper gutters are a bonus; the metal fetches a good price for scrap. When I was a kid, my grandfather would often pay me for my help by giving me the rights to the copper scrap. At the end of the summer we'd take a truckload of old gutters and spouting to the scrap yard and leave with a small fortune.

Raising the Roof: *Remodeling the attic*

The steep angle of the roof, the severe, unadorned lines of the house, the chimney pointing an accusatory finger at the leaden sky, its bare boarding a somber and threadbare frock coat—the old house is a Puritan preacher. The faint odor of mold, a trace of brimstone, the taste of judgment from above, clings like soot to the soiled rafters. Under these cobwebbed gables—the children of a lighter age—look out the cracked window and see gardens growing where before was stone-and-iron-bound spirit.

The attics of old houses were not meant for living. At first they were used for storing the onions and squash, which were kept dry and healthy by the heat rising through the floorboards. As families grew, tiny cubicles were built under the eaves, where the overflow of the family slept—far from the warmth of the hearth.

> . . . I passed some cheerful evenings in that cool and airy apartment, surrounded by the rough brown boards full of knots, and rafters with the bark on, high overhead. My house never pleased my eye so much after it was plastered.
>
> [Henry Thoreau, *Walden*]

As Thoreau observed, the attics of old houses do have a rough and pleasing beauty. The play of light upon the richly hued old boards and the smooth curve of the rafter poles seems to kindle a gentle and strong warmth within the wood itself. An attic is a treasure worth living in. To leave the beams and boards exposed, the insulation must be applied to the top surface of the roof deck and a new deck devised to cover it.

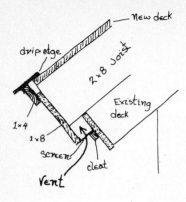 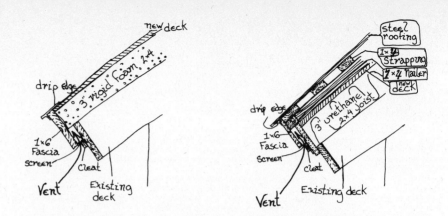

3–43 *Cold roofs and vented walls*

3–44 *Roof pitch and living space*

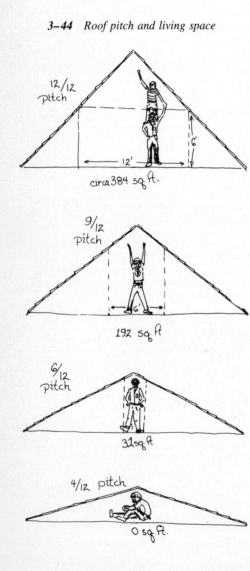

Insulating the outside of the roof deck is similar to the construction of a cold roof. The old shingles are stripped from the deck and 2 × 8 joists laid parallel to the rafters, 2 feet on center. For 9-inch insulation, 2 × 10s should be used. Lay a polyethylene vapor barrier over the entire deck before installing the joists. Avoid ripping or puncturing the membrane; patch any tears with duct tape or punctures with silicone caulk. Affix 1 × 8 or 1 × 10 trim boards to the existing fascia trim. A 1 × 4 filler piece can be used over a large gap to save wood (and costs). See Figure 3–36. Fill in the spaces between the joists with fiberglass insulation, paper side to the roof. Unbacked insulation can be used to save additional money. A ⅝-inch CDX plywood deck is applied and shingled as with a standard roof. Construct an appropriate ridge ventilator.

A roof of this type will result in a very wide cornice, as much as 12 inches. If this width is objectionable, 3-inch urethane-board insulation can be used to reduce the thickness of the joists that support the deck. A waterproof mastic or beads of construction adhesive will adhere it to the deck. Allow a ¾-inch minimum air space between the top of the insulation and the bottom of the roof deck. The ultimate roof would include an additional layer of 1 × 4 strapping to support a cold roof on top of this first deck.

Before the shingles are torn off and the new roof goes on, stand in that space under the peak of the house and consider how well it suits you. Be satisfied that the pleasures of attic living will be worth the expense of the conversion. Remember also converting an attic into a living space is the cheapest addition you can buy. The foundation already exists, there is no expensive excavation or concrete work, and the floor platform is already framed.

Before you raise the roof, pick up a pencil and consider: The effective living space under a gable roof is equal to about half its floor space—with a 3- or 4-foot-high knee wall (a one-and-a-half-story house) slightly more. This figure is based on the traditional 12–12 house pitch. With a floor dimension of 24′ × 32′, as the pitch decreases, the effective living area also decreases.

The addition of a shed or gable dormer will increase the living space under the roof quite dramatically. Decide if you wish to do this before you rebuild or replace the roof. If the roof deck and rafters are rotten or the pitch of the roof too low to allow use of the attic, consider radical surgery: Raise the roof. Remove it entirely and reframe a new roof. A 6–12 roof pitch has no use other than as a dusty closet for the storage of things no one wants to remember. Rather than clutter up our attics, we should empty our lives. As a family settles and grows, its needs blossom into possessions, like lush new growth in the orchard. Attic cleanings are but the pruning of the wild growth. Growth is the natural expression of life, and families sometimes outgrow their houses. As the nautilus adds another chamber to its shell, we add additions to our houses to make the space for our burgeoning needs and desires. Converting an attic avoids pouring money into a hole in the ground to fertilize this growth.

Side walls can be framed to the desired height to support the new roof. If you wish to maintain the traditional lines of the house, a dormer will provide space under the eaves without doing violence to the integrity of the frame. Rebuilding the roof is an opportunity to correct any mistakes in the original construction. Of course before you go live on your ceiling, determine whether the framing of the joists will support your weight. A fellow I know not only reframed his roof but added an entire set of new joists to carry the attic floor-turned-living-space, which previously had been supported by mere 2 × 4s. In his case, the house was only a temporary shelter, a tarpaulin to keep off the weather while he rebuilt the real house inside. Like those strange wasps that lay their eggs inside a host body, he slowly and methodically devoured the original house from the inside out, until all that remained was an empty husk, a few warped and shattered boards piled in the dooryard for kindling. This man is a beacon of inspiration, a true champion rebuilder. The original $2,000 hunting camp has metamorphosed under its cocoon into a $40,000 country cottage. It was raised off its shaky, rotting, post foundation, a cellar excavated almost by hand into the hardpan, the entire back wall removed, porches torn off and rebuilt, the roof raised, dormers and gables framed, new walls, sheathing, ceilings, floors, windows, doors, plumbing, wiring. There is a small relic of the original

house preserved in a glass case on the living-room wall to remind him of what the place once was. The triumph of this poor man's and woman's determination and folly has a moral: However bad it seems, someone has been there and back already.

If you are living in the house when you decide to remove the roof, gather all the possessions that can be removed and store them in a safe, dry place. Your house is about to become a camp, a spartan life-support system, which will provide for the basics of living while you plunder its very vitals. If you can, stay with friends or sleep out in the van for the duration. Cook on a Coleman stove or outdoor barbecue. If you cannot find other quarters, get the job done as quickly as possible. Invite a few strong and handy friends over one fine day, arm them with wrecking bars, and hope for a run of good weather. It's a kind of gambling game.

I used to tease that same friend about his lack of running water. His spring had developed a chronic case of dyspepsia, and his new plumbing languished unused for lack of the time to excavate a new spring. I was building my place at the time, and although we had cold running water to the kitchen sink, the plumbing was not yet finished. The standing bet was as to which of us would get to have a shower first. The night after his roof was torn off, I was at home, listening to the rain falling gently on the roof, when the phone rang. It was my friend. All he said was, "You lost."

Covering the exposed floor deck with a poly sheet after the roof is removed will not keep out all the water, but it will help prevent the entire house from turning into a gigantic shower stall. Water will work under the seams and around places where chimneys and pipes puncture the membrane. If possible, tape the edges of the poly to the protruding element so that the water will drain off. Poly sheet comes in widths to twenty-four feet. Use the widest sheet to minimize seams. Batten the edges securely to the sidewalls of the house. Elevate overlapped seams above the floor deck by folding them tightly over each other, like freezer wrapping meat, and staple the seam to a length of strapping. Where the plastic is unsupported, for example over a staircase opening, it is better to puncture a drain hole and collect run-off in a waiting bucket.

First remove all the shingles from the roof deck. Do this the day before your help arrives, and cover the deck with tarpaper or plastic sheet, in event of bad weather. Clear the old shingles from around the house, and truck them to the dump. Avoid cluttering up the work area. When your commandeered friends arrive, begin removing the decking. You may wish to salvage the tongue-and-groove boards for reframing or building pigpens. Start at the peak and work down—

3–45 *Protecting exposed floor from weather*

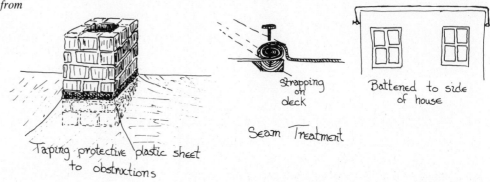

Taping protective plastic sheet to obstructions

Strapping on deck

Battened to side of house

Seam Treatment

standing on the deck if possible—and using a rafter as leverage, pry off boards with a crowbar. They can be loosened by pounding them up from the inside of the deck. On steep roofs, staging brackets or even temporary cleats of 2 × 4 tacked to the deck will be needed. A ground crew (women and children usually seem to be assigned to this role) pulls the nails from the salvaged boarding and stacks it out of the way. Split pieces are put into a kindling or burning pile. Cleaning the area as you work will prevent accidents and time lost stumbling around piles of trash when you rebuild.

All the trim boards are removed from the eaves and rakes as you move along the edge of the roof. Save them for reuse if possible. After the roof is completely stripped, the rafters can be removed. Standard dimensional lumber rafters are easily taken down by pulling the nails at the birdsmouth (where the rafter joins to the plate) and then twisting them free of the ridge board. Often a crowbar will be all that is needed to twist and pry a rafter free of the plate.

Lowering pole or heavy-timber rafters is not quite as simple. They must be handled delicately, as their weight could crush you as well as the deck if they were to topple uncontrolled. If there is a ridge beam, the end rafter is cut free of it with a chain saw. The upper end of the beam is then lowered to the deck with a rope and, if possible, is pried free of the plate at the same time. A stubborn rafter can be loosened at the plate with a chain saw. Use a rope to lower the pole or beam, cinching the rope onto the ridge beam itself. Start at the middle and work toward each end if the ridge pole is one continuous piece. That leaves the end wall-rafter pairs supporting the ridge and, since you will be working from a ladder against it, the ridge supporting you. Nail temporary diagonal braces to the end-rafter pairs and cut the ridge free, lowering each end with a rope. If the ridge beam is spliced in the middle, leave a rafter pair on each side of the splice and take down each half of the frame separately. The end rafter pairs are roped to a secure hitch, with one rope used to pull them over and another to slow the descent. This same technique can be used to lower a complete rafter pair where a ridge beam is not used. The rafters are cut at the plate and carefully lowered to the deck. The timbers can be saved to be exposed as part of the new roof framing. Wear gloves when working with ropes, to prevent burns if the ropes should slip.

End rafters will be studded and sheathed to support the gable walls. Remove the sheathing, working from the peak down, pounding the boards free of the studding from the back side. A sledgehammer will remove the studs. It is also a convenient tool for loosening recalcitrant rafters from the plate. Remember that the great weight that anchors a timber roof to the plate is converted into energy when the roof falls. You want to harness this momentum, not be carried away by it.

Piles of framing lumber are stacked, ready for use—your drawings and your quart of good cold ale are in hand—the twilight gathers around your friends now helping themselves to the potluck sagging the table stretched over the sawhorses. You pray for the good weather to hold.

Follow the standard framing methods of new construction when rebuilding the roof and walls. The pleasures of working with new materials and a clean and open work area will be a true intoxication. You will swear on a pallet of plywood never again—*never again*—to rebuild an old house, never again to use old lumber, not one single warped, twisted, nail-studded, four-dimensional stick. This intoxication is as deep as your pocketbook. Consult Willis Wagner's *Modern Carpentry,* the bible of the straight rule and square timber, or L. O. An-

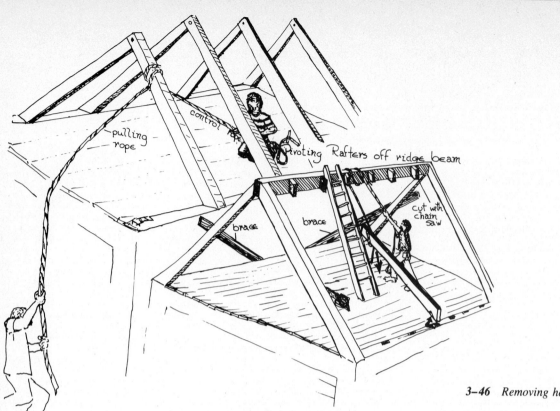

3–46 Removing heavy-timber rafters

derson's *Wood Frame House Construction* for the details of framing you will need. Your copies of these books will undoubtedly become dog-eared, smudged with the signatures of torn knuckles and smashed fingers, worn with reference. You will know them chapter and verse. It is not my intention to duplicate the excellent technical information they contain, but rather to provide general guidelines and to elaborate on the principles underlying the specific techniques.

Let your needs guide your imagination when planning your attic addition. The cost differential between the various options will not be great enough to make any particular choice more attractive than any other. Figure 3–47 suggests some of the possibilities.

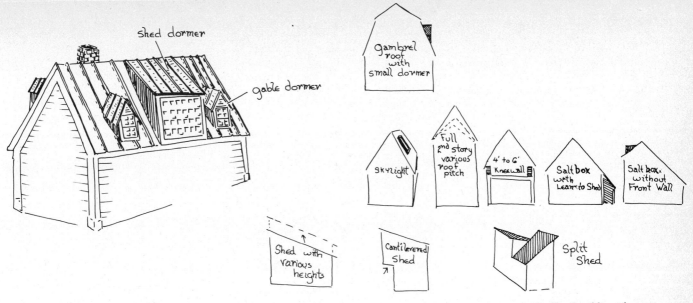

3-47 Roof-line changes

Dormers preserve the integrity of a steep, pitched roof, while creating usuable space. A common mistake is to make them too small. It takes very little more time or money to build a good-sized dormer instead of a small one. In a gable dormer, the pitch of the roof is perpendicular to the pitch of the main roof. A shed dormer is parallel to the main roof. Gable dormers are the most complex to frame and require a fair degree of competence on the part of the builder. Unless you feel capable of figuring it out, hire a carpenter. Perhaps you can work along as a helper, and learn a few things. Shed dormers are far simpler to build. Knee-wall spaces (the area at the bottom of the triangle formed by the roof and the floor deck) are awkward to use except as storage areas. Raising the height of the side wall of the house can overcome this difficulty. Adding an entire second story may present too severe a facade, particularly for a narrow house. Maintain a sense of proportion: A two-story house with a steep roof, set in the middle of an open field, will look like Aunt Em's house in Munchkin land. Lost in the deep woods, it may seem friendlier and less imposing. The vertical lines of a façade can be counteracted to some degree by a lower roof pitch, the addition of porches or decks, and the use of horizontal siding and jet shingles.

A reasonable alternative to a full second story is a 4-foot (half-story) knee wall. Many of the old houses were framed with 10- or 12-foot side walls for just this reason. Unless the house is ''balloon'' framed (the studs run continuously from sill to plate and the floor floats from them on a ledger), it is not advisable to platform-frame a knee wall less than this height. The 4-foot dimension is easily adapted to the use of full 4 × 8 sheets of plywood, which will be necessary to give sufficient rigidity to the frame. A shorter wall will be unstable. Even a 4-foot wall should be tied and braced securely with diagonals let into the studdings at the corners and with braces concealed in interior partitions.

The narrow spaces under the peak of a traditional northern farmhouse can be opened up by a skylight. The Velux® skylight is perhaps the best available commercially built ventilation unit available. It is easily installed, opens and closes, and is watertight. Although building a venting skylight that is watertight is very ticklish, a fixed-light unit is not beyond the skills of the novice framer. There is a lot more to recommend the 12-12 pitch than tradition alone. The angles of such a roof are either 45- or 90-degree cuts. These cuts are easily done, and with little chance for error, using a skilsaw and combination square. No complicated computations are necessary. The amateur builder should keep that in mind. The rafter-tail overhang, which will frame the eave, can be either "square-cut" (resulting in a "railroad jet," after the old rural stationhouses where this style eave was popular) or "plumb-cut," i.e., cut at the same 45-degree angle as the rafter peak, plumb to the wall of the house.

The gambrel roof will cover a larger volume of usable space than any other standard roof design, which is why it is the familiar and traditional barn roof. It is also easy to frame, since shorter lengths of rafters are used. Dormers can be added for windows in the steep bottom-wall section. A shed roof may give usable space under its entire length, depending on the height of the front wall. It is the simplest of all roofs to frame. The timbers must be heavy enough to carry the snow load. Any span of great length must be supported by a carrying beam. The shed can be cantilevered out beyond the existing front wall of the building if new floor joists are spliced along the existing joists. The protective overhang will shelter firewood and shade solar windows from the summer sun. The shed design can be varied by alternating the pitch of the roof, from one side of the house to the other as in Figure 3–47.

The saltbox roof combines the shed and gable design. The long, steep, rear slope encloses storage space and can be extended to the first story for a lean-to shed or entrance porch. Skylights can open this floor to light. The saltbox is every bit as traditional a design as the gable roof and will harmonize well with a variety of settings. A more contemporary variation on the saltbox theme is a sloped front wall. A 45–60-degree slope will be ideal for solar-heating collectors in Northern areas. Windows can be framed into projecting or inset dormers.

The suggestions above by no means exhaust the possibilities for roof framing. The only real limitations are those imposed by budget and skill. The budget may be fixed, but the skills can continue to grow. A novice would do well to visit a building site, perhaps after hours, or on a weekend, and just walk about, carefully observing the way things are put together. Try to grasp the feel of the framing, to fathom the logic of stress and balance. Standing before a project outlined in real wood makes more sense than reading about it in a book.

If you feel the need, build a small model from balsa or cardboard. Show it to a carpenter friend, who may be able to point out impossibilities in the design. Often lumber yards provide free design services, especially if you order the materials from them. Common sense and careful observation will do more for you than any expensive architect.

If you can organize another work party, try to frame the roof in a single day. You will be that much closer toward getting in under the weather. At least two pairs of hands are needed to frame a roof in any case. Precut the rafters and organize your materials before help arrives. Utilize the extra bodies to their maximum potential by having them raise the rafters and nail decking instead of carrying about boards. When dormers are to be built, raise all the common rafters first, leaving out those under the dormer course. The dormer can be framed later by a single worker, if help is limited. Plywood decking will keep out some of the water and, when covered and battened with tarpaper, will keep you dry for a winter or longer. The object is to get the bulk of the work done while you have the help and weather. The gable-end walls and other details can be filled in later. Make sure that the work area is secured before the help

arrives. Nail down loose board flooring and put temporary boards over any exposed ceiling areas. (My same friend almost lost his mother when she stepped off the floor platform and fell across the joists, breaking three ribs on the way.) Save the plastic sheet to lay across the rafters for weather protection if the work must stop before the deck is applied. Dormers and gables can be closed in with a sheet of poly tightly battened to the studding. Staple an additional layer on the inside surface, and you will have a warm and secure, albeit somewhat noisy, temporary wall—the night winds will play that plastic like a sail in a storm when you try to sleep.

When you are not resorting to the wholesale removal of the entire roof, the addition of a dormer is a simple way to increase the living space below. The same basic module can shelter one window or an entire wall. A saltbox house is actually nothing more than a continuous shed dormer across the front wall. Cut the roof back along the line of the rafters that mark its outside dimension. Always plan the width of a dormer to fit into the rafter-spacing module. Work in multiples of two; for 2-foot centers, use 16-feet, not 15-feet. Sawing through a roof deck is easiest with a reciprocating saw, (known as a *sawzall*® or *tiger saw*®). This tool, which resembles a science-fiction weapon, is the remodeler's friend. It can cut through roofing and decking, and even nails, at a single pass. Cut the sheathing boards to the outside of the rafters and leave them unsupported until a nailer is scabbed onto the side of the rafter, after the required decking is removed.

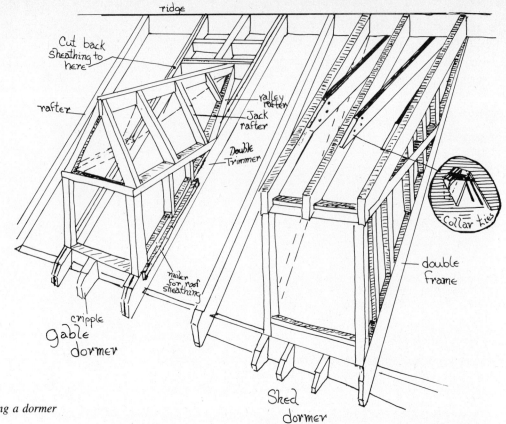

ridge

Cut back
Sheathing to
here

rafter

valley
rafter

Jack
rafter

Double
Trimmer

Collar ties

nailer
for roof
sheathing

double
frame

cripple

gable
dormer

Shed
dormer

3–48 Basics of framing a dormer

Remove the rafters on the inside of the dormer area. Since the dormer will not extend to the outside of the eave, being framed off the plate, small stubs (''cripple'' rafters) will be left to fit against the studding of the dormer's front wall. These are nailed to the wall studding or to the face of the sheathing. The rafters that support the dormer itself are called *trimmers* and should be doubled to carry the extra weight. The peak of a gable dormer can be framed directly

over the deck of the existing roof. Pull up the shingles along the valley line and lay the new valley. Replace broken shingles as necessary and snap a chalk line to cut the valley line. The top course of the roofing on a shed dormer is simply run up under the main deck roofing or to the ridge. The junction between the dormer rake trim and the old roof should be sealed with flashing cement.

Ideally, a new dormer is added as a part of a reroofing project, enabling both roofs to be shingled together and simplifying framing.

CHAPTER IV

OF SKINS AND SHELLS:
WALLS, WINDOWS, AND DETAILS

Life began in the cradle of the sea. Drifting in the warm currents of these primordial waters, simple creatures absorbed their needs from a soup of dissolved nutrients, returning their wastes to replenish what they took. The first terrestrial life forms were like astronauts, confronting a terrain as inhospitable as the empty reaches of deep space. To crawl from the sea, they had to take it with them. The skin, a selectively porous membrane, which not only filtered out the harshness of the outer world but enclosed the real environment safely within, evolved to fill this need. In time these living water-bags colonized their new environment so extensively that they forgot where they came from.

The skin of the house, the wall, is that membrane. It hangs on the strong bones of a timber frame. Like a pelt, like feathers or scales, clapboards shed the weather. Sheathing boards are its web, insulation the fat of the house, windows and doors, it ventricles and pores. Within, the ebb and flow of life is nurtured. The smoke rises from the flue, the garbage goes out the back door . . . and so easily have we forgotten the patterns upon which we build. So easily we fail to see the model and the connection: We think somehow that we and what we do, are separate from the world. The salt of the earth flows forever to the sea, and the blood pounding within us is as salt in the sea. If we listen, we will hear its ancient rhythms, beating on the shores of our minds, unchanged since the dim red light of that first dawn.

Houses age just as their builders, from the open and naked rawness of the new wood and paint, through the mellow softness of the middle years, the beginning of sag and settlement, to the decay of old age. They grow and change, springing new and full blown into the world, growing fat with family life and finally abandoned to neglect, put aside like the old people no one wants. The only difference between old houses and old people is that the house can be rebuilt. People can be born again, but they usually die first. Fortunately, houses are a lot easier to resurrect than people. Only one man is reputed to have managed the act so far.

A house wears its age on its face. The fissures of weathered boards and peeling paint, like eczema and baldness, the arthritic disjointing of cornice and trim, the debilitating diseases of internal rot—the house shares the wrinkles and scars of life passed. Like those beautiful people who fly off to exclusive Swiss clinics for face liftings, the skin of an old house can be restored to a semblance of youth. There is nothing exotic or mysterious to the process, and it need not be expensive. It is fairly necessary to the well-being of the house and can even be fun for the rebuilder.

> To keep three or four spots of eczema in a private part of my body and now and then scald or bathe it with hot water behind closed doors. Ah, is this not happiness?   [Chin Shengt'an, seventeenth century]

Walls have two sides: an inside and an outside. The function of each is almost totally different. This obvious fact is often overlooked.

The outside wall consists of two elements, the exterior finish and the sheathing, which roughly correspond to the epidermal and subdermal layers of the body. The finish is in direct contact with the elements. Its tightly overlapping structure is designed to shed water. This outer skin is fastened to an inner layer of sheathing boards, which not only support it and form a secure barrier against wind infiltration but give the frame added structural rigidity, much like connective tissue. The inside wall of the house is a marriage of structural necessity and aesthetic feelings. It is decorative and, in this sense, arbitrary. But, it also

makes the house livable. It covers and protects the nerves and circulatory systems of wiring and plumbing, regulating internal temperatures. It controls the flow of humidity and warm air and is, in this sense, vital. The space between inner and outer walls is a transition zone, filled with a vital fluid: air. This fluid is held in the pores of insulation, much as fat is stored in the connective tissue.

Like the shell of a clam or the skin of a beetle, the wall of a stud-framed house is structurally integral with the sheathing. It is an invertebrate design, much older than the skeletal design of the timber frame. The "primitive" cultures of the world build houses in the images of insects and shells. Wall and roof are one. The first houses were arches of bent poles, saplings covered with skins or thatch. Masonry shells of later cultures recapitulate, but do not surpass, the intricacy of the nautilus or the oyster. As humans discovered their bodies, they discovered the timber frame. And as their culture reached the stage of modern industrial-ant society, they built the stick-frame house.

The wall then, is both structural and cosmetic in function. It extends into the spiritual realm as well as the physical. Because it is the face the house presents to the world, changing this face has profound psychological reverberations. After the traumas and frustrations of foundation work, the results of which are largely buried and intangible, a renovation of the exterior or interior walls is a stimulating and by comparison, pleasurable, tonic. Painting the wall may save your marriage.

To consider the outside wall as a "defense" against the environment implies an antagonism, an extension of the way in which Western man has brutalized his world. It is the madness of poisoned rivers and polluted mother's milk. Our monuments may well be our gravestones. Simpler and, perhaps wiser, people have sought to live with nature, not to ignore or "conquer" it. The wall is a membrane, not so much a barrier as a zone of transition. It is selective, allowing transfers of energy across its surfaces. Like an air lock, it equalizes the temperature and pressure differentials, allows sunlight and fresh air to enter what might otherwise be an unwholesome cave. A membrane is not a fortress but rather a point of equilibrium. A good wall utilizes the environment as a vital part of its design.

Because the exterior wall is in direct contact with the harsher aspects of the climate, it suffers most from erosion. Constant cycles of wet and dry, hot and cold, will wear down mountains, let alone houses. It is a testimony to the unique durability of wood that it weathers so well and so long. Examine an old board taken from a barn. It will be noticeably thicker where it has been protected by an eave from direct exposure to the weather. The wind and rain have scoured the very grain of the wood, leaving a fantastic landscape of ridge and valley, the dense layers of fall wood like the desert buttes, standing out against the softer spring wood. If kept dry and well ventilated, wood will wear away before it rots. Except in a rain forest, the normal air movements accomplish this drying and ventilation process quite well.

As the outer wood wears, the nails draw moisture. They rust away, leaving small cavities for water and rot to gather in. The constant shrinking and expansion causes cracks to open along the grain. As water works into these crevasses, the wood leaches away, the cracks open wider, and sections of clapboards break loose. Nails are pulled as the boards warp and curl. The skin becomes loose and flaccid, allowing both water and wind to penetrate the walls. The house develops a chronic cold; it is drafty. Like a deathbed revelation, the old boards glow with a strange beauty in their decay, "grey" is a mere ap-

proximation of their being, an average of the many subtle shifts of color and density as they respond to light and weather. The grain is a map, a book of verse, a journal of the house's passage through time.

But poetry will not necessarily keep you warm and dry, and analogy is not firewood; the connection between words and buffalo chips is only metaphorical. Tourists may think it quaint to live in a weather-beaten old house but its inhabitants know it for the energy sieve it is. Driving the backroads in winter, one will often find entire houses swaddled in plastic sheets, battened with tarpaper, in the fight to slam the door on winter's icy fingers.

Infiltration and Heat Loss:
Tightening up the house

It is a common misconception that heavy insulation alone is the most important requirement for a warm house. While that may indeed be true for the roof, insulation in the walls is nowhere as critical. A *tight* house is far more effective, since infiltration of air is the major cause of drafts and high heating bills. Cold outside air will move into a house when a negative pressure differential is created. Wind blowing against one side of the house causes a partial vacuum on the opposite wall. In attempting to equalize this pressure, the wind moves *through* the house via whatever pores are available. Negative differentials are also created by exhaust vents, furnace flues and, especially, fireplaces. Fresh air is drawn in to replace the air escaping up the chimney. The temperature difference between outside and inside air will also cause the same negative pressure. Warm inside air tends to move through the walls toward the outside drawing in cold air to replace it, as if through thousands of tiny chimneys.

Negative pressure is not in itself a bad thing. The same principle can be utilized to obtain summer cooling and ventilation in lieu of an air conditioner, which is nothing more than energy-eating compensation for poor design. The ventilating roofs described in chapter 3 are examples of the creative use of pressure differentials. Controlled air infiltration is ventilation. Uncontrolled infiltration is the cause of winter troubles. A general program of tightening up the house is the first step toward control. Plugging up as many of the obvious points of entry as possible will go a long way toward lowering heating bills.

Weatherstripping should be applied to all doors and windows. Threshold gaskets are particularly important. Caulk all cracks around doors and windows

4–1   Causes of air infiltration

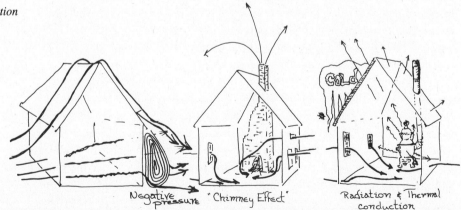

where air might infiltrate, especially where clapboards butt against the trim. Use only a good grade of caulking. Oil-based caulking compound is useless—it soon dries out, cracks, and breaks off. It has virtually no resistance to the movement of joints caused by normal expansion and contraction of the wood. Butyl and neoprene caulkings are better. Phenol and latex-base compounds also tend to dry out and shrink away from the joints. All these caulkings will break down after a few years of exposure to weather and sunlight. In the long run, they are a waste of money. Silicone caulk is more than twice as expensive as any of the above-mentioned compounds, but is far superior. It is flexible, virtually indestructible, and unaffected by extremes of temperature—something you will appreciate if you have ever tried to use any other compound at temperatures below 40° F. As with any other caulking, silicone must be applied over a clean, *dry* surface for a good bond.

The Tremco Company of Newark, New Jersey, manufactures a product called MONO®, which is one of the best general sealants available at a reasonable price. You may be able to order it by the case lot (caulking an entire house requires at least a dozen standard tubes) through your lumberyard or from a plate-glass window installer. MONO will stick to almost anything and is very flexible. It must, however, be applied warm (85° F.) and should be preheated in a low oven or behind the wood stove. Tremco also manufactures the fiberglass emulsion compound used for patching holes in steel roofing and rusted fenders mentioned in chapter 3.

Caulking is applied in an even bead with a caulking gun. Large cracks (over ¼″) should first be filled with oakum, or better yet, Mortite® rope caulking, a claylike material that will adhere to most surfaces. Smooth the bead with your fingertip to help it adhere tightly to the substrate and give it the proper concave, water-shedding shape.

Like caulking, weatherstripping comes in a bewildering variety of materials. Wool felt can be used where the surface is not subject to repeated movement, but otherwise it is impractical except as a temporary expedient. While it is a suitable backing for storm windows, it will soon tear loose and rip, soak up water and rot, and generally fail when used on a door jamb. There are several grades of foam weatherstripping. Avoid the self-adhering foam types; the adhesive dries out, and the strip separates from the jamb. Painting over foam will destroy its flexibility and effectiveness as a sealer. Most synthetic foams tend to break down after a few years' exposure to the weather. The best general weatherstripping for doors is retailed under the trade name Porta-seal® and consists of a vinyl gasket embedded in a strip of wood door stop. A single package contains enough to weatherstrip a standard 3′ × 6′-8″ door. The gasket strip is nailed to the door jamb forming a positive seal against the door when shut. It is available in 1½-inch widths for entrance doors and a ¾-inch width for storm doors and windows. If the door fits too loosely to make a tight contact, add a shim behind the weatherstrip of the required thickness. The bottom of the door should be equipped with a threshold gasket or a weatherstrip mounted on the edge opposite the direction of closing. Vinyl strips tend to crack and split after use, especially in cold weather, in this application. Nylon sealers are better. Figure 4–2 shows some of the applications of caulking and weatherstripping.

Infiltration along the foundation wall can be cured by *banking,* an old country remedy for a freezing cellar. Spoiled hay or spruce boughs and brush piled against the outer wall will break the wind force. Snow accumulation adds insulation. Banking paper is nothing more than tarpaper cut to width, battened

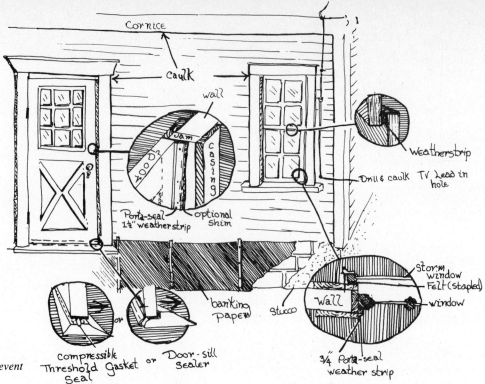

4–2 Tightening up the house to prevent wind infiltration

to the bottom edge of the wall sheathing, and held in place with stones or earth. It is removed in the spring to prevent rot. A coat of stucco, which is a mix of cement and sand, can be applied over a block wall to seal gaps. Remember to plug all foundation ventilators for the winter with a batt of fiberglass insulation.

Weatherstripping and caulking will reduce infiltration significantly. Storm windows are another important step. The heat loss by infiltration through a single pane of glass can be reduced by one-third with the addition of a storm-window panel. Although thermopane glazing will reduce additional heat loss by *radiation* it will not significantly lower infiltration loss. However, factory-built windows are much tighter and less prone to infiltration than old or home-built windows, to begin with. A wood-frame storm window equipped with felt weatherstripping is the most economical solution to winter infiltration problems. A temporary expedient is the polyethylene storm window. The poly is cut several inches larger than the window and folded around a one-inch strip of cardboard or wood and stapled to the casing. If the poly is stapled to a wood frame made of firring strip and angle irons, it will last more than one season. The frame is secured to the wall with storm-window screw eyes. Drill a hole slightly larger in diameter than the screw eye through the storm-window sash. A screw-driver blade makes an excellent lever for turning the eyes into the casing. New storm windows are expensive. Look around the attic or cellar, the garage or the barn when you buy the place. The old windows will often be stored away. Aluminum storm windows lose a great deal of heat through their frames in the North, but they do have the advantage of never having to be removed.

Wind-related air infiltration can be tempered by a windbreak. Evergreens planted at a distance from the house equal to five times its height will help cut down the force of the wind. Deciduous trees will slow the wind very little unless densely planted. A windbreak planting is a long-term investment. In most locations, there is little that you can do immediately to prevent wind infiltration.

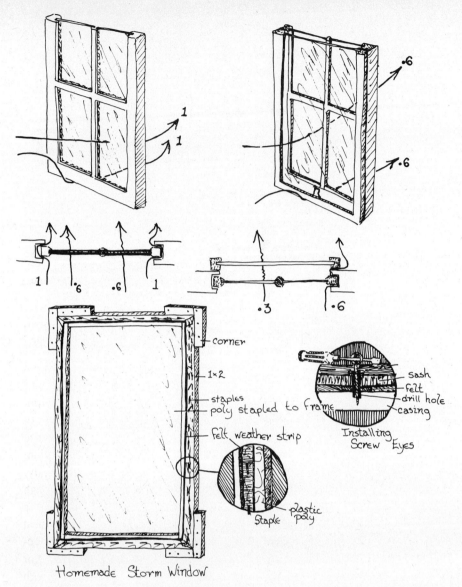

corner

1×2

staples
poly stapled to frame

felt weather strip

Staple

plastic
poly

Homemade Storm Window

sash
felt
drill hole
casing

Installing
Screw Eyes

*4–3 Storm windows and heat-loss
factors through windows*

But you might consider installing a wind generator to recoup part of your energy losses.

Fireplaces are the main cause of the "chimney effect." If you must have a fireplace, at least remember to shut the damper when it is not in use. The same thing applies for all wood stoves. Some heat will be lost through furnace flues, but that is a necessary evil. Furnaces need to breathe. You cannot really get an old house too tight. Despite your best efforts, there will always be sufficient numbers of pores to feed the fires.

Perhaps even more important than weatherstripping and caulking as a factor in reducing chimney effect and increasing the general comfort of a house is a tight vapor barrier, which is an impermeable membrane installed behind the inside wall finish. It prevents warm, moisture-laden air from moving through the wall and condensing on the cold side of the exterior sheathing. Such condensation would otherwise rot the wall framing and studding. The vapor barrier also helps minimize air infiltration and maintain internal humidity. It is best applied when refinishing the interior walls.

From the foregoing discussion, it is obvious that there is much that can be done to tighten up a house that is in otherwise good condition. Even new houses are seldom properly caulked and weatherstripped—an unfortunate legacy from our days of blind energy profligacy. Most builders have yet to reorganize their priorities to reflect the economics of energy conservation. For some who do know better, it is just too much of a bother and expense to do it right.

Exterior Siding and Trim:
Repair and replacement

If the existing exterior siding is threadbare and loose, infiltration cannot be prevented. The material will have to be replaced. This investment will pay off not only in increased resale value, since it improves the outside appearance, but in reduced heating costs as well. Clapboards and wood shingles are two of the most widely used exterior wall coverings. Asphalt shingles are somewhat less common and nowhere near as pleasing to look at. Aluminum or vinyl siding is all too frequently used to cover any of the other types of siding. While they do have a longer life than painted wood surfaces, they are neither attractive nor morally justifiable in an age of energy consciousness. There are other more ecologically sane alternatives to the problems of protecting houses. (See Afterword for further discussion on the subject of synthetic building materials in general.)

Old clapboards or shingles are easily removed with a flat steel pry bar, (the carpenter's Wonderbar.®) As with stripping a roof deck, large sections can be pried loose at a stroke. It is best to pry from under the butts. Remaining nails are hammered back into the sheathing boards. Strip only one wall at a time; otherwise the entire house may be left exposed to a sudden turn in the weather. As you strip the finish, observe the condition of the trimwork. If the window or door casings are badly cracked or weathered, they should be replaced. Use your flat bar to pry them free of the jambs. Cornices and frieze boards, returns, or "rebates," will all suffer frequently from pockets of rot. Even sound trim is almost always in need of repainting.

Early homes were strictly utilitarian. Their builders had difficulty enough tending to the rigors of mere survival and little time to spare for embellishment. Whatever trim they may have added to the house was plain board, serving only to close in the gap between the rafter tails and the side wall. As life became more settled and secure, the desire for ornamentation was indulged. Architectural fashions of Europe were imported along with tea and china. During the eighteenth century, the Georgian influence resulted in the elaborate cornice work that was typical of country manors and the townhouses of the well-to-do. Freed of the structural restraints of the stonework that was the prototype for this work, wood moldings could be applied in successive layerings of pure decorative fancy. Even humble farmhouses were often graced with a fluted pediment or layered cornice. This decorative impulse reached its apotheosis in the extremes of Victorian gingerbread. Wonderful to look at but hell to maintain, it was a true talisman of class distinction: "Will you be needing the painters again this year, madam?"

Before the days of factory millwork, moldings were cut by hand, using a special plane. Each plane was equipped with a blade designed for a particular cut. Several planes were used to make a single piece of molding. Every carpenter owned his own set of molding planes, and the resulting work was very much

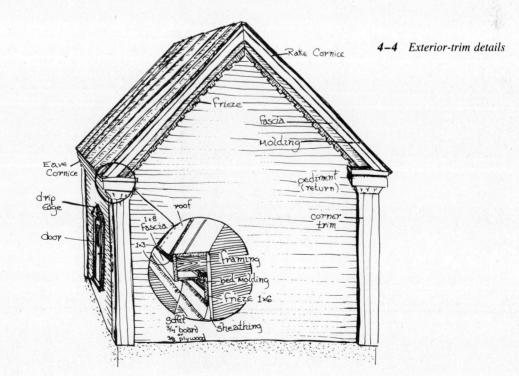

4–4 *Exterior-trim details*

a product of his own inventiveness, which accounts for the wide variation in design. The path of one man's travels through a region can often be traced by the distinctive moldings he left behind.

Replacement of original moldings will be impossible unless you can locate a set of old molding planes. These are a common item in antique shops. With patience, you should be able to duplicate the original pattern. The match need not be perfect; you won't be able to see it from the ground. There are stock moldings available at the lumberyard, which can be used as a substitute for the original trimwork, re-creating the effect in spirit, if not in detail. Of course, all the original moldings will then have to be removed to avoid a patchwork appearance. If your budget cannot accomodate the considerable expense of new molding, a simplified version can be built by replacing all the original cornice work with one-inch boards. Modern carpentry, by dint of economy, has come full circle to the exigencies of the pioneer days. Soffits and fascia on contemporary homes are most often completely lacking in embellishment, fulfilling only the bare functional minimum of a stop to fit the siding against.

Remove and replace all doubtful trim boards. Small pockets of rot can be cleaned and filled with a nonwater-base wood filler (plastic wood). Water-base putty is easier to use but must be sealed immediately upon drying, to prevent it from washing away. It cannot be equaled for interior use. Durham's Rock-Hard® is an excellent product of this type. Holes and cracks and any obvious gaps where air can infiltrate are likewise puttied or caulked. When working under cornices, keep a can of wasp-killing spray handy. While wasps fill a valid ecological niche, it is better that they do it some place other than your cornice. Remove any boards carefully, listening for the telltale buzzing of wasps. An angry swarm can result not only in painful stings but in a fatal fall as well.

All loose and scaling paint should be removed with a wire brush or paint scraper. Primed woodwork should be finish painted within forty-eight hours. Many primers begin to lose their adhesive properties after prolonged exposure to air. Paint the trim *before* you put up any new siding. This will save cleanup and spattered walls.

Once the walls have been stripped of the old siding and the trim repaired, decide whether you wish to add or remove any windows. It will be easier to do now than after the new siding is added. The margin for error is quite generous when working in the substrate. The wall is covered with a rosin-coated paper (building paper) to seal out wind. Lay the paper from the bottom of the wall up, overlapping each course by two inches. Lay right over windows and cut them out after the paper is stapled in place. If the casings are to remain in place, loosen them enough to slip in the edge of the paper. Pay particular attention to the top of the window casing. Water can enter the wall above the window if it is not properly flashed and sealed with a *drip cap*. The drip cap should be protected with an aluminum or copper flashing nailed up under the siding. A simple sheet of metal flashing folded over the casing can be substituted for a wood cap. A cant strip should be inserted behind the siding (see Figure 4–5).

Clapboards are the traditional siding in regions of driving storms and hard winters. In colonial days, bolts of oak were riven with a froe. Today they are cut to produce the typical bevel shape on band saws, from spruce, cedar, or redwood. Their tightly overlapping pattern sheds water easily and seals the wall against wind penetration. Clapboards are manufactured in several grades

4–5 Protecting the window from water damage

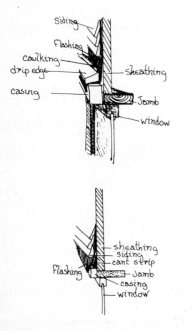

and widths, affecting the price and the labor required for installation. Extra-clear grade is free from any knots or defects. It is the most expensive and is used where the finish is to be painted. Knots bleed through paint and must be otherwise sealed. (BIN® shellac sealer is the standard product for this task and is used wherever resinous knots are to be painted over.) Cottage-grade clapboards are the most economical but are also filled with defects that must be cut out to avoid rot or leaks. Second-clear, or clear, grade is the best compromise: Any knots or defects are in the portion covered by the succeeding course. Exposure to the weather is equal to half the width of the clapboard plus ¼ inch; for 5-inch clapboards allow 2¾ inches, for 5½-inch allow 3 inches for 6-inch, 3¼ inches. To estimate the amount of clapboards needed to cover a given area, multiply the square footage you must cover by the width of the clapboard and divide the result by the width of the exposure. The resulting figure is the number of feet of clapboard to order.

Start by leveling a line ½ inch below the bottom edge of the wall sheathing. A string can be stretched across the length of the wall. Lay the bottom of the first course of clapboards to this line. Insert a ⅛-inch-thick cant strip, cut from the top portion of a clapboard, under this first course to give it the proper bevel. Nail clapboards with 4d galvanized nails spaced about 12 inches on center within ½ inch of the butt. Do not drive the nails too deeply into the wood as it can easily split. Rip a 16-inch length of 1-inch stock to the width of the exposure and use it to guide the alignment of succeeding courses. A more accurate jig is shown in Figure 4–6. Check the run of the courses from time to time with a 4-foot level.

Unless you are very careful about checking the run of your courses it is very easy for them to run off level, particularly on long walls, unbroken by windows or doors. There is another method, preferred by many carpenters, which, although it takes more time for the initial set-up, results in greater accuracy and actually allows faster application of the clapboards once the lay-out is completed. The wall surface should be covered with rosin-coated builder's paper as above. Builder's paper also provides a legible surface for chalk-lines.*

Make a *story pole* from a straight length of 1 × 2 and carefully divide it into increments equal to the width of the desired exposure for the clapboards. Lay the story pole plumb along the wall and, starting at the bottom of the wall, transfer the markings onto the wall. Repeat this operation at the other end of the wall and around all windows and doors. Be sure that the bottom line is level across the wall. Continue until you reach the top of the wall. Connect the

4–6 Laying clapboards

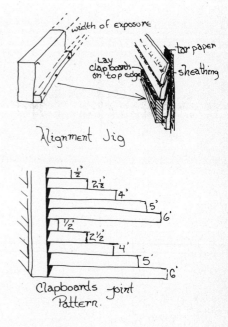

Alignment Jig

Clapboards Joint Pattern.

*Never use tarpaper (*saturated* asphalt-felt paper) between clapboards or any other finish siding and the sheathing boards. The felt is an effective vapor barrier and can cause condensation of moisture (and eventual rot) between itself and the sheathing boards. Rosin paper or *unsaturated* asphalt felt paper is permeable to water vapor and allows its passage through the siding. Condensation of the sort described above generally should not be a problem in a well-insulated house equipped with an adequate vapor barrier on the interior wall surface. Not enough water vapor will escape to condense within the exterior walls. But an old house with poor or non-existent insulation and crumbling plaster or peeling paint for an inside vapor barrier is another case. It would be wise to hold off painting the exterior walls of such a structure until you have corrected the insulation problems. Otherwise moisture escaping through the walls will tend to be stored by the relatively porous wood siding, particularly during the winter months, and then, as it migrates through to the outside during warmer weather, will cause the non-porous paint to blister and peel. Good insulation and a tight vapor barrier are critical factors in determining the life of an exterior paint job, as well as protecting sheathing boards from moisture-related damage.

markings with a chalk-line. You will now have a line for each course of clapboards marked on the wall.

Starting at the top of the wall, nail the first full clapboard in place so that its bottom edge is even with your chalked line. Be careful to drive the nails of this first course only in the unexposed (upper) portion of the clapboard so that you will be able to slip the next course up under the butt. Continue down the wall, slipping each course up under the one above it. Tack your nails in place rather than driving them home and use only two nails per length of clapboard, always leaving the bottom-most edge unnailed until another clapboard has been slipped up under it. If you were to drive the nails home it would be harder to slide the clapboards up under the edge and you could easily split a clapboard trying. You may need to use a block of wood to hammer the edge up into place in any case. When you have finished a section (all you can reach from a ladder or staging), nail it off. Try to make your nailing pattern run in more-or-less straight lines down the wall.

You might wonder, why couldn't one lay the clapboards from the bottom of the wall up, thereby avoiding all this slipping and sliding, simply aligning the top edge of the clapboards to the chalk-lines? This would indeed be the preferred method were it not for the fact that the top edges of clapboards are so thin they rarely are straight. Thus a nominal 6-inch wide clapboard might actually be 5½ or 5¾ inches wide or taper unevenly, making it impossible to align with your guide lines.

Take care to maintain spacings around windows. The courses should work out equally at the top of the windows. Often the old window frames will not be set level or plumb in the wall. If you are laying the clapboards level, they will appear to slant against the lines of the window. Measure the distance from the butt to the window from a point at least 20 inches below the sill. By dividing the distance by the exposure of the courses, determine the number of courses needed. Measure the difference between one end of the window and the other. That is how much you will have to slant the courses to make them appear level against the sill. Divide this figure by the number of courses to find approximately how much each particular course will be crowded. If the courses are slanted gradually, the deviation from true level will not be apparent. The same technique compensates for variations over a window header as well. It is useful when running clapboards up against a frieze board or under a cornice to avoid having the last course working out to a (hard-to-nail) 1-inch strip. (*Example:* Figure 4–7 shows a difference of 1½ inch from one side of the sill to the other. The 24-inch area to be covered at a 3-inch exposure divides into eight

4–7 *Compensating for crooked walls*

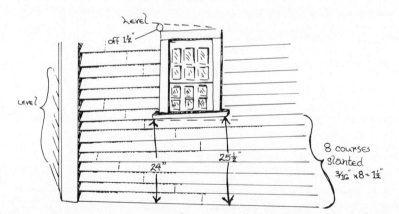

courses. 1½ ÷ 8 = .1875 or ³⁄₁₆ inch. Hundredths can be converted into sixteenths on a special conversion scale in the upper corner of the framing square. Each course is therefore slanted about ³⁄₁₆ inch to work out evenly under the windowsill.)

Clapboard joints should never break above each other. Allow at least three inches between joints. It is better to use a consistent pattern when breaking joints. That allows the nailing lines to remain fairly straight and creates a neater job. Clapboards come in bundles of different lengths. You should buy several. Not only will it simplify staggering the joints but waste will be minimized when cutting boards to fit in between windows and against corner boards. When using a handsaw or skilsaw, the cut should always be made from the backside of the material. The cut on the finish side will then be smooth. A table or radial-arm saw cuts from the top down, so always cut with the finish side up. Saw butts as accurately as possible. A cut-off guide is a great help when using a skilsaw. Use a rip guide for cuts along the length.

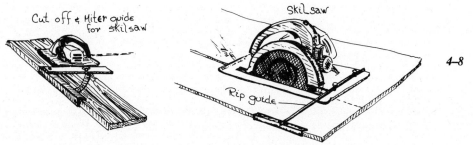

4–8 *Skilsaw aids*

The application of clapboard can be speeded up considerably if you drive only enough nails to hold each piece to the wall. When the surface is covered, the remaining nails can be driven all at once. One worker can cover the wall while a helper cuts clapboards to length. Clapboards must be nailed to a firm substrate. One-inch boarding is quite suitable. For new construction, ⅝-inch CDX plywood is generally used. Additional protection from wind infiltration can be obtained by sheathing a rough board wall with ½ inch asphalt-impregnated sheathing panels.

Wood shingles are an equally popular siding material. They are less expensive than clapboards and provide an equally watertight and durable surface. Cedar shingles need no painting or other finish, as the wood is naturally decay resistant and will weather to a beautiful silver grey. Shingles can be applied over masonry walls using nailing strips as well as over conventional wood sheathings. The main difference between cedar shingles as roofing and as wall siding is the maximum permitted exposure. It is equal to half the length of the shingle less ½ inch. Thus for a 16-inch shingle, the exposure should be 7½ inches.

Begin by laying shingles to a straight edge made from a length of ship-lapped board tacked level to the wall. Allow the first course to project ¼ to ½ inch below the sheathing. Building paper should be used as a backing for shingles. (Use it for all wood siding.) As with roofing, the shingles should be blind-nailed and spaced about ¼ inch apart to allow for expansion. Shingles can be butted against corner boards or, unlike clapboards, mitered or lapped at the corners. Caulk all joints against windows and doors.

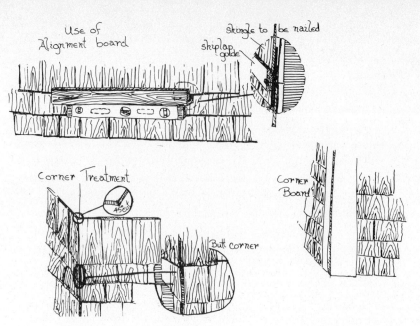

4–9 *Laying wood-shingle siding*

To lay shingles over masonry, fasten 1 × 4 strapping to the wall, using hardened masonry nails and a four-pound hammer. These nails can be driven into concrete without bending. Use a bead of construction adhesive for extra holding power. A special hand-held shield is sold for driving hardened fasteners, or a gunpowder-charged driving tool called a *Ramset*® can be rented for large jobs. Wood shingles are nailed with two nails, within 1 inch of the edges. Use three nails on shingles over 8 inches wide.

While cedar shingles and spruce clapboards are among the most traditional and handsome of exterior sidings, they are also among the most expensive. The careful attention required for alignment, the many small pieces with relatively little coverage per unit, the number of nails needed to fasten them—all make for a slow and (if hired out) expensive job. There are several contemporary alternatives equally pleasing in appearance, low in cost, and easy to apply. The board finishes shown in Figure 4–10 are typical.

4–10 *Exterior wood finish*

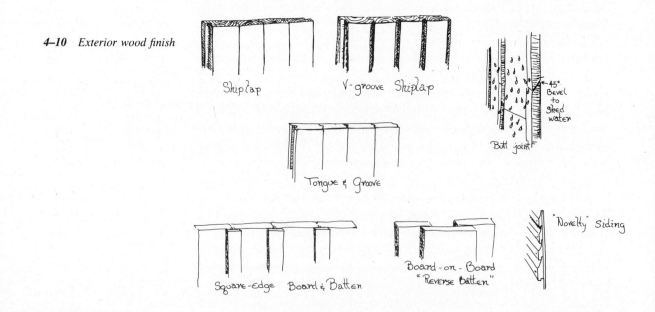

A variety of texture effects is possible using these natural products. Boards can be either roughsawn or surface planed. The roughsawn boards will show the marks of the saw teeth, an effect that many consider rustic. If the board was sawn on the circular saw, the blade will leave the familiar pattern of curved ridges. A bandsaw leaves a somewhat smoother pattern of horizontal ridges, which can be more pleasing than the rougher circular-sawn board and is more suited for use on interior walls.

Whatever surface finish, all boards should be "thickness" planed. Roughsawn lumber will vary considerably in thickness. Often a board may taper from one end to the other as much as ½ inch. Rough boarding is fine for a barn where precise work and tight fit are not necessarily the highest priority, but a house requires a different order of precision. Have the boards run through a single-side planer at the sawmill. That will remove any excess width, resulting in a uniform board with one rough and one smooth side. The edges should also be planed for width. It is then a matter of choice which side is exposed to the weather.

If a board does not run the entire height of a wall, the horizontal butts should be beveled on a 45-degree angle to prevent water from working behind them. For the same reason, board sidings should not be laid horizontally. An exception is a special tongue-and-groove siding called *novelty* siding. The scooped-out upper edge will shed water as will the bevel of V-groove siding.

Shiplap siding is generally considered the most versatile. As shown in Figure 4–10, the edges of each board are cut out, or *rabbeted*, on opposite sides. When lapped and nailed the rabbets create a watertight seal. Shiplap can be applied so as to duplicate the effect of wide clapboards simply by laying the rabbets to overlap the course below. See Figure 4–11. As with clapboards, the overlapped boarding must be butted to trim and corner boards, which will have to be a full 1½ inches thick. Otherwise the boards will protrude beyond the edge and leave a gap behind them. Use kiln-dried dimension lumber for this purpose, to avoid opening of cracks after the wood dries out. Corner trim boards should be mitered together, otherwise one of the corner boards will have to be ripped down to width to form an even corner when overlapped. Cut the corner boards to length and nail them together before installing them on the building. Align them with a single tack nail while they are adjusted for plumb with a level. Window trim will have to be narrow enough so that there will be sufficient jamb studding behind the sheathing to attach the clapboards to as well. Generally the width of the trim should not exceed two inches. Additional jack studs or blocking can be added behind the exterior wall if the inside is also exposed to repair. Nail clapboard shiplap through the lap about ½ inch from the bottom edge with 8d galvanized box nails. These nails must always penetrate the boarding and substrate through to the studding below. Sheathing board does not have enough nail-holding power to prevent the boards from curling and working loose over time.

Variations on the clapboard theme are the use of 10- or 12-inch wide rough boards overlapped as clapboarding with a 2-inch lap. These boards can be square edged, or left with the rough edges of the log intact for a more rustic effect. Wide boards are more prone to curling and twisting than narrower widths. Use 10d or 12d galvanized nails for better holding power. Lay boards with the heart side out (the growth rings should be convex when you look at them). This makes a surface that tends to seal tighter as the boards shrink and curve.

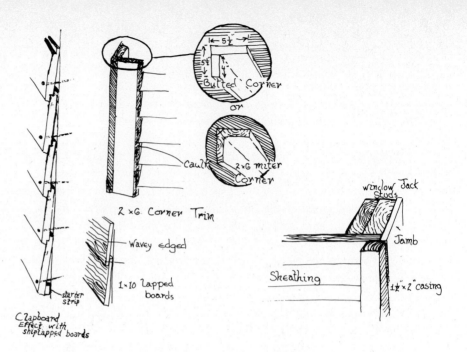

4–11 *Siding and corner-treatment details*

Butted Corner

or

Caulk

2×6 miter Corner

2×6 Corner Trim

Wavey edged

1×10 lapped boards

starter strip

Clapboard Effect with shiplapped boards

window Jack Studs

Jamb

Sheathing

1½"×2" casing

Vertical boards must be nailed into blocks set into the wall framing. Unless you plan to gut the interior walls, it will not be possible to install these nailers. Instead 1 × 4 strapping nailed across the studding over the old sheathing on 2- or 2½-foot centers will make a firm base for holding the siding. The dead air space between the boards and the sheathing will add extra insulation.

Tongue-and-groove board is not often used for vertical finish sheathing because that type of board is much more difficult to draw tightly together. The structural rigidity of the interlocking joint, however, makes it an excellent material when applied horizontally or diagonally, as a substitute for plywood in flooring, roof decking, and wall sheathing. Shiplapped boards can be applied much quicker; a bowed board can be driven tight by hammering a 16d toe nail through the lap. Avoid using wide boards for exterior surfaces where the tightness of the seal depends upon the lap—6-inch boards are the optimum width. The wider the board, the faster the coverage, but the greater the shrinkage. An 8-inch board can sometimes shrink enough to expose the joint.

4–13 *Toenailing out a bowed board*

4–12 *Laying siding over strapping*

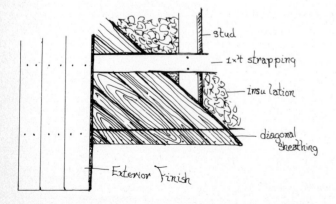

stud

1×4 strapping

insulation

diagonal sheathing

Exterior Finish

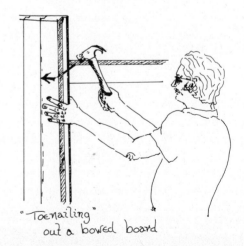

"Toenailing" out a bowed board

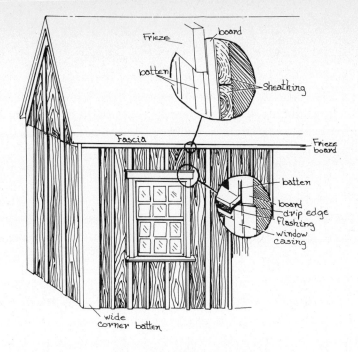

4-14 *Board-and-batten siding*

Board-and-batten is the simplest way to cover a wall tightly. Shrinkage of the joints is no longer a problem because any gap is completely covered by a narrow strip of wood (the batten). Vertical-board siding should be checked from time to time for plumb. The advantage of a board-and-batten wall is that any deviations will be hidden under the batten.

Drive the nails at opposing angles to each other. That prevents the board from splitting as it dries out. The board will actually slide down the nail as it shrinks. A variation on the board-and-batten idea is reverse batten or board-on-board. The first layer of boards is nailed to the wall, separated by a spacer block, and a second layer nailed over the gap. You can experiment with the width of the boards and the gap to create interesting effects. 6- and 8-inch or 8- and 10-inch exposures are standard.

Windows and door casings are treated as if they were wide battens. The tops of windows should have a drip cap, to which the battens are fitted and carefully caulked. Wide battens are used for corner trim if desired. Battens can be butted to a frieze board under the cornice, nailed over the top of the boarding itself. All horizontal joints in both boards and battens should be beveled at 45 degrees. An unusual effect is gained by offsetting the boards on the gable ends. Additional strapping is used to fill out the base. Other possibilities are to shingle the gables or board the gables and shingle the walls.

An argument often advanced in support of prefinished, factory-made exterior siding, is that it does not require painting. Hardboard sheathing with a baked enamel finish and aluminum and vinyl sidings are touted as the answer to the expense and bother of repainting the house every few years. That is the right answer to the wrong question. Has anyone ever stopped to ask, why paint at all? Good paint is expensive. Painters, good and bad, are expensive. Painting means repainting. The idea that a house must be painted is another example of how notions of fashion become accepted as cannons of nature. It is argued that paint protects the wood and adds years to its life. While that is arguably true, there are far less labor-intensive ways to accomplish the same objective. As long as it is kept dry, unpainted wood will last a lot longer than the house's owners.

4-15 *Treatment of gable end wall*

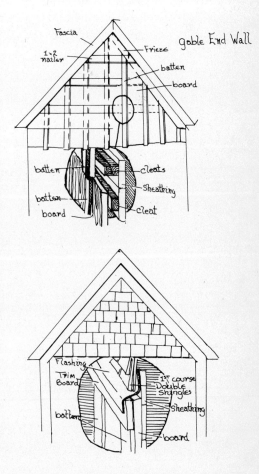

The sun and weather will play upon it like an artist at a palate. No paint can ever duplicate the enchanting hues and delicate beauty of naturally aging wood.

Stains that contain wood preservatives are now available in a wide range of colors and transparencies. Stain will apply much quicker than paint and need not ever be repainted. It will weather along with the wood, blending quite harmoniously. When the stain has worn entirely away, the house can be restained without scraping and sanding of blistered and peeling paint. The new opaque stains (which are so dense as to appear like paint) even do away with the necessity for painting trim boards.* If you are one of those people who feel a house is naked without paint somewhere, indulge your fancy by painting the trim. The contrast between a dark wall and a light-colored trim can be very pleasing. Accept the responsibilities of your whimsey and buy the highest quality paint and apply it to a thoroughly dry and clean base. Recoat every few years to prevent blistering and peeling. If your house is already painted and the exterior walls are in good condition, you are most likely condemned to the vicious cycle of paint and repaint. You have my condolences.

Windows and Doors: *Repair and replacement*

When the exterior walls were undergoing their face lifting, we assumed the windows were to be left intact. In fact, that is not always either possible or desirable. I remember examining a small pocket of rot alongside a window sill. As I removed the sheathing board, I could see that the rot went a bit deeper yet. Another board was pried loose. An hour later I stood before a gaping hole where there once had been a window. The entire wall had been torn off from window to sill. Gangrenous stumps of studs hung suspended from the plate. The rot had worked several inches into the sill itself. The entire wall shuddered in the stiff September breeze. It was the same for each window along that wall of the house. What was left of the window frames held rotten sashes.

If all a window needs to restore it to usefulness is a simple patching or reglazing and a coat of paint, it should be repaired and left in place. A storm window will help keep the house warm. If the sheathing and the window itself have seriously deteriorated, however, it must either be rebuilt or replaced. Unless you are an experienced cabinetmaker with a fully equipped shop, you cannot build a movable window as good as one you can buy. Factory-built double-glazed or "thermopane" windows are one of the great revolutions in building; they are easily installed and provide an air- and weather-tight seal. They are also very expensive, costing upwards of $25 per square foot of thermopane glass surface. The windows for an average new home can represent 10 to 15 percent of the entire construction budget. Even so, this money cannot be much better spent. Good windows pay for themselves through years of trouble-free service and savings on the heating bills by preventing air infiltration. If you can afford the expense, buy new windows.

---

*Paint or a varnish-type sealer is necessary only to seal movable surfaces such as doors and windows against absorption of moisture which otherwise would cause them to warp, swell, and stick. Particular care should be taken to seal *all* edges thoroughly, especially top and bottom, to insure stability. These are the only wood elements of the house that actually *require* painting. Exterior paint actually may further internal rot by preventing moisture movement through poorly insulated walls.

Whenever possible, choose a size similar to the window you intend to replace. It is better for them be slightly undersize than over. Windows are sized according to the dimensions of the rough opening needed to fit the unit into the wall. Additional measurements are given for the installed exterior size, that is, what you see looking at the wall, and also for the size of the glass itself, should it need replacement. If the new window can fit into the old space with a minimum of blocking and filling, you save the labor of hacking out the frame to accommodate an oversize unit.

To remove an old window, first pry off the interior trim. The exterior trim follows. Remove the stops, allowing sashes to be pulled free and stored for safekeeping. Old sashes make good barn or shed windows as well as cold-frame panels. All that remains are the side and head jambs and the sill. Sometimes the entire unit can be pried free intact, but chances are that it will be nailed so securely that the dry, half-rotten wood will split. Remove the jambs however you must. Measure the opening to see if it corresponds to the necessary rough-opening size. If it doesn't, and must be enlarged, remove the subsill first. Windows look best when their tops are at the same height on a given wall, which is fortunate, as hacking out a heavy header at the top of a window is hard work. Remove the subsill and cut down the jack studs the required amount. Renail the subsill. Cut back the wall sheathing flush to the new height. A sawzall will prove an invaluable tool for this kind of work. The jack studs along the side jambs may also need to be removed. If possible, they should be replaced with a one-inch board to support the header. With a post-and-beam frame, a header will not carry any appreciable weight, and its support is not critical, as with a stud-framed building. It will hold itself in place with nails alone. If the opening must be greater than the width of the jack studs, the wall sheathing is cut back to the next stud and a new window opening framed.

If a new window opening is to be cut into the wall of a stud-frame structure, a header will have to be added to carry the weight of the wall and the ceiling joists above. A small header (three feet or under) can be replaced without any special support. Tear out the wall finish to expose enough space above the window to fit the new header. For headers much over three feet in length, support the ceiling joists with a post of 4 × 4 fastened to an upright 2 × 4 and a plywood gusset. Shim and drive it up tight under the ceiling joists to hold up the ceiling while you remove or add the header.

4–16   Enlarging a window opening

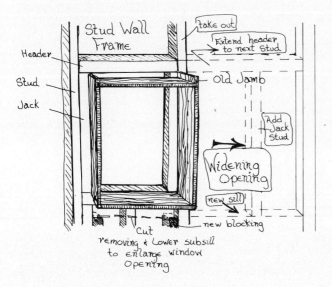

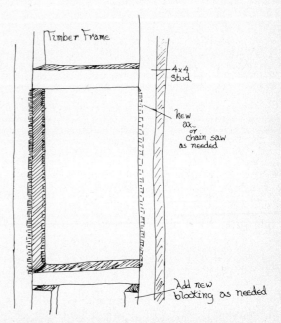

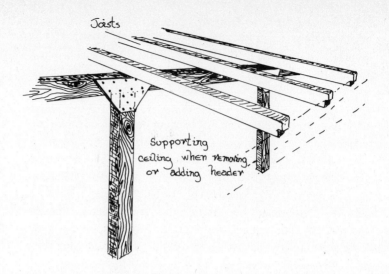

4–17 *Supporting the ceiling when removing or adding a header*

Once the interior and exterior sheathings have been cut back flush with the edges of the opening, the new window is inserted. Check for level and plumb. Scribe a line on the siding along the edges of the window casings, remove the window, and cut the siding back to this line. Reinstall the window, nail it in place through the casing and caulk the joints tightly. Use 16d galvanized-finish nails. Do not forget to insert flashing or drip cap above the head casing. The inside finish should butt flush to the jambs. If necessary, rip "extension" jambs to fill in any gap. Interior casings are then nailed to secure the window. Offset casings ⅛ to ¼ inch from the jambs around the window. A flush edge is difficult to match perfectly, and unless it is perfect and painted over, it will look unfinished. This slight offset creates a pleasing detail and allows for minor adjustments in plumb.

Unwanted windows, particularly those on the north side of the house, should be filled in while the exterior siding is being replaced. Once the window and jambs are removed rip a 1-inch board to the width of the wall studding and nail it around the entire frame. Additional studs are cut as needed and nailed

4–18 *Installing a new window to fit siding*

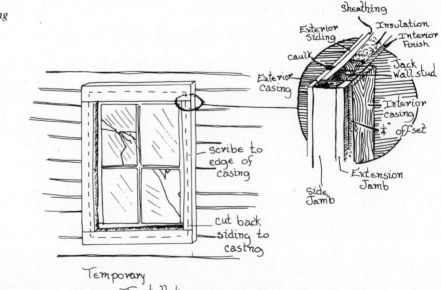

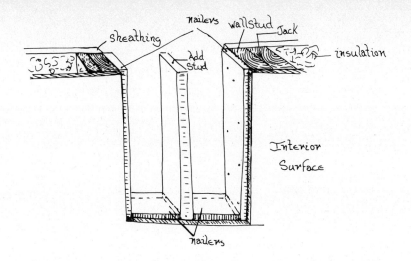

4–19   Blocking in a window hole

into the opening to maintain the 16- or 24-inch framing module. Insulate the cavity and nail matching interior and exterior sheathing to the nailers.

To patch a window hole with clapboards, align each course with the butts of the old clapboards. Where large sections of clapboards must be replaced or added, it is good practice to start from the top and work down toward the sill, as described earlier. Try to stagger the joints where the new clapboards join the old by removing sections back to a joint. The top course of clapboard is gently pried up and the nails loosened and pulled. Use a chisel to loosen the nails before inserting the pry bar. A new clapboard is slipped under the butt. Tack it in place with two nails. Each succeeding course is slipped up under the butt of the previous layer and tacked. The entire wall is then nailed at once. This method enables you to align the new clapboards with the ends of the old where the spacing or run is not even or level. Snap a chalk line across from end to end of the existing clapboards, if needed.

When your budget does not afford replacement of all old windows, or if wholesale replacement is not really necessary, individual window units can be rebuilt. The difficulties inherent in the construction of a truly weathertight opening window can be avoided by separating the ventilating and the visual functions.

Fixed-glass windows are inexpensive and easily built. Because there are no moving parts or seals to maintain, no great skill is needed. Thermopane insulating glass can be ordered to size from wholesale distributors at a fraction

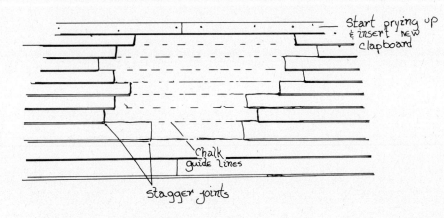

4–20   Filling in missing clapboards

of its installed cost. Set the glass against an inside stop nailed to the jambs. Use 1 × 1 clear pine for stops. Seal the window with clear silicone caulk and nail an outside stop in place. Caulk the joint between stop and glass, as well. Single sheets of glass can be doubled, separated by a ½-inch × ½-inch spacer strip inserted between them. Caulk only the inside sheet of glass and leave the outside uncaulked. This allows moist air to escape rather than be trapped between the panes, to condense with the changes of internal temperature. Clean the inside surfaces of the glass very thoroughly before installation, as once they are in place, they cannot be cleaned again. This same technique can be used to double up a single-pane picture window for added insulation or to protect a stained-glass piece from the weather. Use only double-strength glass and handle large sheets carefully. A home-built frame crate may be needed to transport such glass from the hardware store to home. Cut rabbeted moldings to carry the glass and hold it in place against the existing wood sash.

Ventilators for houses equipped with fixed windows can be installed in an opening framed between the studs. A ceiling-level vent used in conjunction

4–21   Construction of fixed windows

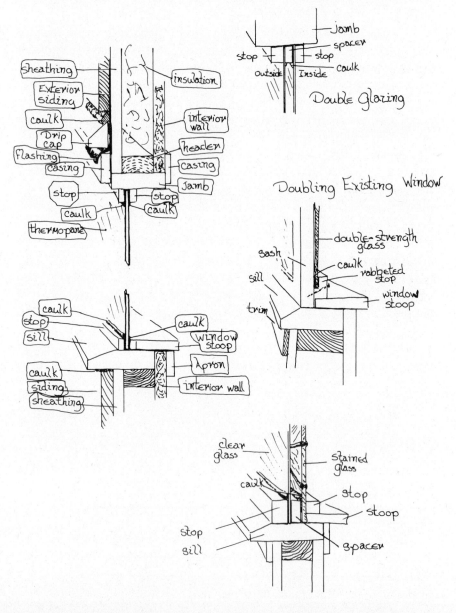

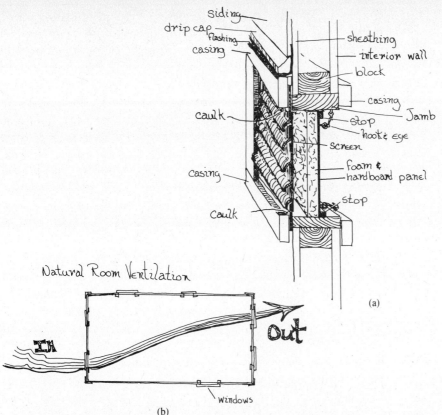

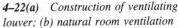

Natural Room Ventilation

(a)

(b)

Windows

4–22(a) Construction of ventilating
louver; (b) natural room ventilation

with a floor vent on the opposite wall creates the greatest air flow for summer cooling. Orient these vents toward the prevailing winds. Inlet vents should have one square foot of surface area. Outlet vents work best with three square feet. The proper placing of ventilation will allow you to use natural convection currents to air condition your house. These vents must be able to shut for the winter.

The simplest solution is to install a louvered and screened ventilator in the wall. Ventilating units are inexpensive and available in a variety of sizes. Extend jambs flush to the wall sheathing. Cut back the siding to butt against the casing. Install the vent, nailing through the flanges. Seal with silicone and add casings. A drip cap is necessary above. The inside wall is cased and a hardboard panel bonded to two-inch urethane-foam insulation board is cut to fit and pushed against a weatherstripped stop for the winter months, secured by eye hooks. You will have to maneuver the panel into the opening by turning it at an angle.

Double-hung windows are the traditional windows used in older homes. In terms of efficiency, they do not make much sense; they leak, rattle in the wind, and stick, and the sashes overlap directly in the line of sight. They do require a minimum of hardware to operate, which might be one of the reasons the design was so popular in the age before machine-stamped steel parts. Also, because they do not swing in or out to open, they do not obstruct the use of wall space.

Examine the sash (the wood frame that holds the glass). It is most likely in need of reglazing. Glazing compound is a kind of putty, which seals the glass to the wood and stabilizes it in the frame. The sash is held in the jamb by thin wood strips (stops). Loosen them with a chisel and then use a flat pry bar to remove them. Sometimes you will find that the stops are screwed to the jambs, covering the hardware and workings of the sash weights, which, together with ropes and pulleys were used to help raise the sash. Replacement parts are still available for this once-popular window system. When the stops are removed, the window sashes will fall from the jambs.

Work carefully with a chisel to remove the old glazing compound. Avoid any pressure against the glass itself, which might crack it. Work against the wood instead. The glass will be held to the sash by small metal wedges called *glazier's points*. Pry them loose with the chisel. Feel for them as you clean out the glazing. Remove the glass. With a paint scraper, clean the rabbet down to bare wood and brush a light coat of linseed oil over the wood. Replace the glass. Insert glazing points with the chisel blade. Use one in each corner and one for every foot of length. Glazing putty is prepared for use by rolling a ball of it between your palms until it softens. Roll it into a long rope about ⅜ to ½-inch thick and lay it against the sash. Press into place with your fingertips and then, with the chisel or putty knife, press it firmly and evenly into the joint against the glass and wood, forming a 45-degree bevel and a tight seal. Remove the excess putty and save for reuse. Clean the sash and glass and reinstall the window frame.

Replacement glass can be cut to exact size at the hardware store where it is purchased. Glass should be ¹⁄₁₆ to ⅛-inch smaller than the opening it is to fit. If you must trim your own glass (perhaps you have several sheets salvaged from old storm windows) use a glass cutter (an inexpensive hardware-store item) and a steel straight edge. Score a single steady and continuous line and snap the piece to be removed downward over an edge. If your line was clean, it will break evenly. Weak corners of the sash can be repaired with a flat-angle iron. If the corner is too rotten to brace, cut a ⅛-inch hardboard gussett and nail and glue it across the corners. Buy a new sash if you cannot build one yourself.

When the jambs and sills themselves need replacement, study their construction and try to duplicate it. Make a drawing of the assembly before you take it apart. Often the sills were cut from a heavy slab of timber, as much as three or four inches thick. You will have to fashion one from standard stock. Measure the width of the wall opening from exterior to interior sheathing. Add the width of the ears, which should project about ½ inch beyond the exterior casing. Cut the sill to the length of the rough opening of the window, allowing for the width of the jambs and the casings and their offset. A 10-degree bevel

4–23   Repair of window sash

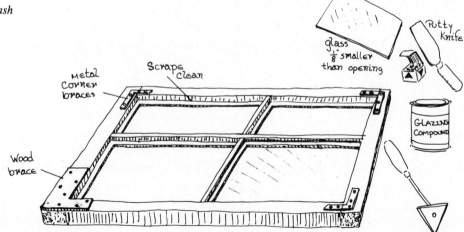

is cut along the front edge of the sill (a table saw is handy for this operation). The bevel should extend to the inside edge of the sash, which is also cut to the corresponding level. Side jambs should be "dadoed" (grooved) at the top to accept the head jamb. The unit is nailed to the side of the sill and checked for square. Nail a temporary brace across one corner to help it hold its shape, and insert in the rough opening. Cedar shingles are used to shim it plumb and level to the jack studs. Drive 8d finish nails through the jambs into the studding. The exterior casings will also help hold the frame securely. A nail is driven through the casing and into the jamb. Another is driven through the wall sheathing and into the studding.

Mark a line with a combination square to align the stops, which are cut from ⅜-inch × 1½-inch clear stock and nailed in place. An alternative is to use 1½-inch stock for the jamb and rabbet out the inside surface to carry the sashes. You may be able to purchase new double-hung sashes at a considerable discount from a lumberyard's discontinued stock. These sashes fit a particular manufacturers' windows and vary in design. Often they are grooved to fit a metal track. Cut a wood strip, and round and wax the edge to make a slide track. A little experimentation will reveal the best way to fit the sash to stops and tracks.

The upper sash of a double-hung window is fixed permanently in place by its stops. Vinyl-gasket weatherstrip is fastened to the bottom inside edge of this fixed sash. Weatherstrip should be nailed against the inside jambs, either as a stop or on top of it.

It is actually possible to rebuild a window from the inside out. I mention this because it is something that can be done while the weather rages outside. You can proceed with the winter work of refinishing the inside walls and remain unhampered by the need to rebuild the entire window first. As the house settles over the years, the windows will no longer be plumb or level, a situation that can have a discomforting effect on your equilibrium. Applying level or plumb paneling around a tilted window will accentuate this perceptual indigestion. If jacking the foundation has not straightened the walls and you have no further intentions of pulling them one way or another, the windows themselves should be realigned square and true. That is best done during warm weather, but schedules and realities do not always neatly dovetail.

The storm window should be in place on the exterior casing. Replace it with a sheet of poly to protect it and you from harm—in case the hammer slips. Now remove the interior casings and jambs. If you can, pry the entire unit free and realign it in its rough opening. Chances are the wall will lean too much to allow sufficient maneuvering space. When the jambs are removed, leave the exterior casings in place. If the sill cannot be reused, remove it and cut a new one as outlined in Figure 4–24. Hew down the window jack studs with a hatchet or wide chisel until they will admit the realigned jambs. You may trim ¼ inch off each side of the sash to gain an extra ½ inch and save that much hewing. Any nails that protrude through the back of the exterior casings are cut back with nipping pliers, and the new jambs are shimmed into place. The window is reassembled. The poly sheet is replaced by the storm window until next spring when the exterior casing boards are removed and realigned. Wider casing boards will be necessary to cover any gaps between the siding and the trim unless the exterior siding is also scheduled for replacement.

The principles for repairing windows are applicable to the repair of doors as well. A door has a sill (called a threshold) and head and side jambs. The

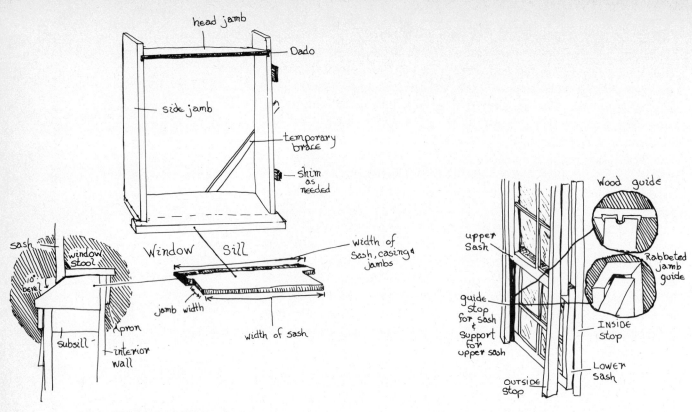

4-24   Window-frame construction

frame is really only a large window frame. There are two kinds of doors—exterior and interior. Exterior doors are heavy and often made of solid wood frames and panels. The standard thickness is 1¾ inches. Interior doors can be 1⅛-inch panel-and-frame or 1½-inch hollow core.

Door jambs and hinges must correspond to the difference in weights. Interior doors are fitted with a single pair of hinges and 1-inch or 1⅛-inch jamb stock. Exterior doors are hung on three hinges and require heavier jambs. A dry, planed 2 × 6 or 2 × 8 free from serious knots will make an inexpensive jamb. Otherwise use five-quarter (full 1⅛-inch thick) clear pine. Cut a ¼-inch rabbet into the sides to form a door stop. Apply weatherstripping along the stop. Lay the door on a flat surface and cut the jambs to the length of the door plus ⅜ inches plus the thickness of the header. Allow for the threshold when figuring the height. The jambs should extend past the header an inch or more, if there is room in the rough opening. That allows a dadoed joint for the header jamb,

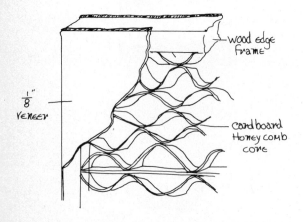

4-25a   Hollow-core interior door

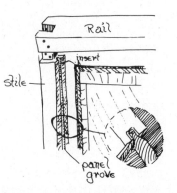

4-25b   Raised panel rail-and-stile door

which is much stronger than a simple butt joint. Cut the header to the width of the door plus $\frac{1}{16}$ inch plus the width of the dadoes. The head jamb is nailed and glued to the side jambs. Attach the hinges to the door. Use butt hinges that are equal to twice the thickness of the door (3 inches for $1\frac{1}{2}$-inch doors, $3\frac{1}{2}$-inch $\times$ $3\frac{1}{2}$-inches for $1\frac{3}{4}$-inch doors, and 4-inch $\times$ 4-inch hinges for 2-inch doors). Longer hinges, (4-inch $\times$ 6-inch, etc.) are used for heavier doors. Always use *loose-pin* hinges. Cut a mortise into the door the depth and width of the hinge. Lay the hinge on the edge of the door and scribe the line with a chisel edge. For a standard 6-foot, 8-inch door, the top hinge should be hung 7 inches down from the top and the bottom hinge 9 inches up from the bottom. The third hinge is in the middle. (The top hinge takes the greatest strain and is therefore closer to the edge.) After the hinges are screwed in place, the door is set into the jamb, resting in the door-stop rabbet. The door is positioned with about $\frac{1}{8}$-inch clearance at the top edge and $\frac{1}{32}$-inch to either side (a matchbook cover will do for a gauge). Mark the position of the hinges on the jamb, remove the door and cut the hinge mortises into the jamb. Use a screwdriver to remove the hinge pins, separate the two halves, and screw the butt into the mortise. Notice that there is a top and bottom to the hinge, as well as a front and back. The face of the hinge will have countersunk holes to seat the screw head, and the hinge should always be aligned so that the pin cannot fall out. Place the door back in its frame and drive the pins into the hinges. Tack a temporary brace across the bottom corner to keep the door jambs together and drive a 6d finish nail through the side jamb into the door to keep it closed. Lift the entire frame and shim it into the rough opening. Use 12d finish nails to fasten the jambs to the framing. There should always be a shim behind each hinge point and behind the strike, as well. Pry the door free of the nail holding it to the jamb and remove the nail with a pair of pliers. Check the door for fit. The striking edge can be planed at a 5-degree bevel to help prevent binding. Take the door off its hinges to plane the edge if necessary.

Cut the threshold to fit and drill it to accept finish nails. Thresholds should be cut from smooth hardwood. Preshaped blanks are available at the lumberyard and will save you the labor of fashioning your own. Seal the bottom of the threshold with silicone caulking or waterproof construction adhesive and install by driving the finish nails through the predrilled holes. Cut the casing boards to a bevel to fit against the threshold, allowing a $\frac{1}{4}$-inch offset, and nail in place. Do not forget to insulate between the door jambs and the studding first.

Unless you find, when determining the length of a door and its jambs, that the sill is absolutely level, it is best to cut the door to the full floor length and then scribe the bottom edge to fit the threshold. Rather than shim the threshold to level, match the bottom edge of the door to the pitch of the floor. If you are installing an old door in a new frame, check the door itself for square. Often one side of such a door may taper or be longer than the other, having once been planed to fit a crooked opening. Trim the door square before the new jamb is built and installed. Once again, leave the bottom edge to be scribed to the threshold. Remove all hardware, and check for hidden or broken nails or screws before you cut. A straight length of wood tacked to the door will guide the skilsaw cut. Smooth the rough edge with a plane before hanging.

Old doors can be given new life by overlaying them with veneer or boards. Glue and nail or screw boards to a solid-panel door in whatever pattern your imagination suggests. Utilize the grain and knots and the different woods to create a pleasing design. Such a door will be thicker than a normal door and

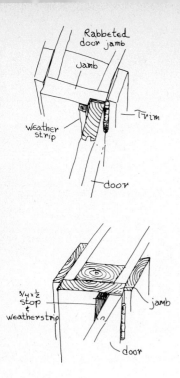

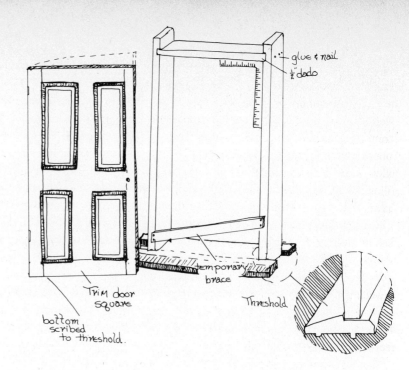

4-26 *Hanging doors*

will require a **T**-strap hinge, which means it must be hung flush with the casing, or else the door itself must be banded with clear grain stock. Screws will not hold in edge grain. Remember that, if you build doors of boards and cleats. Standard hardware will not fit doors over two inches thick. Latches or doorknobs can be custom extended at a welding shop.

A good exterior door is an expensive investment. To work well, a door must remain stable in adverse weather conditions. It should be built from clear, dry stock, usually select hardwood or fir. The rail-and-stile design allows the panels to float freely in the frame, which remains unaffected by their shrinkage or expansion. Protect your investment and seal the door with two coats of paint or clear varnish immediately upon installation, if not before. Doors should always be stored standing up, prior to use. Do not forget to seal the top and bottom edges, to prevent the wood from absorbing atmospheric moisture.

Install the lock-and-strike plate after the door is hung. Standard hardware is available that will simplify the task. The Kwikset® line is one of the best.

4-27 *Hanging home-built doors*

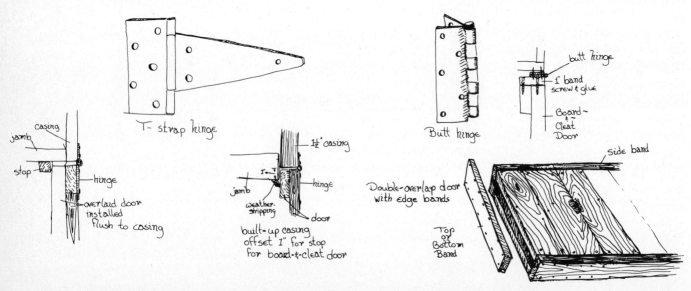

Complete instructions and all necessary templates to insure an accurate and easy installation are furnished with every lockset.

Interior doors are installed according to the same general principles as exterior doors. Panel doors can be 1¼ inches or 1⅛ inches thick. Hollow-core doors are generally 1⅜ inches or 1½ inches thick. Old panel doors salvaged from the dump or torn-down buildings, when repainted or stripped, make excellent interior doors, with far more character than the motel-room finish of a hollow-core door. Recycling an old door is preferable to the expense of purchasing a new interior panel door. Buy your doors first and plan the openings to fit them. Tolerances are not critical on interior doors, and because the door itself is light, one-inch stock will be sufficient for the jambs. Nail door-stop molding to the jambs, after the door is hung. Latches of forged iron or even hand-carved wood can be used instead of locksets. Allow ½-inch clearance between floor and door bottoms, with additional clearance for a carpeted floor. A threshold is not necessary, but a *saddle* (a narrow, beveled oak piece) is used under the door to cover any unsightly joints in the floorboards, which are frequently matched under a door.

Old doors can be restored to life with a good coat of paint. First fill all holes with wood putty and seal all cracks with caulking. Damaged panels can be removed by pulling the moldings that secure them and then replaced with new panels of ¼-inch plywood or hardboard. For the novel effect of a stained-glass appearance, replace wood panels with colored acrylic panels. Do not expose acrylics to direct sunlight without a cover sheet of glass, as the ultraviolet radiation will cause it to deteriorate. Angle irons can be used to secure weak or rotten corner joints. A dog-eaten door can be filled with putty and sanded smooth, but personally I find this canine artwork pleasing if the paint is stripped and the wood sealed with a clear finish.

In cold climates, a single entrance door should never open to the outside. A tight storm door creates an air lock, which helps keep in the heat. Aluminum storm doors, unless filled with an insulated core, loose a great deal of heat through their frames. Wood is infinitely preferable. Storm doors are available with removable screened and glass panels, which are changed with the seasons. Take care that the handle of the storm door does not strike against the handle of the entrance door itself. Avoid setting the handle so close to the door stop that it pinches your hand or knuckles as you use it. Hang screen doors flush with the casing. If the offset of the casings is increased to ⅜ or ½ inch, the jamb itself can be used as a stop.

Doors can be owner built. Unless premium wood is used, they will not hold their shape for long but will twist and warp as the wood works against itself. A tongue-and-groove door of vertical plank should be braced with a diagonal layer on its reverse side, either cleated strips, or as a complete overlay. Using kiln-dried wood only and sealing the door with two coats of paint or varnish will help keep it stable. A functional, if not beautiful, door can be made from a sandwich of ¾-inch foam insulating board and ½-inch plywood. The plywood is screwed and glued to butted 1 × 6 top and side rails. The bracing effect of the plywood will help keep the door stable. Simple doors can be built from tongue-and-groove boards and cleats of good dry stock. Brace the door from the hinge toward the handle side.

Owner-built doors, unless built like fine cabinetry—i.e., rails and stiles, floating panels, and so on,—are best confined to interior usage or for mudrooms, cellar hatchways, and barns. A properly installed, factory-built entrance door,

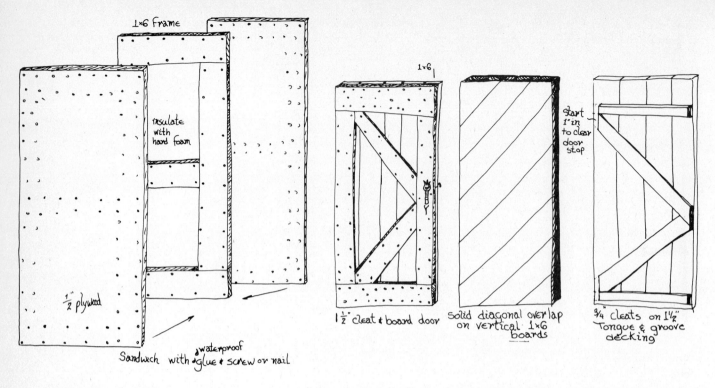

1×6 frame

insulate with hard foam

½″ plywood

Sandwich with waterproof glue & screw or nail

1½″ cleat & board door

1×6

Solid diagonal overlap on vertical 1×6 boards

start 1″ in to clear door stop

¾″ cleats on 1½″ tongue & groove decking

4–28   Home-built doors

like a factory-built window, is an expense that will repay you in durability and trouble-free operation.

Plaster: *Gutting the walls*

Plaster was an almost universal interior-wall finish in old houses. It was cheap, the raw materials were readily available, and it made a tight wall with good vapor resistance, a fact much appreciated in the days before insulation. That is why the old homes are still, in fact, standing. If warm, moist air had been able to work through the walls and condense upon the cold inner surfaces, the resulting water would have collected on the sills and studding, and rot would soon have eaten away at the very fiber of the house. Plaster helped retard this process to a great extent. Over the years, though, it dries out until, one day, even the many layers of wallpapering can no longer keep it hanging on the walls. It tears in great sheets and sags and buckles like the flabby bottom of old age. Settling of the house causes even sound plaster to crack. Small cracks can be repaired with spackling compound and small areas replastered as necessary, if the material is otherwise sound. Joint compound used for sheet-rock taping will do an excellent and inexpensive job. Gypsum plaster is used for larger areas.

Insulation becomes ever more critical as heating costs continue to rise. Good insulation is plenty of insulation. If the plaster is in an advanced state of decay or if you are planning extensive interior renovations, it makes a lot of sense to strip all the plaster from the interior walls and ceilings. Although insulation can be blown into the walls from the outside, that is not always the best way to install it. Blown insulation is prone to settling. Even at densities that will not settle, the problem of providing an adequate vapor barrier remains. The contractor will tell you that the material itself is treated to be water resistant,

vermin proof, and a fire retardant—for example, cellulose fiber. What that actually means is that if water condenses behind the wall, the insulation will hold it like a sponge without rotting. It may take a while, but the wood eventually suffers from the moisture. Chemical-foam insulation has a built-in vapor barrier, but it is very expensive to install, and since the field is so new, reliable installers can be scarce.

Complete removal of interior plaster not only will allow easy insulation with relatively inexpensive materials but will simplify revamping of the wiring and plumbing systems. Plaster can be removed from the ceilings to expose the old beams. Originally these beams were covered over as soon as the householder could afford to hire a plasterer. Exposed beams were a sign of poverty. A successful man put distance between himself and the origins of his wealth with successive layers of plaster and paint. Ornamentation and artifice underscored the triumph of will over what was seen as hostile nature. Today we are starting to understand the cost of ignoring our roots. Artificial materials require great expenditures of energy to manufacture and transport and often cause great pollution. They need specialists to install them. There is a movement afoot to restore Simplicity to the pantheon of the Virtues. A house is now perceived in the old way, as an expression of the possibilities inherent in the environment. Native wood is chosen over plastic laminates as a wall finish, the beams of the house are exposed. The feeling of security that emanates from these massive timbers—their rude strength—is a revelation of structure as connection with nature.

If the plaster is, then, to be removed, the job is best done all at once. Piecemeal removal only means extended mess, continued uninhabitability. Walls that may appear sound upon initial examination will begin to crumble the first time a molding is removed or a window casing pried. Start from the attic and work to the cellar. Plaster alone is gritty and dusty; mixed with generations of mouse droppings and the dust of decades, it is near lethal; wear a dust mask and finish the job as quickly as you can. Unless you plan to bulldoze the waste material underground, avoid dumping it in outside piles. Haul it to the dump immediately.

Rebuilding a house at this stage requires a tool seldom mentioned in the how-to-do-it books—a good ordinary pickup truck. No other investment will return as much service for the money. There is little you can do in the rebuilding business without one. The daily needs and tasks of rural living require the transportation of incredible amounts of things, few of which will fit very well into the trunk of a car. Sooner or later, if you plan to work on your own place, you will need a truck.

With a temporary chute built of old boards, funnel the debris from the upper story into the bed of the truck. A plank ramp and a wheelbarrow will do for what can't be thrown into the truck through the windows. Separate the lath from the plaster, to keep for kindling and to reduce the bulk of the dump loads. Although this dried wood is very good tinder, your enthusiasm for it will wane after you snag yourself a few times on the needle-sharp stubs of rusty lathing nails. Pile it out back and save it for a celebration bonfire when the job is done, if local ordinances allow burning.

Plaster and lath can be removed simultaneously. The hooked end of a crowbar is smashed through the wall and then used to pry free sections of wood and plaster. It may help to bash the wall a few times to loosen the plaster first. (A historical aside—the type of lath you find will be a fair indication of the age of the house. The oldest were split from a single bolt of wood, like an accordion, or else handsplit, making them uneven in shape and thickness. After 1850, lath was sawn on power mills and became more regular.) Tearing down plaster is a great outlet for fantasies of destruction and revenge. It can be a job for the whole family, at least as cathartic as television and far more healthy. Use snow shovels and wear dust masks to gather up the debris for removal. This cleanup is best done in summer, when an afternoon dip in the pond will wash away the memories and grime of a miserable day's work. After the walls are cleaned and the debris removed, the walls can be insulated and left covered with tarpaper or poly sheets while other, outside, structural work proceeds.

If the wall cavities or ceilings have been blown full of fiberglass or mineral wool at some point during the houses's past history, the material most likely has settled enough to make it worthless. In any case, these materials are useless without a proper vapor barrier and should be removed. The joys of insulation, the itch and choking dust of its removal, will add a new dimension to the tortures of plaster removal. It seems to expand as it is torn from the walls, until the entire house is full of it. Days later you will feel it in your clothes and between the sheets and taste it in your food, even after several passes with a good industrial vacuum cleaner. This insidious itch becomes more psychological than physical. You can never be quite sure if you are imagining it or not.

Is all this trouble worth it? There are alternatives to the complete gutting of the interior, even if the plaster is unredeemable. Although insulation can be blown into the walls from the outside and the blow holes plugged, the technique leaves something to be desired as far as accuracy is concerned. The operator works blind—never quite sure if a cavity between studs has been completely filled. If the plaster is stripped from the walls but the lathing left intact, the walls can be blown full of insulation from the inside, allowing the operator to see how well the wall spaces are being filled. The lath will hold the insulation in place. A polyethylene sheet or builder's aluminum foil is stapled tightly over the lath before it is covered with a new wall finish. Nail strapping horizontally across the studs, over reflective foil. This strapping also provides a convenient space to run electrical wires through, although they can be worked behind the lath itself. Shims behind the strapping will even out the wall surface. A vapor barrier can also be applied directly over existing plaster, with strapping nailed directly over the old walls, to carry new finish walls. All existing electrical outlets will have to be remounted flush to the new wall thickness, and door and window casings must be removed and extension jambs used to fill them out to the new width. There are a couple of disadvantages to this otherwise satisfactory system. For one thing, the removal and replacement of jambs and casings requires a lot of time and exacting work, whereas wholesale destruction is fast. Also, the walls will be thicker, shrinking the size of the room as much as four inches overall, which may be a critical factor where space is limited.

Blown-in insulation is expensive if done right. Loose-fiber types must be installed at a density that will prevent them from settling. The cost is a function of the volume of material (cubic footage) as well as square footage. The greatest disadvantage is that you rarely can do it yourself, unless you can find a blower to rent. This is particularly true of the more esoteric materials such as urea-formaldehyde foam, which is touted as a superior insulation. Extreme care must be taken in its application. Not all contractors really know what they are doing, especially since the technology is currently undergoing rapid changes. Besides problems of odor and toxicity due to improper curing or mixing of chemicals, there also seems to be a problem with product shrinkage after curing. Such shrinkage, of course, will seriously diminish the effectiveness of this material against air infiltration. The manufacturers claim only minor shrinkage; test results seem to reveal much greater percentages. Far more promising are the cellulose-fiber based spray foams which have been used extensively as an insulating coating on the steel walls of industrial structures and are now being used in residential work. K–13® is one such product. While installing fiberglass insulation is not the most pleasant pastime, it is not difficult, and the material is inexpensive. Most important, it is a job you can easily do yourself. With careful attention to quality, owner-installed fiberglass will be as effective as professionally blown-in materials. As an owner-builder the less outside work you hire, the more you save in money and the more you spend in time. If the repairs are to be extensive it is more efficient to start with a clear deck; gut the walls completely. If only one room needs work, strap directly over the plaster. If you remove ceiling plaster but leave the lath intact, a 4-mil (thinner than regular) poly sheet stapled over the lath will prevent dust and grit from falling in your eyes and mouth as you hang the new ceiling.

4–29   New walls over old plaster

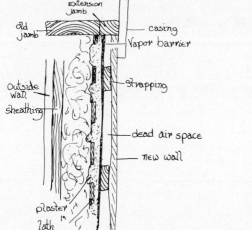

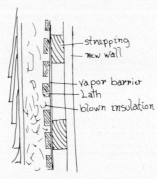

So far, we have discussed insulations and vapor barriers with nothing more than a cursory explanation of the terms. It is important to have a thorough understanding of the art and science of proper insulation. Much damage can be done by incorrect application.

An Insulation Primer

The passage of heat through solid materials is called *conduction*. An insulator is anything that retards this movement. Trapped air (dead air) is an excellent insulator. A hollow wall itself is not a dead-air space because the volume of air it contains is large enough to allow the creation of heat transfer by *convection;* Currents of air transfer heat through moving molecules. These currents arise whenever a temperature difference exists across an enclosed volume of air, and they are a prime cause of infiltration. A space more than ¾ inch wide will allow the formation of convection currents. Insulators used in the home work because they contain a tangled web of surfaces that trap air and prevent its circulation or, in the case of foam insulations, contain closed cells filled with inert gases. These nonconductive materials include spun glass and mineral fibers, organic materials such a paper fiber, and synthetic plastic foams. The old-timers understood the principle of dead air when they filled the walls of their houses and barns with corn cobs or sawdust. Unfortunately, they didn't know about vapor barriers, and the walls often rotted as fast as the insulation itself.

A wall, as we have seen is a porous membrane. In cold weather, the inside temperature is much higher than the outside air. Heat tends to move through the wall by conduction and convection to the outside as well as by infiltration. The tendency is toward equilibrium. Because people and plants live in the house, the inside air is heavy with moisture: Life gives off water vapor. This warm, moist air also moves through the wall until it encounters the cold surface of the outside wall, where it condenses and freezes. Although much of this water will evaporate, some will remain liquid and flow along the wall to collect on the sills and start rot. It can actually condense within the wall, depending on its moisture content, which will, together with the temperature, determine the *dew point* (the temperature at which saturated air gives up its water.) The dampness can rot the wall sheathing from inside as well as cause paint to blister and plaster to dampen.

If an impermeable (water-resistant) membrane is installed between the inside wall and the insulating material, water vapor will not pass through the wall to the cold side. This vapor barrier can be a polyethylene film, aluminum foil, or specially treated paper backing on the insulation itself. Tarpaper is also an effective vapor barrier.

4–30 Effect of insulation on wall temperature and humidity

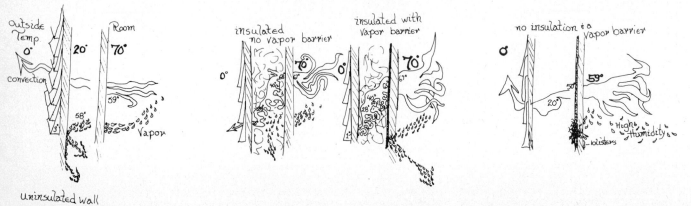

A vapor barrier without insulation will cause condensation on the interior wall surfaces or, even worse, behind the wall. Painted walls in kitchens or bathrooms will soon peel or sweat, as moisture condenses on their relatively impervious surfaces. High-gloss, oil-based paints over plaster can be an effective vapor barrier, when fresh. Vinyl wallcoverings are also resistant to vapor passage. These wall finishes, when used with proper insulation (which should have its own barrier), will help keep the house comfortable. Humidity is a prime factor in how comfortable we feel within a house. If the humidity is low, it will require more heat to feel warm because our bodies evaporate more moisture from the skin surface in dry air than in moist air, and body temperature is lowered. This is a strong argument for storm windows; the moisture condensing on a single pane of cold glass is just so much water removed from the air. Maintaining the proper humidity level will enable us to lower our thermostats and keep our mucous membranes from drying out, and since the mucous membranes are the first line of defense against disease, will thereby help us stay healthy.

Insulation is rated according to its ability to impede the passage of heat. This resistance of insulation to heat or cold is called the *R factor*. Because the resistance varies with different materials, the R factor is related to the thickness of the insulator as well—an important point in determining costs and the suitability of a particular material to a particular application. Two inches of styrofoam may cost twice as much as four inches of fiberglass but give a greater total R value.

Table 4–1 lists the common residential insulators together with their R values and methods of use.

TABLE 4–1 Common Residential Insulators

Material	Description	Application	Approximate R value/inch
Fiberglass	Rolls, precut "batts" to fit stud- and joist-spacing modules, with/without applied vapor barrier; loose fill for blowing	Stapled between studs, or friction fit	3.5
Mineral wool	Similar to fiberglass; more prone to matting	Loose fill, blown in; prone to settling	3.0
Styrofoam sheets	White: open cell	Use around perimeters	4.0
	Blue: closed cell, rigid type	Under slabs and floors; friction or mastic over roofs; great fire hazard, releases toxic gases, cover with firecode sheetrock if used inside building	5.0
Urethane sheets	Rigid, with or without backing or nailing surface	Same as styrofoam	6.5
Urea-formaldehyde	Self-adhering foam, permanent	Blown in; noncombustible; application and curing problems reported	5.5
Cellulose fiber	Loose-fill, treated-paper product; can settle unless very dense	Blown in; install w/vapor barrier	4.5
Cellulose-fiber adhesive foam (K–13®)	Self-adhering	Sprayed on, noncombustible; can flake off where exposed	5.5
Vermiculite, perlite	Loose-fill, expanded-mineral product, very light	Pour into attic joists, concrete blocks; requires vapor barrier	2.5
Fiber boards	Asphalt impregnated or cellulose, sawdust sheets	Sheathing boards; will smoulder	2.0
Wood, sawdust	Prone to settling; barn-wall filler	Can rot, burn	1.0

Generally speaking, the price of the material is directly proportional to the R value per inch. The blown-in plastic types are the best insulators but also the most expensive, in both initial cost and the hiring of professional applicators.

Fiberglass is ubiquitous, exactly because it is low in cost per square foot and easily installed by the homeowner. It is available with an aluminum-foil, reflective facing or with a kraft-paper vapor barrier. The shiny foil surface helps radiate heat back into the room. To be effective, it must be separated from the back of the inside wall surface. The batts are designed to be stapled between the studs so as to create the desired air space, but in practice the insulation sags, touching the back of the wall. Nailing strapping over the studs is the only effective way to maintain this spacing. Staple insulation between the studs, not over them. The paper will bunch up if face-stapled and can create lumps under the wall. But although the argument has raged on both sides for a long time and every carpenter has his theory, it doesn't seem to matter much which way you install it. In fact, stretching the paper flanges over the studding prevents "fish-mouths," puckers in the paper that reduce the effectiveness of the vapor barrier.

4–31 Installing insulation

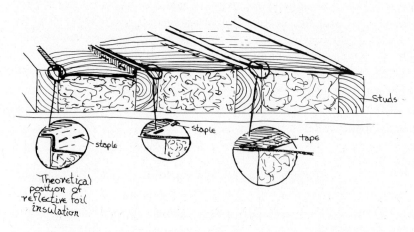

When calculating the total resistance of a wall, the R values of the wall finishes and the thin films of air that actually adhere to the inside and outside surfaces, should be taken into consideration (see Table 4–2). R values are given for insulation only and do not include this incidental resistance as part of the design specifications. I mention this example only as an indication that the type, thickness, and number of layers of wall construction material can significantly affect total insulation value.

Table 4–2   Determining the R Value of a Wall

Factors to Consider	R value/inch
Outside air film	0.2
¾" wood siding	0.8
½" sheathing board	1.0
Air space, inside wall	1.0
Sheetrock	0.5
Inside air film	0.7
Total	4.5

The figures in Table 4–2 reflect the R value of an uninsulated wall. As heating costs rise, adequate insulation becomes an economic imperative. There is a point of diminishing return for insulation use: 2 inches in a wall may save 80 percent of the heat, and 4 inches will save 90 percent, but 8 inches will only save 95 percent. Is the extra cost justified by the savings in heat over a short-enough pay-back period? The terms of the equation are shifting as heating fuel increases in cost. Standard practice mandated 4-inch walls and 6-inch ceilings, with R values of R11 and R19 respectively. Architects and builders now recommend R values of 19 and 30, or 6 inches for walls and 9 inches for ceilings. This requires 2×6 wall studding and 2×10 rafters.

Insulation is only part of a general program of energy conservation, which also includes tightening up the house by caulking and weatherstripping, avoiding heat loss through windows and chimneys and use of nonfossil fuel alternatives. The major portion of heat is lost not through the walls but through the windows by direct radiation. A well-insulated house with expanses of open glass is an expensive house to heat. Heavy curtains or insulated shutters drawn across that glass at night will prevent heat loss through it. Other than through windows, most heat is lost through the roof, which is why extra R values are required in ceilings. That is where your insulation dollar is best invested.

Practically speaking, you cannot increase the thickness of the wall studding to accommodate more insulation. A urea-formaldehyde spray foam will have that effect because it gives more resistance per inch. But it is an expensive alternative to the 4-inch wall and an extra cord of wood. A tight house will save more energy than a drafty, well-insulated one. Urea-formaldehyde or cellulose foam will accomplish both these objectives. The use of wood for inside and outside finish and dead-air spaces behind strapping will add to the insulating value of the wall.

An unheated basement is another area that can be profitably insulated. Four inches of fiberglass insulation under the floorboards will help keep the floors warm. It will also create a cool cellar, useful for the storage of vegetables and other foods. A bucket of live coals from the wood stove, left next to the food-storage shelves will prevent freezing on those really cold nights. Electric heaters will accomplish the same task at a greater cost.

While the outside wall is exposed for foundation work, styrofoam perimeter insulation can be glued to the wall with mastic. The material is stuccoed above ground level and simply buried below. This will help tremendously to keep the cellar warm. It can also be glued to the inside walls.

Strapping may have to be nailed across the floor joists to support the insulation batts if the joists are spaced farther than 24 inches on center. Heavy timber frames often employ a 32-inch module. Stuff the insulation between the strapping. This technique can also be used to insulate between timber rafters. The strapping then becomes a nailing base for the finish-wall paneling. Chicken wire can also be stapled to joists to hold insulation in place. The E-Z Insulator Hanger Co., (5317 Rogue River Hwy., Gold Hill, Oreg. 97525) manufactures a steel bracket in lengths up to four feet which hammers between joists and supports the insulation batts. If you must insulate under a porch or crawlspace over bare earth, nail a sheet of preservative-treated ¼-inch plywood or homosote under the joists to prevent rodents from making their nests in the insulation.

One of the chief causes of infiltration is the failure to stuff the cracks between window jambs and the framing. Use a tapered wood shingle to stuff thin strips of fiberglass into these gaps. Avoid packing it tightly, as fiberglass loses its insulative properties if compressed. A better job can be obtained by filling any such cracks with Polycel-One® urethane spray froam which dispenses like shaving cream. A special applicator nozzle enables you to tightly seal even small cracks. It is well worth the expense and trouble to seal these areas.

Remember that the vapor barrier must always face the heated side of the wall. A reversed vapor barrier will cause condensation inside the wall. A special type of insulation, *reverse flange,* is used for insulating under cellar floors. It comes in batts, which are covered with a kraft-paper vapor barrier on one side and a paper wrapping on the other. When it is installed, it is stapled with the kraft side facing the floor boards. The paper wrapper keeps the applicator from getting a faceful of fiberglass. Remember also to leave an air space between the back of the insulation and the underside of the roof deck. This channel provides for the free flow of ventilation air from under the soffits to the ridge or gable outlets. Ventilation is particularly important when using steel roofing. Escaping moisture, unless otherwise vented, will rapidly condense on the underside of a steel roof. Installing a decking of plywood or insulating board between steel and insulation will prevent such problems. Vapor barriers are only as effective as they are tight. Avoid puncturing the membrane. Patch rips and holes in poly with tape. Take care to cut carefully around electrical boxes, and fill the space behind them with insulation. Do not mash the fiberglass to fit under or against pipes. Instead, score the back of the batt and fold the insulation around the pipe. Split the batts to fit around and behind obstructions and wires. Cut the batts to fit tightly against the top and bottom of the wall cavity. There should be no gaps between butted pieces. Overlap the vapor barriers at a joint. Stretch the covering tightly between the studs; do not jam or wrinkle it and avoid puckers, or fish-mouths, when stapling the flanges. The more gaps you leave, the more heat you waste. Because, no matter how carefully you work, it is impossible to avoid some puckers and tears when using paper or foil-faced fiberglass insulation, it makes sense to cover the insulation with a continuous poly film stapled over the studs. The expense and labor is small and the effectiveness of the vapor barrier is greatly increased.

4–32   Installing insulation around obstructions

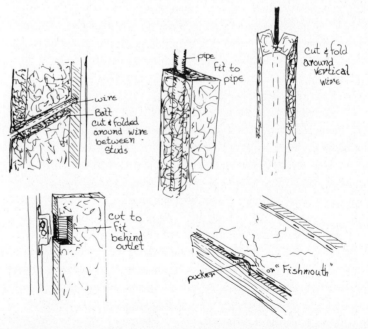

An excellent type of fiberglass insulation is the unfaced *full-wall* batt, which is designed to stay between the stud cavities by friction. The entire wall is covered by a poly sheet after the material is in place. Windows and electrical outlets are cut out after the plastic sheet is installed. Full-wall insulation has a slightly higher R value than conventional 3½-inch insulation—R13 as opposed to R11. It installs much more tightly than paper-faced types and is easily cut to fit around wires and pipes or against angled framing.

If you do use standard fiberglass insulation and plan to leave the walls uncovered for a while, staple tarpaper or building paper over it to keep the dust from sifting into the rest of the house. Foil-face decor can grow more pleasing everyday, especially as your energy for further work slips away. The house is warm, there is no urgency to do more. There is even a particular brand of insulation that is printed with a woven-mat pattern, as if the manufacturer expected the product to double as decorative wall finish. Some householders have lived two years or more with their exposed insulation, becoming almost fond of the reflections of the fireplace on its shiny surface.

I remember spending the night in such a house, sleeping on a guest bed next to the wall, and waking up feeling as though I'd slept on a bed of nettles. A fine rain of fiberglass slivers had worked its way into the blankets, covering the bed, and from them into me.

Interior Partitions and Staircases

It is easy to remove old walls and to frame new partitions once the interior of the house has been gutted. Electrical and plumbing runs can be made from old walls to new. There are many reasons why you might find it desirable to remove an interior wall. Dramatic changes in the sense of space and the quality of light in a room can be achieved through the strategic removal or addition of a wall. You may simply need more space or the feeling of space; the rooms of an old house tended to be smaller and more numerous than our modern notions of proportion allow. In the age before central heating, this arrangement served a practical purpose. Rooms were heated by fireplaces or individual parlor stoves. Rooms that were not used were unheated and closed off from the core of the house. In the winter months, most of the living went on in and around the kitchen, with perhaps a parlor opened up on warm days or when guests came to visit. Today this zoned living makes sense to preserve fuel when living in a large, rambling country house, which would then expand and contract with the seasons.

The average outside dimensions of the typical farmhouse are 24 × 32 feet, which is not surprising, as it is about the upper limit of the space that can be heated comfortably by a single wood-burning heater or central fireplace as well as the maximum length of an easily maneuvered hewn timber. Most larger houses have grown up around this basic core. Heating a house of this size with a wood stove is simplified if the floor space is kept open and the heater centrally located. There is no real need for a dining *room;* an *area* can be defined by the placement of furniture, fireplaces and masonry work, half-partitions alone or in conjunction with open shelving, even the clever use of hanging and potted plants. All allow the free circulation of heat from the central stove and yet retain a sense of space and division of function. Bathrooms and guest rooms, pantries, and perhaps even a private study furnished with its own small heater can be independent of the main areas. Heat flow to these outlying rooms is controlled by opening and closing doors. Of course, they will still tend to be colder than the rest of the house. That is not a problem for a guest room, as a warm quilt-comforter will be all the supplementary heat required, but the same quilt will be less helpful keeping the bathtub warm. I solved that problem in my house by building the bathroom door behind the stove. Before taking my shower, I would stoke up the fire, and when finished, I could dry off directly in front of a blazing stove. It was cheaper than a space heater. Leaving the door open at night prevented the dripping faucet from freezing solid in the bottom of the tub.

If you were involved in the restoration of an old house rather than its remodeling, you would most likely retain the existing walls and rooms as given and install a modern central-heating plant to keep the wash basins from freezing. A wood/oil system will eliminate the *necessity* for opening up a house but only at a greater cost. There is also a psychological benefit to the open house; the kitchen can flow into the rest of the living space, and the cook is not then ostracized from social life while preparing dinner. An open house is strong preventive medicine against the onset of cabin fever come the tail end of the winter.

Whatever the reasons to remove a wall, there are two kinds of partitions: those that carry weight and those that do not. Removing a load-bearing partition is not likely to be a problem you will encounter in a post-and-beam framed house. The weight of the floor and ceiling joists is carried by a continuous girt or massive central beam called the *summer* beam. (The word is probably a derivative of the archaic English ''sumpter,'' which was a pack mule capable of shouldering a heavy load.) Partitions were merely nailed to the underside of weight-carrying beams. There may be the rare case of a beam cut to allow a stairwell or otherwise weakened by later alterations. In more modern houses, framed with studs, the bearing partition wall is a common means of supporting the ceiling joists in the middle of their span. It transfers the weight to a girder under the floor joists. You can almost be certain that any partition wall running

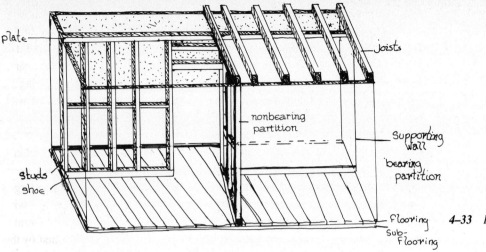

plate

joists

nonbearing
partition

Supporting
wall

bearing
partition

studs
shoe

Flooring
Sub-
Flooring

4–33 Interior partition types

parallel to the length of the building, i.e., perpendicular to the run of the joists, which divides the building in half or thirds, is such a wall.

The nonload-bearing partition is simply an arbitrary division of floor space and contributes nothing to the structural support of the house. Any partition running parallel with the joists is almost always nonbearing. The only complication in the removal of such walls is the necessity to reroute existing wiring or plumbing. Consider this possibility before trying to remove any wall. It would be an unpleasant surprise to discover that you had torn into a wet wall (the wall that contains a good deal of the supply, drainage, and venting pipes for both the bathroom and kitchen, usually framed with 2 × 6 or 2 × 8 studding to conceal them). It might be more trouble and expense to remove and relocate the plumbing than the results would justify. Don't be afraid to tackle the job, however, if you are absolutely certain that it is necessary. There are many ways to disguise plumbing in dead spaces behind a closet, or boxed into corners, in lieu of complete removal. Of course, if your plumbing is in need of replacement anyway, consider putting the entire plumbing core somewhere else.

Moving electrical wiring is nowhere near as large a task as changing the plumbing. Cutting the circuits and pulling the wires back under the floor will be sufficient in many cases. Unless the walls and the plaster have been gutted, you must first remove the ceiling and baseboard moldings. If they must be cut, use a sabre saw or a small handsaw to begin the cut and finish with a sharp chisel. When you are removing a plaster or sheetrocked wall, especially if it is papered, score the division between it and the remaining wall with a sharp utility knife. That will prevent the plaster or wall covering from ripping when you tear away the wallboard. If the cut is to be covered over by new trim, a sabre saw alone will do the job. Clean up all loose plaster and lath before going any further. If the rest of the house is being lived in, you might want to hang a poly sheet or curtain to keep the dust from drifting.

The wall-partition studding is either toenailed or nailed directly through the plate and shoe. The simplest way to remove a stud is with a good blow from a heavy hammer or sledge at the joint of stud and shoe. Although quick, this method produces large amounts of kindling. It depends on whether you need kindling or studding more. Many times the lumber used for partitions in old houses may not be worth much more than kindling. If you wish to salvage the wood for future use, use a cat's paw to remove the toenails at the shoe (base of shoe), and then, using the stud as a lever upon itself, twist it free of the plate. If the stud has not been toenailed into place, you will have to smash it free or saw through it at the bottom on a line above the nails that hold it in place, using a sawzall or skilsaw. Any small blocking in between the studs can easily be removed with a few sharp hammer blows. Pull all the nails out, or drive the points back into the wood. Do this immediately. It will not take long to get the point if you forget and step on a rusty nail. Even if you do not plan to recycle the lumber, bend the nails over; they will be less dangerous and will lay flatter and pull apart more easily when you dump them in your truck.

Any wiring in the wall will have to be removed. Shut off the circuit breaker or remove the fuse that controls the particular circuit. You can locate the right fuse by plugging a light bulb or tester into the outlet and having someone turn off the circuits until the light goes out. But use a pair of electrician's pliers to cut the wires, in case you made a mistake. The insulation on the handles will prevent a nasty burn or shock. Remove the outlet box and pull the wire back through the hole by which it entered the partition. Tape the bare ends and turn the circuit back on. Later, you can splice into the feed line and run it where you wish.

Wires that feed circuits to or from the floor above will now be exposed. If your ceilings have already been removed, reroute these wires through the joists to the side walls or to a convenient partition where they can be run down the wall cavity and into a basement or attic feed. If the ceiling is already in place and not scheduled for removal, use a fish wire (a stiff, hooked wire used to feed cable through walls) to run the cable along the joists to a place where it can be run through a baseboard or partition and rejoined to the cut circuit. Floorboards can be taken up to give access to wire runs, and base or ceiling mold can be removed and the plaster grooved for a wire. Surface-run *wiremold* is a convenient way to avoid working the wire into the wall or ceiling. Floorboards can be cut along a joist and renailed to a cleat if necessary. Large holes left in the floor by the removal of wires or nails can be filled with a plug of

4–34 Removing partition studs

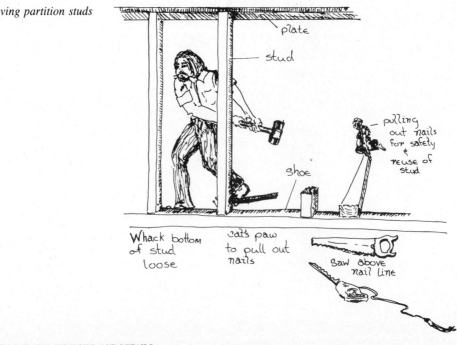

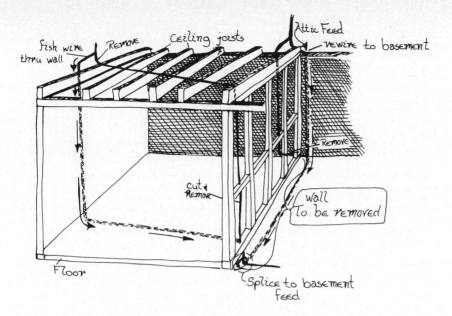

4–35 *Rerouting wires when removing a partition*

matching material or similar wood, stained to match the original. The same method is used to fill in any hole in the floor left by the removal of a chimney, stovepipe, or the like.

If the ceiling beams are to be exposed and a plaster or wallboard finish laid between them, the cable can be run in the space between the finish and the subfloor, alongside the strapping. If the subfloor boards themselves are to be the finish ceiling, force wiremold or dark wire into a crack against the beam and the subfloor. Eliminate ceiling fixtures, to avoid running additional wires across the ceiling.

Before you do any electrical work, check local ordinances. In many towns a licensed electrician is required. An owner may be able to do his or her

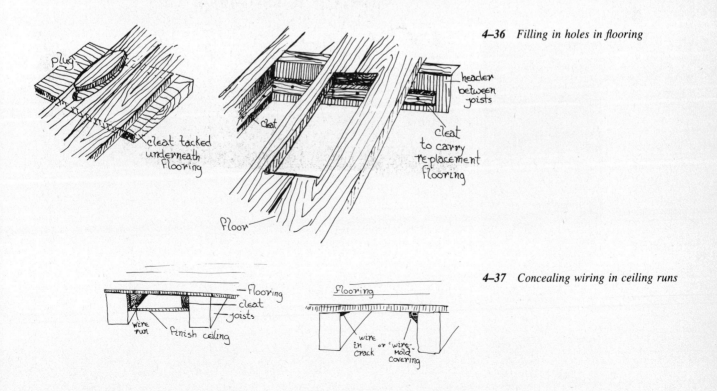

4–36 *Filling in holes in flooring*

4–37 *Concealing wiring in ceiling runs*

own work if it is inspected by the proper authority. Fire-insurance and mortgage institutions may have their own regulations concerning the need for professionals. Consider hiring an electrician if you are not comfortable with rewiring work. A heavy-duty half-inch drill and several electrician's auger bits are the minimum rewiring tools. An experienced electrician can make sense of the tangle of wires and feeds, three-way switches, and other incomprehensibilities that may greet you upon ripping into a wall and have it neatly rewired before you can figure out which plug feeds which switch. If there is only a single circuit to move, do it yourself, but complicated jobs are sometimes best done by professionals. They have the tools and parts, as well. If the walls are gutted completely, rewiring will be done as easily as new work. You will have access to all circuitry, which you can add or remove as desired. That is a strong argument in favor of tearing down the walls. The need for professional help is reduced.

After the wall studding is removed, the plates and shoes are pried free. Spackle over any nail holes or bare patches in the plaster. Panel adhesive can be used to glue a filler of sheetrock to the lath left exposed by the removal of a partition, forming a base for spackling.

If you wish to add partitions, snap a chalk line on the floor for aligning the shoe. The important thing to remember is that your floor probably will not

4–38   Adding a partition wall to a crooked room

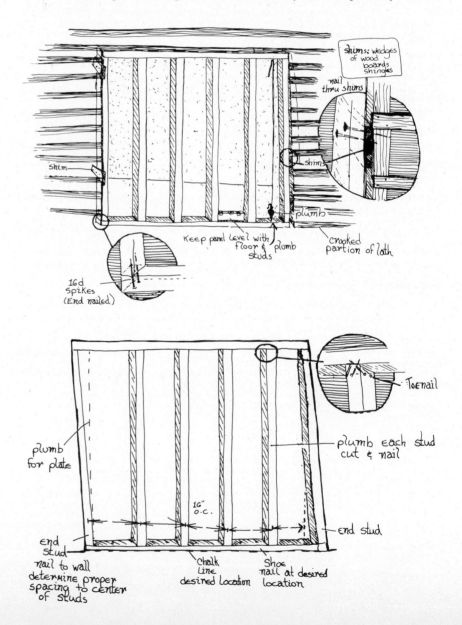

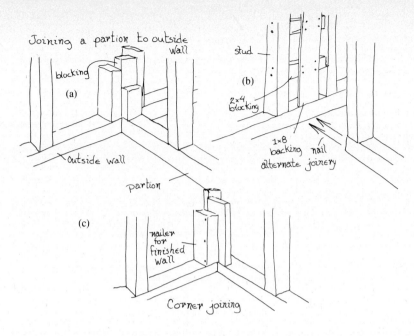

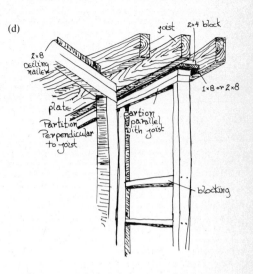

4–39a–d *Partition framing details*

be level. If you are framing up the partition as a complete unit and tilting it into place, frame to the height of the lowest end and shim into place. This works when there is only a small variation from one end of the partition to the other, not more than about an inch. A simpler method, especially when the surfaces are badly out of level, is to nail the shoe and plate into place with the stud spacing premarked. Each stud is then cut and measured to length and toenailed in place. Check the wall against which the partition is to be fastened for plumb. Add or subtract the amount the wall is out of plumb from the length of the plate or shoe, as needed. If the new partition is laid perpendicular to the run of the ceiling joists, it is simply fastened to them. If nailers cannot be inserted between joists to carry a parallel partition (as when the ceiling is already in place), secure the partition with *moly-bolt* dry-wall anchors and construction adhesive. Figure 4–38 shows methods for building partitions in unsquare rooms. Figure 4–39 shows some partition-framing details. If vertical board sheathing is planned as a wall finish, nail horizontal blocking into the partition to carry it. Otherwise strapping will be necessary, resulting in a thicker wall.

The load-bearing partition carries the considerable weight of the ceiling joists and the floor or ceiling above it. This weight must be supported while the wall is removed and an alternative means of support installed in its place. A temporary support beam is jacked up under the joists as close as possible to the original wall. After the wall is removed, a carrying beam is added to take the weight. Posts are needed to support this beam at either end and, if it spans much more than sixteen feet, in the middle as well.

Follow the same general procedure as in removing a nonbearing wall. When the studs are exposed and the work area clear, assemble your jacking equipment. You will need a length of jacking timber, a 4 × 8 or even two 2 × 8s spiked together will do, as will a few lengths of 4 × 4 or doubled 2 × 4, for jacking posts. Keep a few odd pieces of plank to use as jacking pads, to help distribute the weight over the floor as you lift. Three screw jacks would be ideal, but with patience, you can make do with just one. Raise the first post slightly higher than necessary to free the partition of its weight, and then let the joists back down onto a second post cut to the proper length. Repeat the process at each jacking point along the jacking timber. More control over the lifting is made possible by using a jack under each lifting post at both ends and also in the middle of the span, if necessary.

With a stepladder to support one end (or the shoulders of a couple of friends), lift the other end of the jacking timber into place and hold it there until the jack post is tight up under it. Repeat at the other end. If you are removing a long section of wall (over sixteen feet), do it in sections of sixteen feet. The longest-length timber that you and your help can comfortably lift into place is just about that long. Longer beams require more hands and more jacks. Once the beam is in place, holding the ceiling joists, remove the partition. In some cases, the joists are lapped by each other and nailed together over the bearing wall. They can be supported by a single jacking timber under their middle. In most cases, however, the joists were simply butted end to end over a partition instead. That enables the flooring above to be nailed in a continuous line, but it means that a separate jacking timber will be required to support each side of the joists. Place these timbers at least two feet away from the partition on either side of the wall to allow ample work space. The flooring itself will prevent the joists from spreading apart; otherwise the weight of the roof and floor would push out the outside walls.

Chances are excellent that the joists themselves will be nailed into the top plate of the bearing partition. If the ceiling is already removed, simply pull the plate free by removing the toenails with a cat's paw. If the ceiling is to be left in place or for some reason you cannot get into the space between the joists, try to pull the plate free with a pry bar. It will not be easy. The bottom of some of the joists will splinter and the plate will split. It may help to split the plate with a chisel first. Place a board under the pry bar when pulling over an existing ceiling—otherwise your bar will push a hole through the finish before it moves a nail. The portion of any nail that sticks through the ceiling can be cut with a hacksaw or nipping pliers or bent over and back under the finish.

4–40   Supporting the floor when removing a load-bearing partition wall

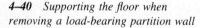

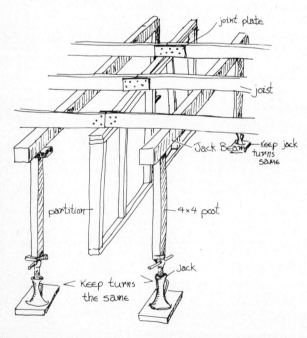

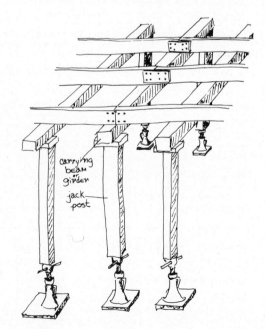

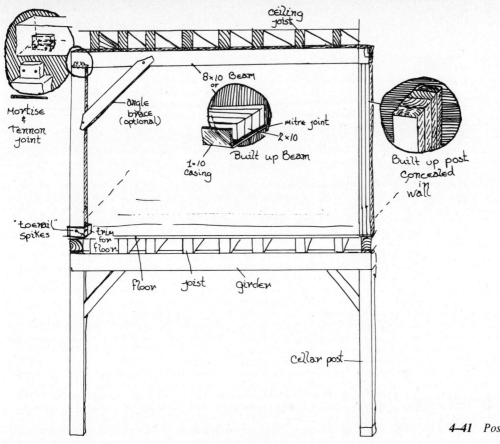

ceiling joist

Mortise & Tennon joint

angle brace (optional)

8×10 Beam or

mitre joint

2×10

Built up Beam

1×10 casing

Built up post Concealed in wall

"toenail" spikes

trim for floor

floor   joist   girder

Cellar post

4-41 Posting a carrying beam

Give careful thought to what your bearing wall is to be replaced with. Use a similar beam to match those in an exposed beam ceiling. Even if there isn't a similar beam showing anywhere else in the house, a roughsawn or hand-hewed beam may still add a pleasing touch. If the beam is not to be exposed, it can be built up of double or triple 2 × 10s. To determine the dimensions of the carrying timber, refer to the load and span tables for floor or ceiling joists in your carpentry manual. Whatever beam you do use, it will be supported at both ends by matching posts. If the beam is in two sections, they should be lap-jointed over a post under the middle of the span. End posts can be concealed in the partition wall on either side. Support the beam with doubled or tripled 2 × 4s, just as you would a door or window header. Use similar beams as posts if they are to be exposed. The center post can be left exposed, boxed in, or incorporated into masonry work or a half partition, if desired.

The carrying beam itself should also be jacked into place. The weight of the ceiling joists will cause some sagging and settling. Installing the beam under tension will compensate. This is the same principle as the one given in chapter 2 for replacing cellar girders. You can also raise the temporary support beams higher than the actual height of the partition. The posts that support the new carrying timber are cut slightly higher, as well. How high you raise the ceiling depends to some extent on how much the floor sags as you jack from it. Distribute the weight across as many joists as you can with the jacking pad. Once the posts are in place under the carrying beam, the temporary support posts are lowered and the jacking timber removed. The beam is attached to the post and the post to the floor with toenailed spikes. Predrill a hole large enough to admit the nail head, and then plug it with a dowel filler. If you are a real perfectionist, you can cut a mortise-and-tenon joint where the beam meets the post and peg the timber to it.

These posts must have solid bearing on whatever is beneath them. Generally a bearing partition rests upon a corresponding partition or girder directly under it. Because you are now concentrating onto a few single posts the weight that was previously carried by several floor joists, you should post under these new posts as well. These cellar posts should rest on flat rocks or cement slabs. If you have planned properly, the upstairs posts should fall somewhere near the cellar posts. If not, an angle brace can stiffen the supporting timber. Touch up any gouges in the ceiling finish and repaint.

Exercise great caution when removing a masonry partition. Such a partition is almost always load bearing. If masonry is above the wall you wish to remove, it will have to be supported by a steel I-beam, hardly a job to be tackled by an amateur.

As you remove or add new walls, you may decide to rebuild or add a staircase. Difficulties with staircases in old houses are generally caused by walls and floors that are out of plumb. Construction of stairs in a new house proceeds on the assumption that the surfaces are level with respect to each other. Calculations can therefore be straightforward. You must measure the proposed stairwell area very carefully before you begin the layout.

An existing staircase needs repair if the treads are badly worn or split. Refinishing may be all that is needed to restore them to life. Stair-tread material

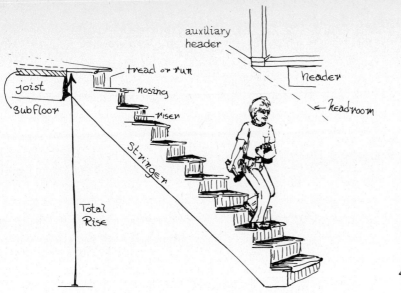

4–42   *Stair concepts*

is available with a preformed nosing in clear douglas fir. Pine is too soft to wear well. Dry spruce plank is a good substitute. Tear up the old treads and cut new ones to match. Replace risers if needed.

A new staircase should be laid out to provide sufficient head room, or clearance, as the stairs are climbed. Head room is often a problem in narrow buildings and tight corner stairs. Nonbearing partitions can be extended into the stairwell with auxiliary headers made of 2 × 4 or by extending the floor and hanging the partition from the ceiling. Joists and headers should always be doubled when cut to make a stairwell opening, Figure 4–43 shows the framing of a typical stairwell. When you are working with heavy-timber frames, a short timber can be mortised between the joist timbers to carry the stairwell. If the stairwell does not fit evenly between the joists, a header beam will have to span

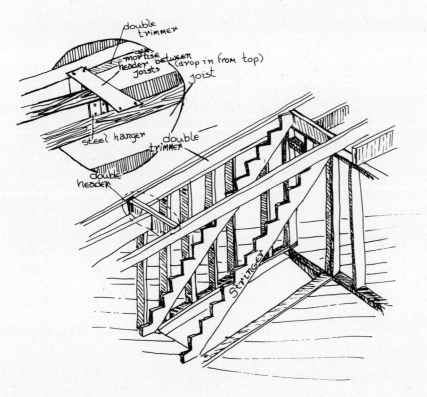

4–43   *Stair framing for heavy-timber structures*

the opening and *trimmer* joists added to it. A partition can help support the trimmers unless the stairwell is to be completely open, in which case, the header alone will carry the trimmers. Support the end of the trimmer joist with a jack post until it is joined to the header. Custom hangers can be substituted for mortise work; the latter would necessitate lifting of floor boards.

Calculate the number of treads and the required rise. The relationship between rise and tread is the most critical factor in successful stair layout. Long practice has demonstrated that the most comfortable and useful stair has a rise of 7⅝ inches, with a 10-inch tread. The general rule for the ratio of rise to run is that the sum of two risers and one tread should equal 25. A rise of 8 inches is about the steepest easily negotiable stair. All treads and risers should be the same size in a given run of stairs; otherwise, there is a tendency to trip where the stair changes height.

To determine the number of risers and treads, divide the total rise in inches by 7. Round off the resulting figure to the nearest whole number and divide that into the total rise. For example: The total rise is 8 feet, 1 inch, or 97 inches. 97 ÷ 7 = 13.85, or rounded off, 14. This is the number of risers. 97 ÷ 14 = 6.92 or about 7 inches, the height of each riser. Using the rule given above for ratios of rise to run: 7 + 7 = 14. 25 − 14 = 11. The tread width should be 11 inches. The total number of treads is one less than the number of risers, in this case, 13. 13 × 11 = 143 inches or 11 feet 11 inches, for the total length of the staircase opening (total run).

This is a rather low stair. The size of the rough opening could be considerably reduced by a slight increase in riser height, using 13 risers instead of 14. 97 ÷ 13 = 7.46 or 7½ inches, which is a comfortable rise. 25 − 15 gives a 10-inch tread width, 10″ × 12 = 10 feet, a saving of almost two feet, for the stairwell opening.

Make a *story pole* to lay out the actual stringer height. A story pole is a straight piece of 1 × 3 set plumb against the finish-floor height above and below the stair opening. Set a pair of dividers to the calculated riser height and mark off the distances on the pole; continue adjusting the distance on the dividers until it divides exactly flush with the top of the finish floor on the story pole. This is the exact riser height, which will vary slightly from the calculated height, enough to make a good fit impossible without a story pole. With a four-foot level and a straight edge, determine if there is a difference in floor level from

4–44   Determining stair rise

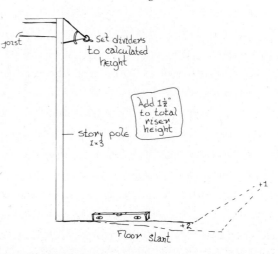

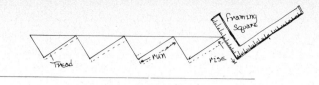

4–45 *Laying out stair stringers*

the story pole to where the stair stringer will sit. Then level across from one stringer to the other end and check for slanting in this direction as well. A difference of several inches is not unusual across a badly sagging floor. Additional height is added to or subtracted from the total rise. If there is a variance across the stringers as well, average the total amount and use that figure as a base for the riser calculations. Check your calculations against the dividers by starting at the top end of the story pole and working down. The difference at the bottom should equal the riser height plus or minus the variation in the floor.

After the calculations are corrected, lay the stringers out with a framing square on a length of 2 × 12. Scribe the saw lines carefully, using a scratch awl. Cut the first stringer and then use it as a pattern for the second (and third if the staircase is more than 3 feet wide and the treads less than 1½ inches thick). Make the initial cut with a skilsaw and finish with a hand saw. The stringers are tacked in place (they can be nailed to the partition studding or to a ledger set in the stairwell header), and shimmed level at the bottom edge if the difference across the floor was averaged. Nail riser boards in place. Treads are added next. Make a provision for a 1-inch *nosing,* or overhang, when figuring the actual width of the treads, as the nosing is not figured into the original calculations. The first riser is trimmed across its bottom edge to allow for thickness of the tread. That automatically compensates for the height of the last tread to finish flush against the floor at the top of the stair run.

There are several ways to finish off the junction of the stringer and the stairwell wall. The wall finish can be applied before the stringers are installed, which is the easiest way to avoid tedious finish work. This method works well when there is no partition covering up the outside wall of the stairwell. The stringers can be nailed to the partition studding and finish walls cut to fit around the stringers. Blocking is nailed between the studding to carry the ends of the wall finish. The treads and risers are then butted to the wall. The most tedious way is to fit the wall finish around the nosings and risers. Avoid this method, as it is impossible to get a tight fit, except where joint compound is used to fill in the gaps in conjunction with a plaster or sheetrock wall. An elegant solution to the problem, which also allows the use of "open" stringers (no riser board), is to fasten good quality 1-inch stock, cut for the stair-tread layout, to a solid 1 × 12 or 1 × 14 backing stringer (called a *skirtboard*). The skirtboard acts as a finish edge, to which the wall paneling is butted. Open risers can also be set in grooves cut into a single stringer. A router will cut the grooves for this "housed" stringer, which supports the treads and risers. The openings are tapered and wedges driven under the treads and risers to prevent them from squeaking.

Straight-run stairs are the simplest to construct. Landings are used to make a turn without major difficulties. The height to the landing is figured as a separate stair run. Post under any projecting joists. While a landing can be added anywhere in a flight of stairs to make a turn, standard practice puts them

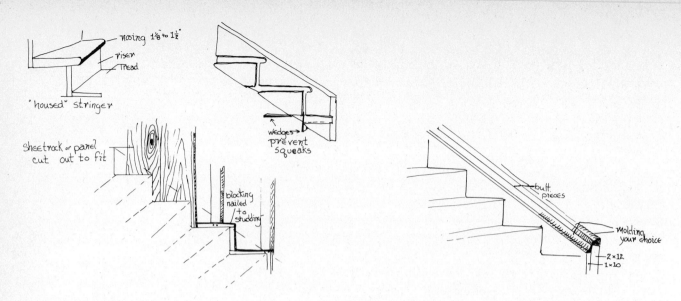

nosing 1⅛" to 1½"
riser
Tread

"housed" stringer

sheetrock or panel cut out to fit

blocking nailed to studding

wedges prevent squeaks

butt pieces

molding your choice

2×12
1×10

4–46   *Stringer finish details*

at the bottom of a run. A single landing, or several landings at different levels, can be used to create dramatic effects in the stair design, but each landing will compound the problem of moving heavy or bulky objects up the stairs. The winder stair makes a turn in a very tight space. This type of stair is quite common in old houses but rare in new construction because of high labor costs. The rule for winder stairs is to locate the point of convergence outside the stair run itself. This allows the tread width at the line of average travel to equal the tread width of a straight run. A stair with the point of convergence inside of the stairwell is extremely dangerous, as the treads will come to a point and offer opportunity for a fall. Since the stringers for these stairs must change their angle as they wind around the stairwell, it is much easier to fasten cleats to the finished stairwell at the appropriate points to support the treads. A full-scale layout should be penciled on a concrete surface, to determine the actual size and angle cuts of the treads. The lines are used for cutting templates. The same principles are used to lay out a spiral staircase, which is a useful way to put stairs into a very small opening. Spiral stairs are fine for access to little-used rooms or as a secondary entrance. Their narrow dimensions make it impossible to carry any large objects up them. When making a full-scale layout, use the center of the stairs for a point of convergence. Lay out the treads to divide the square stairwell

4–47   *Stair-landing combinations*

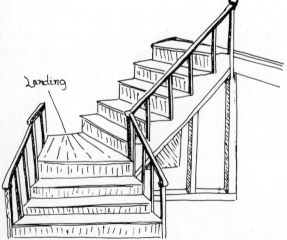

Landing

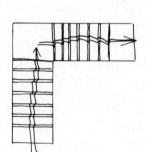

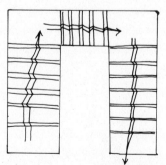

opening into four equal parts. A three-quarter turn is easier to negotiate, but a full turn allows the use of extra treads. Allow sufficient head room under any landing. Open stringer stairs are simplest to construct. You can screw and glue 1½-inch cleats to the wall finish and to the center post to carry the treads. The treads can be cut from 2-inch slabwood. Align the blanks so that the grain of the tread runs parallel with the nosing.

A space-saving solution to the problem of cellar access is the time-honored trap door. A trap door frees you from the necessity of running opposing flights of stairs in a closed stairwell. The access to the upper level can be completely independent of the cellar. Trap doors are simply constructed and can be easily concealed under a rug, if desired. The cellar joists are cut to the desired opening size and headers and trimmers doubled as required. A rough flight of ladder stairs at a 60-degree angle will provide entrance to the cellar. The door itself rests on cleats nailed to the sides of the joists. It can be hinged with concealed butt hinges or surface-mounted T-strap hinges. Build the door from cleated 2 × 6 tongue and groove or doubled 1 × 6s nailed perpendicular to each other. Special recessed trunk handles can be used for the top side and regular door pulls for the underside. A length of chain fastened to the underside will prevent the door from opening too far or falling back in. A trap door behind the wood stove is a real step saver.

Besides its simplicity, the trap door is archetypical. It recapitulates the portals of the underworld. And from those dark depths where potatoes lie dreaming and cider mutters to itself, we draw out sustenance.

The old house has come full circle: From outside to inside, from top to bottom, it has been kneaded and cajoled into a fairly pleasing shape. Its cancerous rot has been surgically excised, its wrinkled walls and glazed windows smoothed, its very bones given new life and strength; the entire house is wrapped tight, like an Easter child in new clothes and haircut.

But the house does not yet beat with life, pulse with the currents of heat and water, light and power. It has no heart, no nerves.

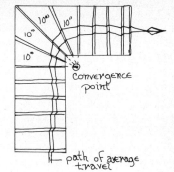

4-48 *A winder stair*

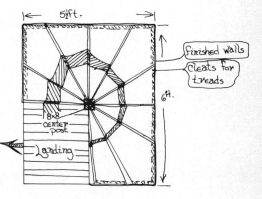

4-49 *Spiral stairs*

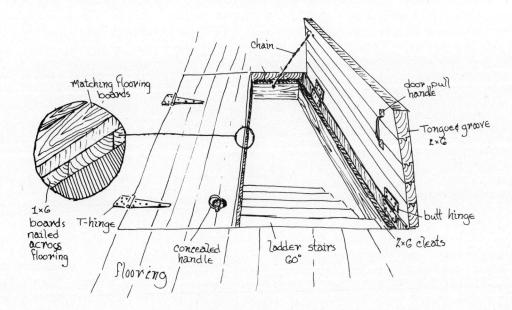

4-50 *The cellar trap door*

OF HEARTH AND HOME:
A PRIMER ON UTILITY SYSTEMS

SECTION 1 **ELECTRICITY**

Theodore Sturgeon once wrote a story describing a day in the life of a fully-automated house whose owners had mysteriously gone away. The house continued blithely about its business, cooking breakfast, cleaning up after itself, watering its plants, picking up its dust, chattering to itself like a pair of silly barnyard geese in a language of electronic pulses and mechanical clatterings until a malfunction in the basement incinerator caused it to catch on fire, destroying itself in a macabre orgy of mechanical mindlessness. The image of automatic dust-eating mice scavenging the debris of the fire is a finely wrought irony on the theme of blind technology and natural forces, a reflection on the potential for self-destruction of technology that is unhindered by intelligent direction.

If the structure of the house is analogous to the human body, if it is made in our image, then its electrical circuits are the nervous system and its plumbing and heating pipes, the circulatory system. Electricity is a form of energy, and "energy" may well be another word for "mind." This idea is not as far-fetched as it sounds. The findings of modern physics and of ancient Buddhist metaphysics are amazingly congruent. On cold nights when the humidity is just right, I hear a noise that seems to come from within the walls of the house. At first I'm not always sure—it also seems to come from the space between my ears. The sixty-cycle hum of electric current is the sound you hear when there is no other sound. Do I hear the radiation that envelops our world, the radio waves, microwaves and electromagnetic currents that pass through our bodies every minute of our lives? Do the very molecules reverberate with these ineffable harmonies? Does all matter sing the song of the wires in its soul?

Lying in bed on those cold nights, poised on the edge of sleep, I'm not sure if the sound does come from within—the boundaries waver. Sometimes the sound fills the entire house, pounding like an idling diesel engine waiting outside the windows. The very walls vibrate. I wake my wife and ask her if she can hear it too. She does. The world shifts back into the familiar chessboard of I-it. We both lie awake, our stomachs tight, listening to the pulsing of the walls, reassuring ourselves with solid rational explanations for this phenomenon, trying to lasso it with talk. We try to be grownup, nonchalant. We requested a service call from the power company, but the man who came said he had no idea what might cause it.

The old gods have been captured, violated, and bound to our service. The first man to tame fire did not feel any different than we do lying in our automatic beds, in our smooth houses. We can almost hear it scratching at the windows. We awake in the belly of night wondering if the stove will turn on us; we return from a late visit, secretly fearful as we round the last turn that our house will greet us as a flaming sacrifice to these outraged powers. Listening to the hum, the line is that thin. Although we have bound the universe in chains of copper and aluminum, with bands of plastic and rubber, we have not come so far as to forget. It does our bidding, but we really don't trust it. It performs tricks for us, but we do not sleep easy. Like a fifteen-year-old on his first date, we've had a few beers, we talk tough, but our hands are clammy. When the mood of the weather is exactly right, the fibers of the wood—its very pores— beat with the rhythm of the wires and we toss in our dreams.

The connection between mind and electrical energy, between the energy of your head and the energy in your home, is not coincidental. How you live your life, the priorities by which it is ordered, are reflected in the needs and desires of the household energy systems. Nothing better epitomizes our relation to the world than the way we heat our houses and dispose of our wastes. Some of us feel it perfectly justifiable to blacken the crystal skies of the southwestern deserts to run the electric toothbrushes of distant cities. A half pint of our own bodily wastes is so abhorrent to us that we must use five gallons of precious drinking water to flush its memory from our minds.

As we become ever more removed from the cradle of nature, we become ever more entangled in a cat's cradle of technological dependencies, an addiction much more insidious than the worst narcotic. Our life-support systems all come from somewhere else; our food, water, heating fuel, our power sources, are at the end of a vast and intricate chain of circumstances beyond our control. The illusion of stability is shattered by the increasing frequency of breakdowns, brownouts, and ever-higher prices. Economics should be based ultimately on ethics. This becomes obvious when a true accounting of the costs of energy is rendered. It is necessary to choose utility systems wisely and to strive as much as possible to shorten the steps between producer and consumer. Learn to think in terms of closed systems instead of linear throw-away progressions. Before you decide what color fixtures you need for the upstairs bathroom, decide if you need a bathroom at all.

Electricity is a convenient form of energy, which is why it is so popular. It is easy to use, to convert to heat, light, or horsepower, to transport and to manufacture. We pay a steep price for this Faustian bargain; the very blood of the earth is burned to fill our hunger for power. Some people are so outraged by this blind appetite and what it does to the earth, that they simply refuse to feed the monster. They choose to live without. It is not a choice most of us would willingly make, as we love our comforts too dearly. Electricity itself is not evil; rather it is the means of production, together with thoughtless consumption that is reprehensible. Those who live without electricity would willingly embrace it if they could produce it in nondestructive ways. Unfortunately, except in areas too remote from the power lines, the initial cost of generating power is very high, at present about $3,000 per 100 kilowatts output (the average home uses 500 to 700 kwh each month). Efforts are being made to improve the technology of wind, solar, and water generation, to increase production to the level of affordability, but it will be a long time before these efforts bear fruit.

Far more promising is the generation of power from renewable resources whose combustion creates useful by-products. Wood- or garbage-burning power plants that generate fertilizer as a by-product of the electricity, investigations into alcohol-fuel production through fermentation of vegetable wastes, the production of methane from manure—all offer the possibility of regional self-sufficiency and ecological harmony. That way seems more palatable than the gargantuan, centralized, and highly capitalized nuclear or fossil-fuel plants that are still on the drawing boards.

Should you tie into the grid? It is a personal decision, made on moral as well as economic grounds. It may not even be a choice. More than likely, your house is already connected. It then becomes a measure of self-discipline, of careful and *conscious* consumption. Thoughtlessness is the major reason why the United States, with 6 percent of the world's population consumes over a third of the world's resources. Scrutinize the way you live with the same careful attention you give to the foundation of the house. Someday the frippery of

appliances that beguile the householder will be seen as baroque variations on the theme of decadence, an elaboration of convenience into nonsense.

Demystifying the Beast:
The basics of circuits and grounding

Electricity frightens people. There are those who cannot fix a plug, who react to a spark with the same terror as primitives fleeing the white god's thunder sticks. Others find it a mystical and incomprehensible force. If electricity is thought of as water, it becomes friendlier. Watering a garden with a hose is not a traumatic experience for most of us. Electricity is really a plumbing problem.

Water flowing through a pipe exerts a pressure expressed in pounds per square inch (psi); this pressure is, electrically speaking, *volts*. The rate of flow of water is measured in gallons per minute (gpm), electrically, it is *amps*. The friction (resistance) of water flowing against the pipe is measured in *poises*, with electrical current, it is measured in *ohms*. Just remember that the longer the wire, the greater the resistance. Large pipes are needed to carry volumes of water without excessive friction, which must be otherwise overcome by increased pumping. The same is true of wires: They must increase in diameter to carry increased currents. Heat is the by-product of this friction (electrically, it is *resistance*), which is why an extension for a lamp will overheat if connected to a portable heater. Volts × Amps = Watts. This basic equation for electricity (Ohm's Law), is a measure of the work done by it, similar to horsepower. Electricity is sold by the power company in *kilowatt hours* (kwh), 1000 watts used for one hour.

Just as water flows through pipes, electricity flows through *conductors*, materials that have low resistance to the passage of electricity. *Insulators* are materials that have a high resistance to electrical currents. They are like the walls of the pipe and the various control valves. As water flows from a source (reservoir), ultimately back to the sea, electricity also flows from its source, the generator—an infinite electrical reservoir—to a ground. The current flows because of a difference in potential between source and ground, like water flowing downhill—the flow is *positive* with respect to the ground which is *negative* (higher versus lower). A lightning bolt is nothing more than a very big spark, the completion of a circuit between positively charged clouds and negatively charged earth.

An electric current will flow only if there is a continuous path between its source and return. Along the way it will work, running motors, heating wires, emitting light, reacting to whatever device is inserted in the circuit, including the human body. If a pipe springs a leak, the current will continue to flow until the reservoir is emptied. An electrical reservoir is, for all practical purposes, infinite. If a leak (a *short circuit*) occurs in an electrical line, all the power, all the way back to the generator can flow through it unless a protective device intervenes first. A short circuit is a way for the current to return to ground without having to complete its continuous path. Figure 5–1 shows how a circuit is protected by a fuse, which is nothing more than a one-time switch set to open the circuit if the current flow should exceed a predetermined safe limit. In this figure, a short is assumed to have taken place in a motor. Because the fuse is in the positive, or "hot", side of the circuit, it will blow, breaking the current flow. Thus, touching the motor will not cause you any shock, even though you

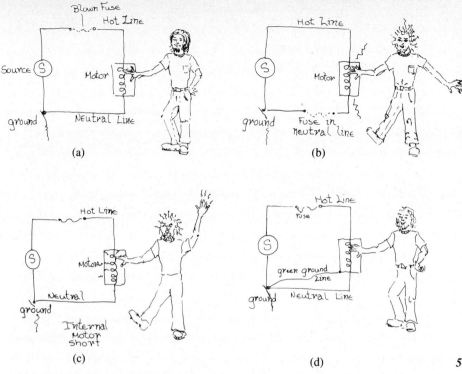

(a)

(b)

(c)

(d)

5-1 a-d *How a ground works*

are in effect inserting yourself into the circuit and providing a path for its flow to ground. Figure 5–lb shows a situation where the fuse is inserted on the wrong side of the line, in the return (negative) leg. Although it has blown, there is still current in the hot end and inserting yourself across it provides a convenient ground for it and a serious shock for you.

In Figure 5–lc, a short has occurred between the motor windings and the body of the motor. Often the fuse will not blow (particularly if the chassis is insulated from the ground until you touch it), but enough current will remain in the circuit to make touching the chassis lethal. Finally in Figure 5–1d, the motor chassis itself is connected by a wire directly to ground as well. Thus an internal short will blow the fuse.

This example demonstrates the importance of *grounding* a circuit. The metal frame of a motor or any appliance and the steel boxes that contain electrical fixtures should all be connected to a wire that runs continuously back to the ground for the system. The ground side of a circuit is never fused.

A basic circuit for residential wiring purposes consists of three color-coded wires; a white or "neutral" wire, a black or "hot" wire, and a bare, or green, "ground" wire. In a 240-v circuit, a third, red, hot wire is used. The white wire should never be fused or interrupted by a switch. It must provide the return leg to ground at all times. When a short circuit occurs, more power will flow through the wires than they can safely carry which increases their resistance and causes heat. With enough heat, the insulation melts, and the wires and the house burn up. Because a fuse is thinner than the wire it protects, it vaporizes first, shutting down the circuit. Circuit breakers are thermosetting switches, which control a magnetic relay that turns off the circuit when their limits are exceeded.

Electrical fixtures are likewise color coded. Brass terminals are always connected to the black wire (hot) and silver terminals to the white (neutral). The continuous ground (bare or green wire) is connected to the green terminal on switches and to steel boxes with special grounding lugs.

Electric current is either *direct,* which means that it flows in one direction only, or alternating, which means it reverses its polarity (in this country) sixty times or *cycles* per second. Thus, if the current is measured across both legs of the circuit with respect to a neutral, both wires will carry 120 volts at a given moment and zero at the next. The voltage is measured as 240 v. The current is said to be "in phase." This is how house wiring can be split from a 240-v feed into 120-v circuits as needed.

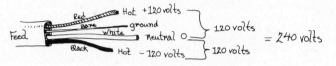

5–2 *Splitting a 240-volt line*

Electricity from the pole enters the house through a *service* drop, which is connected to the meter that tells the power company how much of their product you use. From the meter, the wire connects with an *entrance panel,* which contains a *main breaker,* which is the basic on-off switch for the entire house, and individual circuits, each with its own fuse or circuit breaker. Each circuit branches out to the various fixtures or outlets. *Subfeed* distribution panels can route large amounts of power to branch circuits with a minimum of voltage loss. They function like the ganglia of the nervous system. The brain stem and spinal column branch out to individual nerve endings in much the same fashion.

Electrical Materials:
 Basic hookups, planning circuit needs

There are several varieties of cable in use today. Steel-jacketed, or BX, cable was once very common and in some areas, local codes still require its exclusive use. Inside the steel jacket (which must always be connected to a continuous ground) are two insulated conductors. The steel must be firmly joined to the metal of the outlet boxes. BX cable is cut with a hacksaw and unraveled. A special protective bushing is inserted into the cut end to protect the insulated wires from chaffing, and the cable is secured to the box with a lock-nut connector.

Romex, or NM (nonmetallic), cable is the most popular cable in use today. It is used for all interior wiring. It consists of two or three plastic-jacketed conductors and a bare ground wire enclosed in a plastic jacket. Standard size for home wiring is 12-2 with ground. The size and number of conductors is always printed on the cable jacket. Thus 12-3/w g indicates three color-coded #12 wires and a bare ground wire. Three-wire cable is used for wiring 240-v light-duty appliances and three-way switches. For heavy-duty circuits, such as water heaters and pumps or small motors, 10-2/w g is used.

Type UF cable (underground feeder) is a Romex-type cable covered with a tight, sunlight- and weather-resistant jacket designed for use outdoors. It can be buried directly underground.

Service-entrance cable is a heavy-duty Romex type. Its resistant outer layer covers a woven-aluminum ground sheathing and two insulated inner aluminum conductors. Aluminum is used because it is cheaper than copper. Sizes range from 2/0 for use with 200-amp feeds, to 4/0 for 100-amp service and

6/0 for 50-amp ranges and dryers and 8/0 for 40-amp appliances. Working with a 2/0 cable is about as easy as trying to bend steel dowels.

Wiring is sometimes run in thin-walled steel or aluminum tubing called *conduit*. Commercial structures are often required by code to use conduits. Exposed wiring in barns and warehouses is often protected by these pipes.

Electrical fixtures must be housed in steel or plastic boxes, which must always be covered. These boxes are available in shapes and sizes designed to

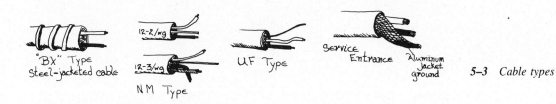

"BX" Type
Steel-jacketed cable

12-2/wg

12-3/wg
NM Type

UF Type

Service Entrance   Aluminum Jacket ground

5-3 Cable types

fill every wiring need. Plugs and switches are rated for different types of service and current loads. There are specific connectors and hardware for each type of cable used, as well.

As mentioned in chapter 4, before entertaining the notion of doing any of your own electrical work, check local code regulations. You may not be permitted to do any, particularly if you have borrowed mortgage money to finance your rebuilding. Even if there are no regulations that prohibit you from being your own electrician, you may still consider hiring a professional. Wiring is not really difficult to learn, but it is a long way from understanding circuit theory to the nuts and bolts of connecting that circuit. Professional electricians

carry an entire truckful of parts so that they will always have exactly the one they need. You will be running back and forth to the hardware store many times over to pick up and return the wrong item before your system is complete. That is no great loss if the store is just around the corner, but if you live nine miles by dirt road to town, it can add up. It takes time and practice to master the techniques of any trade. You will more than likely have enough to do working at carpentry without trying simultaneously to learn wiring. Someone who does it all the time can do it a lot faster than you can. What for you may be a complicated puzzle to reason out is, for the professional, an intuitive procedure.

The arguments above notwithstanding, electrical work has a pleasing logic of its own. If the basic principles are understood, you can certainly manage to wire your own place. It may take longer, it may be an energy-draining confusion but if time is cheaper than money or if wiring turns you on, by all means go to it. First, get a copy of the National Electrical Code, which will tell you what you can and cannot do. Actually, it will tell you what you *should* do, you can do anything you wish but if you expect to sell the house or borrow money on it, it is best to stick to approved practices. The house may not last long enough to resell if you do it wrong. You may wish to buy one of the many wiring books that make the code accessible to the ordinary mortal. *Wiring Simplified* by H. P. Richter is an excellent guide to the science of wiring. Sears and Roebuck publishes what has to be the all-time bargain in wiring books, *Do-It-Yourself Wiring Handbook,* which costs only 50¢. This booklet tells you just about anything the homeowner will need to know to safely wire a house or barn.

If the walls of the house have been completely gutted, rewiring will be no more difficult than new work. Examine the condition of the existing wiring. When houses were first wired, single conductors mounted on ceramic standoff insulators routed electricity through the attic and into gas-lamp pipes. Your house has probably been rewired since those days. If not, it will present a serious fire hazard. Watch for a metallic, cloth-sheathed cable, which was a forerunner of Romex cable. The insulation deteriorates over the years, becoming a potential danger. The inner insulation as well as the outer can break down. If your house is wired with this old cloth cable, you should strip all the old wire. Build a fire and burn off the insulation to salvage the copper for scrap.

Older houses are often wired with a two-wire Romex cable lacking a separate continuous ground wire. Of course, the white neutral wire is connected to ground, which theoretically should insure your safety. The problem is that the individual steel boxes housing the outlets are seldom adequately connected to the neutral wire, and a dangerous shock is possible. Wall plugs that have only two openings with no provision for a ground lug are indicative of a two-wire system. While chances are good that you will never suffer electrocution because of it, never plug appliances or motors designed to be grounded, into a two-wire system without using a grounding adapter. The wire from the adapter should be fastened to the screw that secures the outlet cover plate to the box. If BX cable was used instead of two-wire Romex and it is free from corrosion, it can be left in place and grounding adapters used to connect three-wire appliances to the system. The armored sheathing creates the necessary ground. You should rewire two-conductor systems to obtain the necessary ground protection.

Inadequate wiring often begins at the service drop. Houses wired before the advent of electric ranges and dryers will often have a 30- or 60-amp service feed. 100-amp service is considered the bare minimum for today's needs. A house fully equipped with electric range, dishwashers, dryers, hot-water heater, and so on, will require a minimum of 150-amp service, and an electrically heated house will need a 200-amp service drop. Farms and homesteads that use heavy power tools and welders should also have 200-amp service. The initial higher cost of the hardware will be offset by the versatility and capacity of such a system. A 200-amp feed can be split into two 100-amp subfeeds, one for the house proper and another for the shop and outbuildings. The shop feed can be further split into a 60-amp welder circuit and several 30-amp feeds for a tool bench or small outbuildings. Consider in the light of their true moral cost, how many appliances you expect to run before you decide upon the capacity of your service drop.

The electric company will furnish the wire to a *weatherhead* mounted on the wall of your building or a *service mast* above your roof. They also provide the meter. You will have to install the rest of the connection to the entrance panel. Local specifications vary, so be sure to contact your utility for advice before you do any entrance work. A fairly standard system is shown in Figure 5–4, both for a rural service-cable installation and an urban conduit entrance.

The utility company has the sole legal right to tinker with the meter in your meter box. They own it. There is a plastic seal attached to the lock. If it

5–4   Service-entrance connections

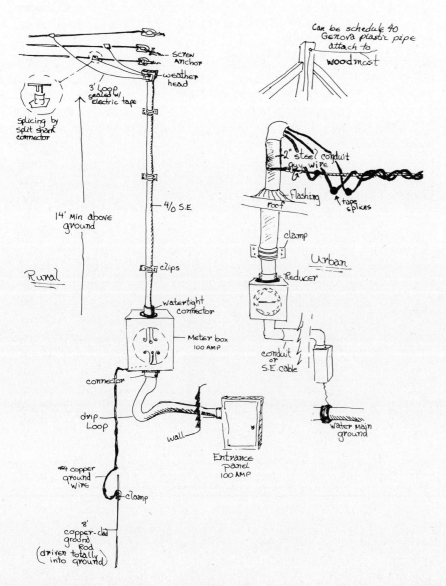

is broken, the power people can hold you liable and impose all sorts of penalties, especially if they think you were trying to tamper with the meter to cheat them out of their rightful profits. Now I happen to know of several people who have had need upon occasion, to disconnect a meter for perfectly legitimate reasons, such as moving or replacing the entrance panel during remodeling. Reversing the meter to make it run backwards and cheat the power company was the last thing on their minds. These people simply broke the seal and carefully unplugged the meter, thereby shutting off the power, since the meter is nothing more than a cartridge-type switch across the main feed. But I certainly would not recommend that to you. Call up the utility repair department and have them come out and charge you to perform this arcane and dangerous maneuver. There will be a reinstallation charge as well.

From the meter box, the entrance cable runs *by the most direct path* to the entrance panel. The code specifies this very clearly. And at what service cable costs per foot, you will not want to waste any. In rural locations, the system is grounded to a copper-clad steel rod driven at least one foot deeper than its full 8-foot length into the earth. The connection is made directly to the ground terminal of the meter socket. Where a municipal water line is available, the system can be grounded directly to it from the service-panel ground lug. The panel itself varies in size with its capacity both in current and the number of circuits. Other than that, all panels are basically the same. The feed from the meter runs to a main-disconnect circuit-breaker or switch. There are three lugs, one for each leg of the 240-v feed and one for the ground. By tapping single legs of the circuit, you will obtain 120-v circuits as needed. Tapping across both sides will deliver 240 v. The white neutral is connected to the ground terminal. So is the bare ground wire. The hot, black wire is connected to the fuse or circuit breaker. Three-wire 240-v circuits are fused across the red and black wires, two-wire 240-v circuits across both white and black legs.

A 24-circuit box is standard for a 100-amp residential circuit. The capacity of the existing panel can be expanded by adding on a smaller 4- or 8-circuit distribution box.

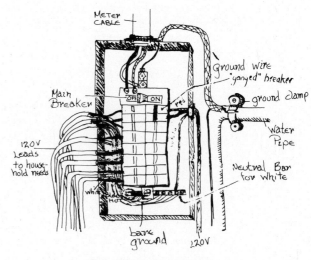

5–5 *The entrance panel*

Circuit breakers have largely replaced fuses as the standard protective device for home wiring. A breaker can be reset when it trips, a fuse must be replaced. People run out of fuses at the most inconvenient times. It is also very annoying to blow a whole box of fuses before the cause of an overload can be found. Although breakers represent initial extra cost, both in the type panel required and the cost of the breakers themselves, they soon repay their costs with convenient service. One precaution to observe with breakers; trip and reset all breakers at monthly intervals; corrosion and plating, which can occur on the terminal points, will raise the rated capacity, causing a 20-amp breaker to remain untripped until the overload exceeds as much as 25 amps. Second-hand electrical equipment is one of the best salvage bargains. New material is unbelievably expensive. But there are many different makes of circuit breakers, not all of which are interchangeable with a given panel, so be sure to match these items properly. An old fuse panel can often be piggy-backed with a separate fused disconnect switch to create a usable system. It is unfortunate that many people think nothing of wiring the branch circuits of a house but balk at wiring the entrance panel. The old terror of the power is surfacing here. Somehow it seems easier or safer to work with the domesticated 120-v end of the circuit than the more elemental 240-v feed.

From the panel, the individual circuits branch out to the various receptacles, lighting fixtures, switches, and appliances that supply the needs of the house. Your wiring book will help you determine the best way to run these circuits and the number you will need for adequate wiring and the capacity of each. A typical panel for a 150-amp service might contain*:

> One 150-amp main breaker
> Two 30-amp, 240-v hot-water heater, dryer circuits
> One 40- or 60-amp, 240-v range circuit
> Four 15-amp general-lighting circuits
> One 20-amp kitchen and appliance outlets
> Four 20-amp general-outlet circuits
> One 60-amp subfeed to garage or shop
> Four 20-amp future-need circuits
> One 20-amp freezer circuit

Notice that outlets and lighting circuits are separated, as are kitchen circuits, which often carry a heavy appliance load.

As the cost of power generation increases, the use of electrical appliances becomes less economical. The all-electric house of the sixties is a casualty of the energy crunch. Electric heat can no longer be justified, except under very special circumstances. Where a house can be entirely closed up and the plumbing concentrated in one small, insulated space, (a machine-room design concept) an electric heater set at minimum temperature can be a practical way to keep the core pipes from freezing. The plumbing system will, of course, be drained back to this core. Electric heaters are sometimes used to protect a basement from freezing, but whenever electricity is used to generate heat, it is done at a great cost in efficiency. Using electricity for heating water, drying clothes, cooking

*Obviously the total power drain of all the individual circuits will exceed the capacity of the main breaker. This is no problem as long as these circuits are not drawing power simultaneously so as to exceed the 150-amp limit.

food, warming space is the fastest way to use up a great deal of expensive power. The use of central air conditioning is difficult to justify, particularly in a temperate climate, and is more a consequence of poor house design than an architectural necessity. A well-built house should ventilate itself, utilizing natural air currents and proper siting and the properties of the materials used in its construction. ''Primitive'' cultures understood these principles far better than we do. They worked with nature rather than trying to circumvent it by expenditures of energy. One would do well to consider alternatives to lavish energy consumption. Wood heating is once again becoming popular in forested regions, and while complete solar space heating is not yet feasible in all areas of the country, it is possible for domestic hot-water needs to be supplied by the sun, anywhere and at a competitive cost.

The proliferation of electrical appliances is a reflection of the lack of awareness with which we go about our daily lives. Very few of these items are absolutely necessary. Too often the time saved by them is used to watch television. Electric clothes washing machines make sense when they use cold water. A small blender or food mixer may be of inestimable help to a serious cook. But it would be hard to convince a starving Bengali peasant that an electric toothbrush is an absolute necessity. The resources of our planet are better squandered on feeding people than on the production and use of extraneous gadgets.

When you sit down with paper and pencil to map out your electrical needs, remember that no man is an island. The choices you make influence the large-scale flow of energy in the rest of the world. It matters not how perceptible this disturbance is, it is still felt. Bear the image of that starving Bengali in mind. You are both connected to the same circuit.

Rewiring Notebook

Wires are run through holes drilled in the studs. Place these holes far back enough into the stud so that nails from the wall finish will not pierce the cables. Where studs have to be notched and wires run close to the surface, mark the location of the cable notch on the wall finish or floor, again to avoid danger of puncture. Cables should be stapled where they run parallel to a joist or stud. Leave a small loop of cable behind each outlet box. The slack will simplify future wiring changes. Convenience outlets are located about 16 inches above the floor, switches 48 to 54 inches. Kitchen outlets should be located above the countertop backsplash.

Installing electrical wires in old buildings without removing the walls and ceiling is a game of hide and seek. It is more a problem of carpentry than electricity. A *fish wire* is indispensable for pulling cables through walls and around corners. Figures 5–7 through 5–24 comprise an illustrated guide to the vicissitudes of rewiring old houses.

The best way to run wiring to outbuildings is to go underground. A two-foot-deep trench should be sufficient, but to be perfectly safe from the breakage that can be caused by frost heaves, the cable should be buried below the frost line. Where it runs under a roadway, it should be encased in conduit or plastic pipe. It is a good idea, even if not required by local codes, to run underground wire through a plastic pipe so that replacement or repair will be possible without having to dig up the entire length of the wire. All runs should be unbroken by splices, as boxes are not designed for underground service.

5–6 *Concealed wiring*

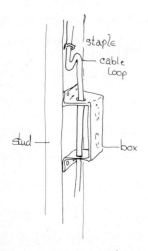

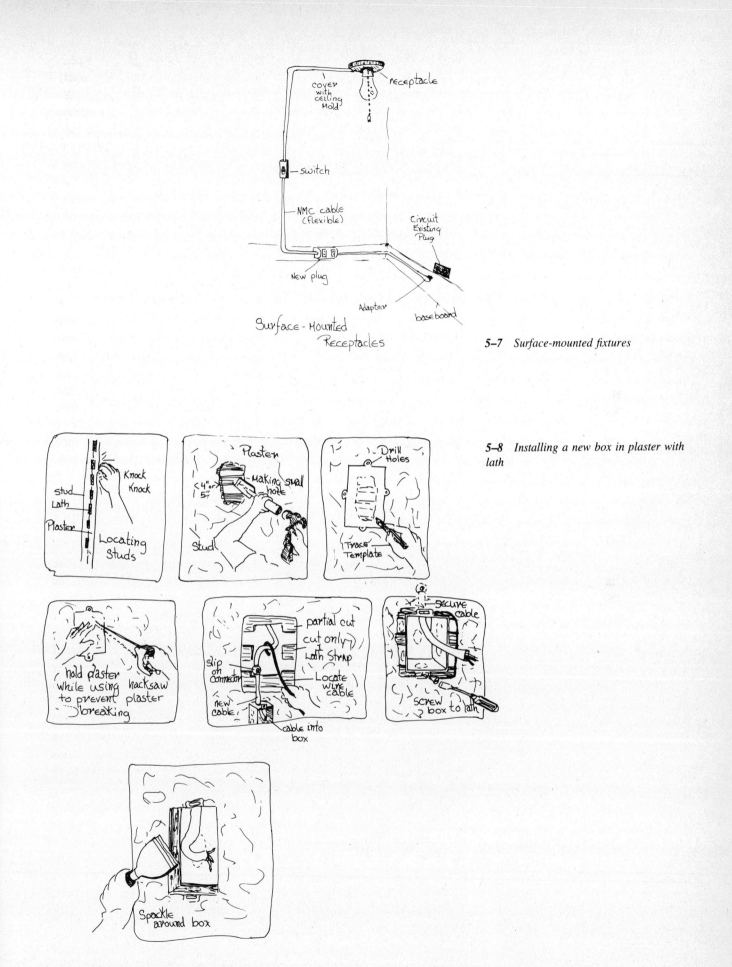

receptacle

cover with ceiling mold

switch

NMC cable (flexible)

Circuit Existing Plug

New plug

Adapter

baseboard

Surface-Mounted Receptacles

5–7   *Surface-mounted fixtures*

5–8   *Installing a new box in plaster with lath*

Knock Knock

stud
Lath
Plaster

Locating Studs

Plaster — making small hole

< 4" or 5"

Stud

Drill Holes

Trace Template

hold plaster while using hacksaw to prevent plaster breaking

partial cut
cut only
Lath Strap

slip on Connector

Locate wire cable

new cable

cable into box

SECURE cable

screw box to lath

Spackle around box

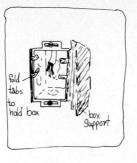
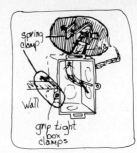

5–9 *Installing boxes without lath or support*

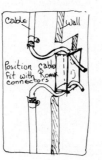
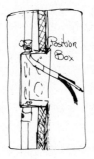
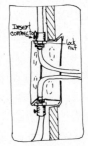

5–10 *Reversible mounting ears on box*

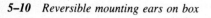

5–11 *Installing a box with two cables*

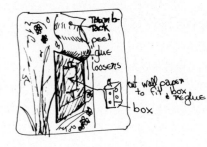

5–12 *Wall surface saved*

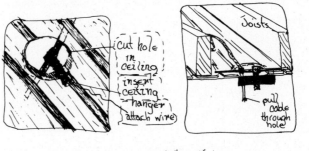

5–13 *Installing ceiling fixture*

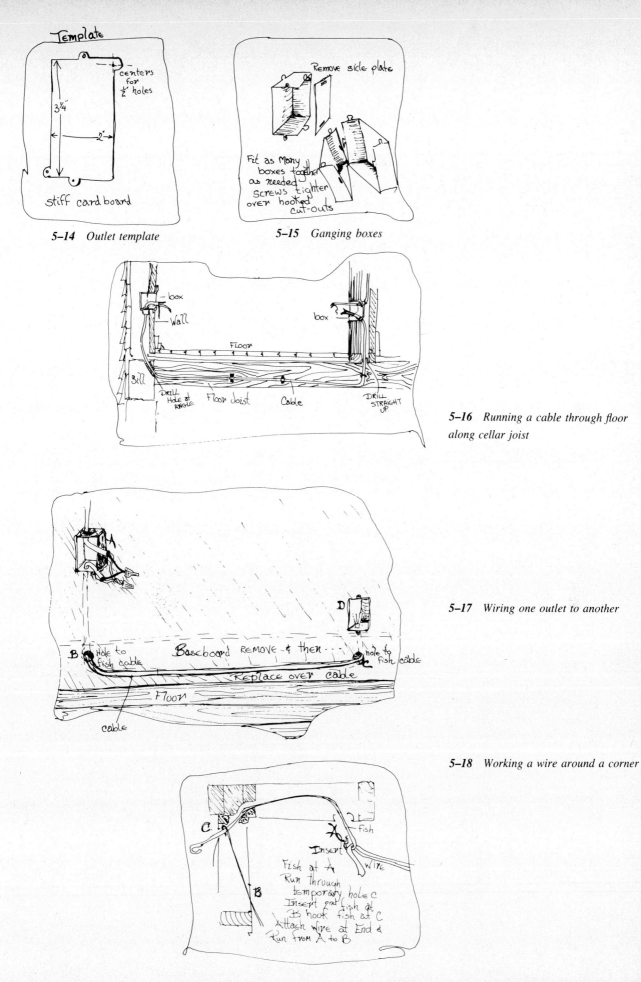

Template

centers for ½" holes

3¼"

2"

stiff card board

5–14 *Outlet template*

Remove side plate

Fit as many boxes together as needed screws tighten over hooked cut-outs

5–15 *Ganging boxes*

box
Wall
box
Sill
Floor
Drill Hole at Angle   Floor Joist   Cable   Drill Straight up.

5–16 *Running a cable through floor along cellar joist*

A

D

B Hole to fish cable   Baseboard REMOVE & then   hole to fish cable

Replace over cable

Floor

cable

5–17 *Wiring one outlet to another*

5–18 *Working a wire around a corner*

C

fish

Insert   wire

B

Fish at A
Run through temporary hole C
Insert and fish at B hook fish at C
Attach wire at End & Run from A to B

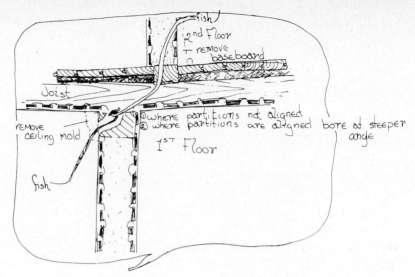

5–19   First- and second-floor wire joinery

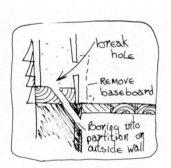

5–20   Running wire through a timber sill

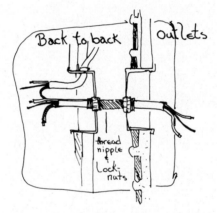

5–21   Wiring back-to back outlets

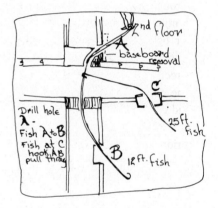

5–22   Wall-to-ceiling wiring

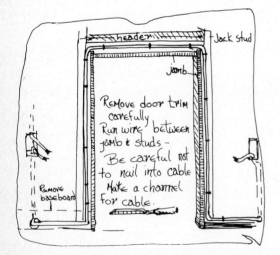

5–23   Wiring around doors

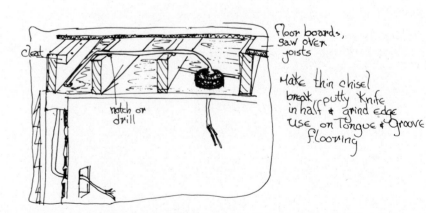

5–24   Attic wiring

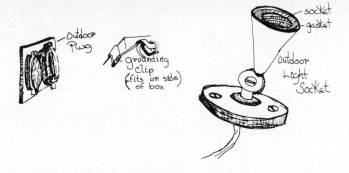

5-25   *Outdoor fixtures*

When installing outdoor fixtures, special waterproof covers are used. These are spring loaded against a rubber gasket. The box, like all boxes, should be grounded. Outdoor lights should also have a rubber gasket, which prevents water from working into the lamp socket.

A radical alternative to the difficult task of running new wiring through old walls—of notching plaster and removing baseboards—is to not run the wire through the walls at all. Instead, build a boxed-out baseboard, which runs continuously around the entire perimeter of the room. This unit can be a base for bookshelves, incorporated into furniture and cabinetry or window seats. Wires are run from cellar feeds to points along the wall. Outlets are installed directly in the face of the unit. Holes can be punched into the plaster where a line needs to be fished up into the wall. This system allows plumbing changes and can be incorporated into baseboard heaters.

Using a baseboard duct system allows you to do all insulation and interior-wall finish without having to wait for the electrician or plumber. It also

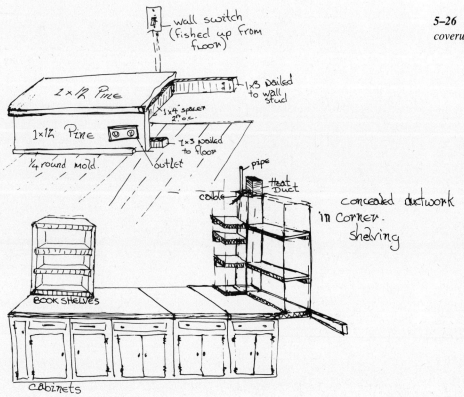

5-26   *Basic wiring and plumbing-duct coverups*

makes it possible to wire or plumb without violating the vapor barrier. Wires, pipes, and heating ducts can be run to the second floor in false corners where two bookshelves come together.

SECTION 2   **PLUMBING AND SEWAGE DISPOSAL**

The word "plumber" is derived from the Latin word for lead, *plumbum*. The basic principles of the plumbing trade have changed very little since the ancient Romans circulated household water and wastes through lead pipes. (As a point of historical interest, it has been argued with some force that the degeneracy of the Roman nobility can be attributed to the mental effects of lead poisoning.) The plumber's trade, like that of the mason's, has been jealous of its secrets. And until recent years, there was some justification for the mystification that surrounded plumbers; they worked with ancient and heavy elements, with lead and cast iron, copper and tin. They were the descendants of alchemists. Like the dwarfish metalsmiths who lived under the ice-rimmed mountains, they plied their trade in dark and moldy basements.

Plumbers have a large investment in specialized tools: pipe benders, threading machines, reamers and cutters, wrenches and torches. They carry a warehouse of fittings and connectors, pipes, solder and fluxes. No wonder then,

that plumbers consider themselves part of the blue-collar elite and adjust their prices and wages correspondingly. But in recent years, there has been a revolution in plumbing. The introduction of plastic-pipe sytems has shaken the foundations of the plumber's time-honored hegemony. It is now possible for anyone, without complicated tools, to plumb his or her own house. Gone is the need for molten lead, oakum, and heavy cast-iron pipes. The plumbers' unions and trade associations, which help to enforce plumbing codes, have fought bitterly against the introduction of the new materials. What latex paint has done to the professional painter, PVC pipe has done to the plumber. While there still are cases where plumbing codes specify cast-iron or galvanized-steel pipes, they generally apply to commercial or industrial uses, and the homeowner will rarely have reason to deal with these difficult materials.

Nevertheless, all of the reasons that justify the employment of an electrician apply to plumbers. They have the tools, the right parts and the experience. As with house wiring, codes or bank regulations often require the work to be performed or inspected by a licensed plumber. There is likewise a Uniform National Plumbing Code, which specifies minimum standards and approved practices. These recommendations should be observed to avoid jeopardizing the resale value of your property. Beyond this, by all means consider doing your own plumbing. It too, has a mystique of its own. I love to lose myself among the plumbing bins of a hardware store, like a kid in his blocks. There is a fascination to those shiny little pieces of brass and copper, the ells, tees, angles, and myriad compound connectors, threaded and smooth. I have often thought of collecting one of each kind, to put in a wall case, to look at, play with, combine in weird sculptures.

The Chief Plumbing Material:
   Pipe

If the wires are the nerves, the plumbing is the circulatory system of the house: The water pump is the heart; the pipes the arteries; the septic tank and waste lines, the kidney and bowels—the excretory system. As the debilitation of old age often leads to breakdowns in our circulatory system and internal plumbing, most old houses suffer from poor circulation and various intestinal afflictions. A diverticular house is not only inadequately plumbed, but like an underwired house, can be dangerous. There are still municipalities where water is supplied through lead pipes. There are homes without properly vented waste lines and homes where the drinking water is contaminated by the effluent from inadequate sewage disposal.

A plumbing system consists of two parts: the supply line and the waste line. The supply is simply a distribution network, which moves water from a source and delivers it to where it is needed. The waste system removes that water after it is used, along with any pollutants it may have acquired along the way. There are four basic pipe systems that can be installed by the homeowner with a minimum of skill and tools: a flexible polyethylene pipe, which is the familiar black plastic; CPVC or PVC, (chlorinated-poly-vinyl-chloride), a rigid plastic pipe sold under the trade name, Genova; ABS (acrylonitrile-butadiene-styrene), similar to PVC, often used for drain and waste lines; and plain old-fashioned copper tubing. When plastic pipe was introduced, one of its major advantages was its low cost; plastic was cheap and copper dear. Over the years the price differential has narrowed, as the price of the oil from which these plastics are made rose and the price of copper dropped on the world market. The advantage now is the ease and convenience of assembly these systems offer. This advantage is also its main disadvantage. Lengths of pipe are joined to fittings with a special solvent cement. If the joint springs a leak, if a mistake was made in the alignment, the entire joint must be cut out and replaced with two new joints. Copper pipe has to be soldered. Soldering requires a certain amount of skill, but it is not difficult to learn. A bad joint can be easily resoldered, as often as necessary.

Flexible polyethylene pipe should be used to deliver water from its source to the house. It can be buried directly in the ground. Formerly, galvanized-iron pipe was used for this purpose. The iron pipe soon develops hardening of the arteries, especially in hard-water regions. As the diameter of the pipe decreases, the friction on the water flow increases; the pump has to work harder to draw less water, and it soon fails. Poly pipe does not corrode, minerals do not adhere to its slippery sides. It is also available in coils of up to 400 feet in length, making it possible to avoid the need for splices and couplings when running water from a distant spring or well. For a discussion of the mechanics of water supplies and splicing, see chapter 7.

Plumbing codes prohibit the use of polyethylene pipe in residential systems, mainly because of its low heat resistance. It will melt at 120° F. A fire in the house would turn it into dripping goo. Since domestic hot water is from about 120° to 150° F., poly pipe is not applicable to hot-water lines in any case. It could be used for cold-water lines except that its low structural strength makes it vulnerable to failure, particularly at the joints. Connections are made with nylon fittings secured by stainless-steel band clamps. In a pressurized water system, the momentum of water movement can cause these joints to develop leaks over time. Poly is often used in rural locations to supply water to barns and outbuildings, where economy and flexibility of installation are important and the pressure is lower than that of municipal systems. It is also suitable for cold-water lines in a low-pressure gravity-feed system.

Rigid PVC plastic pipe is strong enough to resist the force of pressurized systems. It will also withstand higher temperatures and can be used with hot-water lines (up to 150° F.). It is available in a variety of diameters and with fittings that allow it to mate with copper- and threaded-pipe systems. ABS pipe will withstand higher temperatures (up to 180° F.). Since it is also stronger, it is somewhat more expensive than PVC. It is used exclusively for drain or waste runs. It is not available in the smaller diameters.* Both these pipe systems are joined by using a solvent (methyl-ethyl-ketone) to dissolve the material itself. The surfaces to be joined are first cleaned with an acetone cleaning compound. Both surfaces are then coated with a bead of cement and the connection made. The joint is rotated slightly (about 5 degrees) to insure a good bond and then allowed to set. Joints set very rapidly; a misjointed piece can be pulled apart for only a few seconds. Do not run water through a pressurized line for at least an hour (specifications recommend twenty-four hours for industrial applications) or within fifteen minutes for a drain line.

There are studies on record that maintain that the material from which these plastics are made are stable and do not, over time, leach into the water they carry. Vinyl chloride, the raw material for PVC is a known carcinogen. When polymerized into a plastic it becomes chemically stable, some say, inert, and apparently, nontoxic. There is conflicting evidence that over time the plastic does break down, depolymerizing into its constituents, releasing minute amounts of this vinyl chloride vapor into the environment. The process is accelerated by heat or sunlight, which is why you detect a characteristic cloying odor when you get into a car that has been sealed shut on a hot day: the upholstery, which is largely vinyl, has been evaporating. While there is no concrete evidence that this process takes place in water lines, that does not mean it doesn't. The validity of "scientific evidence" is no more objective than the scientists who prostitute themselves and their research to the corporations paying their salaries. My water flows into the house through 350 feet of buried 1¼-inch polyethylene pipe. I know that the first glass of cold water drawn from the tap in the morning tastes and smells like polyethylene. This is a relatively simple hydrocarbon. It has none of the chlorinated structures that are characteristic of the carcinogenic compounds and is reputed to be environmentally safe. But hot water is a potent solvent. There is no really "safe" level for chlorinated hydrocarbons in the biosystem. A few parts per billion may well be the straw that gives the camel cancer of the liver. I'd think twice about using PVC or ABS pipe for carrying anything hot or cold I wanted to drink.

Copper tubing is not much more expensive and is strong, noncorroding, and unaffected by heat. Soldering is a fairly simple technique once you get used to it. And copper is a trace element that is actually vital to the proper functioning of our nervous system. The few molecules that could conceivably leach into hot water would do us no harm. Use ABS or PVC for drain and waste lines. Copper would be prohibitively expensive in these large-diameter pipes. Cast iron, the traditional material, is not only expensive but difficult to work with and requires special tools.

---

*Although PVC pipe is used by home plumbers for both supply and waste lines, it actually is not approved for use by the plumbing codes, ostensibly because of the toxic gases that it would give off if the house were to catch fire. The code does allow ABS pipe which burns less harmfully.

The Distribution System

The distribution system, however it enters the house, from a well or a city water main, should be planned so that all lines can be drained back to a low point and the entire system shut down. This not only enables a rural weekend house to be left unheated, except for the pump room itself, but facilitates repairs on any system. Half-inch, thin-wall, copper tubing is normally used for supply lines. Type L is used for indoor applications and the heavier type M for outdoor and underground or heavy-duty work.

Copper is also available in two types of flexible tubing—type L and the heavier type K. Flexible tubing is very handy when making connections in areas where solder would be awkward or for making odd bends with a minimum of fittings.

When water must be supplied to more than one fixture from the same line, the supply feeder should be ¾-inch pipe. Otherwise a pressure drop occurs when, for example, you run the shower and the sink at the same time. The increased-diameter pipe allows more water to be delivered, preventing the demands of one fixture from preempting those of another and helping you avoid a scalding or chilling experience. Individual shutoff valves should be installed on all supply lines, both hot and cold, to each individual fixture. In the event of repairs, only the particular fixture, rather than the whole system, will have to be shut down. The body of these valves is stamped with an arrow, which should always point in the direction of the flow. The valve will not seal properly if the arrow is pointing backwards.

Never run pipe in a plumbing system horizontally. All lines slope at a slight angle, to drain to their lowest point. Long runs can also slope toward a valve in the center of the line. This valve should be fitted with a hose coupling or a screw-type draincock. Although not absolutely necessary, such valves are very convenient when a line has to be drained for repair, or new lines spliced in. The individual fixtures can be shut off above, and the supply line below, the

5–27 *Simple distribution system*

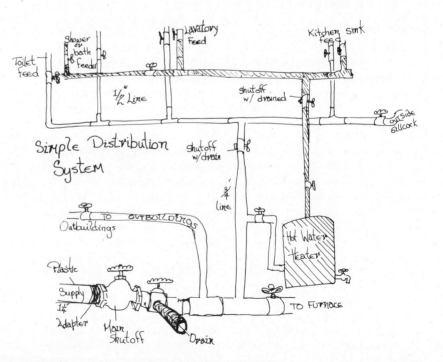

repair point. Water in the line then runs back to the draincock. It is important to empty the line completely, since the repair fitting cannot be soldered if the line contains water. The water absorbs the heat of the torch before the metal can become hot enough to melt the solder. Even a slight drip, if constant, will prevent a good joint. Drain lines and shutoffs at convenient points facilitate drainage.

Copper pipe must be clean for a good solder joint. Even the oils from your skin will prevent a tight bond. Clean the surfaces of the pipe with steel wool or emery paper until shiny bright. The edges of any cuts should be smooth and free from burrs. A tubing cutter makes a neater cut than a hacksaw blade. These tools are inexpensive and available at any hardware store. Coat the polished surfaces with soldering flux (apply with a stiff brush or splinter of wood) and slip the tubing into the fitting. Heat with a propane torch until the metal becomes hot enough to melt the solder. The wire solder is held against the rim of the fitting. As it liquifies it is pulled into the space between the fitting and tubing by capillary action. The solder must be evenly distributed to be leakproof. A thin band of solder forms just above the rim of the fitting when the solder is properly distributed. Surprisingly little solder is needed to make a tight joint. Any excess only collects inside the tube and can cause future plugging. Plan your joints so as to avoid the need to solder upside down. Upside-down soldering can be done, but it is more difficult to get a good fit. Melting a band of solder onto the tubing before it is inserted into the fitting will help. Heat the fitting as well, to expand it enough to fit over the tubing.

In a new house, the plumbing system can be planned completely. Unless you are replacing the entire system in your old house, your plumbing will be limited to repair and upgrading of existing facilities. If all your existing lines are galvanized iron too corroded for use, you might have to replace everything. If the pipes are in usable condition, you will have to live with whatever insanities of design come with the place. The existing plumbing will be a weedlike tangle, having been patched together during the different epochs of the house's previous

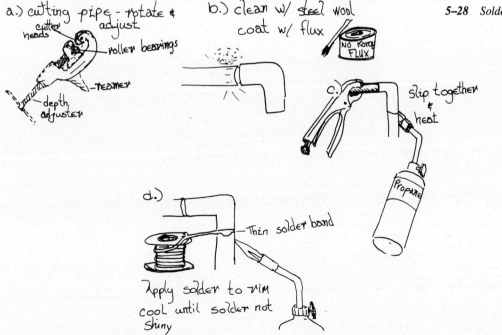

a.) cutting pipe - rotate & adjust
cutter heads
roller bearings
reamer
depth adjuster

b.) clean w/ steel wool coat w/ flux
NO KORO FLUX

c.) slip together & heat
Propane

d.)
Thin solder band
Apply solder to rim cool until solder not shiny

5–28   *Soldering copper tubing*

tenants. But make the best of the situation. Plumbing materials are expensive, and if you can live with what you have, there is little sense in redoing it solely in the interests of a more rational plan. If, however, the service does not deliver enough water to where it is needed or the drain and waste system backs up or emits foul odors through the bathtub drain, you will have to make sense of this bramble patch of pipes and valves. It can be an accomplishment worthy of Sherlock Holmes just to locate the shutoff valve for the toilet supply.

An intelligent plumbing system is a concentrated one, a point that is often overlooked by remodelers who change rooms around without provision for running pipes back to their sources or who put bathrooms at the opposite end of the house from kitchens. Cutting down on the length of pipe is the first and greatest step toward cost savings. Bear that in mind when planning any room changes that will involve plumbing. I know of one unhappy homeowner who decided to heat his water from the oil-fired boiler that vented into the chimney. This unit was thirty-two feet across the other side of the basement floor from his water pump and inlet and the kitchen and bathrooms, directly above. Not only did he have to pay for the extra copper tubing to span the basement but the hot-water runs had to be insulated (which they should be in any case) with a great quantity of expensive foam jacketing, to keep them from cooling off over the distance they spanned. Plumbing should be designed around a centralized core: The *wet wall* is a standard method for minimizing pipe runs. The house is designed so that the kitchen and bathroom plumbing share a common wall. Upstairs bathrooms are directly above the first floor kitchen and bathroom and the laundry room is directly below. The hot-water heater, pump, and central drain all share the same basement room or wall. The wet wall is framed with 2 × 6 or 2 × 8 lumber, to accommodate the thickness of the vent stack, which is a three-inch pipe running, treelike, from the main drain in the basement through the roof.

Working with Cast-Iron Drain Lines

Avoid having to move pipes whenever possible. One exception is when the supply lines run inside an outside wall. In cold regions, they will freeze. Move them to run on the surface of the finish wall. Tear into the walls with care—you may unleash a monster beyond your control. Moving a cast-iron vent stack is not a job to cut your plumber's teeth on, and even professionals prefer to avoid it. The only time a homeowner should have to install new cast-iron pipe is when lines have to be run under a concrete slab. The plumbing codes require all such drain lines to be cast. Unfortunately, since the existing system will have been assembled before the days of plastic pipe, you may have further occasion to deal with this intractable material.

While it is not impossible to learn the techniques of working with cast iron, you will probably be better off hiring professional help. Planning your new work to avoid the necessity of reventing into the existing cast-iron vent stack will help. If you add a new drain line beyond the existing soil pipe, look for a point where it can be tapped into the line without removal of a cast-iron section. The threaded end of a cleanout trap is a good place to tap in such a line.

Removing a section of cast-iron drain pipe to allow tapping in a tee can be done if absolutely necessary. Bell-hub-type cast-iron pipe is sealed at the joint by driving oakum (tar-soaked hemp fibers) with a caulking iron (a flat, offset, blunt-steel chisel) between the hub and the pipe. Use about one foot of oakum for each inch of pipe diameter. Molten lead at a rate of one pound per inch diameter is then poured around the joint to seal it. Take care the pipe is dry; droplets of water inside the hub can turn to steam with explosive force, splattering hot lead about the immediate vicinity. Wear safety glasses and avert your face from the joint while pouring.

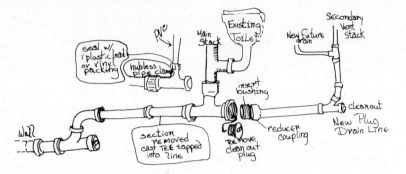

5–29   Cast-iron drain work

5–30   Filling a cast-iron hub joint

Cast-iron pipe is sold in five- and ten-foot lengths. It can be cut by scoring with a hacksaw completely around the diameter. The cut must be even for a good fit. Support the pipe on a block and strike the free end sharply with a hammer until it breaks cleanly along the scribed line, which is easier in theory than in practice. Alternatively, hubless drain pipe is joined with rubber-gasketed, stainless-steel pipe clamps. This is a convenient way to replace a section of pipe without the trouble of lead and oakum.

A horizontal or upside-down joint is sealed with an asbestos joint-runner, a type of band clamp with a hole in the top that fits around the joint. The lead is poured from the top until it fills the hole. I mention these methods for the fanatical and determined do-it-yourselfer. Unless you have a plumber friend who can loan you the tools, it is a lot easier to hire help. Once you have removed the old section and replaced it with a tee, the PVC drain can be adapted to fit.

5–31   Breaking cast-iron pipe

Galvanized-Iron Pipe

Because of the specialized tools needed, working with galvanized pipe also should generally be avoided by the home plumber. A pipe-threading machine is one of those tools you will have trouble finding and rarely have occasion to use again. It is, however, a simple matter to disassemble galvanized connectors and adapt them to PVC or copper fittings. The threads are interchangeable and will accept a variety of adapters. Two pipe wrenches are needed, one to hold the pipe and another to turn the fitting. Old fittings require considerable torque to move them, as they rust solidly together. Whenever galvanized fittings are to be joined, wrap the threads first with teflon joint tape or coat with pipe-thread compound. Either treatment makes a watertight seal that can be easily disas-

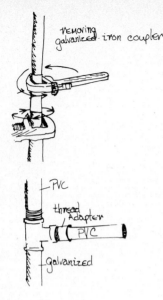

removing
galvanized-iron coupler

PVC

thread
Adapter

PVC

Galvanized

5–32 *Adapting galvanized pipe to PVC or copper*

sembled should the need arise. If you are modernizing your entire system, consider removing all existing galvanized lines, especially in hard-water regions, and replacing them with noncorroding PVC or copper. It can save expensive future work—tearing out newly installed walls to gain access to clogged pipes.

Simple Operations:
Installing toilet bowls and sinks—the wonderful basin wrench

Occasionally when a wall is removed, plumbing will be found lurking within. Avoid this embarrassment by examining the cellar or attic for a pipe that might run into the partition slated for removal. Sometimes, though, there is no way you can tell what might be running through a wall. A horizontal vent pipe is a case in point. Call a plumber or fetch your sawzall. The pipe will have to be moved to a ceiling run or, if found in a proposed door opening, to a run above the door header. Vertical pipes can be concealed by boxing them behind pine boards. Cabinets or valances can also hide pipes, horizontal as well as vertical. A hollow post may be an unplanned-for design necessity. In the excitement of remodeling, it is easy to forget that walls often contain more than old plaster and mouse dust. Dropped ceilings are another solution to the replumbing problem, and so is the baseboard duct work previously mentioned.

One alternative to the wasteful water usage of a standard toilet is to replace it with a new low-volume flush toilet. You may wish to replace your old toilet in any case. Removing a toilet is a matter of unscrewing the mounting bolts in the base. There are four of them, generally concealed under a porcelain or plastic cap. A socket wrench or small pair of vice grip pliers may be needed. Disconnect the supply line from the tank (it should be turned off first), flush the toilet with the supply shut, to empty most of the tank, then ladle the remaining water from the tank and bowl. Lift the stool and tank off its mounting flange. Before replacing with a new unit, clean the mounting flange and install a new wax gasket (available at the hardware store). Set the new tank in place carefully and remount. Do not overtighten—you can crack the bowl. If you wish to seal off the old waste drain and move the toilet to a new location, first plug the hole tightly with rags. The mounting flange is broken back below floor level. Seal the stump with asphalt cement or molten wax. Cast-iron pipes can be stuffed with oakum above the rags and then filled with lead. Lead pipe itself can be smashed tightly shut. When marking the center for the new toilet, be sure which size bowl you have. Standard toilets are made to fit a twelve- or fourteen-inch center, measured from the finish wall. Too small, and the tank will not fit against the wall, too large and there will be a space behind it. Toilet-tank supply lines are generally ⅜-inch chrome-plated brass tubing. This material is used for all exposed plumbing-supply lines, not only because it is flexible but because it has a more finished appearance. It is also very expensive.

Lavatory sinks are either wall mounted or set-in, like kitchen sinks. You may wish to remove the old-fashioned sink because of the inconvenience of the separate spouts for hot and cold water. The wall-mounted sink is attached to a cast-iron or steel bracket screwed to the wall. The water feed and drain lines are disconnected and the sink simply lifted off the mounting bracket. Contemporary lavatories are made to fit into a hole cut in the countertop. A template is furnished for the correct opening when you buy a new sink. If you plan to install a used sink, scribe the outline of the sink on the countertop or a piece of cardboard (the sink is turned upside down) and scribe the actual cutting line ⅜ inch inside this outline. Set the sink in place over a bead of either white or clear silicone adhesive caulking and reconnect the feed and waste lines after the caulking sets.

A kitchen sink is often secured to the underside of the countertop by means of mounting clips, which are screw-tightened clamps that fit into a special flange under the sink and draw it tightly to the countertop. If you attempt to set a standard sink into a two-inch-thick butcher-block countertop, you will have to rout a channel under the edge of the cut-out, as the clamps will only fit a standard ¾-inch-thick counter. The sink is likewise set in a bead of adhesive caulking. Ordinary wrenches will seldom fit into the spaces between fittings and the wall. The *basin wrench* is a tool designed to fit into these awkward places. It will be indispensable when connecting or removing faucets. The head of this wrench will fasten onto the lock nut of the fixture and can be turned by the T-lever handle. No other specialized plumbing tool will be quite as useful.

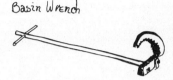

5–33   *The basin wrench*

Waste and Drain Systems

A rational plumbing system derives from the patterns implicit in nature. The arteries of the distribution system bring water into smaller capillaries, which supply the fixtures that service the household. Waste water must be removed through a corresponding system of pipes. The drainage system is often compared to a tree. The central vent stack is the trunk and the various wyes and tees the boles of the main branches, which carry smaller drain lines from individual fixtures. The waste-water system works by gravity; there is no pressure other than weight of the water itself. The pipe need not be as structurally rigid. ABS pipe is often used for such work.

A proper waste-water system must meet two main requirements. First, like the tree that increases in size from leaves to roots, the pipe must never decrease in diameter as it flows downstream. Drain pipes must be smaller than the main stack. Branch lines are never perpendicular to the trunk but must enter it at a slight angle. These requirements help prevent clogging and aid in cleanout. Second, the drain system must be vented. The decomposition of human and household wastes produces hydrogen sulfide (rotten-egg smell), which is toxic, and methane gas (swamp gas), which is flammable as well. The easiest path for these lighter-than-air gases to follow is from the sewer back up into the house. Traps are installed on every fixture drain to block the passage of these gases and force them up the vent stack. A trap is a bend in the drain line, which forms a water seal. The gas is prevented from exiting back through the fixture. If the pipe were ever completely filled with water the momentum of the draining water could create a siphon effect which would break the seal. The longer the pipe, the greater the possibility of its filling completely. Therefore, plumbing codes specify that a fixture cannot be more than ten feet of horizontal distance from the vent stack. Any fixture that exceeds this distance must be equipped with a vent of its own or a *revent*, which is a line that runs from below the fixture trap up into the ceiling and back to the main stack.

Where installing a secondary vent stack or revent is impossible, a special fixture (the V-200 Auto-Vent®) is now available that will vent a line without

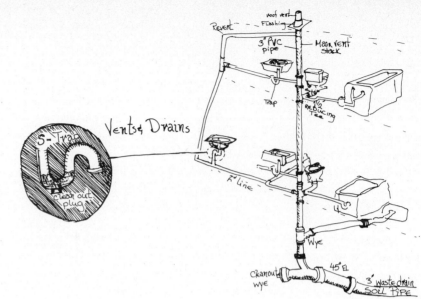

5–34 *Vents and drains*

the necessity of a pipe through the roof. It acts essentially like a valve in a radiator line. Check with your hardware store for this inexpensive and simple solution to an otherwise complex problem.

There are two kinds of waste water: *Grey* water and *black* water, or *"soil."* Grey water is the effluent from washing machines, sinks, and tubs. Black water carries human waste. It is common practice to run both of these wastes into a common drain pipe and from that into the municipal sewer or, if you live more than 500 feet from such a sewer, into a septic tank.

Fear and Loathing:
Septic tanks and waste disposal

The disposal of human waste in the United States is a triumph of fear and superstition over common sense. Our attitudes toward our bodily wastes stem from the same philosophy that allows us to destroy our environment: "Out of sight, out of mind"—the curious idea that somehow, if you flush it away, it goes away. This linear mode of thinking ignores the basic reality that one person's downstream is another's front yard. Indoor plumbing became widespread only in the late-Victorian era. It is no mere coincidence that our attitudes toward disposal of human wastes are grounded in the same abhorrence of bodily functions that characterized that age. Rather than recognize waste as a profound link in the natural cycle of growth and decay, as a resource to be husbanded, polite folk are horrified by the mere mention of it, while others make it the subject of infantile "dirty" jokes. Sewage is a simile for that which is cast aside, buried, forgotten, and useless. There is no such thing as "waste." We read that the Chinese have used human excrement to keep their fields productive for more than forty centuries, and we smile smugly at their benighted primitivism and meanwhile grimace at the ever-mounting costs of fertilizers.

Most building codes reflect this perverse and irrational attitude by refusing to allow any alternative to the wasteful flush toilet that might treat our by-products as a resource. The average American family uses 88,000 gallons of water per year, 40 percent of which is flushed down the toilet. It is insane to use five gallons of pure drinking water to carry away one-half pint of waste into the rivers and then spend millions trying to figure out how to clean up rivers. Unfortunately, until public-health officers can see their so-called wisdom for the prejudice it really is, most of us have no choice but to continue using the flush toilet. You can cut down water consumption by the simple expedient of placing a brick (or two if it doesn't interfere with the flushing mechanism) into the tank. The water displaced will cut down on volume and still leave plenty for the normal flush. There are also several, unfortunately expensive, toilets on the market designed to use less water per flush than their standard counterparts. There is little more than this that concerned residents of urban areas can do, other than disciplining themselves to flush only when necessary, to leave the liquid wastes unflushed until evening, and generally limit toilet use. The problem of what to do with those wastes once they pass into the sewer remains.

The Privy

In rural areas, septic tanks are the standard method of on-site sewage disposal. Although they too, are connected to the wasteful flush toilet, they are at least, if properly designed, a very efficient and ecologically sound means of sewage disposal. It is quite possible to buy an old farmhouse completely lacking indoor plumbing. The outhouse is a viable alternative to the expense of a septic system.

The privy can be a temporary expedient, employed until money can be raised for a septic system and conventional toilet. Or it can be a permanent addition, used year-round or seasonally. In warmer regions of the boondocks there is little justification for the expense of septic systems. The health hazards associated with raw sewage and its disposal into the water table can be avoided by building a closed, concrete-lined composting privy, a structure that aerobically digests human waste and renders it pathogen free and suitable for use as a high-grade fertilizer. The Farallones Institute (at Point Reyes Station, Calif.

94956) has designed just such a privy. You can order plans by mail. Ask for *Technical Bulletin No. 1* and enclose $1.50 plus postage. In any case, a good privy must be screened to prevent insect infestation and vented to relieve odors and should be sited so that it is at least 100 yards downstream of a water source, to avoid contamination. Other than this it can be as whimsical a structure as one's fancy allows. The rigors of elimination in the winter can be abetted by the time-honored expedient of keeping the toilet seat in the house, warming up under the stove until needed. The technological-overkill approach dictates the construction of an insulated outhouse (with its own TV or reading light) equipped with a small radiant-electric heater, which can be switched on from the main house, prior to use.

Composting Toilets of the Indoor Variety

There are at present about a half dozen indoor composting toilets commercially available and a number of companies are about to enter this lucrative field. The toilets are roughly of two types. The larger, bulk units, have few or no moving parts, require infrequent maintenance, use little outside energy, and need be emptied only at long intervals. These units, typified by the Clivus Multrum® and the Toa Throne®, are quite expensive—in much the same price range as the conventional septic-tank installation. The smaller units, typified by the Mullbank Ecolet® or the Bioloo®, cost about half as much as their larger competitors but require electric fans or small heaters and do not have great capacities. They must be emptied more frequently, and the user must be careful about how much of what goes into it.

These systems are designed as alternatives to the flush toilet and therefore require no water to operate. They also compost kitchen wastes, significantly reducing garbage disposal problems (the smaller units, of course, cannot handle as many kitchen scraps as the larger ones and can be easily overloaded). Unlike a conventional flush toilet which typically utilizes the same sewer drain as the sinks and tubs, none of these alternative systems are intended to absorb or process grey water, which must be drained into a separate dry well. In some areas, plumbing codes prohibit the use of dry wells and require that even grey water be discharged into a septic tank. Although disease-causing microorganisms are not a serious hazard in grey water, this untreated effluent, if discharged directly into the soil without the beneficial bacterial action of a septic tank, can pollute water supplies. The biological oxygen demand (B.O.D., a measure of how much oxygen is needed to digest a particular substance and therefore how much will be removed from the water, depleting aquatic life systems) of the detergent residues in grey water is as great as that of raw sewage. A dry well is really nothing more than a holding tank for a large volume of waste water, which it allows to slowly percolate into the surrounding soil and water table. Since there is almost no bacterial digestion of solid particles taking place in a dry well (the dry well is mostly filled with air and septic tank bacteria are *anaerobic*), it can often become clogged with grease or food residues, reducing its storage capacity and effectivness. Thus the need for additional facilities to handle grey water adds considerably to the cost of a waterless toilet and eliminates one of the main reasons for installing a waterless toilet in the first place. Fortunately, there are ways for enterprising and ecologically-conscious individuals to recycle grey water directly into gardens or holding tanks where excess heat can be extracted first. Grey water pollution is less a problem in the middle of a fifty-acre homestead than in a surburban plot. Other than this, these toilets are more of an ethical statement than an economic necessity. At present very few states approve their use, although acceptance is growing, as public health officials become familiar with them. A waterless toilet that has been approved is the Destroilet® which does its work by incinerating the wastes in a gas-flame jet. Destroilets may be practical on rock ledges where there is no alternative system available or in areas where larger systems and materials cannot be brought in, but they suffer from the disadvantage of a seat that can become uncomfortably hot in prolonged use and a downwind odor while operating that would gag a maggot.

An excellent publication that discusses the current alternatives to the flush toilet is published by the Minimum Cost Housing Group of the School of Architecture, McGill University, Montreal, Canada: *Stop the Five-Gallon Flush (A Survey of Alternative Waste-Disposal Systems)*. It is obtainable from the address above for $2 postpaid.

Septic Systems

A septic system is actually a holding tank in which anaerobic (without oxygen) bacteria consume wastes and convert them into a nonpathogenic effluent, which is then released into the soil. The same process takes place aerobically in the soil itself. The amount of water and waste generated by human activity is so great that it would exceed the self-purification capacity of the soil were it to be directly released. That is the reason for the septic system. Primary digestion takes place in the tank. The effluent is further purified by natural soil action in the leach field before it is absorbed into the immediate area.

The cost and design of an on-site sewage-disposal system is a function of the soil type and the seasonal water table, as well as the level of the bedrock below the ground surface. A sandy soil is ideal. A heavy clay soil is virtually impervious to water and will not absorb much effluent. An opening corresponding to the capacity of the septic tank must be dug and various layers of crushed stone and gravel and light soil laid down over a system of leaching pipes. A percolation test will determine the size of the field since it indicates the absorptive capacity of your soil. This test is best performed by a professional soil engineer.

Septic-tank ills are often chronic and vary with the seasons. The first symptom of catarrh of the tank is a toilet that will not flush properly and

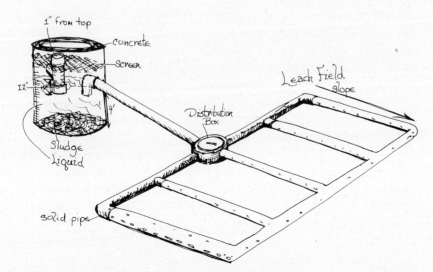

5-35 On-site sewage system

continuously backs up. If efforts with a plumber's snake or drain router fail to find or clear any obstruction in the sewer line itself, suspect the septic tank—especially in the spring, when the ground-water level is at its highest and the carrying capacity of the soil therefore at its lowest. If the addition of a package of bacterial enzymes fails to bring any improvement, the tank will have to be pumped. First you must locate the tank itself. Follow the line of the sewer outside the house. Plunge a pointed steel bar or crowbar into the soil until you strike something solid and hollow. This method will work in the spring, when the soil is soft. Otherwise you will have to trust to chance and dig wherever you think the tank may be. Generally the tank is fairly close to the house and within two feet of the surface—often only a ten foot length of pipe separates it from the wall. If there is snow on the ground, you will be aided in locating the tank by the melting snow. Because bacterial action generates heat, the snow over a tank will thaw first. You can then expose the cover with a hand shovel.

Another symptom of a sickly system is a noticeable sewage odor in the ground over the leach field. Lush vegetative growth will give further evidence of leakage. The odor and the nutrients indicate that the system is not digesting the sewage as well as it should be and that raw sewage is being released from the tank directly into the ground. The capacity of the tank may be exceeded, or the bacteria themselves may have been killed. Flushing toxic chemicals and paints down the household drains is a good way to plug up your septic tank. To solve the problem you can obtain new bacteria cultures, although in most cases, the old bacteria will reestablish themselves if given a chance.

A handful of fresh sludge left when the tank is cleaned will see it off to a good start. Often the old tank is too small for the needs of the flush-fanatical family, especially when compounded by a garbage-disposal unit. These days 750-gallon tanks are considered barely standard. A family of two adults and children, who compost their kitchen wastes, should be able to get by on a 500-gallon tank. Most new homes have 1,000-gallon tanks. A normal tank will require pumping only once every five years. Pumping is too expensive a ritual to have to attend to an overloaded tank every year. A leach field that is too small or has become compacted by the passage of heavy machinery over it (remember that cement truck that got stuck last fall?) can cause a tank to back up. The entire leach field will have to be dug up and replaced. If you are plagued with chronic septic-tank troubles, consult a soil engineer to determine the needs of your system in relation to the soil type and the capacity of your tank. A professional design and opinion, even if not required by local or state ordinances, will be the best insurance you can buy for guaranteeing a trouble-free sewage-disposal system.

The considerable expense of excavating the old tank and replacing it with a larger one can sometimes be avoided by a change in living habits. Flushing the toilet only when solid wastes have accumulated will help reduce the amount of empty water clogging up the soil, as will restricting flushing to mornings and evenings in times of high water tables. Composting the kitchen wastes will provide valuable garden fertilizer. A garbage-disposal unit requires 50 percent more capacity than a standard household tank. Tank sizes are based on a figure of about 100 gallons per person above a base of 500 gallons for a four-person household.

> What chemistry! That the winds are not really infectious, That all is clean forever and forever.   [Walt Whitman, "This Compost"]

There's an old New England saying—"what with the high cost of heating, the average icicle on a roof costs about five dollars a foot."

[Eric Sloane, *A Reverence for Wood*]

Residential use accounts for 20 percent of all the energy consumed in the United States. Half of this energy is used for space heating. Efficient heating systems are necessary to lower operating costs and to conserve dwindling energy supplies. The heating system in an old house is rarely either efficient or in top working condition. Cleaning the furnace and having it periodically adjusted alone can result in a 10 percent savings in total heating bills. Add to that a program of good insulation and a tight house, and further substantial reductions in costs can be achieved. A heat exchanger inserted in the flue to extract heat that would otherwise go up the chimney and circulate it into the duct system is another cost-saving investment that can easily be added to an existing system.

Domestic heating systems use a medium to transfer the heat generated by combustion in the furnace to radiators, which give up that heat to the rooms. This medium is a liquid, either steam or water or air. Radiant heaters, either gas or electric, heat by blowing air across a hot surface grid and directly out into the room. A wood- or coal-burning stove is also a radiant heater. Heating systems, while simple in theory, are actually quite complicated to design and install. The job is best left to an experienced plumber. Forced hot-air systems can be installed by the homeowner with stardard parts and a few sheet-metal working tools. The labor is not difficult, but it is important to design the system to fit the needs of the house. This requires considerable expertise and a lot of calculation. The Audel *Plumbers and Pipefitters Library,* Vol. 3 will show the would-be heating contractor how to figure heat loss per square foot, calculate infiltration and transmission heat losses, radiator selection, boiler and pump sizing (boilers and pumps are always needlessly oversized, a situation that should be considered in the light of energy scarcity), and the other information needed to design a system for his/her needs. Another Audel book, *Building Construction and Design,* chapters 1 and 5, in particular, give good background information on heating-system theory.

The simplest hot-water heating systems work by gravity or pumped circulation. Hot-water systems give very mild heat and, because of the latent storage capacity of the water in the radiators, can deliver heat even after the furnace has been turned off. Figure 5–36 outlines the basics of a two-pipe gravity system and a two-pipe forced circulation system. The gravity system works because of the difference in specific gravity between hot and cold water, which causes hot water to rise. The water is heated by the boiler to about 190° F. and as it cools slightly (to about 170° F.), it falls down to the radiators where it gives up further heat to the room and then returns to the boiler. Gravity systems work very well in small homes or concentrated apartment buildings. They are simple to operate with a low installation and maintenance cost. But they suffer from danger of water damage in the event of leaks and freezing if the furnace goes out. Large (expensive) pipe sizes are required to overcome internal resistance. The system responds slowly to temperature changes. Forced hot-water systems use a pump installed in either the flow or return line to suck water through the system. The advantage is that smaller pipes can be used and the

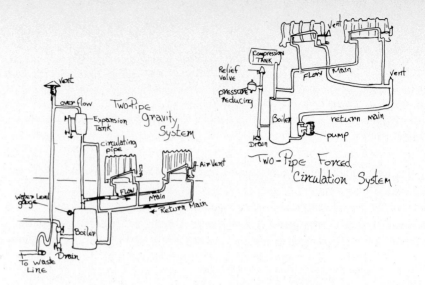

5-36   *Domestic hot-water heating systems*

response to temperature changes is more rapid. Room temperatures can be thermostatically controlled. All high points must be vented to prevent airlocks in the pipes.

Steam heat is another popular heating medium, particularly in urban buildings. There are many variations on steam-heating systems, utilizing low-pressure, high-pressure, and vacuum circulation to name a few, but basically water is heated in a boiler until it turns to steam, which has a slightly higher pressure than outside air. In the radiator, it gives off its heat and condenses into water, which flows back to the boiler to be reheated. Steam heat systems use smaller diameter pipes than hot-water systems. The installation is simple and the initial cost low. Radiators need not be as large as with hot-water systems because the steam gives off its heat by evaporation. The temperature is relatively higher (about 220° F.). Steam heat helps maintain household humidity at com-

5-37   *Single-pipe gravity steam-heat system (with conversion to vacuum system)*

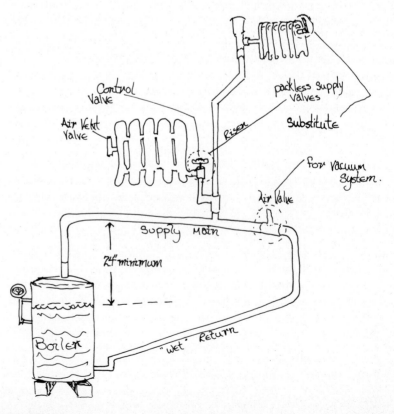

fortable levels. In a single-pipe steam system, condensate flows back along the same pipe as the steam flows up, resulting in the familiar water "hammer" as the steam tries to force the water back up the pipe.

Air must be eliminated from the radiators by the valve in order for steam to enter. As the radiators cool, more air is drawn in through the valves, thus further cooling the radiator. This makes a one-pipe, gravity-steam system somewhat uneven in its heating. The problem can be solved by converting a gravity system to a vacuum system by installing air-and-vacuum valves in place of the original air valves and special packless supply valves for the ordinary radiator control valves. These valves prevent air leakage, and that must be done to insure the proper functioning of the system. The vacuum valve allows air to escape but not reenter as the radiator cools. As the steam condenses in the cooling radiator, a partial vacuum is created, which draws more hot steam into it. Thus the system maintains a more even temperature. Water hammering is also eliminated in a low-pressure steam system.

Beyond routine maintenance, the average homeowner should leave tampering with hot-water or steam systems to a professional. It is a good idea to know the principles involved in the operation of your heating system in any case. Too often we are at the mercy of the machines that are our slaves, and we live our lives surrounded by systems whose functioning is beyond our comprehension, leaving us feeling powerless and abused by forces outside our control. Our forefathers, who made everything they needed themselves, would wonder at the state we've come to.

In the course of your remodeling, it may be necessary to move a radiator or baseboard-heating unit. The homeowner can do this without resorting to a professional. The entire heating system must be drained back to the boiler. Then with the appropriate wrenches, the radiator can be disconnected. The cover plate of a hot-water baseboard unit should be removed and the solder joints in the supply and return pipes heated until they separate. The supply and return lines are cut and capped directly under the floor joists or their point of origin, wherever it is convenient. If the radiator is to be relocated near the same line, a tee inserted in the line can extend it to the desired location. The return line must always slope toward the boiler, at a minimum of 1 inch/20 feet.

Forced hot-air systems are similar to hot-water systems in that they employ a system of ducts to deliver the heated air to registers mounted in the floors, generally along the outside walls under the windows. Cold air is returned by means of a floor grate back to the cellar where it is heated again. A blower

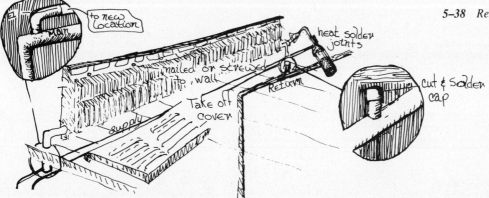

5-38 *Removing a baseboard radiator*

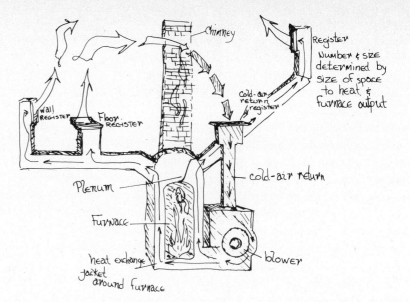

5-39 *Basics of a forced-hot-air heating system*

is used to force the air through the ducts, giving much more rapid and even heat than would be possible through the use of natural convection currents alone. The hot air would otherwise cool too rapidly by the time it reached the second story. The blower is fitted with a sheet-metal jacket that is connected to the cold-air return ducts. Thus the blower actually sucks the cold air from the house and forces it into the furnace, where it is heated and forced into a *plenum*. The latter is a sheet-metal hood over the top of the furnace, a heat chamber that distributes the hot air to ducts that feed the various registers. The surface area of the return register must equal the total surface area of the hot-air registers. Thus a 12 × 12 return is needed to service three 4 × 12 outlets. The number of registers and their size is determined by the space to be heated and the output of the furnace.

An advantage of a forced-hot-air system is that it can be easily connected to operate in conjunction with solar-heat supplementary units.

Alternatives to Conventional Heating Systems:
Solar heating

Conventional heating systems are becoming increasingly expensive to operate as the costs of the fuel upon which their furnaces feed continue to escalate. Radiant electric heat, which was once touted as competitive with oil or gas heat, is now prohibitively expensive. Indeed, electric heat was competitive with fossil fuels only as long as it heated an extremely well-insulated house. An accurate comparison of the true costs of electric heat could be made by comparing the costs of each system in a house equally insulated. Since electric power is generated by the primary combustion of fossil fuels (except for regions where hydroelectric or nuclear plants are operating), the efficiency of the process is low to begin with. A further loss occurs when that electricity is converted back to heat. At least with a home fossil-fuel plant, the fuel is burned only once.

Whatever their efficiencies, heating a house with gas or oil now consumes an inordinate share of the domestic budget. Other options, which were not utilized so long as fuels were cheap, are now becoming competitive. Solar heating is one of these. Completely retrofitting an existing structure for solar heating can be done. The technology and hardware are currently available, and the pay-back period continues to shrink. Architectural firms and solar-heating consultants with the necessary knowledge and skills are proliferating. The owner-builder should consider converting all or part of his or her heating system to solar, as a realistic alternative to fossil-fuel heating costs.

While it is theoretically possible to supply all of the domestic heating and hot-water needs through solar power alone almost anywhere in the country, it is not always economically feasible to do so. In the far North and in habitually cloudy areas like the Pacific Northwest, a conventional or wood-fired back-up system will be necessary to take up the slack on those days when the sun refuses to shine and the wind continues to blow. The outside temperature does not affect the amount of sunshine available, but it does increase the need for heat, often to a point greater than the system can deliver. Even in Canada, the energy contained in the sunshine striking an average house is three times greater than the energy required to heat and light that house each year. The problem is one of efficiency; no system yet operating can recapture anything but a fraction of that munificence.

Solar-heating systems are either active or passive or some hybridization of the two. Passive solar heating is as old as the earth itself. The sun's rays are absorbed by the mass of the planet and slowly radiated back into space. The insulating layer of the atmosphere prevents what would otherwise be a rapid heat loss through this radiation. The mean temperature of the planet remains remarkably stable. Primitive peoples understood this principle intuitively when they built their homes of thick-walled mud to absorb the sun's heat during the day, allowing the interior to remain cool. The cycle reversed at night, enough heat releasing into the cool night air to keep the house comfortable. Passive solar collection utilizes the thermal storage capacities of massive materials such as concrete or rocks, water or mineral salts, to collect large amounts of heat when the sun shines and release it during the night or on cloudy days. The heat can be collected and transferred by circulating fluids or forced hot air into ducts to heat the house.

Active systems begin at this point. They amplify the natural convection patterns of passive systems or even reverse its flow, sucking hot air from the peak of a house and feeding it into the cold-air blower of a furnace, thus preheating the air and lowering fuel consumption. Active solar collectors involve the use of coated plates, which absorb sunlight and transfer heat to a circulating fluid, such as water or—in cold regions—antifreeze, which is pumped or flows by thermal convection to an exchanger that extracts the heat and circulates it throughout the house. These systems can be simple or amazingly complex. The more moving parts, the greater the expense, and the more that can go wrong. Complicated and expensive systems are not necessarily better systems. Technological overkill may satisfy the gadgeteer but do little to return the investment.

Retrofitting the Old House for Solar Heating

Retrofitting an existing structure involves a three-phase operation. Phase 1 should be carried out with any house, solar or conventional, and involves the installation of thermopane windows, tight caulking, and good insulation. Heavy curtains (with weights or velcro tabs sewn into the bottom hem to keep them in place) or insulated shutters should be installed for each window. They are drawn at night to prevent the loss of heat directly through the glass by radiation. Concentrate the windows on the south and southeast walls of the house and reduce or eliminate northern windows. Any coniferous trees that would block the winter sun on the south side should be cut down. Deciduous trees are an asset. They provide summer shading and yet allow the winter sun to penetrate their branches.

The heat collected by a south-facing solar window can be stored if the sunlight is allowed to strike a masonry slab or wall. The construction of such a storage wall is the beginning of phase 2. An exposed-brick or stone hearth or dividing wall that is struck by the low winter sun can be built for the wood stove to sit upon. It will also absorb heat from the stove, which it will then radiate out to the room when the fire dies down. It can easily incorporate the furnace and chimney flues as well. A lean-to greenhouse added to the south wall, with a concrete-slab foundation, not only is a very efficient solar collector but will add much-needed humidity and fresh air to a stuffy winter house as well as the spiritual and nutritional benefits to be derived from growing plants and vegetables. Fresh salad greens in December are a health asset. Ducts running under the concrete slab and into the house help circulate stored heat. The wall between the greenhouse and the main house should be insulated to avoid summer heat build-up and allow the option of shutting the greenhouse down during the coldest winter months.

If your old house has a steel roof with a southern orientation and a 12-12 pitch, it can be painted black and covered with a double-thick layer of Tedlar®/Calwall®, or other plastic coverings. Or a new metal roof can be installed over the existing shingle deck. That brings us to phase 3, the most expensive aspect of the retrofitting project. Cold air is pumped from the basement by the disconnected furnace blower to the roof-top collector, where it is heated by the sun. The heated air is drawn through ducts into a heat exchanger (which can be a recycled truck radiator) in the basement. The duct can be fitted with a damper, which can collect excess heat from the wood stove as well. A small pump circulates water from a 1,000-gallon cistern through the exchanger. This resulting hot water is stored in the well-insulated cistern. At night and on cloudy days, the hot water is circulated through the exchanger, which heats the air to be circulated through the home. A special temperature-differential thermostat with roof-mounted sensors and cistern sensors controls the cycling of the system so that no air is circulated through the roof collector when a heat loss could result. This storage system could also use a rock- or gravel-filled bed to absorb the heated air. The blower would force it into the heating ducts. Such a system would eliminate the need for the liquid heat exchanger and, consequently, for water storage. The ducts to supply basement air to the roof top collector can be built into the outside corner trim of the house or run through the walls.

Finally a commercially available solar panel (costing from $1,000 to $1,800) or a home-built model (costing as little as $300) is installed to supply the domestic hot-water needs. These units are practical anywhere in the country if you are willing to pay the price. Northern conditions require complicated valves and sensors and a nonfreezing fluid cycled through a heat exchanger, to function year round. It is considerably simpler to heat water with a collector until cold weather sets in and then shut it down, drain it, and transfer over to a wood-fired system or conventional gas system.

The cost of retrofitting can vary according to how much of the work is contracted out and how large a percentage of heating needs the owner wishes

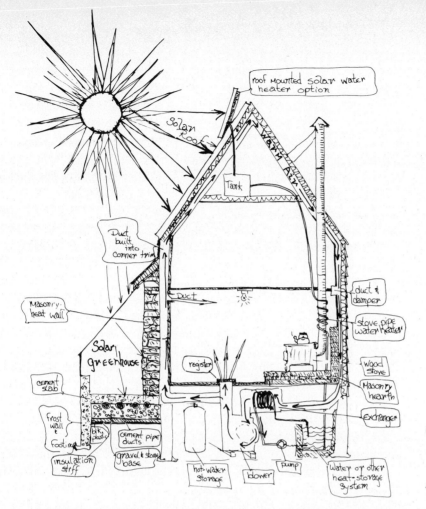

Labels within the figure:
roof mounted solar water heater option
Solar Roof
WARM AIR
Tank
Duct built into corner trim
Masonry heat wall
Duct
duct & damper
Solar greenhouse
stove pipe water heater
register
wood stove
cement slab
Masonry hearth
Frost wall & footing
blk. plastic
cement pipe ducts
exchanger
insulation stuff
gravel & stone base
hot-water storage
blower
pump
Water or other heat-storage system

5–40 *Retrofitted solar house*

to fill with solar power. An actual conversion as outlined above has been done by an owner-builder in Canada, guided by a solar-heating consultant, for a total cost of about $5,000. See ''Dis Ole House Got Sol,'' as reported in *Harrowsmith Magazine,* II, no. 10 (1978), 4. Even at twice the estimated cost, the system could pay for itself in less than fifteen years if conventional heating costs were $700 per year or more.

Wood-Burning Stoves and Furnaces

After languishing in exile in the rural backwaters, wood heat is gaining new respectability. Hard winters and power breakdowns have revealed the fragility of the energy-supply network, which we have heretofore taken for granted. The Constitution does not guarantee our right to oil and gas. The technology that gave us this system is consuming its very foundation. All across the country people are cutting fuel costs by cutting wood. Wood- and solar-heating systems have one thing in common: They both demand involvement. No longer can homeowners simply set their thermostat and let the house heat itself while they go about their business, oblivious to the workings of the system. With a solar house, you must open and shut curtains in response to the weather. It is no longer something external—you learn to live with it, not ignore it. Wood heat requires even more participation.

Wood is an excellent fuel. It is a well-known saw that wood heat warms you three times over: once when you cut it, once when you split and stack it, and finally, once more when you burn it. Basking in the glow of the old wood-burner, the feeling of warmth is more than skin-deep. The winter storms howl outside the walls in vain fury. You are safe and secure, unaffected by the intrigues of Arab sheiks and the machinations of power brokers. More than this, you are heated by wood that you yourself have cut; every piece is a well-known and treasured friend. The memory of clear October skies under a flaming canopy of leaves floats into your mind. You remember the knotty old hollow beech and the limb that pinched the saw bar, the piece that was too tough to split that you saved out to carve the stool you are sitting on; the images dance in the flames as you feed the fire with a piece from that very tree . . . the memories melt, the warmth in your belly rises to your head, you drift with the old dog into the strands of sleep.

Wood heat demands complete attention. You cannot leave the house for extended periods lest the fires go out and the pipes freeze. Many people balk at wood heat for exactly these reasons. Wood heat makes sense for a dairy farmer who is bound to his cows anyway, but for those addicted to outside stimulus and activity, having to return home to stoke the fire is akin to a prison sentence. A back-up heating system, oil or gas fired, that takes over as soon as the fire dies and the temperature drops to a predetermined level is the solution to the dilemma. At present there are a bewildering variety of wood/oil/gas/coal/electric burners that work in conjunction with, or are themselves, the primary heating unit. All of these units function like a conventional forced-air furnace system and are quite expensive, at least three times the cost of a good wood stove. A wood-gasifier system is currently being developed that may revolutionize wood burning by offering the convenience of conventional automatic systems. This system will burn chips or pellets of waste wood in a special automatically fed hopper, which will convert the wood to volatile gases. The gases will be burned in a conventional-type furnace burner, producing high-efficiency combustion and pollution-free exhaust. A whole new local industry may develop to supply the wood chips needed for such a furnace.

Straight wood-burning furnaces are somewhat less expensive than the combination systems and can heat a large house quite comfortably. Stoves are limited in the volume of space they can effectively heat. The upper limit of a single stove is reached with a single-story, Cape Cod farmhouse of five rooms and dimensions of about 24' × 32' (about 10,000 cubic feet). A furnace is really nothing more than a big stove fitted with a sheet-metal plenum and a jacket that warms cold air to circulate either by natural convection or forced blowers. Furnaces can also fire boilers that turn water to steam for heating or heat water for domestic use. A stove is simply a metal box, which holds a fire and heats by radiating to the room from the hot surface and by natural convection currents. Furnaces hold considerably more wood because they consume more wood.

Designing for a totally wood-heated house, utilizing only a stove, requires careful attention to the floor plan. "Central" heating is called such because isolated rooms are served by ducts emanating from a central source, the basement furnace. It is a misnomer of sorts; a one-room cabin heated by a stove in its middle is a more accurate application of the term. Heating with wood stoves involves opening up the house as much as possible to facilitate the circulation

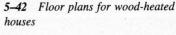

5–41 *Installing registers*

of heat. The alternative is to close off extraneous rooms, to centralize the house around the stove. Bedrooms require little heat during the daylight hours, as they are used only for sleeping. Studies have shown the beneficial health effects of sleeping in cold rooms. The logical extension of this concept of closing off sections of the house is to enclose the entire plumbing system, including pump, water heater, and all pipes, in a single room, insulated from the rest of the house. This boiler-room module can be kept from freezing by a small electric or gas space heater, which is set at the lower end of its range while the owners of the house are away. Indoor plants, of course, will not be possible in a house that is subjected to freezing temperatures.

Floor registers are a simple way to distribute heat throughout the house from the single-source heater. The registers are kept closed during the day, allowing the stove to heat mainly the downstairs areas. At night the registers are opened to warm the bedrooms, while the downstairs cools off somewhat. Registers can be bought new from heating suppliers. Often, used cast-iron registers of quite exotic ornamentation can be found in antique shops.

Where large areas of the house are remote from the main stove, an additional smaller stove is used to heat them. The flexibility of stoves as direct heat sources enables you to supply heat to areas only when needed. A study, office, or den, equipped with its own stove, can be warmed quite easily. Figure 5–42 indicates the basic layout of a wood-stove-heated house. All bedrooms are upstairs except for a guest bedroom/study, which can be heated with its own stove if desired. The key to successful stove heating is to approximate the ideal

5–42 *Floor plans for wood-heated houses*

of that one-room cabin. Spaces can be divided with half partitions, furniture, even plants. The chimney can extend into an exposed masonry wall/hearth that helps hold heat.

The pattern of life is centered around the stove. This is the true difference between "central" heating and point-source heating. In a conventional house, there is no place to go to get warm. All zones are roughly the same temperature. If you enter from outside, chilled to the bone, your body perceives this uniformity as cold. You wander about, uncomfortable, unsatisfied until you gradually thaw out. With a wood heater there is a very definite place to warm up: in front of the wall of radiant heat emanating from the stove. As your body warms, you move farther away from the stove. Nothing could be simpler or more directly satisfying. No thermostats, no motors or blowers, nothing but the relaxing massage of the stove.

Because of natural convection currents, the floor of a house heated by a stove tends to be cold and drafty. Wendell Thomas of North Carolina solved this problem by building his house over a sealed crawlspace. The floor boards stop two inches short of the walls around the perimeter of the house, creating a cold-air return register. As the cold air flows down the outside walls into the basement, the heat stored in the earth floor warms it enough for it to rise through a grate directly under the wood stove. Thus the cellar acts as a plenum. The air cools and flows down the walls to be recycled. The result is a draft-free floor and remarkably steady temperatures. Once the house was left without a fire during a 0° F. winter night. So great was the store of latent heat in the earth that by morning, the temperature had only fallen from a high of 70° to a quite tolerable 50°.

Wood heat is also dry heat. The boards covering the walls behind the heater will begin to shrink. Gaps open between boards that were tightly butted when first nailed. This shrinkage can be minimized by bringing interior sheathing board indoors at least a month, preferably longer, before they are used. The boards are stacked to allow air-free circulation around them. Scraps of boards called stickers are used to separate each layer by at least half an inch. Boards within a layer should not touch each other; separate them about ⅛ inch. Stack the boards in the room in which they will be used, if possible. They will slowly adjust to the average humidity of the room. This step is a necessity for air-dried lumber, as well as for "kiln-dried" lumber that has been stored outdoors for any length of time. The amount of shrinkage increases with the width of the board, as well as with its moisture content. A ten- or twelve-inch-wide board is very attractive as wall paneling but, if green, very unstable. It will shrink enough to expose a ½-inch shiplap joint. Narrow-width boards are preferred unless you are sure that the wide boards are dry. In any case they should be stored indoors. Six-inch paneling with a ½-inch shiplap is an optimum width from the standpoint of speed of coverage and amount of shrinkage. Normal shrinkage will not expose the joint.

When using straight-edged boards, particularly old barn boards, gaps are quite normal and cannot be prevented. The wall itself should first be covered with tarpaper (unlined side out) before the boards are nailed. That creates a plain black background behind the gaps, which actually helps highlight the boards, outlining each with a broad stroke.

Besides drying out the wallboards, wood heat will dry out your lungs, nose, and throat. Radiant heating causes very low humidity, which leads to stuffy noses and dry skin. The hot-air currents set up by convection are like desert winds, depositing a fine dust throughout the house. As the relative humidity is lowered, the air temperature must be raised for the body to feel comfortable. This means that you will need to burn more wood to feel warm. The technological solution is to add a humidifier. Humidifiers heat water and release the vapor into the room air, or else they are installed directly in the furnace heating duct. They require energy to run. A time-honored and less energy-expensive solution is to keep a large basin of water on top of the stove when it is in use. The larger the surface area, the faster the evaporation, and the more moisture released into the room. Old, enameled wash basins are excellent for this purpose. A handful of aromatic herbs, such as rosemary or lavender, can be added to the water and will give off a pleasant scent that relieves stuffiness. Another bonus of this stove-top humidifier is additional heat. As the stove cools during the night, the water gives off the heat it has absorbed while it was being warmed. It functions like a small radiator. Green plants will help keep up the humidity of the house, also. Plants give off water through transpiration, as a by-product of their life processes. It may still be necessary to run a vaporizer at night in rooms where small children are sleeping as their mucous membranes are very vulnerable to drying out.

Of Chimneys

The combustion gases generated by the stove must be vented to the outside. A proper stovepipe installation and workable chimney are crucial not only to the proper functioning of the stove itself but to the life and safety of the house and its occupants. An inadequate installation is a very serious fire hazard. In the rush to convert to wood, all too often not enough attention is given to the stovepipes and chimney.

Your initial inspection of the house should have included the chimneys. A bad chimney is a structural problem that must be given high priority—as high as the foundation or roof problems. Plan to complete any masonry work before cold weather; it will be easier on your fingers. A safe chimney must have a liner, or flue tile. Individual tiles are made of fire clay and are cemented together from the fireplace smoke shelf or chimney base to the top of the chimney. These tiles create a tight, fire-proof duct for combustion gases. These gases would otherwise work between cracks in the mortar and circulate in the house, resulting in soot-blackening and sometimes fires. A chimney fire can easily heat the bricks to the combustion point of the wood frame surrounding them. The liner insulates the bricks from direct contact with any fire. Also, equally important, a drafty chimney will not draw properly.

If a chimney you plan to use is lacking a flue liner, it must be demolished and rebuilt. A *temporary* expedient, which will last until the chimney can be rebuilt, is to run galvanized stovepipe up the chimney directly from the stove or furnace. Don't use the fireplace if the flue is unlined. The chimney must be sealed at the outlet between the brick and stovepipe.

Even if a chimney has a liner, quite often the portion projecting above the roof will need replacement. The mortar crumbles from exposure to the weather, leaving the bricks in place by virtue of their weight alone. Rotten mortar is grainy, is white in color, and crumbles quite easily. Tap the bricks with the butt of your palm. If they move or can be lifted free of the mortar bed,

5-43   *Chimney construction*

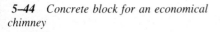
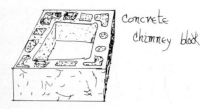

5-44   *Concrete block for an economical chimney*

ready the trowel. Remove the old brickwork until a sound layer is reached. Most likely that will be just below the roof line, unless the chimney is old enough for the mortar to have rotted along its entire length. Examine the bricks themselves as you remove them. Old chimney bricks can be reused if they have not become brittle or crumbly from exposure. The topmost bricks will most likely shatter or ''spall'' and should be discarded or used to line your garden paths.

A loose chimney will not draw well but will tend to smoke and downdraft. Fissures between the bricks negate the chimney effect. That effect is directly related to the height. The draw of a chimney is also affected by its width: the wider the chimney, the less friction between the walls and the rising smoke. That is why the flue tiles have rounded corners. A round flue is even better. Conversely, unlined, rough brick will slow down the smoke, even if all else is tight, causing substantial creosote buildup. An increase in flue diameter will not compensate for lack of height. It merely reduces the velocity of the smoke, increasing cooling and condensation. Thus there is a definite relationship between height and volume. A one-story house with a low roof does not permit a high-enough chimney to produce an ideal draft. The tip of the chimney should be at least 15 feet above the thimble.

In older houses, it was quite common for upstairs bedrooms to have individual stoves that vented to a chimney built upon a base of upright boards. The chimney extended only through the attic. Sometimes the stovepipe from a heater on the lower floor passed through the ceiling and warmed the bedroom before it entered the half-chimney. Although half-chimneys saved on brick and labor, because of their short length, they were susceptible to the problems outlined above, as well as causing floors and ceilings to sag.

The top of the chimney must project at least 2 feet above the ridge line of the house, or any other ridge line that is within 10 feet (horizontally) of the chimney. Chimneys not centered directly over the ridge should extend at least 2½ feet above it. A chimney draws because of a change in temperature. When the difference is great enough, hot air will flow toward the cooler outside air, which can actually be drawn down the chimney at the same time (causing down-drafting and poor draw). Air moving across the lip of the chimney creates a partial vacuum, which also helps to create the draft, especially when the chimney is cold and the fire newly kindled. If these air currents are obstructed, the chimney will fail to draw properly. A low chimney is a frequent cause of down-drafting. Large trees overhanging the roof can create turbulence and eddies, which allow cold air to sweep down the chimney. If raising the height of the chimney does not solve the problem, the trees will have to be cut down.

Once the chimney is torn down, several options are available for rebuilding. A masonry chimney is the safest, most permanent, and most labor-intensive type you can build. It takes considerable experience to lay brick or stone with speed and accuracy. The amateur mason will find that laying up a chimney is slow work. If the chimney is to be completely concealed within the walls, a lot of time and expense can be saved by building it from concrete chimney blocks. These are special hollow blocks, which form the outside and inside walls of the chimney in a single course. A flue liner is necessary. For multiflue chimneys, standard concrete blocks are used instead. The disadvantage of using concrete blocks is that for anything larger than a single flue, the outside dimensions of the chimney become cumbersome. A concrete block chimney can be faced with brick veneer or slate flagstones after it is constructed. This enables the homeowner to build a solid chimney quickly and then undertake the labor of facing it when time is available. Block chimneys can also be stuccoed with cement or plaster for a pleasing effect. Several coats will be necessary to prevent the joints from showing through.

Each individual heating element connected to the chimney requires its own flue. Two stoves should never vent into the same flue unless the flue size is increased at the point of connection of the higher stove. But this method should be used only if no other solution is possible because it does lower the efficiency of the draft. An exception to the rule is the vent from a gas or oil hot-water heater, which can be connected to the furnace flue.

Brick makes a very beautiful chimney. There is a wide variety of brick types, colors, and textures. If the old bricks are in good condition they can be reused. Clean used bricks by knocking off any mortar that may still adhere to them with the point of a brick hammer. Avoid striking the brick itself, as it may split. A wire brush will remove the loose scale, soot, and mortar. Old bricks should be soaked in water prior to use to prevent a rapid absorption of moisture from the mortar. If you are using old brick, remember that you will need additional bricks because the new chimney will be larger and will require more bricks per course to accommodate the flue tile. The old bricks from the chimney can be mixed with other used brick if they are of the same size. Genuinely antique bricks will be handmade and of odd sizes. They will not mix with machine-made bricks. Save them for a special project. If you do use them in your chimney, hide the change from one style to another between floors and ceilings.

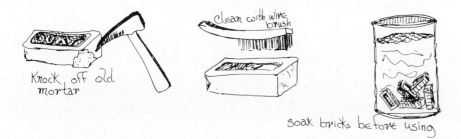

5–45 *Cleaning used bricks*

To lay up a chimney, begin in the cellar with a solid footing. A concrete pad at least 1 foot deep and 3 feet square will carry a single-flue chimney. Footings for larger chimneys should extend at least 6 inches beyond the sides of the chimney. Fieldstone chimneys require deeper and wider footings because of the tremendous weight of the stones (such chimneys weigh 50 tons or more). A 4-foot depth is recommended. Pour an 8-inch walled hollow square and fill it with concrete and loose stones. Pour a slab over this. The concrete should cure for at least three days before the chimney is laid.

The flue tiles are set in place before the brickwork. Each tile is leveled and plumbed and will serve as a rough guide for the brick laying. A plumb bob hung from the underside of the roof or ceiling opening to the foundation will mark the outside corner of the chimney. Stretch a string tightly between the roof and slab. Tie the end to a masonry nail driven into the slab. Do this while the cement is still ''green.'' Repeat the operation to mark all four corners. Although a skilled mason will lay up a chimney with only a single line and a level, the novice will find it helpful to use the string method to keep the chimney plumb. Lay brick up to the height of the first flue tile and then spread a bead of mortar on the edge of the tile and carefully set the next tile in place. It is neither

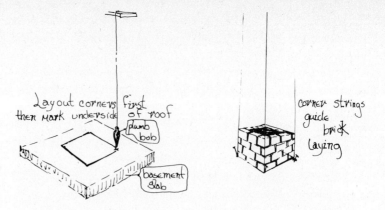

5-46 *Laying up a plumb chimney*

necessary nor desirable to fill the space between the tile and the bricks. Enough mortar will drop down between to hold the flues in place. The air space acts as an insulator between the flue and brickwork. Check each course of bricks for level and use the thickness of the mortar bed to compensate for any slight irregularities or deviations from level.

It is possible to offset a chimney so that it will fit around an obstruction and avoid cutting a rafter. In no case should the angle of the offset be greater than 60 degrees, nor should the center line of the upper flue fall beyond the center line of the lower chimney wall. Flue tiles must be cut to the complementary angle of the offset. Chimneys can be *corbeled* (extended-outward) by projecting each course out beyond the lower one, no more than 1 inch at a time. Not only is corbeling decorative but the larger amount of masonry will withstand the weather for a longer time. The section should extend down below the roofline at least 6 inches, unless only the upper few layers of the chimney lip are to be corbeled. Corbeling is a way of increasing the size of the chimney to accept an additional flue from a second story or attic stovepipe.

The chimney must be flashed where it passes through the roof. Because a masonry chimney is a stable structure relative to a wood frame, *counterflashing* is recommended to compensate for changes in the height of the roof to the chimney. If the chimney were tightly tied to the roof by its flashing, the metal

5-47 *Offset chimney*

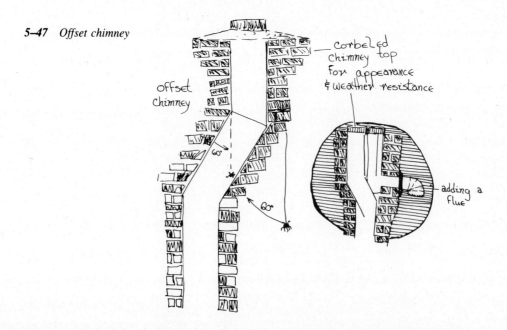

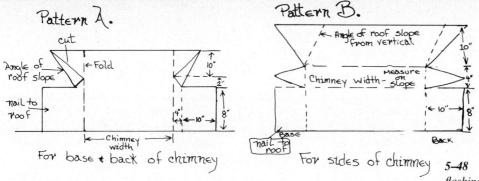

5–48 *Patterns for perfect chimney flashings*

would tear or leak as the roof sagged or the chimney settled. The brickwork could also crack. Lead or copper should be used for the flashing inserted into the brickwork. It is more expensive but will outlive the building and can be very easily bent to conform not only to brick but to stone work as well. A layer of flashing is also fastened to the roof between the shingle courses. This in turn is covered by the layer inserted into the joints of the masonry. The overlap of the two layers seals out water. A pattern for cutting the base flashing is shown in Figure 5–48. It requires 22-inch-wide flashing metal. It looks complicated and it is, but it works perfectly. If you are more interested in getting the job done rather than doing it perfectly, trust to flashing cement and the malleability of the metal to seal over any gaps. You won't be able to see it from the ground.

The flashing for the side of the chimney is either a single continuous piece that runs under the shingles, as in pattern b (the shingles are cemented to it) or else it is *stepped* (cut into 8-inch-wide strips inserted between each layer of shingles). A layer of flashing is then covered by a course of shingle. Use the pattern for the side flashing to lay out the base and back-corner pieces. Measure in 18 inches from either end and cut square across the piece. When using these flashings with steel roofing, fasten them to the roofing with sheet-metal screws and lay a bead of flashing cement between the flashing and roofing.

On any roof slope that exceeds a 5-12 pitch, you will need a saddle or staging platform to work off of as you lay your bricks. When the chimney runs through the ridge, a simple saddle will allow you to work from all four sides. Where the chimney enters the roof below the ridge, roof brackets are used to support a staging plank. A wider staging can be constructed with custom brackets

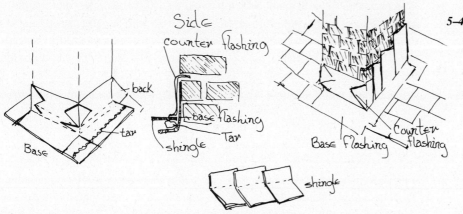

5–49 *Flashing around the chimney*

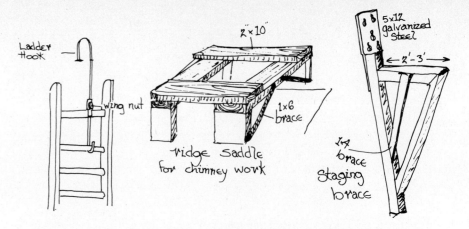

5–50   *Working on the roof*

of 2 × 6 lumber. Use a blunt ladder hook over the ridge to provide access to these platforms. A sharp hook could puncture the old roofing.

The flue should project at least 4 inches above the last layer of bricks. A 2-inch-thick layer of mortar is used to cap off the opening. It should slope away from the flue to shed water and help the wind sweep over the chimney top. Various ornamental treatments are possible for finishing chimneys, as well. The capped chimney will prevent the rain water from entering.

Install a cast-iron clean-out door at the very base of the chimney, to enable the periodic removal of ash build-up.

5–51   *Chimney cap treatment*

Cutting flue tile requires patience. The material is very hard and brittle. A skilsaw equipped with a special masonry cutting blade will cut entire tiles by repeating scoring cuts along the line of the cut until the tile breaks cleanly when struck with a hammer. You should cut about half-way through. Another method is to pack the tile with sand, which will act as a shock absorber and carefully break a hole through the section to be removed with a carpenter's nail set. Expand the hole bit by bit. Do not worry about getting an exact line, as gaps can be filled with mortar. This method is especially useful for cutting round openings for stovepipe thimbles.

When a chimney extends through a steep-pitched roof at a point below the ridge, a chimney saddle will be necessary to prevent leakage caused by ice and snow build-up on the back side of the chimney. A saddle is nothing more than a small gable dormer framed directly over the roof boarding and flashed and shingled exactly like a standard valley. It can also be completely covered with sheet metal and coated with tar. The saddle keeps snow from accumulating. When a chimney penetrates the roof close to the eaves, and therefore must rise high above the roof, wrought-iron reenforcing angle braces should be fastened into the mortar joints to help anchor it to the roof.

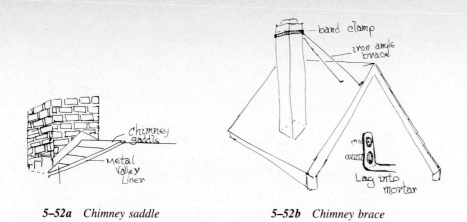

5–52a *Chimney saddle*   **5–52b** *Chimney brace*

The connection between a chimney and a stove is made through a metal collar (thimble) inserted in the brickwork and flue. The bricks are cut with a brick hammer or 3-inch brick chisel to fit close to the thimble. Any gaps are filled in with mortar. The stovepipe passes through the thimble into the hole cut in the flue.

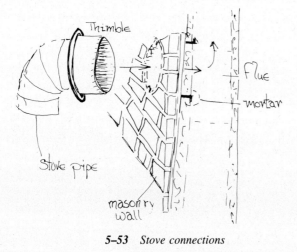

5–53 *Stove connections*

Where a chimney passes through a floor or roof, a minimum clearance of 2 inches between it and all combustibles should be maintained. Do not stuff insulation into the gap. Although the material itself will not burn, it can become hot enough to cause whatever it is touching to catch on fire. The gap between the chimney and wall is covered with a metal trim-collar (which will dissipate heat quickly) or by extending the sheetrock wall flush to it (sheet rock does not absorb heat well). For the same reasons, asbestos shields should never be mounted directly to the wall behind a stove but, instead, should be separated by a minimum 1-inch air space. Porcelain-fence insulators will keep an asbestos sheet away from the wall and are themselves noncombustible.

If a chimney must pass through a beam that cannot be cut without weakening it, the last full course of brick is laid tightly up under the beam, and the next courses are laid on edge. This results in a savings of over 2 inches. If additional clearance is needed, notch the beam itself (no more than one-quarter of the total width).

The masonry of a fireplace can be used to support heavy beams that would otherwise pass through it. Lay the mortar and masonry up to the beam.

5–54 *Running a chimney to a beam*

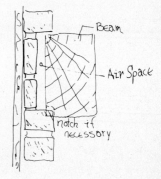

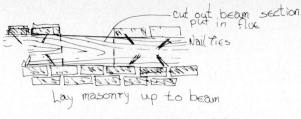

5–55   *Cutting a beam for chimney hole*

Pole-barn nails or large spikes are driven into the beam to act as ties to the masonry. Once the supporting mortar has set, the beam can be cut out and removed. Additional ties are driven into the butt ends and the masonry work completed. Steel plates can be lag-screwed into the beams for extra-strong masonry anchors.

The flue liner of a chimney will withstand temperatures of up to 1800° F. without cracking. This makes them safe for any type of fire and, so long as proper clearances between combustibles are observed, virtually unaffected by chimney fires. But as mentioned elsewhere, a masonry chimney requires a great deal of labor to build and a certain amount of skill and a great deal of not inexpensive brick. A far more flexible system is afforded by the prefabricated chimney made of double-walled stainless-steel pipe sections filled with asbestos insulation. The most popular of these systems is sold under the trade name Metalbestos®. These chimneys are expensive by the linear foot, but can be assembled in a matter of hours, require no foundations and can be hung from the ceiling or roof, and will give years of trouble-free service. The cost of a Metalbestos® chimney is far less than a chimney of brick or block built by a hired mason. It is slightly less expensive than an owner-built masonry chimney as well. Metalbestos® systems are complete with installation instructions and fittings that allow the unit to be fitted to the roof slope and properly capped. Because they require so little space, they can be concealed in a wall or closet. They will withstand a temperature of 1400° F. for a short period and are designed to operate at 1000° F. for extended periods of time—more than adequate for a wood fire.

Stovepipes:

Basic principles of heating with wood

The stovepipe that connects the stove to its chimney is the weakest and most potentially dangerous link in the entire system. Improper stovepipe installation, coupled with poor wood burning practice, leads to creosote build-up and, eventually, chimney fires. A fire in a flue-lined masonry chimney is not a serious threat. Indeed the old-timers often cleaned their chimneys out by deliberately lighting a chimney fire to consume accumulated creosote. It is a much more sensible idea to clean out the chimney periodically rather than to burn it out, intentionally or accidentally. A burlap bag full of chains or sand lowered down the chimney will help scrape the liner free of creosote. Do this in the fall before you start your fires. A chimney fire in a thin-walled steel pipe is another matter altogether. As the pipe changes color from cherry red to orange and begins to melt, great gouts of molten metal fall to the floor, and the remaining stovepipe becomes a blowtorch that can ignite the house.

When wood is burned, volatile gases are given off. So is a large quantity of water, which exits as steam. If the temperature of the pipe drops to around 240° F., these unburned gases combine with the water vapor to produce a brown liquid, pyroligneous acid. As more water boils off from the acid, it turns blacker, until it is deposited as evil-smelling and flammable creosote. Because the creosote is sticky, the friction against the draft increases, allowing even greater amounts to build up. These deposits remain in the chimney until the coldest night of the year, when the old stove is really cranking. The temperature in the pipe or chimney finally reaches the flash point of the creosote, and a ferocious chimney fire rages into being. It is a fact that more fires occur on the coldest nights in wood-burning country.

Creosote build-up can be prevented by:

1. BURNING DRY, HARD WOOD. Green wood contains a large amount of water, which must be driven off before the wood will burn much at all. The temperatures at which this process takes place do not much exceed 212° F. That makes green wood an ideal creosote generator. Hardwood is preferable to the coniferous species, which tend to be naturally high in creosote-producing resins. Pine is the worst offender of all and should never be burned green. Balsam, cedar, spruce, and hemlock, in roughly decreasing order, are not nearly as resinous but do not give up very much heat per cord.

2. DO NOT DAMP DOWN A NEW LOAD OF WOOD. Allow the wood to burn well before turning down the damper. New wood lowers the temperature of the stove gases drastically and requires a good air supply for efficient combustion. Poor air produces many unburned by-products.

3. USE A GOOD STOVE. Modern stoves are designed with a series of baffles that lengthen the combustion path, allowing for secondary, and even tertiary, burning. The greater the amount of volatile gases burned in the stove, the greater the heat given off, the more even and controllable the fire, and the less creosote formed.

4. KEEP THE PIPE RUN AS SHORT AS POSSIBLE. Single-wall pipe is an excellent radiator of heat. Black pipe emits more heat than galvanized. As the length of the pipe run increases, the flue gases cool. Avoid horizontal pipe runs or excessive bends, both of which cut down on draft and provide places for creosote and soot to collect. Horizontal runs are especially dangerous, as enough soot can collect in them to plug the pipe completely. Keep all seams on near-horizontal runs opposite the bottom. A split seam can spill hot ashes on the floor.

5. NEVER PASS SINGLE-WALL STOVEPIPE DIRECTLY THROUGH A ROOF DECK, FLOOR, OR WALL. Avoid using it outside the house. Stovepipe should run into a Metalbestos® chimney at the ceiling. If it must run through a floor, separate it by 12 inches from combustibles. Support the stovepipe with a sheet-metal collar. If pipe is run through a wall, the same metal collar should be used to maintain safe clearance. Pipe used outside a house will quickly cool the flue gases and cause condensation. Outside pipes, if they are used at all, should be Metalbestos®. A single-wall pipe will sometimes fail to draw unless a wad of newspaper is lighted and stuck up the bottom of the outlet to start a warm-air flow.

Creosote has a nasty habit of dropping down the stovepipe from the seams. Besides staining the floor, it will often burn, giving off an odor similar to frying hog hairs. The conventional method of assembling stove pipe should be reversed. The crimped sections should point down. Any creosote will then flow down inside the pipe, to be consumed in the fire. A double-crimped section may be necessary to fit the pipe into the collars of some stoves or into a Metalbestos chimney. Sheet-metal crimpers can be bought at the hardware store, although many sheet-metal shops have a crimping machine that you can use for a small charge.

If you heat with wood stoves and would like to heat your hot water from the stove, a coil will be needed inside the top of the stove. Winding a pipe around the stovepipe alone will not transfer sufficient heat to raise the water temperature. Any joints on this heating pipe should be brazed with a welding torch rather than soldered, as the heat of the stove fire will melt a solder joint. The storage tank for the hot water will have to be mounted above the stove to utilize the thermosiphoning effect. Plans for such a system and the necessary hardware are available from Blazing Showers, Box 327-A, Point Arena, Calif. 95468, for $2.50.

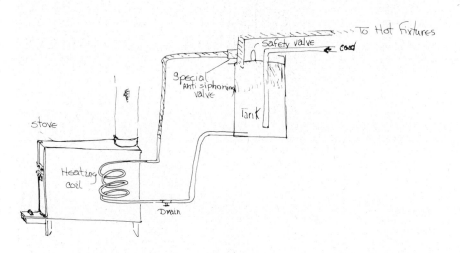

5–56 *Heating water from the wood stove*

Various heat extractors are manufactured that can be installed into a stovepipe. They provide an additional surface for heat radiation and are often equipped with a small blower to circulate the hot air. Keep the length of the stovepipe short because these units can extract enough heat to lower flue temperatures drastically.

Fireplaces

Much has been written about the inefficiency of fireplaces as a heat source. While exact figures vary, it is quite likely that their overall efficiency does not exceed 15 percent. Because fireplaces heat only by direct radiation, the bulk of the fire's heat goes up the chimney. The chimney sucks in much more air than is required for combustion of the logs. This air is supplied by infiltration, which means that the warm air in the house is constantly being replaced with cold outside air. A chimney used in conjunction with a central-heating furnace could actually result in a net heat loss. The amount of heat required to warm the infiltrating air may be greater than the heat radiated by the fireplace. The rest of the house will be frigid while the family huddles in the small circle of warmth by the hearth, or else the furnace works overtime to compensate for the heat loss.

No matter how true or compelling the arguments against fireplaces may be, the notion that a house is not a home without a fireplace still persists. No amount of reasoned analysis can alter this dimly understood but deeply felt conviction. Prometheus bound . . . in the dim and smoky womb of a rock cave the first man tamed the breath of the gods. Fire was safety from the dangers of the night. These ancestral memories are inscribed into the frame of our consciousness. The common origin of the words "hearth, home, and heart," their association with centering, of drawing around the fire, reverberate back through the ages to that ancient family of hunters huddled around the glowing embers, warm and well fed, while the night wind howls outside this magic circle.

When someone is asked to draw an image of home, invariably a fireplace is included. It is the icon of the family, which gathers together by a blazing hearth. The fire is frequently described as "cheerful" or "cozy." When our presidents address us with their words of assurance, they are frequently seated beside a flickering grate. Although wolves of real flesh and blood no longer howl outside the door, the memory lingers. As we stare into the dancing flames, visions are revealed, and old feelings, like ashes under the grate, are stirred. The room softens and draws closer, dreams shimmer beyond the sphere of sight. For a moment the mind's clutch slips—who are these planners and designers that could counsel us to forsake these depths for the sake of efficiency? And yet they are right. A fireplace is an unconscionable luxury, a fuel-squandering beast living within the walls of our cave. What alternatives are there?

The gross inefficiencies of fireplaces can be overcome to some extent. A new fireplace should never be built on the outside wall of the house. The old-timers realized this when they built their houses centered around the chimney. The bricks of an outside chimney are kept cold by the air, and a great deal of heat is lost through them. Creosote build-up is a problem, and such chimneys frequently do not draw well. By providing a direct connection from the hearth of a central fireplace to an outside air source, you can avoid having the warm air of the house consumed by the fire. A register installed in the hearth in front of the fire grate and connected by a six-inch stovepipe duct that runs under the floor and out the basement wall will draw outside air directly to the fire. A damper should be installed in the pipe, so that it can be closed when not in use. The damper can be operated from above the floor by remote control if it is a sliding-disc type.

Additional heat can be recovered by constructing or buying a C-shaped grate of hollow pipe. Cold air drawn in under the fire is warmed and circulated into the room as it exits from the top of the pipes. Such units are commercially obtainable under the name Thermograte®. You can also build into the chimney itself ducts that allow cool air to be warmed as it passes along the brick liner and flows out into the room from an opening above the firebox. The Heatilator® chimney works on this principle. Small electric blowers will increase the air circulation. A damper should always be installed in the throat of the fireplace below the smoke shelf. The damper is kept closed when the fire is not in use. Good firebox design will help increase the amount of radiation. There are standard tables that list the dimensions of the various parts of the fireplace with respect to each other for a given size opening. These relationships are very precise and must be observed if the chimney is to operate properly. The Audel *Carpenter's and Builder's Library,* Vol. 3 and Willis Wagner's *Modern Car-*

5–57   An efficient fireplace

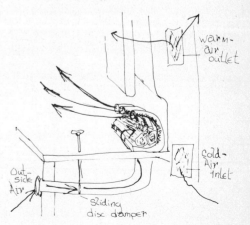

pentry both include complete tables. The definitive treatise on the subject of fireplace design was written by Count Rumford and forms the basis of Vrest Orton's *The Forgotten Art of Building a Good Fireplace*. The ruminations of this eighteenth-century English nobleman are based on sound theory and minute empirical observations and have been irrefutably validated by actual construction. The Rumford fireplace is characterized by a very shallow, sloping firebox. The fire seems almost to rest on the floor. It radiates a good deal more heat out into the room than the traditional designs and always draws perfectly.

A well-designed inside fireplace, with an outside air supply and a circulating grate, will operate with far greater efficiency than the unengineered fireplace. Its efficiency can approach that of some of the draftier wood stoves. Since the fire seldom dies down enough to shut the damper until long after the householders have gone to bed, heat loss is still a problem. A pair of insulated steel shutters or glass doors that can be closed when the fire starts to die down will mitigate this problem. An automatic damper, which would shut down by barometric or temperature differences, would be a boon to the wood burner. (There is an opportunity for an inventive entrepreneur.) The Chimilator® is a damper mounted at the chimney top which, to some extent, accomplishes this. When the chimney is shut off at the top, the heat-robbing column of cold air is replaced with insulating dead air. If you have an existing fireplace that cannot be retrofitted with shutters, consider bricking it up completely and installing a good tight Franklin-type stove.

The construction of a complete masonry chimney and fireplace is precise work. The dimensions of the various parts are critical, and the framing of the opening requires considerable experience. The home mason would do better to install a prefabricated steel firebox (the Heatilator®). Such units are properly sized and, in addition to providing extra heat circulation, are also a fool-proof form for the brickwork. The brick itself must be kept from direct contact with the steel by a one-inch layer of fiberglass insulation. If the masonry were laid against the metal it would crack because of the rapid expansion of the steel when heated. Although Heatilators® are fairly expensive ($500 or more), their cost is offset some by savings in materials and labor. They are backed by a guarantee of twenty years, which is a long way short of forever. A masonry fireplace can be built to incorporate the Heatilator-type venting system within the brickwork. In modification of this principle, you can install the inlet in the back of the firebox and heat the air as it rises through a chamber and out a register in the front of the fireplace. Figure 5–58 shows construction details of a typical fireplace. Notice that the hearth is not set directly upon a wood floor. If it were, shrinkage and settling would cause it to crack. Hearths are built on cantilevered slabs or brick arches supported by a wood frame until they are set. Considerable time and expense can be saved by constructing the base portion of the fireplace from concrete blocks.

Fieldstone fireplaces are built exactly like brick fireplaces but on a larger scale because of the greater size of the individual structural units. Working with stone requires patience and a careful eye, both in selecting good-quality stones and creating a pleasing pattern when they are laid. Stones must bind each course together exactly like brickwork, and running joints are to be avoided. Stagger the joints between layers.

If the arguments in favor of architectural efficiency have triumphed over your archetypical needs, there is still a compromise that allows you the psychological benefits of an open fire without the financial drain of the fireplace

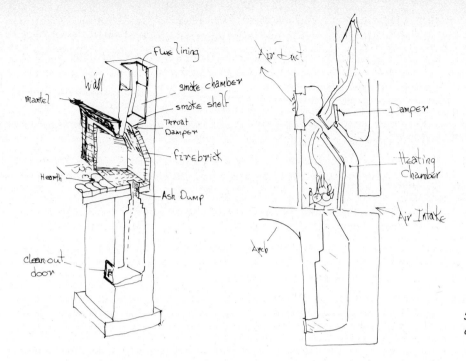

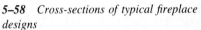

5–58   *Cross-sections of typical fireplace designs*

itself. Even the most efficient fireplace will require an extra cord of wood because of its very presence in the house. The so-called Franklin stove, the original of which was invented by the redoubtable Dr. Franklin himself, is the answer. Most of the Franklin stoves on the market are useless ornaments and drafty and inefficient heaters, to boot. But the Jøtul Combi®, the Vermont Casting Company's Defiant®, and the Hearthstone® are all built with doors that really seal tightly. These units work like conventional wood stoves when the shutters are closed, and when they are open, you can ponder the mysteries of the universe as you stare into the depths of their flames.

> . . . you now realize that your consciousness was feeding upon appearance like a flame upon fuel. With the cessation of the process of combustion, physical and mental consciousness cease to function, with the result that the basic consciousness of being emerges with greater clearness.
>
> [Pir Vilayat, *Toward the One*]

CHAPTER VI

THE VISIBLE REWARDS AT LAST: FINISHING TOUCHES

For the important thing in a living house is not splendor, but refinement.

[Li Liweng, *The Art of Living*]

The interior finish of the house is the mirror of the builder. No other aspect is so personalized, so indelibly stamped with the signature of individual character as the treatment given to the walls and cabinetry. We have seen how the roof, the frame, the walls, the wires and plumbing of a house reflect the bodily image of its builders. As a smile reveals the mood of the smiler, the interior finish of a house is a window of the builder's soul. We speak of the "feeling" of a house, and there is that impalpable, but nonetheless very real, vibration that arises out of the form of a house but is composed of something more—the relationship between the house and those that live in it. It is a synergistic partnership, a marriage of mind and matter. Ideally, the design of a house is an expression of the felt needs of a particular individual, the play of a discreet personality, a tapestry of wood and stone. The house is a kind of ego play.

It can easily become a seductive obsession, a millstone of misplaced purpose: the goal rather than the means. But as the true craftsman loses his or her ego in the work, becoming one with it, there is something that happens between a house and its builder. The form and content merge, to give it the breath of life. The house and builder together are the brush with which the spirit writes upon this world. Thus does the house extend beyond its builder in fulfillment of a larger and older pattern. As houses remain and their builders depart, like leaves from the tree, something of that love is left behind, absorbed into the walls, where it reverberates, like ghost tracks of plankton in the night sea. We swim in these waters of long-lived lives, are bathed and renewed and carried off into our own sleep.

The interior of the house is the bridge between the builder and the building. It is on the interface of the inner walls that the labors of structure, the roots and necessity, the branches, finally burst into bloom. And lived within, they at last bear fruit. Because the visual results are so immediately gratifying, the psychological satisfaction is great. Building is the art of making what is seen only in the mind's eye visible in the eye of the world. Images in the mind acquire weight. As an image is expressed in the work, a tension grows between the weight of the image and its expression. A sense of balance must be maintained, or the weight of the image will overwhelm the imagination, like concrete bursting a weak form, and drown the spirit in a hardening slump of ego. When the work is completed, the tension is relieved and the weight dissolved, the forms are stripped, the real work begins.

Finish work requires a new mind, a different pace. The sledgehammer is put aside, the plane iron honed. The secret of finish work is to handle finish wood as you handle your food, with clean hands and a respect for its nature. Washing your hands before you pick up a board will save hours of sanding smudges off cabinet surfaces. Stacking boards where they will not be walked upon and where they will stay dry will keep them usable. Select each piece with an eye for the grain, both structurally (straightness) and compositionally (the flow of knots, twists) as a picture. Remember above all that steel is harder than wood. A "hammer blossom" is the issue of this misbegotten union, and about as desirable in finish work as a wart upon your nose.

And what is the mind of the woodworker like?

Woodworker Ch'ing carved a piece of wood and made a bell stand, and when it was finished, everyone who saw it marveled, for it seemed to be the work of gods or spirits. When the marquis of Lu saw it, he asked, "What art is it you have?"

Ch'ing replied, "I am only a craftsman—how would I have any art? There is one thing however. When I am going to make a bell stand, I never let it wear out my energy. I always fast in order to still my mind. When I have fasted for three days, I no longer have any thought of congratulations or rewards, or titles or stipends. When I have fasted for five days, I no longer have any thought of praise or blame, of skill or clumsiness. And when I have fasted for seven days, I am so still that I forget I have four limbs and a form and body. By that time, the ruler and his court no longer exist for me. My skill is concentrated and all outside distractions fade away. After that, I go into the mountain forest and examine the Heavenly nature of the trees. If I find one of superlative form, and I can see a bell stand there, I put my hand to the job of carving; if not, I let it go. This way I am simply matching up "Heaven" with "Heaven." That's probably the reason that people wonder if the results were not made by spirits.

[Chuang Tzu: *Basic Writings*]

By the time you are ready to finish off the interior walls your original plans will have changed many times. As you live within your evolving work, new possibilities and directions are suggested. Materials may become available by happenstance, the cash flow may have switched channels. Before you pick up the hammer and saw, pick up the pencil and paper again. During the process of construction, you may have found it helpful to keep a design notebook, almost a scrapbook, in which you jot down brainstorms, fantasies, ideas for arranging

your house, clippings from magazines, articles, and sources for materials. Despite their slickness and emphasis on expensive surfaces, many of the home-building and remodeling magazines may carry ideas or photographs that will be springboards for your own concepts. I find the photo backgrounds of advertisements a particularly rich inspirational lode. Also, browse through a copy of *Handmade Houses: A Guide to the Woodbutcher's Art* by Art Boericke and Barry Shapiro. Hone your imagination. Let it simmer like the stewpot on the back burner, adding what is needed as the smell and taste evolve.

And then pick up your hammer.

Interior Wall Finishes:
The great debate—gypsum wallboards versus wood paneling

For some strange reason gypsum wallboard, familiarly known as sheetrock or dry wall, has become almost the only finish used for interior walls and ceilings. Speed of application and low cost are given as the reasons for the aesthetic halitosis that allows every wall and ceiling surface of a house to be reduced to a blank and arid expanse, smothered with this overused and underutilized material.

Although sheetrock possesses many desirable characteristics, ultimately the labor and material costs saved in initial application are more than offset by the costs and labor of taping the joints and papering or painting the finished surfaces. It is really not much more economical than other finish options when all costs are considered. *Real* wood paneling is nailed to the wall, and no further finish is necessary other than a coat of linseed oil or urethane varnish. The use of native woods, purchased from local sawmills, results in a wall that not only compares favorably in price to sheetrock but is infinitely more pleasing to look upon than the dull surfaces that mirror the vacuum of imagination that is a typical house interior.

Prefinished wood paneling is considered the ultimate low-cost interior finish. It has all the hallmarks of a product of modern high technology: fast, convenient, no fuss, no mess, easy to install, inexpensive, consuming great amounts of energy in its manufacture, transported from far away, and totally inferior to the product it purports to replace. Prefinished wood paneling sheets, unless they are of the highest quality (and therefore more expensive per square foot than the real thing), do not in the slightest way resemble real wood. Plastic at least can honestly be itself and can be used creatively for its inherent properties of boldness and durability. Bogus materials, such as imitation bricks, fake beams, and prefab wall panelings have no soul of their own. They negate what spirit the house may be struggling to give voice to. If people could feel the emptiness of these products, they would never consider living with them. Unfortunately this hollowness is often an expression of the unfelt void within the builder and the homeowner.

Sheetrock is undeniably a versatile material. Unlike the objection to wood ''paneling,'' it is not the nature of the product that is in itself offensive but the way in which it is so thoughtlessly used, without appreciation of its possibilities as a design element. Sheetrock is above all a neutral material. If used with wood, or a contrasting surface, the tension between texture and space is highlighted. Dramatic planes are delineated, dark rooms lightened. Low ceilings in a dark room seem higher when covered with blank white. A hard, glaring surface is softened and made interesting by the use of textured paint. Sheetrock can be used as a noncompetitive background for furniture, pictures, household talismans and tokens, or as a strong contrast to relieve what might otherwise become a tyranny of busy grain and linearity of wood. It can add or subtract space. The key is to vary the rhythm: to use sheetrock in combination with other materials or finishes to create interest and tension, to enhance the best qualities of each material.

Unfortunately that is rarely done. Builders or homeowners slap the stuff over every wall and ceiling surface and give no thought to the system or lack thereof that they are creating for themselves to live within. The fundamental psychological effect of our environment upon our well-being, our emotional equilibrium, is ignored for reasons of false economy.

Sheetrock: *Installation and finishing*

Another popular misconception about sheetrock is that finishing is a job easily done by the amateur. The picture of the smiling woman, trowel in hand, tailored jeans (if a woman can do it, anyone can), is an outright lie, unless she happens to be a veteran mud hen. It may well be that the average woman will do a better taping job than the average male simply because she has had to develop a high level of patience to survive in a male-dominated world. Patience, a steady hand, and practice are required to finish the joints between dry-wall panels; it takes a good deal of experience to get the feel for the material, (the mud, as sheetrock pros call it). Nothing looks worse than a poor taping job, which is all that most first-timers can accomplish. Here is a strong argument for hiring a professional finisher (one who works by the square foot, not by the hour), or else figuring out a clever strategy to avoid both sheetrock or exposed joints.

The long edges of a sheetrock panel are slightly beveled. Align the sheets so that the seams fall along the beveled edges wherever possible. Butting the unbeveled sides creates a much more difficult seam to tape. Sheetrock is cheap: Use a full sheet rather than piecing together several small pieces to cover an area. The fewer seams to tape, the easier and faster (and better) the job. If you must use pieces, save them for the insides of closets, where the joints will not show. Occasionally a full piece will not fit through the door opening of a closet— sheetrock does not bend around corners. Score the piece on the paper-backing side and fold it carefully. Do not fold it completely over; otherwise a crease will show on the finish side. Manoeuver the piece into place. The crease should fall over a stud if possible.

Plan the length of the sheets to minimize seams. Sheetrock is available in 4-foot wide panels in lengths from 8 to 14 feet in 2-foot modules. (For example, a ceiling 13 feet 6 inches wide would benefit from the use of 14-foot panels.) Thickness of sheets varies from ⅜-inch light duty to ½-inch standard and ⅝-inch "fire-code." A special moisture-resistant type is manufactured for use in bathrooms and other high-moisture areas. Long sheets are raised into place by two workers and supported in the middle by a "deadman." That is a length of 2 × 4 nailed and braced to another to form a tee, which can be wedged between the sheetrock and the floor, holding it tight to the ceiling. Rental units have an adjustable height control that allows you to actually raise the panel up

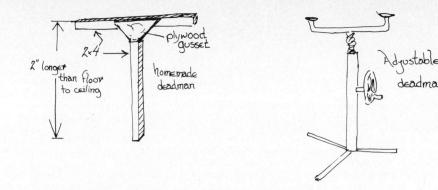

6–1 *"Deadman" for holding long panels in place*

into place. Whenever possible, all long seams should run horizontally. Vertical butted seams should then be offset from each other by four feet. This makes for easier and neater taping.

Special ring-shank nails (sheetrock nails) with a rust-resistant, blued-steel finish are used to hold the wallboard to the studding. Nails must be driven *straight* into the stud. A bent nail or crushed head will puncture the paper surface and lessen its holding power. Drive the nail so that the head rests in a dimple formed by the hammer blow. Nails that protrude above the surface will show through the joint compound. Take care that the last blow of the hammer does not actually break the paper covering or crush the sheetrock. Space the nails 8 inches apart along the studs. An alternate method, especially recommended for ceilings, is to drive the nails 2 inches apart every 12 inches. Special sheetrock screws are made to fit an attachment operated by a power drill and will speed up application, particularly on ceilings, as only one hand is needed to run the drill that holds the screw, instead of two hands (one to hold the nail while the other runs the hammer).

Gypsum wallboard should never be nailed to green framing lumber. As the wood dries out it will shrink away from the nails, causing them to pop out of the wall and through the finish. When using green lumber, wait six months, preferably during the heating season, so that the framing can dry out before you apply the sheetrock. Where ceiling joists are 2 feet on center, 1 × 3 strapping is nailed perpendicular to the run of the joists and along the edges of the ceiling between each course of strapping, spaced 16 inches on center, to carry the sheetrock panels. If the panels were nailed directly to the joists, they would tend to sag over time, and the nails would pull through the surface, especially if the ceiling has a floor above it.

Cut sheetrock with a knife (the Stanley "utility" knife with replaceable blades is recommended, also known as a Matte Knife). A scoring cut is made on the face side against a straight edge, and the core is snapped by pressing the sheet downward over an edge. The backing paper is cut through. Keep the knife blade sharp to avoid tearing the paper backing. A small Surform® block plane is useful for smoothing any rough edges if a tight joint is necessary, although, normally, there is a fair degree of leeway when fitting joints. Since small gaps (up to ¼ inch wide) can be filled in with joint compound, panels need not fit so tightly against a wall or corner that you must force them into place and risk breaking an edge. However, take care to butt all factory edges snugly, as it will help keep each sheet aligned and running square and true. Holes and other irregular cuts are made with a keyhole or electric saber saw. Holes for electrical outlets and pipes are first scored with a knife, around their perimeter, and then

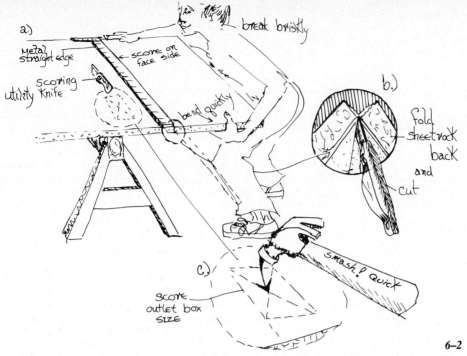

a)
break briskly
Metal straight edge
score on face side
scoring utility knife
bend quickly

b)
fold sheetrock back and cut

smash! quick

c)
score outlet box size

6–2 *Cutting sheetrock*

once more, diagonally. The center is struck with a hammer and the pieces trimmed out.

After all the sheetrock has been nailed into place, the floor areas should be swept clean and odd pieces of sheetrock disposed of. The dust and debris will otherwise be tracked all over the house. Even worse than the mess on the floors, small particles find their way into the joint compound and cause streaks and gouges. Wallboard joint compound (''mud,'' or ''goop'') comes in both one- and five-gallon pails. Unless you are patching only a small area or a few joints, buy the larger size. It costs less for five gallons bought as a unit, than it does for three bought separately. As soon as you empty a five-gallon pail, fill it with water to prevent the remains from drying out. Later, you can rinse out the pail. These buckets have a thousand uses around the home and farm, everything from stock-watering pails to garden pails, from ash to trash.

Stir the mud before use. Sometimes the liquid medium will separate out from the solids. A special aluminum hod is used to hold the compound for application. The surface is kept clean and the mud kept together to prevent its drying out. A bead of mud is applied to the depression between the tapered edges of the butted seams and over all flat joints, using a 5- or 6-inch-wide taping knife. Keep the bulk of the mud in the center of the knife. Paper joint tape is embedded into the mud, centered over the joint. Smooth the tape into place and remove excess mud from under it with the knife. Apply a light skim coat over the tape when done.

After the first coat is dry (usually overnight if the room is kept at the optimum temperature of 70° F.), a second coat must be feathered over the first, using the full width of the taping knife. A wide taping paddle (11 or 14-inch) is then used to smooth the mud over the joint. This coat should extend about 2 inches beyond the last coat. Avoid making the mud build-up too thick at the edges of the seams. It should blend or feather smoothly into the paper surface.

A third and final coat is applied over the first two and feathered out an additional 2 inches.

Inside corners are taped, using the edge of the knife to fill in each side. The tape is creased and folded down the middle to fit the corner and bedded into the compound. Some people prefer to use a special corner trowel for smoothing both sides of the joint at once. Personally, I find that it is just as easy to use the standard knife. Outside corners are first covered with a metal corner bead. The compound is spread over the metal using the edge of the bead as a guide. The mud should cover the full width of the knife. Give nails at least three coats with the knife. Any protruding nails are set with the hammer. Where the edge of a sheetrock panel is to butt directly against finished wood, metal "J" or "L" head is used to ensure a clean edge.

Sand the final coat smooth with 120-grit coat sandpaper folded over a wood block. A Rockwell Speedblock® orbital sander is an ideal tool for finishing sheetrock joints. The mud should blend into the wallboard without ridges and without showing traces of successive layers. The slightest imperfections will show through the paint. If a seam is covered too thickly or too thinly it will be obvious. Wear a dust mask when sanding. Although wallboard compound no longer contains asbestos fibers, as previously, the dust is still to be avoided. An alternative to sanding, which works for a job that was initially well done, is to sponge the surface with a damp cellulose sponge. The compound will soften enough to remove ridges and minor imperfections. If the mud becomes too muddy, however, the sponge itself will leave gouges in the surface.

6–3   *Taping sheetrock joints*

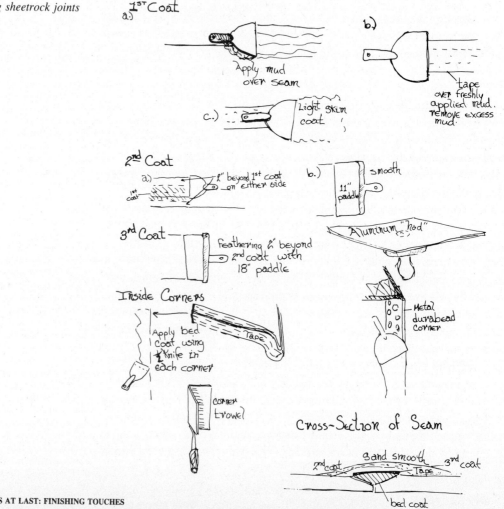

On paper, that is the procedure for taping. The actual practice is usually more frustrating than it might appear. Craters (pockets in the mud) will refuse to disappear, ridges will show where one layer crosses over another, humps and valleys will indicate the intersection of seams, and gouges will show the scars of hardened particles that worked their way into the mud. Wherever the knife has lingered, a telltale ripple will be left behind. Exert a *steady* pressure when running the compound down the joint—try to move the knife in as graceful a sweep as you can without pausing. When you lift the knife off the joint, return it gradually, like an airplane coming in for landing, to avoid leaving ripples. Always keep the edge of the taping knife and the hod itself clean. Wipe them off at intervals to avoid build-up of dry particles. Keep the cover on the mud bucket so that the chips and dirt do not fall into it.

The amateur sheetrock taper should consider the advantages of "texture" or sanded "stipple" paints. These heavy latex compounds contain grit, which can be worked up into a variety of textured effects with a brush, roller, or sponge. They are much thicker than conventional paints and will hide a multitude of sins. Two coats of well-finished mud will generally suffice if covered with a texture compound. Do not use these materials on surfaces you may wish to wash or that might be exposed to dust accumulation, as the rough surface will be impossible to keep clean.

The taping of long seams can be avoided entirely by covering them with ½ × 4 or 1 × 4 wood battens. These battens should be stained or painted first and applied after the sheetrock itself is finished. With careful attention to the layout of joints, it is possible to create a symmetrical pattern of battens and to use them as a design element. Of course, the nail heads must still be finished in standard fashion with joint compound. Fabric or burlap can also be glued directly over wallboard surfaces to completely avoid any taping. If the cloth has a loose weave, the wallboard is best painted dark or a matching color.

Plaster and Some Modern Alternatives

Before the invention of sheetrock, plaster was the universal interior wall finish. That alone explains the popularity of gypsum wallboard. The proper and even application of plaster requires a great deal of skill and is a laborious process. A *lath* (which is the structure that gives the plaster a bonding surface) of gypsum board, wood strips, or perforated metal sheet, must first be nailed to the wall framing to carry the plaster. Wood strips called *plaster grounds* are nailed around door and window openings and at floor level to guide the plasterer in maintaining the even thickness of the plaster coat. These grounds were often left in place as a nailing base for the finish trim. The casings and trim can also be applied first and the plaster laid to the edge of the wood, but as the casings shrink, a crack develops at these joints. The object of the old-time plasterer was to obtain a smooth, evenly polished surface finish, similar to the feel of wallboard. Needless to say, that is hard to do. Also popular was a sand finish, which approximates the look of a texture paint applied with a roller.

A modern version of plaster, which can be applied in one, rather than two or three coats, over inexpensive gypsum lath (Rocklath®) or directly over sheetrock, is sold under the trade name Structolite.® This premixed material is applied with a trowel in broad strokes and gives a grainy appearance. It is not possible to produce a smooth finish with this material. Instead, the application

is varied to create textured effects and a primitive sort of finish. Apply before the trimwork. When combined with wood paneling or as a filler between rough-hewn beams, it gives a rugged and pleasing surface that is also unfortunately an excellent dust collector in a wood-heated house. Another product, Imperial QT,® contains tiny plastic beads and creates an even coarser-textured surface, which is also much whiter than the dull grey of Structolite.®

Painting Walls: *Color theory*

Paint or wallpaper is the standard finish for sheetrocked walls. If the use of paint can be justified anywhere at all, the interior walls are probably the best candidate. There isn't much else you can do with a sheetrock wall. Modern paints have taken much of the art and science out of painting. Over 80 percent of all paint applied today is applied by do-it-yourselfers. All you need to know about applying paint is generally printed on the label. Be sure that the brush or roller is suited to the paint type you use. Latex paints (water-base) are different from alkyd paints (oil-base—actually a misnomer, since modern "oil" paints use a synthetic vehicle rather than linseed oil to carry the pigment) and must be applied with appropriate rollers or brushes. Also, an oil paint will adhere poorly to a wall painted with water-base paints and vice-versa. The class of application will also determine the best type of paint: Alkyd paints seem better suited to outdoor trim work than latex paints. The latter are excellent for interior wall and ceiling finish, although manufacturers now claim to have developed a latex that surpasses oil paints for exterior durability.

The ancients often described a person's character in terms of color. Just as we are only beginning to understand the correlation between the complex symbolic systems of astrology or the *I-Ching,* and the revelations of modern physics and science, we are just beginning to fathom color. Extensive research into the theory and nature of color has shown definite relationships between color and personality types, color and mood, and even color and physical well-being. As a home painter, you should analyze the qualities you wish to enhance before you decide on the color of a given wall surface. The function can be coordinated with mood.

The effect of a color is related to its *hue,* as pure color—its basic character if you will—and to the *intensity* of that hue—its *tone* or *value.* The relationship between one color and another—its *harmony*—is also important. Colors are either *similar* or *complementary.*

Colors at the short end of the spectrum we see as the rainbow—colors such as green, blue and violet—are perceived as cool, sedative, heavy, introverted. Yellow, orange, and red create the impression of warmth, activity, lightness, and extroversion. That alone would indicate that a warm color is better suited to a northern room that receives little light. A cool shade would be best in a sunny exposure. The tone of the color as it varies from strong to pale is very important. Bright, stimulating colors are preferred by children. Red heightens nervousness and sexual and hormonal activity. Light blue tends to lower the blood pressure, and dark blue leads to depression. Yellow is universally perceived as cheerful. Green is reputed to be relaxing, which might explain its use in hospitals and institutions. Darker greens may help one ease into meditative reveries in a den or study; time slips by faster in green rooms than in red rooms. Warm tones are sociable, cool tones more formal: The dining room can be

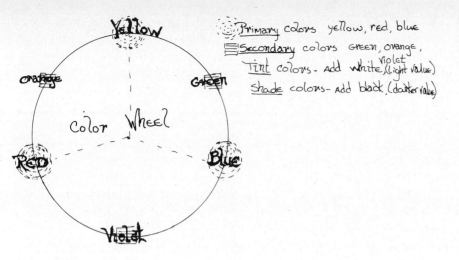

Primary colors yellow, red, blue
Secondary colors green, orange, violet
Tint colors - add white (light value)
Shade colors - add black (darker value)

Color Wheel

6–4   *The color wheel*

painted to reenforce the household's feelings about eating as ceremony or celebration. White can be harsh as well as bright, sterile as well as the most clean
of colors. Grey is the most soothing and harmonious color if relieved of a
tendency toward depressing blandness by occasional strong contrasts or a mixture
of warm colors.

The relationship and the harmonies of particular colors is best illustrated
by a color wheel.

Those colors directly opposite each other are complementary. Those
closer together are analogs. Complementary colors offer the eye relief from
overexposure to one particular shade; analogous colors help ease transitions from
one room to another.

If paint must be used at all, use it intelligently. Color is a way of designing
the fourth dimension into a room.

Wallpaper

Wallpaper is the alternative to painting wallboard. Two coats of mud will generally suffice for a papered wall so long as they are smooth and even. Small
defects will not "telegraph" through the paper. The wall should be sealed with
a flat latex primer and then sized with a thin solution of special wheat sizing
glue, to create a good bonding surface for the paper. The paper is applied after
the sizing has dried.

Before applying the paper, check the wall corners for plumb. If the corner
is out of plumb, mark and plumb a pencil line to align with the edge of the
paper. Although it would be easiest to start in the middle of a wall, waste is
avoided by beginning in the corners. This starting line is scribed at a point no
farther than the width of the paper from the corner, less the amount of paper
that will be folded around the corner itself—1 inch or less. For example, in
Figure 6–5, the wall is 2 inches out of plumb at the bottom. Twenty-inch paper
is used. Allowing a 1-inch corner lap, the guide line must be scribed plumb 17
inches from the top corner. When the adjacent sheet is applied flush with the
corner, there should be no gap. Subsequent sheets are laid to the starting piece.
The starter piece for the adjacent corner is trimmed to fit flush into that corner.
A plumb guide line is likewise scribed onto the wall surface. Any overlap caused
by ceiling and floors being out of level is trimmed off. The paper need not fit

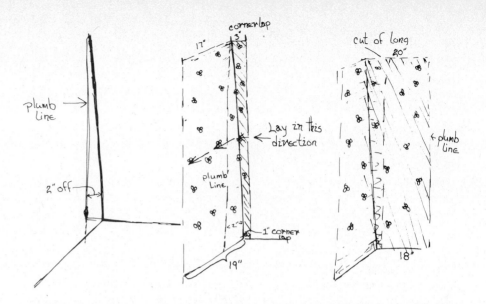

6–5 *Starting wallpaper in a crooked corner*

perfectly to floor and ceilings if baseboard and ceiling moldings are used to cover the joint. These wood moldings are often painted to match or complement the colors of the paper.

To prepare the wallpaper, first set up a table, fashioned from a scrap of plywood or particle board, on sawhorses. Ideally, the table should be as long or longer than the height of the wall to be covered. Guide lines to mark repeated lengths can be squared onto its surface with a pencil. Use a carpenter's square as a straight edge when cutting paper. Apply the paste evenly and do not spread too thin. Wallpaper patterns are designed to lap continuously; observe the proper alignment. The sheet is placed on the wall and wrinkles smoothed with a wide papering brush. Any excess paste should be wiped off the joints or paper immediately—otherwise it will stain. Change the water in the wash bucket frequently, to keep it from becoming a gluey soup. Sponge any spattered paste off the table each time a sheet is pasted.

When ordering paper, be sure to buy a few extra rolls for future repairs or room changes because wallpaper designs are the product of ephemeral fashion and are seldom available for more than a year or so. You can find special books showing traditional patterns that are often especially suited to older houses.

Wood Paneling:

Application techniques and advantages

Matched boards would be more popular as a finish-wall surface if a number of widespread misconceptions did not make sheetrock seem preferable. Wood is thought to be too expensive. To this misconception can be ascribed the roots of the success of the prefinished, imitation wood panelings: ''The look of Real Wood without the bother and expense!'' While wood is undeniably more expensive per square foot than sheetrock, the net cost of either material is about the same when all factors are considered. Prices of wood paneling vary according to type, grade, and source. In northern Vermont, for example, native spruce paneling costs about 26¢ a board foot and pine about 42¢. Hardwoods run upwards of 60¢ to 95¢. Half-inch sheetrock could be bought (in 1979) for about

13¢ a square foot. Wood paneling is nailed to the wall and either left as is or finished with one or two coats of linseed oil or two coats of urethane varnish, both of which are less expensive and give greater coverage per gallon than standard wall paints. There are no joints to painstakingly tape and sand, no footprints tracked all over the house and no expensive wallpaper or paint (two coats) to apply. Individual wood boards can easily be installed by the owner without any worry about the problems of lifting and aligning cumbersome sheets or back-wrenching wallboard on the ceiling. If the costs of labor and materials to finish sheetrock are added in to its initial low cost as a basic material, the differential will be narrowed. The total costs of finished sheetrock would be about the same or more (if hired out to a contractor) than native wood paneling installed by the owner. A professional taper charges 12¢ to 18¢ a square foot to finish sheetrock, and at $15 a gallon, a single coat of paint works out to about 3¢ a square foot. Where the wood must be purchased from a lumberyard instead, at almost twice the native price, the use of wood paneling becomes a question of aesthetics over economics. Likewise, if the job were done with hired labor it would cost considerably more than sheetrocking.

The same types of board used for exterior work can be applied to the interior walls of a house (see Figure 4–10). The restriction against horizontal lapping and the need for battens is, of course, no longer applicable. Thought should be given to the eventual interior wall finish when the walls themselves are being framed. Unless all paneling is to be laid horizontally or diagonally, make some provision for nailers, either by inserting blocking between the studs or by overlaying strapping boards on them or over the original plaster walls. If wall framing has blessed you with a pile of cut-off ends of sufficient length (the result of poor planning, since 6-foot, 9 inch studs should be cut from each half of a 14 footer rather than a single 8-foot piece), or if you happen to have a pile of miscellaneous and misshapen used lumber of varying thicknesses and widths, which are best utilized if sawed into blocks, it makes sense to use these pieces between the studs as nailing blocks for vertical paneling. Cutting up new lumber for this purpose would be very expensive.

If you plan to use vertical siding on both the interior and exterior surfaces of the wall and are framing the studding from scratch, the requisite blocks are often nailed between the studs when framing. That avoids the need for strapping, which slows down application, but requires that the insulation be cut to fit between the blocking—an invitation to air infiltration as well as a bothersome chore. If solid sheathing is already in place on the exterior wall (as in the case of clapboards) the insulation can be installed first and nailing blocks fitted between the studs, with their width parallel to the studs rather than perpendicular. If there is danger of this blocking compressing the insulation too much, it can be scored across the face of the batt to fit around the nailer (see Figure 6–6).

Applying 1 × 3 or 1 × 4 horizontal stripping over the wall after it has been wired and insulated avoids the difficulties. It also creates a ¾ inch dead-air space between the back of the paneling and the insulation itself, which is very desirable for extra insulation. Strapping will, however, subtract an additional 1½ inch from the inside dimensions of the room. That can be a critical factor in deciding whether or not to use it.

A bonus from the use of wood paneling is the added structural stability created by the sandwich of studs, nailers, and paneling, which duplicates the principle that gives plywood its great strength. Whatever nailer system you use, measure the centers to divide the spacing into modules that break on 2-foot centers. That helps you avoid excessive waste when cutting boards to be butted end to end. The center lines are measured from the floor and snapped across the studs with a chalk line. The base line should be leveled across the wall with a 4-foot level and the center lines of the next nailers taken off the base.

Paneling should either be shiplapped or tongue and groove; square-edged boards will require a tarpaper underlayment stapled over the strapping, which not only will help prevent air infiltration from the outside but will fill in unsightly gaps between the boards as they shrink. Tongue-and-groove paneling is most often blind-nailed, a method that leaves no nails showing on the surfaces of the boards. Drive 8d finish nails at roughly a 45 degree angle through the tongue

6–6 *Installations of wood paneling*

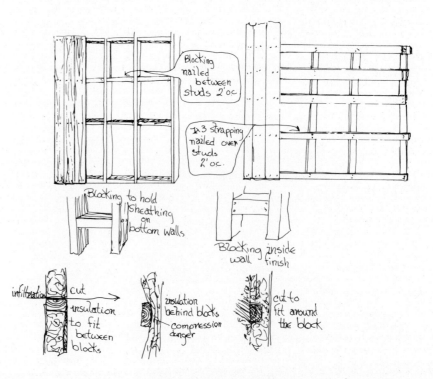

into the nailer. The nail is driven home with a nail set. That is usually enough to pull the board in tight. If a board does not fit tightly, never strike the edge with a hammer. Instead use a short block of matching paneling to drive boards together. Often a slight bow will be enough to prevent the tongue from fitting into the groove. No amount of pounding will bring it together, whereas the pressure of your palm is often enough to flatten the hump and allow the boards to mate, almost as if by magic. Boards can also bow away from the joint. If the nails do not pull the board in tight enough a wedge can be driven against a tapered block tacked across the nailers. Any board that can't be drawn tight by this method will crack first. (See Figure 6–7.) Select your boards with care and avoid having to go to this extreme. Any badly warped boards should be cut through at the worst part and saved for a space that needs a short length.

One-inch paneling will bend with relative ease. If the finish nail does not draw it in sufficiently, carefully drive an 8d box nail (thinner than a common nail) through the tongue and set it. If you think you still need more pull, use a 12d nail alongside the first nail (if there is anything left of the tongue to hold a nail). As the paneling nears the corner of a wall, blind nailing will become increasingly awkward.

The bottom edge of the groove on the very last board will have to be shaved off with a knife or ripped on a bench saw. The board can then be forced at an angle into the last space. For a snug fit, use a block of wood to pound the edge flat. Do not overdo the tightness of the fit, as you will succeed only in splitting the board. Most likely the edge will be covered by the first board of the adjacent wall anyway. The first and last pieces of paneling will have to be face-nailed on their outside.

The first board of each wall section must always be installed plumb. Check the corner with a 4-foot level. Scribe the board to a taper that corresponds to the actual corner. A simple way to determine how much must be trimmed from the board is to measure the distance between the wall and the level, held plumb, and convert that amount into a ratio. For example, if the 4-foot level

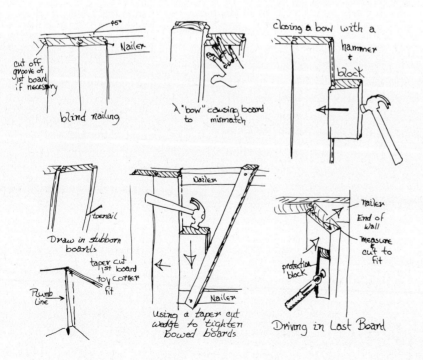

6–7 *Installing tongue-and-groove paneling*

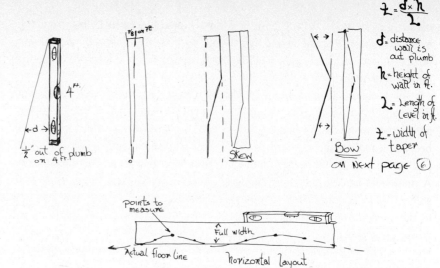

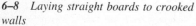

6–8 *Laying straight boards to crooked walls*

shows the wall ½ inch out of plumb at the bottom, the wall will be 1 inch out of plumb over 8 feet or about ⅞ inch over a typical 7-foot interior wall. Thus that amount will have to be trimmed from the top of the board. Snap a chalk line from the top ⅞-inch mark to the bottom corner of the board (zero point) or mark with a straight edge and pencil. The taper is reversed if the wall is out of plumb in the opposite direction. This assumes that the wall is skewed in only one direction. Check along the entire length to see if in fact it is, as often the edge may straighten or bow in the opposite direction. The taper will have to be cut to conform.

The same principles apply to starting horizontal paneling. A leveled chalk line is snapped across the studs at the height of the board width from the floor, measured at the lowest point of the floor. (If baseboards are to be used, the board is simply laid full width to the studs and leveled; any resulting gaps will be covered by the baseboard itself.) Measurements are taken at intervals along the length of the board to give the actual width relative to the rise and fall of the floor. These points are marked along the board, and a line is drawn between them and the board cut to it. Small adjustments are made with a block plane.

Another problem you may encounter is a tilt in the plane of the wall itself. There is little that can be done about gross bows and sags. They are simply among the givens of old houses. The paneling itself will conform to the shape of the wall with little difficulty. Where small dips cause ill-fitting joints, shims cut from cedar shingles are nailed behind the strapping itself. If a line is stretched over spacer blocks from one corner of the wall to the other along the center line of the strapping, a third spacer block will reveal the amount of correction necessary for a straight wall where the line crosses a stud. Hew out the extra wood or shim where needed. The strapping is then nailed to the corrected wall line. This technique is particularly helpful where the wall must

6–9 *Straightening a crooked wall*

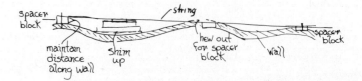

be straight to accommodate built-in furniture or cabinets. It helps provide an even base. Also, when laying hardwood flooring over cupped and dipping boards, the same principle is used to shim irregularities and to prevent the new floor from squeaking.

Occasionally it is necessary to fit a board against a very rough and irregular surface, such as a brick or stone fireplace wall. Theoretically, dividers are used to scribe the line against the board. The practice does not work so well because it is difficult to keep the dividers always aligned perpendicular to the plane of the wall. Tilting the dividers causes inaccuracies in the scribed line. A makeshift pantograph is much more accurate; use a tapered length of wood shingle. Drill a hole in it large enough to hold a sharpened pencil. The point of the stick traces the actual contour, and the pencil transfers it to the board, which is tacked plumb against the wall. The area within the line is cut away with a sabre or jig saw. It is easiest to start by laying the paneling at the edge against the rough surface. If this cannot be done and a piece must be scribed to fill in the gap between the last board and the irregular wall, the line should be adjusted to compensate for the straight board needed. Any gaps between the finished cut and the wall can be filled with clear Phenoseal® (a caulking compound), which will dry to a translucent amber color that matches the wood well.

6–10   Scribing a board to a rough edge

Shiplapped paneling is applied the same way as tongue-and-groove board except that it must be face-nailed, as there are no locking grooves to hold the joints tight. Some builders prefer to use finish nails, set below the surface and filled with stained putty. I find this a great deal of bother. The small bit of nail head that shows is not offensive so long as attention is not drawn to it by a hammer blossom. Nails can be sunk into the wood with a nail set if you prefer, but as you develop control of the hammer, you will be able to drive them flush with the surface without bruising the wood. The last blow is held back—it barely strikes the wood. Rather than try to conceal the nails, you can utilize them as part of the overall design effect. Decorative wrought-iron nails with large, forged heads can accent a barnboard wall. These same nails would also appear too busy on lighter, narrow paneling. Use smaller-headed ''cut'' nails instead or a cement-coated, narrow-headed box nail (sometimes called a sinker) for a more subdued finish. The dark brown coating on sinkers looks very good against any wood paneling. Avoid using bright nails, which distract, or ring-shank underlayment nails, which are brittle and seem to snap before they will bend. Look in the back room of the lumberyard when you buy nails and you might find an odd carton with just the nails you are looking for. Always buy the whole box,

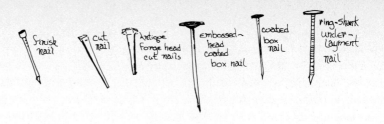

6–11   *Paneling nails*

because it may be one of a kind. It is generally best to buy nails in 50-pound boxes rather than in 10- or 25-pound lots anyway, as there is a considerable discount over the per-pound price.

Use a template similar to the one described in chapter 5 for marking electrical outlets to be cut with a saber saw or keyhole saw.

Wood paneling need not always be applied horizontally or vertically. Interesting decorative effects are possible by laying the boards at 45 degrees or 30- and 60-degree angles to each other. Herringbone patterns can be quite exciting. Avoid too many different angles in a single room as they will only create confusion. One bold stroke is more pleasing than a hodgepodge of chicken scratchings. Since these creative methods result in a lot of odd scraps, plan for a rough figure 25 percent above the board footage needed for straight wall coverings.

An even greater variety of effects can be achieved with straight-edged boards because it will not be necessary to fit laps or tongue and grooves together. Tapered or wedge-shaped boards can be used to create striking sunburst effects. Thinner tapered battens can be laid over the joints of these boards to add additional depth and texture, especially if they are cut from a contrasting

6–12   *Patterns for paneling*

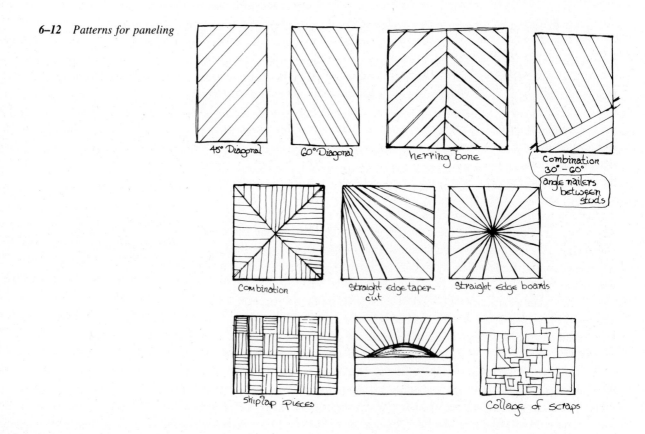

wood. The ultimate in wall sculpture is achieved by building a collage of odd pieces and scraps of varied length, finish, and wood types. These are layered over a solid backing of particle board or plywood, either natural or stained dark, with nails and mastic. The versatility of wood as a sculptural medium is limited only by your imagination.

A less fantastic, but very pleasing, effect is the traditional combination of wood and plaster. The walls are paneled only to a height of from 3½ feet to 4 feet from the floor, either horizontally or vertically, and the upper portion is finished with plaster. (Sheetrock and texture paint or wallpaper can be substituted for the rough Structolite®.) The upper portion of the walls is finished first. A narrow shelf called the *chair rail* caps the junction between the two surfaces. A plain, rabbeted trim molding can substitute for the more elaborate rail. Horizontal paneling makes a room appear wider; vertical paneling seems to raise the ceiling height.

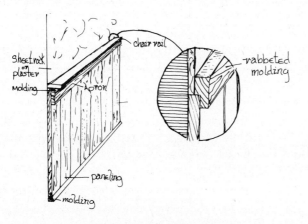

6–13 Wainscotting

A popular wood-paneling material is weathered board salvaged from old barns. It is prized for the subtlety of its grain and texture and the visual interest it creates. Particularly beautiful are boards that still bear traces of the old barn paint or sun-weathered creosote stain. In general, barnboards are applied exactly like new straight-edged wood paneling. Several precautions must be observed: Boards should be thoroughly cleaned with a broom or wallpaper brush before they are brought into the home. They often harbor insect eggs and various mold spores. In cleaning, avoid harsh strokes, as the patina is very delicate and the surface easily scratched. Boards can be sprayed with a bug bomb if necessary. All boards should be thoroughly dry before use. Never store them outdoors uncovered or in direct contact with each other, as mold will bloom if they are moistened and will ruin the surface. If possible, keep the boards in the room where they are to be used for at least two months.

Check the barnboard carefully for broken nails before you make a cut. They will be hard to find and sooner or later you will hit one with your blade. Barnboards also tend to vary in thickness. The portion protected by the eaves from direct exposure to the weather will be as much as ¼ inch thicker than the remaining board. Trim this end off, if you can afford the waste. Otherwise lay the thick butt toward the bottom of the wall where the baseboard will cover it. Barnboards also can taper along their width, making it difficult to keep them running plumb. Keep a careful eye on the run, checking them with a level every few boards. Measure suspect boards across both ends. Tapers can be alternated.

Occasionally you will have to trim an edge. The cut wood will be a different color and texture. Smooth the saw scars with a block plane and run a wire brush over the surface. Touch up the raw wood with a grey barnboard stain. Vermont Weatherboard manufactures a water-base stain which will weather naturally and Cabot's makes a far less expensive oil-base type, which won't. Use the oil-base for interior surfaces and the water-base for exterior boards.

If you desire the effect of barnboard without the difficulties inherent in working with the real thing, Vermont Weatherboard manufactures and distributes a product made from new wood that is treated and stained to resemble barnboards. While no one could honestly confuse it with the genuine article, if thought of as a unique wood paneling rather than as true barnboards, it does in itself possess a distinctive and pleasing quality. It is shiplapped and available in a variety of widths. Besides the standard grey, there is a North Forty® dark brown. The one drawback of this otherwise versatile product is its expense. It costs over twice as much as comparable unfinished new lumber. Some of this extra cost is offset by the fact that it needs no additional finish. When applied to the exterior of a building, it weathers naturally, rapidly developing a very fine character.

Wood used for interior paneling can be applied either roughsawn or smooth planed (on one side). Not only do you have the option of using either the smooth or the rough side out but because the boards are of uniform thickness, edges will match and the entire wall will look better. The type of wood is a matter of personal preference and economics. The characteristics of commonly available woods in the northeastern regions of the country are detailed below. Wood types and costs vary with locally available species. Redwood is relatively inexpensive in California but very high in Vermont. Maple is just the opposite.

Types of Wood for Paneling

Softwoods are generally preferred because of the ease with which they can be worked as well as their comparatively low cost. Because of its softness, pine works easiest of all. Its fine grain makes it somewhat more resistant to cupping and warping than other softwood species. "Knotty" pine has to be a landmark in the history of marketing science. Originally virtually a waste product, this knot-filled, structurally worthless, No. 3 grade pine has been foisted off on the public at premium prices. Advertising and image molding have given it prestige value far exceeding any intrinsic merits it may have. Recycled packing crates would do just as well. But plain, ordinary, No. 2 pine, which has fewer knots (or No. 3 if you really like lots of knots) makes a very beautiful wall finish, especially when rubbed with one or two coats of linseed oil, and it is relatively inexpensive if purchased from local mills. Since No. 2 pine can also be used for window casings and all trim work, you can utilize leftover paneling boards, whereas No. 3 pine is rarely of suitable quality. In any case, both grades can be purchased locally. In fact, many smaller mills do not grade their lumber at all and unless you personally make the selection, you are bound to find a wide range of quality in your order.

Spruce and hemlock are also used for interior finish. They are about 25 percent less expensive than pine. Spruce is a pale-white-to-yellow wood with a pronounced grain and fairly small knots. Hemlock (the eastern variety) has an even stronger grain and a pinkish tint and is quite a bit heavier than spruce. It also tends to split very easily, especially when dry or nailed close to an edge. Spruce does not crack as easily and also is somewhat more stable than hemlock, which often seems to be half water and half pretzel. Larch (hardpine or tamarack) is similar to spruce except for its green-brown tint. It is a durable wood, often used for barn floors, and will suffer much abuse. It is also very prone to warping and shrinkage and should not be used unless dry.

Cedar, either eastern white or western red, is a very versatile wood, both for interior and exterior finish. The wood has a pleasing and characteristic aroma, is resistant to rot, and is characterized by a rare beauty of grain and knot. It is similar to pine in the ease with which it can be worked, although because of its very straight grain, it is more prone to splitting. Cedar is not cheap. It costs about three times as much as spruce or hemlock and is growing more expensive every day. A cedar tree takes about two-hundred years to grow to marketable size. Old stands are not being replaced when harvested but instead are planted with faster-growing, and therefore more profitable, species.

Aromatic cedar has the pungency most people associate with the name cedar. This is the wood used for closet and blanket-chest linings. It can also be used for cupboards and panel doors as well as small finish walls. It should never be used in a structure that will store food, as the volatile resins that give it its odor will be absorbed by the food.

Butternut is a curious wood. It resembles a cross between spruce and walnut, and while technically a hardwood, works like a softwood. It is expensive, something of a native specialty item, but for cabinets or trim details is well worth the cost.

Hardwoods are difficult to work with hand tools. There is no tolerance or give. A slightly oversized piece cannot be forced into a joint as with pine. Nail or screw holes must be drilled first. A warped or bowed hardwood board is apt to stay that way, so selection of good stock is vitally important. Hardwoods also cost considerably more than softwoods, with prices varying according to locale. The grain and color of these woods plus their durability makes them suitable for flooring as well as for fine wall paneling, wainscotting, and cabinet work. Popular native species are oak, cherry, maple, ash, and birch.

Whenever possible, buy native wood from a local sawmill. Not only will you be supporting your neighbor and the local economy, as opposed to filling some corporate till, but you will save a good deal of money. Lumberyards import their products from large wholesalers, and there is a considerable markup to cover the costs of distribution and inventory, sales staff, delivery trucks, and the like. When the lumberyards themselves buy locally, they pocket the difference. All too often the ''kiln-dried'' label, which might justify the higher prices, is little more than a label. Air-dried wood of equal or better quality can be bought from a respected local sawyer. The prices are lower because his overhead is lower.

Be careful to buy only wood that has been air dried for at least a year, preferably under cover, for interior use. Buying at a local mill will give you the freedom to pick and choose your wood. In a given area, there may be more than one sawmill, and the quality of the lumber they produce can vary greatly. Not all sawyers are artists, and some are butchers.

Novel Interior Wood Finishes

Interior wood finishes are not limited to the use of boards alone. Walls can be covered with clapboards. Inexpensive cottage grade or seconds can be used for this purpose. I have seen the successful recycling of weathered clapboards on living room walls. The builder must have had the patience of a saint and the touch of a surgeon to remove those delicate shadows of once-sound wood and renail them in whole pieces.

Cedar shingles can also be used for finish walls, as well as cedar clapboards, rough or smooth, particularly in shower stalls or on bathroom walls. The exposure can be much wider than exterior walls would permit.

These materials suggest one of the drawbacks of the excessive use of wood as paneling. Wood is both fibrous and porous. Unless protected, it will absorb grease, oils, and dirt and be easily stained by water. Linseed oil or a hard sealer such polyurethane varnish or tung oil must be used to seal the pores and make the surface cleanable. Roughsawn wood should not be used in dirt-prone locations or around food-preparation and storage areas. The fibers will effectively prevent cleaning, catching not only dirt but pieces of the cleaning cloth or sponge. Barnboard cabinets may seem like a fine idea but will prove difficult to live with. Unsealed wood should only be used on ceilings or walls less likely to be dirtied.

The standard treatment for finishing the joint between one wood wall surface and another, particularly where the wood meets the ceiling—whether the ceiling is wood or plaster—is to cover the junction with stock moldings. Molding (by which I mean a band of wood used to conceal the inaccuracies of the joint between two surfaces) is not in itself a bad idea. It saves considerable time by allowing an approximate fit to suffice for a perfect one. However, you may feel that it is well worth taking the time to fit boards against a wood ceiling or a beam. A spare, neat line, unencumbered by any trim, is its own adornment. Achieving that line requires a radial arm saw to repeat exact cuts. A hand-held circular saw will be too inexact for all but the most careful craftsman. Moldings are the lazyman's helper. The edges against a ceiling or beam in an old house are often very uneven and fitting boards to them exactly will require more than ordinary patience.

Stock moldings are a relic of neoclassical notions of embellishment. The cove and the Roman ogee, the bed and casing molds, are not only complicated to cut and fit, necessitating coped joints (the coping saw, a thin-bladed hand saw, is used to follow the curves of the piece to be fitted), but are expensive to buy. The baroque frills of conventional moldings have absolutely no relation to the clean lines of a contemporary home. Instead rip a length of the same material as the paneling boards with a table saw. Proper proportion is important: Moldings should not be too wide or thick. A ceiling molding should be unobtrusive; a ½-inch-thick by 1½- or 2-inch wide band is ideal. Exposed edges are planed smooth. Break the edge, giving it a slight bevel. Such a molding is easily cut and finished. Simple 45-degree miter cuts are used to join outside and inside corners. Inside corners can also be square butted if the joint will not be exposed. Where one length meets another, the joint should likewise be mitered. Any small gap will not show because of the surface below.

Baseboards, or "mopboards," are a necessity. They protect the bottom of the paneling from damage by shoes and furniture and from splashes and stains

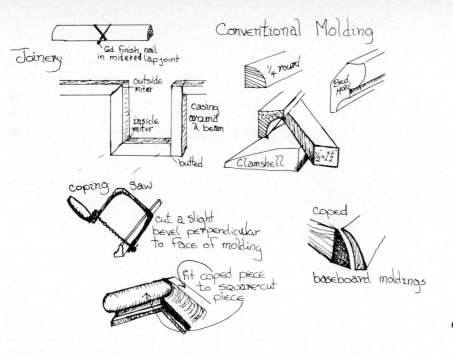

Conventional Molding

Joinery

Gd finish nail in mitered lap joint

outside miter

inside miter

casing around A beam

butted

¼ round

Bed Mold

core

Clamshell

½ × 1½

coping saw

cut a slight bevel perpendicular to face of molding

coped

fit coped piece to square-cut piece

baseboard moldings

6–14   *Moldings*

during floor cleaning, as well as allow for a margin of error when butting the ceiling joints tightly. A 3½-inch or 4½-inch-wide board will be quite sufficient. Use planed boards, well-sealed even over rough-paneled walls, as they will be subject to the most dirt. There is no excuse for a molding where two walls come together, a gap is sloppiness, pure and simple. Take the time to plumb and scribe the paneling, and it will fit tightly the first time.

Ceiling Finish

There is a natural logic to interior finish. The work starts with the ceilings, proceeds to the walls, trim, and cabinet work and then concludes with the floors. Whatever drops from the ceiling does not stain a finished wall. Splatters and spots from the walls strike only a rough floor. A great deal of tedious labor and annoying touchup is saved by working along the curve of gravity.

The ceiling of an old house is subjected to a wide variety of treatments. If the original plaster has been removed, new sheetrock can be nailed to strapping boards fastened directly over the old lath. A film of poly stapled to the lath prevents grit from falling into your eyes as you nail this strapping into place. The lath itself should be removed if changes in the plumbing or wiring are needed. Wood paneling can be nailed directly over the joists if the lath has been stripped but should be nailed to strapping if the lath is left in place. Otherwise the small pieces of plaster sticking between the lath boards make it difficult to lay paneling flat.

Joists can be deepened to accommodate plumbing changes by nailing filler strips to their bottom edges. It may be a good idea to frame an entirely new false ceiling if the old ceiling is very high. This change will result in considerable savings on heat and an increase in comfort, as all the warmth will not accumulate above your head. Although suspended ceilings that use acoustical or insulating tiles are promoted as a solution for high ceilings, unless you enjoy

the look and feeling of living in a church basement or hospital corridor, I would strongly suggest you do not use them. A good job with these tiles requires careful attention to the layout of the supporting frames. Even a good job leaves much to be desired. Textured or embossed tiles cannot overcome the distracting regularity of appearance, the tawdriness of a machine-stamped origin. They do complement prefinished ''wood'' paneling very well, which is why suspended ceilings are so often found in real-estate offices and house trailers.

A high ceiling is lowered by building a grid of 2 × 4 joists at the desired height, to carry the new ceiling. On ceilings of more than a 12-foot span, the joists should be 2 × 6s or else braced to the existing joists by a 1 × 4 tie. Headers are nailed directly over the wall studding at a line leveled around the perimeter of the room. If the room is greatly out of level, a level ceiling will look very crooked. You may decide to split the difference or take your measurements directly off the existing ceiling or up from the floor, whichever will

6–15 Ceiling treatment

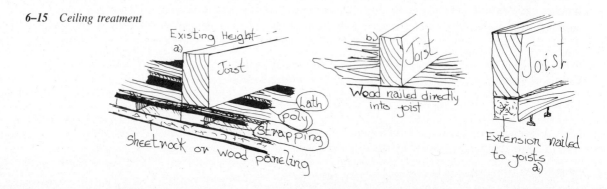

look best. A room that is out of plumb but parallel to itself feels less confusing than a room in which the planes of floor and ceiling are obviously different.

> It would be all right for officials to live in halls twenty or thirty feet high, if their bodies were nine or ten feet. Otherwise the taller the building, the shorter the man appears, and the wider the space, the thinner the man seems. Would it not be better to make his home a little smaller and his body a little stouter?
>
> [Li-Liweng, *The Art of Living*]

There is more good reason for exposing the beams of a heavy-timber frame than mere fashion alone. The beams were covered up perhaps because of an attitude derived from the puritan concern for modesty in dress, which demanded that the bones, the raw flesh of the house as it were, be concealed under a plaster petticoat. Plaster on the ceilings and walls was also a fashionable sign of wealth. Today our more relaxed attitudes toward the body and a rediscovery of beauty in naturalness and of the elegance of simplicity, coupled with a genuine appreciation for the skill of those long-gone framers, adds respectability to what might otherwise be seen as mere fad.

The exposure of ceiling beams creates the problem of how to finish the spaces between them. Some people are quite enamored of the rough-sawn subfloor boards, which will now be revealed. They simply brush them clean, cut away any protruding nails with a pair of nipping pliers, and leave it at that. In a wood-heated house or one heated by forced hot air, these spaces will tend to collect dust and must be run over with a vacuum to keep them clean. The darkness of the wood may give the room a dense and gloomy feeling. This cavelike atmosphere may suit a den or private retreat, but it will put a damper on the mood of the household forced to dine under its somber umbrella. The amount of sunlight entering the house, the height of the ceiling itself, and the finish of the walls need to be considered. Bright walls and light floorboards may well benefit from the counterpoint of a darker ceiling, particularly if it is a high one: The heaviness will seem to bring it closer to the floor. If the subfloor boards are not particularly beautiful, or if their effect is not what you desire, there are two options: plaster (or sheetrock) or wood paneling.

Strapping of some sort will be needed to panel the spaces between beams. A single length of 1 × 3 ripped in half will do. Likewise pieces of scrap paneling can be ripped into 1 × 1 lengths. These cleats are nailed directly to the side of the beam against the subfloor boards using 6d or 8d box nails. (I prefer box nails to common nails for almost all carpentry work as they drive with less effort and do not split the wood as easily, especially when toenailing. They are not as strong as a common nail and should be not be used where the nail itself is relied upon for weight-bearing strength, e.g., fastening the end of a joist to a header when no other support is provided. Also, a glancing blow from a hammer will bend a box nail much more easily than a common nail, and a knot will stop it cold. They require a bit more skill with the hammer. But you also get more nails per pound to make up for the ones you bend.) Wiring can be run through the corridor between a new ceiling and the subfloor. Shallow ½-inch ceiling boxes are used for light fixtures where needed, screwed to wood support blocks nailed between the beams.

Wood paneling is cut to length and nailed to the cleats with finish nails angled toward the beam. Unless the beam is sawn straight, it will prove difficult to fit these pieces tightly to the beam. A hewn beam will often lean inward or out and present a generally uneven surface. Scribing each piece to fit will take too much time, and the results will seldom be worth the effort. A simple ¾-inch, quarter-round molding or flat ½ × 1-inch band molding should be used to conceal the joint.

Select the wood for its effect on the color psychology of the room. Spruce is pale enough to give the desired lightness. Planed side out, it will reflect light, especially when sealed, and is easily kept clean. The subtlety of the rough-sawn side will soften the glare but will be harder to clean. V-groove pine makes a particularly fine ceiling finish. Spruce can also be stained with light tones. Experiment with several stains on scrap pieces before you make your final choice. Thinning down conventional white alkyd paints with turpentine may create a pleasing whitewash effect. Adding small amounts of darker pigment can vary the tones. A light grey or pale sandy wash may be very soothing. Unlike paint, stains do not deny or mask the nature of wood. They can often enhance it by accenting the grain and knots. Why use wood as a medium if it is to be smothered with a coating that negates its essence, that denies it its uniqueness? Wood is used as a base for paint only because it is easier to form and fashion than metal or plastic is and holds paint better. This abuse should be avoided by a respectful builder. Would you bronze your children to avoid the need to bathe them?

There can be such a thing as overusing wood. Wood walls and floors may feel right, but a wood ceiling may throw the house out of balance. It is a matter of personal preference. Sheetrock can be nailed over those same cleats to create a more neutral or very bright ceiling.

Half-inch sheetrock will span beams laid up to 32-inch centers without requiring a center cleat if the floor deck above does not bounce when walked upon. It is better to use a wider cleat to give the sheetrock nails enough wood to grab into. If nailed into a ¾-inch-wide cleat, the nails will be so close to the edge of the sheetrock that they will break through the paper. Cut cleats to 1½ × 1½ inches out of 2 × 4 stock, or lay a 1½ × ¾ inch cleat flat and nail securely into the beam with 12d box nails. Blunt the ends to prevent splitting. (A sharp-pointed nail acts like a wedge, causing splits. A blunt nail crushes the fibers as it is driven through them.) The thickness of the cleat is determined by how much of the beam you wish to expose. The thinner the cleat, the more beam showing. Using ½-inch sheetrock instead of ¾-inch boards will save only ¼ inch, but that same ¼ inch may be very noticeable to your eye. Before nailing the cleats to the beam, staple a strip of poly film wide enough to hang past the beam. Nail the cleat over this strip. It will protect the beam and save painstaking cleanup when you finish and paint the installed sheetrock. After the ceiling is finished, the plastic is trimmed with the point of a utility knife, forced slightly into the joint.

Lay the sheetrock in as long a length as you can to minimize joints. A single piece saves a lot of trouble. Where the space between the joists is greater than half the width of the full sheet (over 2 feet), do not try to piece together the waste. Use full sheets. This may seem extravagant, but sheetrock is cheap and taping joints a bothersome task. It may be worth the extra $10 or $20 in additional wallboard to avoid it. It will not be possible to match the sheetrock perfectly to the bays between the beams, particularly where the beam tilts inward. Measure at several places along its run to get an idea of how much it may vary. A large taper should be cut to fit but a tolerance of about ¼ inch per side is not only acceptable but desirable to ease the fitting of the sheet. The gaps and the nail heads as well will later be filled in with joint compound. A scrap of sheetrock can be forced into gaps over ½ inch and taped over. If a piece is only slightly tight, it can be trimmed in place with the edge of the knife and forced with a block of wood at least 1½ feet long to help distribute the force of the hammer. Any pieces that really are too tight should not be forced, as the edges will crumble before they move, leaving a hard-to-tape mess.

An alternative to using sheetrock is to use gypsum lath (Rocklath®) as a base for Structolite® or Imperial QT®, which, unlike sheetrock, are finished and require no painting. Metal lath can also be used where ceiling thickness is critical (it is thinner), but it must be supported at least every 16 inches, which requires nailing cleats into the subfloor boards. Use ring-shank underlayment rails (for holding power) short enough not to penetrate the flooring above (6d should manage). A slight decrease in length of the nail is gained by driving it at an angle.

A matte-white ceiling paint is applied over the sheetrock. Personally I find smooth white finishes too harsh and prefer to use textured paints, which diffuse the light. They do tend to collect more dust, but I prefer that to the glare. Both smooth and textured finishes can be tinted to offset the contrast between housedust and blank white ceiling finishes as well as soften the mood of the room.

Before any cleats are nailed, the beams themselves should be cleaned. A stiff-bristle brush removes all the clinging dust and cobwebs. The beams are then scrubbed with soap and water. While no further finish is necessary, a lot more can be done. The beams can be stained to a uniform tone; darker colors look good against light ceilings, especially if the beams you are exposing are sawn from dimensional lumber rather than hewn. Rough-sawn lumber appears smoother and more uniform when stained dark. The transparency of the stain can be enhanced by adding turpentine to it. Old beams are darkened by time. Often the wood will appear featureless. A wire brush mounted on the end of a drill can be used to remove this accumulated obscurity. It also wipes out the major part of the stains left by previous plaster lath. (It will not really be practical to completely remove all traces of the lathing.) Sanding the beams would take forever. Each length would have to be gone over twice with a coarse- and fine-grade paper. A sander would fit with difficulty into the crevices of a hewn beam, and the results would appear unnaturally smooth—the ax marks on the beam would make no sense. A wire brush does an amazingly good job. It removes all the grime and scale, and because of its rapid rotation, scratches are minute. The dark grain of the wood is left to contrast with its lighter background in a swirling dance of delight. A coat of oil or sealer will accentuate this effect even more.

6–16 Lowering a ceiling

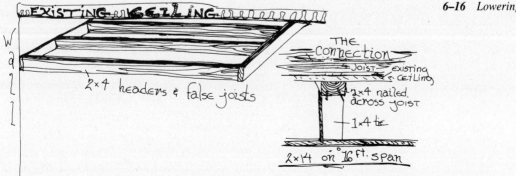

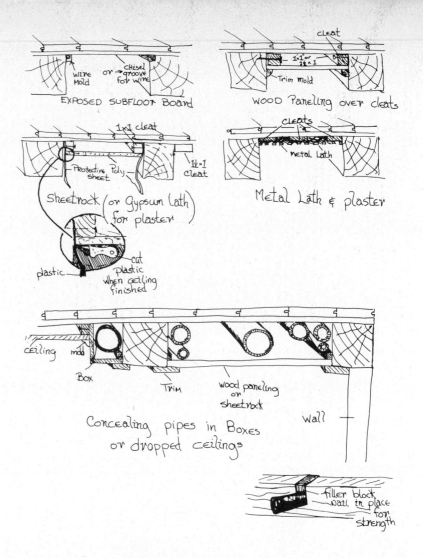

6–17 *Problems of exposed ceilings and their solutions*

Wires that cannot be concealed under the false ceiling should be run through formed-metal channels called *wiremolds,* or else runs should be made with type NMX wire, which lies flat and bends easily. Pipes are a different problem. If they can be concentrated in one bay (for example along the sink wall), the ceiling is dropped for that particular bay. A trim piece finishes the joint. Individual pipes can be boxed where they run parallel to a beam. In no case should a large beam be drilled through for a pipe greater than 1½ inches in diameter. When a section of a standard joist must be removed to accommodate a large pipe, the cutout should be filled with a block to help relieve the compression stress on the remaining portion. (See Figure 6–17.) Rather than fight it, consider painting the pipe ochre or brick red and leaving it exposed. When rewiring or plumbing, try to concentrate runs into a particular bay to avoid these problems. Partition walls under a beam are another good hiding place for wires. Wires can also be laid in the cracks between subfloor boards, or into grooves cut over beams, if the finish floor is taken up or to be replaced.

Finished at Last: *The floors*

The floors of an old house are an archaeological adventure. The various dynasties and epochs of the house's history are chronicled in the strata of the flooring. Rare is the old house without at least one layer over the original floorboards.

Before the ceilings and walls are finished, the floor should be excavated, or liberated from the husk of grime and congealed traffic. This prevents dirt from marring the new finish. Also if you are removing several layers of flooring, your wallboards will need to extend down to the new floor height. Most often the uppermost layer is a battered sheet of linoleum, which the harried housewife ordered from Sears and Roebuck after she had finally had it up to here with waxing and polishing those damned hardwood floors that you are now exhuming. Old linoleum generally comes off quite easily. The cement will be dry enough so that the sheet is barely held and should rip up with no trouble. Asphalt floor tiles should likewise lose their grip with the passage of time. An ice scraper or stiff putty knife or even a shovel will help loosen them. In some cases, wall-to-wall carpet is laid over a backing that is actually glued to the floor. It will have to be scraped with a flat, square-edged shovel, much like stripping a roof of old shingles and just about as tiring.

The narrow, tongue-and-groove hardwood flooring that is usually under the linoleum can either be left in place and refinished or removed entirely. Unless the flooring is miserably patched and uneven, squeaky or mismatched, there is no compelling reason to do other than refinish it. Personally I despise narrow hardwood strip flooring. It is much too busy and too reminiscent of a junior high school gymnasium to imagine living upon. Its very essence reeks of the bowling alley or church or union hall. It definitely has an aura of the institutional, lacking in depth and life. It seems *hard*. For some reason, hardwood plank floors do not feel that impersonal. They are robust, they glow with strength and grain, a deeper fire, like the dull bottom of some slow tropical stream. Why the width of the floorboards should make such a difference defies analysis. Why is it that wide-board floors should be prized above all others? Perhaps it is the difference between the stamp of the machine, the mechanistic repetitiveness, the uniformity of strip floors, that contrasts with the gaps in wide-board floors, the curves of their surfaces—the filet of a tree, they just contain more of the life of wood.

It is most unlikely that a hardwood plank floor will be lurking beneath your linoleum. If you share my feelings about hardwood strip floors, there are further depths to be plumbed. Save the old hardwood—it makes excellent countertops and workbenches as well as very good cookstove wood. Use a crowbar to pry up the old flooring. It will be blind-nailed, so expect a certain amount of loss. The old nails will most likely be more rust than metal, and the boards should pull free without great difficulty. Pry from under the tongue end, opposite

6–18 *Pulling hardwood strip floors*

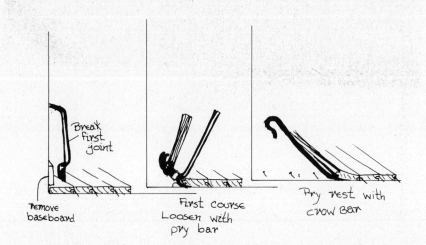

Break
first
joint

remove
baseboard

First course
Loosen with
pry bar

Pry rest with
crow Bar

to the direction the boards were laid. Find the last board (the narrow strip against the wall) and work it free. Drive the end of a flatbar into the joint, chisellike, and break or otherwise pry the board free. Use the curved end of the bar to pry up enough courses to the point where you can begin to use the crowbar. Stand facing the flooring with the bar and lift it with the blunt end. Pulling with the hooked end will split the tongue-and-groove joints.

When the flooring is completely stripped, pull any protruding nails from the subfloor and sweep the surface clean. Under the debris should be the original layer of flooring: those wide, clear boards that were cut from trees larger than any growing today. They probably won't look like much. The grain will be masked by a dingy pallor, pocked with nail holes, and wide rubble-filled gaps will separate each plank. In places, the boards may have rotted or be cratered with the scars of ancient chimneys and the passage of stovepipes. These boards should be smooth surfaced. The ultimate subfloor that supports them will be roughsawn, and often bark-edged and staggered over the joists.

The floors are finished after the ceilings and walls are complete. The art of sanding and refinishing old floors is a lot more difficult and exacting than most people imagine. There is more to it than simply renting a floor sander, running it over the boards, and slapping on a few coats of urethane.

The machines available for rental use are not the same as those used by professionals. They are smaller, 120-v versions of the 240-v professional machines—less powerful and more prone to gouging. The professional machine is equipped with a stabilizing wheel that can be set for depth. A professional job will be mirror smooth but will also be expensive: upwards of a dollar a square foot. You may be able to save some of this expense by applying the finish yourself. If you are not terrified of a few imperfections, you can do the entire job yourself. An average 700-square-foot floor should take a day or less. At a rental rate of $20 a day for your sander and $1 a sheet for the sandpaper and $0 a day for your lack of expertise, you will save a good deal of money.

Before you rent the sander, take a nail set and drive all the flooring nails well below the surface (⅛ to ¼ inch). The sander will grind down the nail heads, but the nails tend to wear the paper faster and can sometimes snag it on a sharp edge and tear it to pieces. The shiny surfaces of the sanded metal will also detract from the finished floor. Fill in or replace all rotted boards. If similar

6–19   *Sanding floor boards*

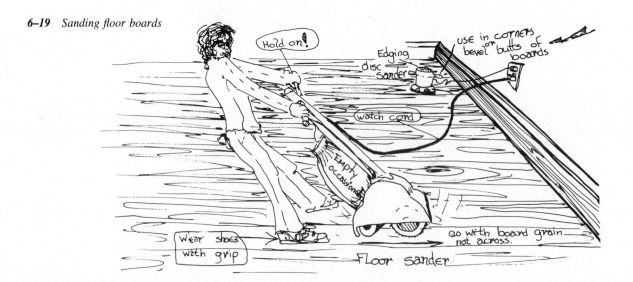

aged boards cannot be found (in a neighbor's barn perhaps or up in the attic flooring), stain new wood to match after the old floor has been sanded. Patch any holes or cutouts. Use a chisel or screwdriver to clean out any loose material, debris, or caulking from the cracks between the floorboards.

The existing floor finish and the thickness of the material to be removed will determine the selection of the grades of sandpaper needed. Heavily painted floors should first be stripped with a nonflammable paint remover, as the paint clogs the sandpaper. Start with a coarse grit (32/0) to remove large amounts of material fast. Always work with the grain, never across it. Cross-grain sanding will leave scratches, which will be difficult to remove, and the sander will tend to follow the dips and cups instead of cutting across them.

Work with a gliding motion, always keeping the machine moving at a steady pace. Never let it linger over an area or it will gouge the floor. The sander is eased into and out of the work by leaning it on its backstop. That avoids ripping the sanding belt. It should be running at full speed when it contacts the surface and only shut off after it leaves the floor. Purchase more sanding belts than you think you will need because, until you get the feel of the machine, a frustrating number of expensive belts will tear themselves to pieces as soon as they touch the floor. Belts are directional and must be not only tight on the drum but oriented correctly. A one-way flange or an arrow should be on the belt. If you are not sure how to use the machine, ask the advice of the people whom you rent it from.

A 60-grit or an 80-grit medium-grade belt is used to remove the deep grooves left by the cutting coat. This step is followed by a fine 100 or even 150-grit finish sanding. The floor should be smooth to the touch. Look at it obliquely. The light should reveal no noticeable scratches. Gouges should be leveled. Hardwood floors may require an additional, very fine grit to remove the last scratches. For softwood floors 100 grit is generally sufficient.

You will also need to rent an edger sander, which is a heavy-duty disc sander mounted on roller bearings and designed so that the disc reaches into the corners, directly up against walls and into areas too small or awkward for the large drum sander. The same grades of sandpaper should be used with this sander also. If the baseboards have been removed first, very little of the floor area will have to be hand sanded or scraped. The edger cannot reach into the very back of a corner or under cabinet toe space. A chisel or block plane and some hand sanding will complete the job. The disc sander is also useful for finishing the bottoms of valleys too deep for the drum sander to reach without removing excessive amounts of the surrounding boards. Because of its circular motion, cross-grain sanding does not leave scratches. The disc sander can be used to bevel any change in height between the butts of sections of flooring. In fact, it may be the only sander you can fit into narrow areas of the floor. If you are lucky, these areas will not be extensive, since the stooped over-position it takes to run a disc sander will be rough on your lower back. Be sure both sanders are equipped with good tight dust bags with no holes in them. You want to minimize the amount of dust that escapes into the air and settles on the rest of the household. Wear a dust mask when operating these machines. If the dust does not contain any ground-up paint, it can be added to the compost pile or used as a mulch for blueberries. If it does, throw it out.

Work in clean stocking feet or absolutely smooth-soled shoes when sanding the final coat. The floors will mar easily before they are sealed. After the sanding is done, the floor is vacuum cleaned, particularly in the cracks between the boards. Any loose material is pried out. Move the vacuum cleaner carefully to avoid marking the boards. Pick up the remaining dust with a tack cloth (a sticky cloth used for cleaning wood prior to finishing and sold at most paint stores). The floor is then ready to be sealed.

Ask the advice of someone you trust at the paint store as to the best floor sealer. You may be able to purchase commercial sealers from a floor finisher or distributor. Whatever product you choose should give a hard-gloss finish that is guaranteed to wear well. Some floor-finishing systems require a special sealer before the finish coats are applied, and others can be applied directly with or without thinning. Often each coat must be burnished with steel wool before the next coat is applied, to avoid dull spots. Use the tack cloth to remove all between-coat debris. A minimum of three coats of polyurethane-type floor finish should be used. Four coats are recommended for high-traffic areas. Apply with a fine-nap roller or wide flooring brush, taking care to pick up stray hairs. Keep the room warm and well ventilated during the application and drying period. This might prove difficult in the winter since the house can be either warmed or ventilated, but rarely both. A large electric floor fan can be used to help circulate the air and heat, and aid in solvent evaporation, if your wood stove can maintain the internal temperature at the required level for the time the floor takes to dry. The drying will proceed much more slowly if the temperature is too low. Use a plank set upon small wood blocks to cross the finish floor to the stove if it is sealed off on its own island. Try to keep the stove accessible or else heat the house with an electric radiant heater or kerosene or propane-powered "salamander," or the like, if you have no backup system. Heating is only one of the considerations when you plan finish work. What will you do with the children and dogs? Will your kitchen and bedrooms remain accessible? Should you plan to spend the night at a friend's house? Sleeping in a house filled with the fumes of evaporating hydrocarbons or the exhaust of a space heater is neither pleasant nor healthy. Perhaps you should leave the flooring finish for fall or spring, when you can camp out in the truck or garage for the two or three days it will require to apply and dry the coats of finish.

There will be gaps between the boards, but they will be filled in somewhat by the dust from the floor sanding which will mix with the sealer to form a kind of paste. Large cracks can be filled with caulking (black or grey)—which runs into money—or tinted glazing compound (use lampblack)—which is cheaper, after the initial sealing and before the final coat. Cleanup will be eased because the material will not adhere well to the smooth, sealed wood. If there are numerous large gaps, consider lifting all the floorboards and relaying them tightly before you begin sanding. An additional board will be needed to fill in the last gap. Occasional wide gaps also can be filled in with strips cut from suitable wood, glued and tacked with small brads.

The beauty of old boards is worth the trouble of uncovering, sanding, and refinishing. As boards age they take on a glow that cannot be duplicated by any stain. More than a color, it is a palpable warmth, distilled from years of living.

One final note on the subject of floors: If you expose the ceiling beams, the removal of the plaster and lath will cause the floors above to act like a sounding board, amplifying whatever sounds are created by someone walking on them. From below, the pitter-patter of little feet above will sound like an

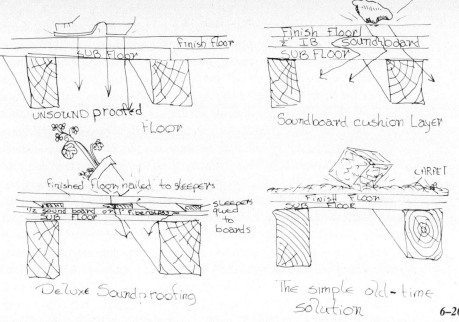

UNSOUND proofed FLOOR

finish floor
SUB Floor

Soundboard cushion Layer

Finish Floor
½" IB Soundboard
SUB FLOOR

Deluxe Soundproofing

finished floor nailed to sleepers
½" sound board on ½" FIBERGLASS
SUB FLOOR
SLEEPERS glued to boards

The simple old-time solution

CARPET
Finish Floor
SUB FLOOR

6–20   Soundproofing a floor

engine with a blown rod. If your ceilings are walked upon by no other persons than yourselves, this will not be a problem. The occasional noise will be something you can live with. The children can have a play area downstairs instead of being allowed to run wild over your head. A more permanent, but costly, solution is to install a layer of sound-deadening board over the existing upstairs floor and lay an entirely new floor on top of it. The sound board should be glued to the floor. This system will help deaden the sound of impact on the floorboards, but some sound will still be transmitted through the wood by the nails that hold it to the subfloor. There is no practical way to solve the problem, and it will just have to be accepted as a side effect of exposed ceilings. The construction of a completely insulated sound-proof floor is too expensive and really unnecessary for the average home. "Sleepers" (strapping) would have to be glued to the soundboard and the nails of the finish floor driven into, but not through, them. Carpeting is also an effective (and simple) sound deadener.

The Principles of Simple Cabinetry

Cabinetmaking is an art all its own. It employs many of the carpenter's tools but, as the experience of Woodworker Ch'ing shows, not every carpenter is necessarily a cabinetmaker. To detail the intricacies of cabinetmaking, were I capable of it, would require a companion volume. But it will be helpful if I outline some of the basic principles of simple cabinet work, to give the novice a starting point. You can develop and refine your own skills according to your inclinations. In working with old houses, the problem is not so much building the cabinets as it is installing them. In a new house the walls are assumed to be level and plumb. Factory-built cabinets are easily mounted by a carpenter, or a cabinet-maker can build the basic units in his shop and install them with little trouble. In an old house, the walls are seldom plumb or the floors and ceilings level. While a good cabinetmaker can install his own shop-built unit

to fit, the process will be slow and expensive. It makes sense to build the cabinets on location.

Figure 6–21 shows the elements of simple cabinet construction. In these drawings, it is apparent that a *level base* is the key to a good cabinet. Check the floor for level before you begin. The base is framed with good, straight-grained 2 × 4s nailed to the wall and directly to the floor. Shims are used to level the base. Allow for a toe space under all kitchen cabinets when constructing the base. Without this space, standing at the cabinet will be uncomfortable; your feet will strike the base and prevent you from reaching across the countertop. Cabinets for bookshelves and wall storage, which are not topped by work surfaces, need not have toe space. The lines for the layout are marked directly on the wall. Allow for the thickness of the panels when laying out frame members. The outside corners of the base should be square with respect to each other and, if possible, with the back wall as well. Panels are built for the ends of the cabinet either from finished plywood (veneer) or from tongue-and-groove boards fastened with glued and screwed cleats.

Check the wall for plumb before cutting the side panels. Any compensation that requires a taper cut should be taken off the back edge. The bottom edge may likewise be cut to conform to the floor. The countertop should be a

6–21   Basic cabinet construction

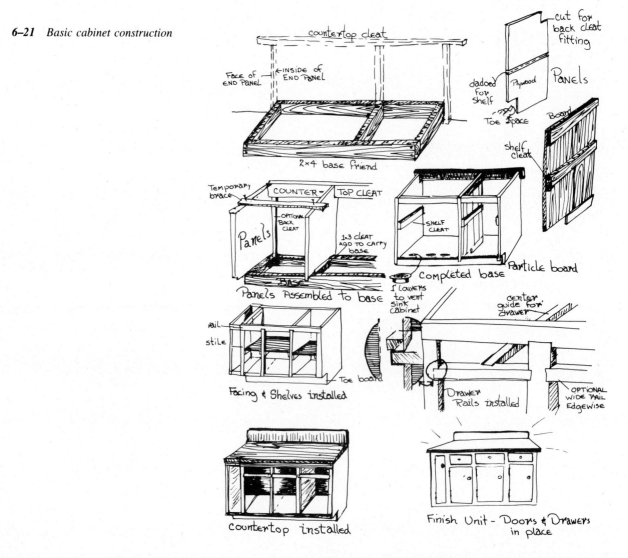

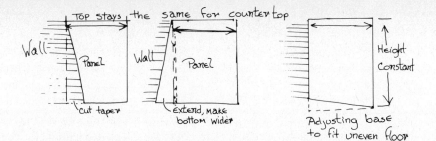

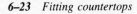

6–22 *Trimming end panels to fit crooked walls*

constant width. Therefore make any compensatory cuts across the back. The principles are similar to those outlined for squaring boards to a crooked wall.

When the back wall itself bows toward or away from the countertop, the difference can be made up on the backsplash. That allows the use of factory-formed (Postformed®) countertops. If the wall is grossly out of square, especially where it forms a corner, it is inadvisable to use a preformed countertop. The unit will arrive with a factory-cut, 45-degree miter for the corner joint, which will cause the backsplash to be conspicuously crooked with respect to the wall if the corner is to fit square. Recutting the miter to the odd angle that fits the actual corner is difficult to do neatly. The procedure is to cut the countertop from the backside with a skilsaw equipped with a fine-toothed or carbide blade set against a wood straight edge tacked to the countertop. Even with these precautions it is a ticklish affair to get the cut accurate, and the resulting gap in the finish surfaces will not look very good. It can be filled with putty and paint, but it is a better idea to make up your own countertops, which will conform to the actual wall. A separate backsplash installed over the countertop surface will fill in any small gaps.

After the side panels are correctly aligned and trimmed, they are nailed to the base and fastened to a cleat against the back wall. A temporary brace will keep the fronts of each panel properly spaced and plumb. A cleat should be added to any inside panels, to carry the bottom of the base where needed. When the base unit is completed, the panels are faced with horizontal lengths of finish wood called rails and vertical pieces called stiles. They are glued in place and secured with finish nails set and puttied. A variety of treatments is possible. The joints can be simply glued and butted or set in shallow dadoes. A dovetail can be cut into the rails. The strips can be secured with countersunk screws or else screwed and plugged. Shelves can be dadoed or simply fastened to cleats.

6–23 *Fitting countertops*

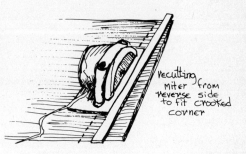

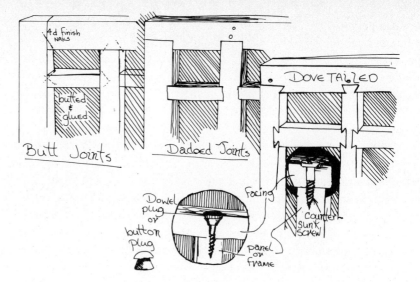

6–24 *Drawer-facing joints and shelving facings*

Particle board is an inexpensive material that can be used for shelving. Exposed edges should be faced with a thin strip of finish wood, glued, and fastened with 4d finish nails. The width of shelving must allow for the thickness of the doors. A ¼-inch facing will not conflict with a ⅜-inch offset door, but if ¾-inch flush doors are used, the shelving must be set back the width of the facing. See Figure 6–25. Drawer frames are built next. You can make side, corner, or center guides, or use commercial drawer guides and various roller tracks and bearings.

6–25 *Fitting doors and cabinet shelving*

Countertops: Materials and Installation

The prebuilt countertop is fastened to the frame with a bead of construction adhesive (Liquid Nail® or PL-200®) applied with a caulking gun over the top of each panel and rail. The countertop is positioned carefully, and weights are rested on it overnight to set the adhesive. Concrete blocks (resting on a board to prevent scratches) make excellent weights. Angle irons can be screwed into the underside of the counter, as well, to secure it to the panels.

Materials for countertops where food is to be prepared should be durable, dense, nonabsorbent, stain-resistant, and waterproof. Plastic laminates, such as Formica®, are one class of material that fit these conditions well and are therefore a popular countertop covering. Formica is also downright troublesome for the amateur to work with. Plastic laminates are *plastic* and should be utilized for the qualities that are the materials' strong point. Nothing seems more foolish than wood-grain or imitation marble patterns that somehow always find their way into kitchens and lavatories. Plastic is hard and bold and homogenous. To disguise it as slate or marble or some weird abstract painting is in bad taste. Instead it should be used for what it is, a hard, impervious surface, maintenance-free and capable of adding a bold color accent to the natural tones of the rest of the room. The newer earth-tone finishes, in particular, harmonize very well with natural wood and stone.

Formica® must be bonded to a structural backing. Plywood can be used for this purpose, but particle board is just as satisfactory and far less expensive. Tenblend® is an extra-dense type of particle board made especially for countertop underlayment. It is sold in 30- or 36-inch widths and lengths from 8 to 12 feet. Allow the countertop to overlap the finish panels and rails by at least ½ inch. The particle-board top is glued and nailed to the cabinet. Contact cement is used to bond the laminate to the substrate. The material can be cut on a table saw or with a skilsaw, using a fine-toothed or carbide-tipped blade. The decorative face should be up when using a table saw and down when using a skilsaw. Cut pieces ⅛ to ¼ inch oversize. Both surfaces are coated with contact cement, using an old paintbrush (animal or fiber bristles, as the solvent will dissolve synthetic materials) or a metal-edged spreader. Set the surfaces aside to dry, usually fifteen minutes or so. Apply a second coat to any dull spots. They indicate insufficient cement. A piece of paper should not stick to the surface when it is dry. The laminate is then brought into contact with the particle board. It must be positioned exactly. Once contact is made, the sheet cannot be shifted. A sheet of wax paper (a slip sheet) should be inserted between the base and the laminate and withdrawn after the laminate is positioned. The surface is rolled with a 3-inch wide rubber roller or hammered by a block of softwood and a rubber mallet to secure the bond. The edges are trimmed next. A file can be used, but a better job is done with a special, 22½-degree-bevel router bit, equipped with an adjustable roller guide bearing. The outside corners can be beveled to about 45 degrees with a mill file and finished with 400-grit emery cloth.

Sink cutouts are made on the finished surface with an electric sabre saw. A skilsaw can be used for the straight cuts, plunge-cutting it through the surface, and the sabre saw used for the corners. Sink cutouts can be ordered precut for an extra charge in a postformed top. Otherwise, it is best to cut them from the

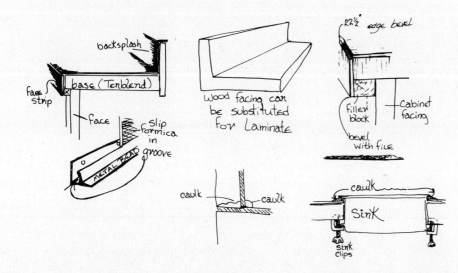

6–26   *Formica countertops*

backside through before installing the top, since the saw will not clear between backsplash and base if cut through the front. Special metal moldings are used to fit the countertop to the backsplash. They are added after the top is in place, but they can be eliminated—resulting in a cleaner joint—by applying a thin bead of clear silicone sealer instead. Thin strips are used to face all exposed edges. Formica can be curved around a corner by heating it gently over a gas flame until it softens and then holding the piece in place until it sets and cools.

Tenblend® used by itself makes a durable, low-cost, and rather attractive counter surface if properly sealed. It requires at least a half dozen coats of urethane sealer to make it water resistant. A special epoxy product, Build 50®, manufactured by the Behr Chemical Company gives an extremely hard, high gloss finish equal to fifty coats of conventional varnish. It can be used to coat any *flat* surface. Coat backsplashes before they are installed. Run a facing strip or ½ × 1½-inch finished wood over the exposed edge of the particle board.

The aristocrat of countertop surfaces is the butcher block. Without a doubt it is a handsome material. But it is actually fairly impractical as a kitchen work surface because of its maintenance requirements. It is easily stained and burned, and the scars from cutting and chopping food are unsanitary. It must be thoroughly washed after cutting raw meat or poultry on it, to destroy disease-causing bacteria. It will have to be periodically sanded and refinished to expose clean wood. Butcher block is also very expensive. Quality home-made butcher block is beyond the capabilities of most amateur workshops unless they are equipped with a planer and jointer. It is an absurd paradox that in order to preserve the material, all cutting should be done on a special butcher-block cutting board. Still, as with fireplaces, there are those who cannot think countertop without imagining butcher block.

A poor man's version of a butcher-block surface, which will perform well and cost very little, can be made from maple floor boards. Do not use oak, as its open grain will absorb food oils and make cleaning impossible. The boards are toenailed to a plywood base, as with standard flooring. Mastic should be spread on the plywood first. The tongues are trimmed off the outside boards. They can be drilled and screwed in place and countersunk with dowel plugs. Old boards can be recycled for countertop material if they are sanded or run through a planer to trim any warp and remove grime. A maple facing strip is screwed to the outside edges.

Butcher block should be protected from water by the application of

6–27   Flooring as a countertop

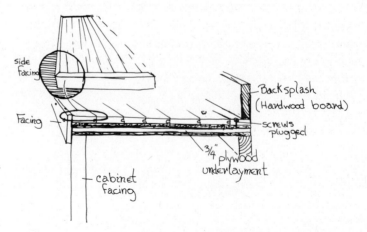

special oil. If it is not to be used as a cutting or food preparation surface, it can be sealed with standard urethane sealers instead.*

Hardwood or softwood slabs are also popular materials for a ''rustic''-looking top. They should be fastened to the frame with angle irons and adhesive or face-drilled, screwed, and plugged. Slabs should always be dry wood. Bring them into your kitchen for at least six months prior to installation, to minimize shrinkage or checking. The backsplash molding will cover any small gap that might open later. Avoid butting end grain against grain in corners, as the shrinkage will be compounded. Instead cut a mitered joint. Remove all bark from wavy-edged slabs, as it will fall off sooner or later by itself. Seal these slabs thoroughly, particularly on the end grain, before they are installed. Softwood slabs must be sealed with a waterproof finish to avoid the absorption of their resins by the food.

Finishing Up Your Cabinets: Shelves, Doors, and Drawers

Wall cabinets are built much the same way as base cabinets except that they are generally made from solid 1 × 12 stock. Dadoes or cleats are cut to carry solid shelving. The sides must be cut to fit flush to the wall. If the wall is out of plumb, not only must the panels taper but the shelves will have to be cut to the proper width to fit. If the wall is not noticeably out of plumb, simply mount the unit in place and plumb it, filling the gap with a length of simple molding. Spaces inside the cabinet are filled with tapered shims glued to the back of each shelf. Sometimes it is easier to mount the shelf unit to the wall as it is and ignore the tilt.

Cabinet units are fastened to the wall studs by the bottom and top cleat or to a side wall. Window casings also make good hitching points when a cabinet fits up against them, as with an over-sink window unit. Large spans of open shelving require additional support, to avoid sagging under the weight of their contents. The stiles can be hitched to a 2 × 4 nailed to the ceiling cornice to help carry the load. Otherwise, use ¼ (four-quarter) stock (planed to a full 1-inch thickness) for the added stiffness. Open shelves can be dadoed or cleated together and built like wall cabinets without facings. Narrow facings, however, will cover sloppy dado joints or the edge grain of the cleats to make a neater-looking finish. Always sand all exposed edge grain smooth. Otherwise it will take a poor finish.

The top of open shelving or wall cabinets can be run directly into the ceiling or closed off and fit into a cornice. Flexibility, especially for bookshelves, is obtained by using steel tracks fitted with removable shelf brackets or clips (K-V® shelf hardware). These tracks will mount either on the surface of the shelf support or else fit into a dado to rest flush with the finish surface.

Doors and drawers are the final phase of cabinet construction. Drawer joinery ranges from the basic and flimsy to the ingeniously complicated. A simple, serviceable drawer is shown in Figure 6–29.

The use of offset panels compensates for any imperfections in the construction of the cabinet or door and drawer and is highly recommended to the

---

*Woodcraft Supply Corp., 313 Montvale Ave., Woburn, Mass. 01801 sells Behlen Salad Bowl Finish, which is an approved finish for all surfaces that come in contact with food. They also are a well-known source for high-quality woodworking tools of every sort.

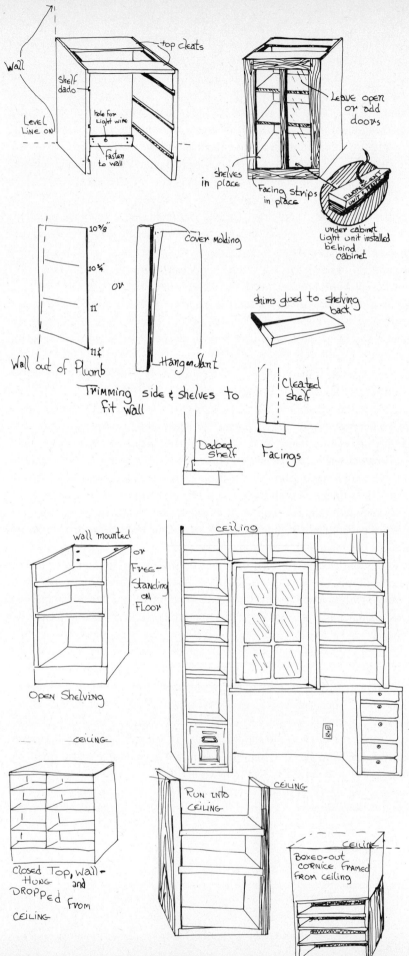

Wall

top cleats

Shelf dado

hole for Light wire

Level Line on

fasten to wall

Leave open or add doors

shelves in place

Facing strips in place

under cabinet Light unit installed behind cabinet

10 3/8"

10 3/4"

11'

11 1/4"

or

Wall out of Plumb

Cover Molding

Hang on Slant

Trimming side & shelves to fit wall

shims glued to shelving back

Cleated shelf

Dadoed Shelf

Facings

wall mounted

or Free-standing on Floor

ceiling

Open Shelving

CEILING

RUN INTO CEILING

CEILING

Closed Top, Wall-Hung and DROPPED From CEILING

CEILING

BOXED-OUT CORNICE FRAMED FROM CEILING

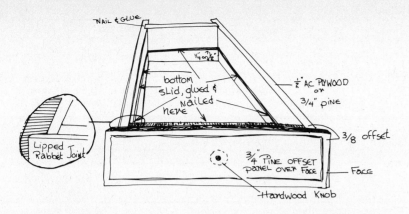

novice cabinetmaker. Flush doors require extremely accurate construction to work correctly and look good. Offset doors can easily be ripped out on a table saw from plywood or cleated boards. When using cleated doors, set the cleats back to allow for clearance between door frame and offset lip. Avoid placing cleats where they will strike against the shelving. Cleated doors will tend to twist and warp. If they are well fastened, when the boards shrink, the cleat prevents them from cupping, and they split apart instead. There is no way you can prevent wood from moving if it wants to. Plywood doors are less prone to these changes. Special veneer plywood faced with hard and softwoods can be used for natural wood doors. Otherwise plywood is best painted. These decorative veneers are more than twice as costly as standard fir plywood, but they do make stable doors, which can be speedily built and require no other finish than a coat of sealer. All plywood edges are sanded smooth.

Use a plywood blade or a hollow-ground blade to avoid splintering the wood. The ultimate in cabinet doors is the rail-and-stile floating panel door. These doors will require a radial arm or table saw for their construction unless you are a patient and superlative craftsman with hand tools. A dado is cut into each frame member that allows the panel to float freely in the groove, contracting and expanding with atmospheric changes without affecting the stability of the supporting framework. Use ¼-inch hardboard, painted plywood, or fancy wood veneers for the panel insert, if desired. The hardboard can be painted with bright colors to create a bold contrast, or clear or colored glass can be substituted for the wood.

6-30   Door details

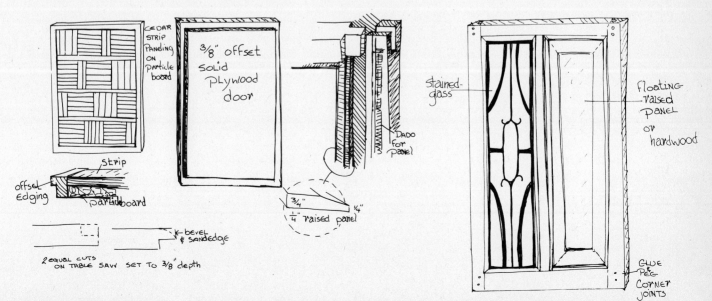

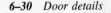

An interesting door can be built by edge-banding ⅝-inch particle board with an offset wood trim and gluing ⅛-inch thick strips of wood or veneer to its surface with a waterproof mastic. Cedarstrip®, 4-inch-wide, 4-foot-long, prepackaged cedar boards cut to slightly less than ⅛-inch thickness and designed for this purpose, are manufactured by Pope & Talbot Lumber Company and distributed nationally.

Flush doors simply fit inside the door frame. Both door and frame must be carefully built to square. Allow a clearance of from ½32 inch to a maximum of ½16 inch. The offset door covers a multitude of sins.

Why use doors on cabinets at all? Why should a kitchen look like a drawing room? Food can be decorative and so can dishware and cooking utensils. Why not display them all on open shelves? A fine idea except for the household plague of dust. Doors do not hide their contents so much as shelter them— reason enough in a wood-heated house. A country house will be home to mice as well as people, and cabinets are one way to keep the food safe from their depredations. Sliding doors are an alternative to the complexities of cabinetry. Metal or plastic tracks (although plastic is much inferior to the former) are available to fit either ⅛- or ¼-inch sliding panels. Panels can be cut from hardboard or ¼-inch veneer plywood and painted or stained. For ventilated cabinets, pegboard, which is perforated hardboard, can be used to form the panels.

The outline above is by no means intended to be a complete dissertation on the techniques of cabinetry, but it will acquaint the beginner with the basic elements of very simple cabinets. You can actually build a kitchen using this information as a guide, but you would do well to research the matter more thoroughly in a volume devoted exclusively to cabinet making. Work at this level requires sophisticated equipment. It may perhaps make more sense to hire a cabinetmaker whose work you know and admire rather than invest in the tools necessary to do it yourself. Cabinetry can be done with hand tools and, in fact, has been for thousands of years, but it requires a consummate craftsman to do an accurate job, which is one reason why the apprentice system was developed and refined to such lengths over time. Woodworker Ch'ing didn't just pick up his ax one day and build a bell stand.

There is another school of thought, which says, let it happen . . . why worry if your joints are not perfect, if surfaces are out of level or plumb? So long as the coffee pot doesn't slide off the counter, it will work for you. It is, after all, your kitchen that you are building, not an entry in a crafts fair. You are building to please yourself and to suit your needs. Build as befits your fancy. Be guided by true principles, but don't let them inhibit you, either. Straight and level cabinetry is sometimes straight-jacket cabinetry. Imagination is a powerful antidote for the lack of polished technique. Remember, only demons travel in straight lines and that ". . . human endeavor must always remain short of perfection; besides no one will ever weed out the tendencies innate in his particular nature; the point is to change their force into life power" (P. D. Ouspensky).

Remember too, that the house should have a resale value. As a modern spiritual leader put it: "No matter how far out you get, always remember your zip code" (Baba Ram Dass, *Be Here Now*).

A COOKBOOK
FOR COMFORTABLE LIVING

We have grown accustomed to finding some sort of lodging wherever we can, if lucky, find employment and then to re-moving (on the average) every three years. This sort of thing cannot fitly be called human living. Today's revolution will occur when employment, including political, economic and technical operations, shall become a means to the tender love, personal growth and spontaneous artistry of settled home life.

[Ken Kern, *The Owner-Built Home*, Vol. III, p. 63]

A house is a tool for living. And since living is, above all, a personal art, the tool should be shaped to the hand of the user. An ill-fitting house, like a poor hammer, causes psychic blisters. Chapter 1 showed how a house design should be analyzed in systematic and functional terms. Living is an energy flow, and the layout of a house can influence the current of this flow, alternating between spillways and dams, locks and waterfalls.

Rebuilding an old house involves a special kind of evolution: The plan is constantly remade as it is lived with and within. Which is as it should be. Structure emerges out of action, form from content. There must be a symbiotic relationship between form and function, just as the chicken and egg are related. It begins with the idea: In the Beginning there was the Word, but as we know, "the Word was the Deed." And the key to getting the deed done is to live comfortably while doing it.

Tearing apart the house while you live under its tenuous shelter is a disconcerting experience. A familiar configuration is suddenly no more, a lunar rubble of plaster and dust appears where once stood the bedroom dresser, a gaping hole opens under the formerly solid floor. Just as you begin to accept the new arrangement, it changes again. Like nomads on a carousel, you are constantly moving your belongings from one level to another, from one corner to the next, trying to keep ahead of the dust, always shoveling out from under. Living within a house that is not yet a home is a problem of logistics. An extensive inventory of the work to be done must be coordinated with the season suitable to its doing and the not-always-predictable flow of finances. The messiest jobs, the jobs that make the house absolutely unfit for living should coincide with those times when the house can be opened up and its people are free to set up temporary quarters outside, or else it must be done in stages, and fast. Work that involves the exposure of the vitals of the house to the elements is most propitiously planned for warm months. More meticulous and less disruptive work—indoor work—can be left for the cold season.

Not only is the work divided into seasons, the house itself should be split into zones that can be quarantined from the flow of family life during the ferment and froth of rebuilding. Start at the top: Rip out the upstairs walls, the plaster and lath, clean it up, and leave it alone. Patch the roof, reshingle it, frame a dormer. Close in the window rough openings with poly. Leave them. Start on the foundation, work on what has rotted. The nights grow crisp: Rebuild the chimney, insulate the attic ceilings.

You will be living in a Cape-Cod bungalow—there is no upstairs, the house is a primitive frame of empty walls, curtains hanging from the ceiling dividing space into discreet apartments. The kitchen is a three-burner Coleman stove set on a scrounged table, the bedroom a mattress on a plywood frame supported above the wardrobe trunk by cement blocks. Winter blankets the world outside, snapping at the plastic sheets battened over the windows. The upstairs rooms, like a caterpillar undergoing its slow and methodical metamor-

phosis, are being paneled, partitions are framed. And one raw day, the floor sander is unloaded from the back of the truck.

With spring, attention turns outward to the gardens. The house moves upstairs, a sheet is hung between the kitchen and the rest of the house, and the inside walls come tumbling down. A tarpaper blanket covers the nettlesome insulation. Windows sprout in blank grey walls, doors are rehung, and a clapboard wall, in its auto-da-fé, is the kindling it longed to be.

The house contracts with the seasons. The kitchen, like a camp follower, moves behind the lines. As the work continues on the downstairs walls, the bookshelves in the new library are stocked with flours and condiments, cooking pots and skillets. The venerable Coleman is resurrected from the garage to replace the cookstove, temporarily disabled due to rennovations. The tomatoes are started in their peat pots under the grow-light by the window as the kitchen cabinet base is leveled. Slowly the panels are built and the countertops set. Doors and drawers are a luxury, to be built next season, after the shop building is finished. For now it is enough to be back home on the range, with places to empty all the old milk crates into, shelves to fill, instead of boxes to rummage.

And so it goes for as long as it must, a rhythm of seasonal breaths, in and out, in and out, until one day that eternal list of THINGS TO BE DONE that has been wearing a permanent groove between your shoulder blades is suddenly very light. Like a bucket that has sprung a leak, there is not much more to carry. You feel empty, strange—it's like realizing that you don't have to get up and go to school every morning, that there's no homework to do at night. Like retirement, suddenly work is no longer a reflex; you have to ask yourself, what am I going to do this weekend? What needs doing? The days expand, your evenings are given back to you, like a discharged mortgage. Your life is your own, your legs are spongy, you move with an unaccustomed lightness of purpose.

Of course, the vessel of desire soon fills, there is always that which must be done. Thinking that there is an end is only the first link in the chain as it is tightened again. But for those first few heady days when it is possible to float, to put attention into yourself and your dimly remembered family, you find that the embers of the feeling have never died entirely, that you can rekindle the blaze and keep something of that freedom as a milepost on the road to the rest of your life.

The work of resurrecting an old house is too great an undertaking to be digested whole. It must be chewed thoroughly. The objective is chopped like spaghetti for a two-year-old into smaller, easily worked pieces. By focusing on limited goals a sense of proportion is maintained, you are not overwhelmed and swallowed by THE GOAL. The reason for which you are doing all this suffering is easier to keep in sight. You are to enjoy and savor the process in and of itself, as a vehicle for self-discovery, not as an accounting of steps taken, of the sum needed to reach the horizon.

An old-timer I once worked with was watching me slam and jam a block of wood into a space too small. I was determined to stretch that opening rather than to take the time to recut the block. I guess he finally lost patience because he turned and said to me, "What's your hurry? You'll be doing this for the rest of your life. You might's well slow down and enjoy it, you damn fool!" Patience and the discipline to remember always that nothing is *that* important, nothing *has* to be done. No one is forcing you to do anything. The house is not the end. It is the path of love, and if it begins to destroy the love of yourself and family, let it go. So much as you become attached to the *idea* of the house, so much does it consume you and become a *thing*. A house should never become a thing but always be part of a larger relationship to the world you live in. And re-member—when you feel the monkey dancing on your shoulders—you knew the job was dangerous when you took it.

> A newcomer to Vermont, spending his first winter, was somewhat overwhelmed by the amount of snow. On a particularly bleak and blowy day he happened to be visiting his neighbor, a crusty old farmer who had weathered many a winter. In the course of the conversation he asked the old-timer, "Think it's ever going to stop snowing?" to which he received the answer, "Always has."
>
> [Anonymous]

SECTION 1   **THE HOUSE-WITHIN-A-HOUSE: THE SHAPE OF THE VESSEL**

The house-within-a-house concept, the movable feast, allows you to live and work under the same roof with a minimum of complete dislocation. The upstairs is the sanctuary, far above the grime and noise of the main-floor dismemberment. The main floor is cordoned off with poly sheets, the workshop is the living room, and the kitchen is found wherever there remains an undisturbed corner.

Plan the work in stages or modules and always leave a refuge. Like rotating fields to different crops, the entire undertaking will benefit. Lay out a flow chart for the entire job and allow spaces to catch up on yourself and your life.

The process of rebuilding is also an opportunity to let imagination and fancy have their day. A good reason for owning your own place is that it can really become your own, not somebody's idea of what you are. It can reflect you as your face expresses your moods. Do not allow yourself to be trapped into or tempted by stereotypes, a mass-produced image of what a house should look like or contain. As we have seen, paint and paper is a convention of fashion, moldings a relic, appliances an Armageddon.

Instead consider how your life is patterned: We spend a good portion of our span sleeping, eating, and defecating. This is our natural body. Our shelters should be designed to enhance the potentials of our physical being. A body in tune with itself grows outside of itself and enters into a harmonious relationship with the broader expanse of the universe. Thus our houses should quietly help further the unfolding of inner nature.

> The enlightened man was asked what he does, having attained such perfect understanding. He replied, "I chop wood, I carry water."
>
> [traditional Zen parable]

The Kitchen

The kitchen is the heart of the home, it is a place for communion—the breaking of bread. Food is a sacrament by which we come to know and be with each other. A kitchen should be a place where food is consecrated, not just shoveled out of a package, bombarded with microwaves, and swilled with television. If the kitchen invites people to gather, if it is not shut off from the flow of the house, hidden away—a kind of alimentary laundry room, the creative flow can happen. The kitchen should not be walled off by partitions. The preparation of food is not shameful, its preparer to be exiled to solitude while the rest of the family gathers in the parlor. A kitchen that is light and airy, that is built of natural materials, will draw people to it. It will be comfortable. The softness of wood and the warmth of brick will not disturb the mind or digestive tract.

All too many modern kitchens are built like automats or hospital galleys: hard, glaring surfaces, banks of gleaming machines—they are places that perform functions devoid of meaning. No one would actually want to spend time there. The dirty dishes are closeted away in a machine. Cleaning up after a meal, washing the dishes can be a pleasant communal way for people to work together. A properly designed kitchen will encourage people to linger and, when the basic energy is harmonious, people will work together. Insofar as food becomes merely a chore or bother, we become that much more alienated from ourselves, and that much more dependent on machines.

The harvest is brought to the kitchen to be put up for the winter. Besides being cozy, a kitchen should be functional. Storage space and work space are the most important aspects of a country kitchen. There has to be enough room to cut up the zucchini as well as cook it. City folks who rarely eat at home think of kitchens as a closet. Their lives are spent in the bedroom or the television den, drowning the daily exhaustion of overstimulus. The kitchen can also, as anything else, become an attachment. The "gourmet" cook confuses ends and means. The experience of food becomes nothing more than an ever-increasing

need for complex stimuli. True food is simple food. The act of eating is as important as what is eaten. Right eating heightens rather than overwhelms the spirit. The kitchen must not become an end in itself—the complete-gourmet-food-preparation-center (this idea, too, is an urban or bourgeois phenomenon), an ego trip—but must remain a tool, and we should always observe the higher level of eating as meeting.

When planning your kitchen, remember the *work triangle*—the principle by which the overall efficiency of a kitchen is rated (Figure 7–1).

The functions of a kitchen are divided into three main work centers, which correspond to corners of a triangle. The sides of the triangle may vary but the total length of all three sides should be no less than 12 feet and no more than 22 feet. The longest leg should be between the refrigerator and the stove or sink. The shortest leg should always be between the sink and stove. More trips are made between these two points than any other. A pedometer might reveal that an astonishing distance is covered during the course of a normal kitchen workday. A poorly designed kitchen can add even more steps to this pattern. No wonder you feel exhausted after a day on the range. A good rule of thumb is that basic functions should be within two steps of the cook standing in the center of the triangle. The refrigerator can be a little further removed because it is more a storage area for perishables than a work place in its own right.

The chores performed in the kitchen will divide the overall space into centers related to a particular function. These centers will have space for storage of necessary tools and work surfaces for performing a particular task. A *sink center* is basic for handling food and cleaning up. Countertops are necessary on both sides of the sink. Storage for detergents and cleaners and for dishes and utensils will be needed. The *refrigerator center* is a food-storage area. It should not be next to the stove because the heat from the stove will overload the refrigerator's cooling system. Ideally a counter should be provided to set food on close to the entrance door and, if possible, close to the refrigerator. The

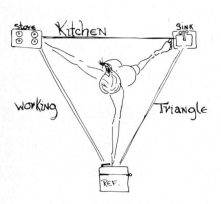

7–1 *The kitchen work triangle*

preparation center is where the food is mixed and chopped and otherwise prepared before being cooked or set out for serving. A space for a chopping block and an outlet for food-processing appliances should be included in the unit. This countertop should be the largest of all. For a house in which all food is store-bought, a 3-to-4-foot surface is enough. A country kitchen, where the harvest may require canning large amounts of bulky produce or cutting up sides of meat, will need more space. From 5 to 8 feet of countertop would be ideal. Storage for baking and cooking supplies measuring and mixing utensils, small appliances and dry goods, is needed. This storage should be located or included with the refrigerator or sink center. An L- or U-shaped area or a central island can accommodate the design.

The *cooking area* contains the stove (or stoves if both gas and wood stoves are used) and a small counter for pots and pans. Space for storing pots and pans and utensils is also helpful. A wall alongside the stove can be used to hang the best cookware on. Any of these centers can be combined to utilize limited space by sharing a common countertop. A *storage center* is an indispensable part of a land- or whole-food-based lifestyle. Families that buy their food in bulk from co-ops or who grow and put up a large amount of their food needs have a requirement for greater storage capacity than the supermarket shopper. The pantry can be part of the kitchen but is best outside the work triangle, nearer to the entrance door. Other specialized work areas can be designed to suit the needs of the individual family: bakery centers with a lower-than-standard countertop to facilitate bread kneading, office centers, eating areas, and so on.

The kitchen is planned so that the main flow of traffic does not pass through the work triangle. A parade through the soufflé is not good planning. A certain amount of space is required for concentration on the task at hand. Kitchens should invite circulation (they are generally attached to the back, or familial, entrance, rather than the front, or formal, entrance), not as a direct highway but more as an eddy off the main thoroughfare.

Flooring for Kitchens: Slate, Vinyl-Asbestos, Particle Board

While on the subject of traffic, note that the kitchen floor bears a large share of the total household perambulations. Food preparation can be messy. And the floor will bear testimony to this. Flooring materials for a kitchen should be capable of suffering abuse with a minimum of maintenance. Wood is not always the most suitable material for kitchen floors. Although a well-sealed wood floor is water repellent, it will show dirt very easily. A daily scrubbing will be necessary to keep the boards from being obscured by a crust of grime. Staining the floors a dark tone before they are sealed will help minimize this problem to some extent. Because of the heavy traffic, a kitchen floor should be sealed with four coats of a top-quality sealer.

One alternative to the maintenance problems of wood flooring, which does not compromise the natural-materials purist, is a floor of gauged slate or quarry tiles. Gauged slate is analogous in thickness to planed lumber. One side is surfaced, to provide for good adhesion and uniform thickness, and the other side is natural. Quarry tiles are smooth-surfaced tiles of either slate or man-made ceramic. Tiles must be laid on a smooth, stable surface. An old wood floor is neither. An underlayment of particle board or plywood is needed over very uneven floors. Underlayment-grade ¼-inch hardboard can also be used if the floor is not too badly warped. Continuous joints should be perpendicular to any joints in the existing floor, except when laying plywood, where it is not necessary because of the greater rigidity of plywood. A coat of panel adhesive troweled over the subfloor will help prevent the popping of nails that can be caused by changes in the stability of the subfloor. Underlayment nails (ring-shank nails similar to sheetrock nails but with smaller heads) are driven 6 inches apart over the entire surface. A 4-inch spacing is used along the edges of each sheet. Sheets of underlayment should actually be separated from direct contact with each other by a $\frac{1}{32}$-inch gap. Use a matchbook cover inserted between the joints to space them.

Random-patterned gauged slate actually is applied in a precise pattern. The basic module will generally be printed on the packing carton. The slate is available in several colors, either solid or mixed. Quarry tile is similar to slate tile but is cut to uniform 6-inch squares, a dull brick red in color. Spread a coat of tile mastic over the underlayment. Do not apply over an area greater than you can finish within the drying period of the cement. Slate and quarry tile require a different mastic than asphalt, vinyl, or porcelain tiles do, so be sure to read the labels and choose the correct product. Mastic is now available with a nonflammable solvent base but there is some controversy as to its durability in comparison with the standard type. Some professional floor installers will not guarantee a floor against separation if it is laid with the nonflammable mastic. (They will use it on walls, however.) When you are working with tile mastic, make sure you have good ventilation as the fumes are poisonous and will cause dizziness and headaches and a generally unpleasant intoxication if inhaled too heavily.

After the tile has set, it must be grouted. Use slate-*cement* type grout for floors, not the less durable *plaster* type used for porcelain wall tiles. The grout is mixed with water and rubbed into the cracks between the tiles with a trowel, cloth, or sponge. Dry grout is sprinkled over the surface to absorb the excess. Cleanup is done with a dry rag followed by several moppings with a damp rag. Any remaining stains can be removed with a wash of vinegar and water. Do not let thick smudges of grout dry on the tiles. They do not clean easily.

Since slate is porous, the floor will have to be sealed. Use clear masonry sealer. Two coats of urethane varnish will complete the finish. Slate tiles can also be used for countertop surfaces and backsplashes as well as for tub and lavatory enclosures. The tiles should be glued to a particle-board underlayment. Edges can be butted to slate or trimmed with wood bandings.

Cutting slate tiles is not difficult if a skilsaw or radial arm saw equipped with a masonry blade is used. Successive scoring cuts are made until the tile can be broken on the line. (Usually about halfway through.) Never try to cut the tile at a single pass, as the blade will only overheat and destroy itself. Wear a dust mask and eye protection. A radial arm saw is the ideal tool for making fast, accurate cuts. Rough edges can be smoothed with a Surform® block plane (which will become dull after a while) or a carborundum block (much slower, but longer lasting). Circular cuts are made by using the edge of the skilsaw to rough in shallow arcs until the tile snaps. The various tungsten-carbide hacksaw blades and other hand tools are far too slow for such work.

Slate is not cheap. It will cost as much per square foot as quality hardwood flooring (about the same as plastic laminates). It also has the disadvantage of brittleness. A heavy object accidentally dropped onto a slate floor can crack the tiles. It will also scratch easily if a metal object (refrigerator, stove, table) is dragged across it. These scratches will not sand out as with wood. Your best protection is a good, hard urethane finish over the tiles. Contrary to popular opinion, slate as a flooring material is actually not any more tiring on your feet and legs than a wood floor. Studies have shown that aching feet are a result more of the shoe material and heel design than the hardness of the flooring surface. There is the psychological dimension of perceived hardness, however, which these studies ignore, and you may decide in favor of wood or carpet for that reason, although I couldn't imagine a more unsanitary surface for a kitchen floor than carpeting.

The same underlayment that will carry a slate floor will also do for a sheet or tile vinyl-asbestos floor (erroneously referred to by many as "linoleum," which is a far less durable material, actually a patterned heavy-duty tarpaper). Vinyl-asbestos, like plastic laminates, do have their advantages. The sheet, when properly installed, is a very durable floor that requires little maintenance and is sound deadening as well as comfortable under the feet. It tends to be warm, whereas slate is often very cold. The selection of pattern should be guided by how well it shows dirt and the relationship between the pattern and the rest of the room. As with the use of color in general, the color of the floor can have a potent effect upon the mood of the people working in the kitchen.

Individual-tile floors have a habit of popping up over the years, but they are easily owner installed. Generally, all you need to know is printed on the package. For guides, snap a chalk line down the center line of the room and another at right angles to it, also dividing the room in two. Use a framing square to lay out the angle. Mark over this line with a pencil, so it will not be smeared and lost when you spread the adhesive. Lay the tiles into position without sliding them, which would cause mastic to ooze up between the joints. Before you spread the adhesive over the floor, make a trial layout of the tile pattern along the guide line to see how well it fits against the end walls. Space the layout to avoid having to fill in with small pieces along the walls if possible. The principle is similar to starting shingles in the center of the roof. You may find that you need to offset the starting (center) line in order to avoid ending up with a narrow strip. Lay all full tiles first, and then do your margin work. The pattern or color of the design is frequently varied around the perimeter of the room.

Vinyl-asbestos sheet requires the skill born of experience to properly cut and fit around fixtures and to minimize seams. It is best laid before the cabinets or plumbing fixtures are installed. A heavy roller is necessary to smooth the material and insure a good bond. Try laying the floor yourself if you feel handy with a linoleum knife and have access to a roller (small, water-filled lawn rollers can be rented or bought. The metal surface of the roller is best covered with a cloth or old towels stitched together to keep it from scratching the floor). Most flooring dealers will be glad to give you advice you'll need to do a good job. If you don't want to do it yourself, you can get a price that includes installation. One note of caution: Although vinyl-asbestos flooring appears flexible, avoid sharp bends when maneuvering it into place, as it can easily crack.

The ultimate in low-cost floors, offering flexibility in design as well as an outlet for creative expression, is a simple, painted particle-board surface. Standard underlayment-grade particle board is glued to the subfloor with panel adhesive and nailed 16 inches O.C. with underlayment nails. The surface is painted with heavy-duty porch and deck enamel or an all-purpose machinery-type enamel, which can be found in a surprising range of vivid colors. Designs can be worked into the floor with a little planning. Use two coats of the lightest shade as a base. When dry, paint over it the darker elements of the pattern. This technique can be used to create the checkerboard effect of real floor tiles or to create much more whimsical or intricate designs, borders, or medallions. A third color can be overlaid on the first two.

Such a floor can be a temporary expedient, which will cover an otherwise drab and unfinished surface until a permanent floor is installed. If the entire floor is given a few coats of urethane varnish, the pattern will last a lot longer between repaintings. It can always be redone if you decide a fresh design would be helpful.

The Bathroom

The bathroom has to be one of the most underrated, ignored, and poorly designed rooms in the house. Our attitude toward bathrooms is paradoxical: On the one hand the number of bathrooms in a house is a sign of prestige and wealth. But its very name denies its real function, its true reason for being. When someone says, "I've got to go the bathroom," chances are good that they aren't about to take a bath. This attitude of shame and secrecy about our basic bodily functions is a barnacle embedded in our cultural conditioning.

"One need not be reminded that modern bathroom systems are ugly, expensive and unhealthful." Until our attitudes about defecation and other body processes change, our bathrooms will continue to conform to Ken Kern's observation. The very name "water closet" implies that whatever happens within should be hidden or closeted away from sight. Thus excrement is considered "waste" and washed away as quickly as possible, to a subterranean limbo where it magically vanishes without any further effort on our part, where someone else does our dirty work. The loss of potentially valuable nutrients and the huge public costs of reprocessing these wastes are not remarked. The role of excrement as a crucial linchpin in the ecology of natural cycles is likewise ignored, at even greater long-term costs. Our uptightness as a culture may prevent us from appreciating those moments of simple communion with the body basic; our unbalanced diets may also make elimination an ordeal. As soon as sitting on the pot is appreciated for the relaxing pleasure it can be, toilets will be designed with the same care and attention to detail and rightful form that we lavish upon our kitchens.

There are several studies that allege that the position the conventional toilet design forces us to assume when eliminating is actually unhealthful, compared to the natural, squatting position used by humans in the open. The bowl is set too high for complete evacuation of the bowels. This condition, it seems, can lead to a host of spiritual as well as intestinal ills. Unfortunately, other than constructing your own squatting toilet (there are designs and molds available— see Kern's *Owner-Built Home,* Vol. III, Chap. 10), there is little you can do to avoid use of the little white god. The installation of a waterless toilet, such as the Clivus Multrum, allows you to set the height of the seat lower than a standard bowl. It also allows you to compost your wastes instead of flushing them away.

If the toilet fixture itself cannot be ideal, at least the room in which it sits should be. Wood, when properly sealed, is as hygienic as porcelain tile, and much more pleasing. The burnished glow of fine oiled cedar or redwood paneling, the warm interplay of slate tops and light from a well-placed window, magazines or *The Farmer's Almanac,* and a few green plants will create a comfortable and meditative atmosphere, which will help induce healthy elimination.

The bath itself should be a soothing experience. The surroundings must contribute to a mood of leisure and relaxation. The sunken bath is an attempt to recognize the sensuality implicit in the act of bathing. The hard, impersonal surfaces of glazed porcelain, or the flaking coating of plastic panels, the dizzying optical illusions of the floor-tile grid—features of the typical bathroom—are not. Framing a sunken bath into an existing house is not a reasonable job for most people, nor is it an inexpensive antidote to the doldrums of the standard undersized bathtub.

It is very likely that the old place will have, firmly planted in the oversized closet that passes as a ''bathroom,'' an old-fashioned, claw-foot tub (also called an Essex tub by plumbers). Don't be in a hurry to cart it off to the dump or out to the pasture for a stock-waterer. Study its shape and construction with a critical eye, notice how roomy, how deep it is, and how invitingly the sloping back asks you to slip into its warm waters, to float and forget. And compare that to the compact cubicle of a modern tub, as functional and as relaxing as an ice-cube tray. The peeling paint can be scraped and sanded or brushed smooth. The tub can be given a coat of bright all-purpose enamel. Its toenails can be manicured. Or, if the fact that dust can collect under its belly really does disturb you, consider enclosing the entire tub and making a raised version of a sunken bath.

The Bargain-Basement Bathtub: Enclosing a Tub

To enclose a tub, it first must be disconnected and removed. A particle-board top is cut to a size that encompasses the whole tub and leaves counter surfaces at top and bottom ends as well as a narrow margin along either side. A framework of 2 × 2s or 2 × 4s is built to carry the top and is nailed plumb and level to the floor and supporting walls. Meanwhile, place the tub upside down on the particle board and scribe its perimeter with a pencil. Using dividers, transfer the outer line at least half the distance between the edge of the lip and the body of the tub (the exact dimensions will vary with the tub—usually they are somewhere near to 1 or 1½ inches). Cut out the opening. Nail the top to the framework.

The choice of surface material depends on your imagination. Quarry tiles, Formica®, or tongue-and-groove boards are possibilities. Secure the material (if not Formica®) with mastic or construction adhesive. If using wood, blind-nail the pieces, or else screw them into the base and countersink and plug the holes. Transfer the tub opening onto the new surface, using the original cutout as a template, and cut any projecting boards or tiles flush to the edge. When cutting slate tiles, do not press too hard with the skilsaw, as they can break free of the mastic. Seal all edges and joints with silicone caulking, paying particular attention to the joint between the top and side walls. The trim treatment can be simple or fancy. Tiles should be glued to a side panel cut to fit before it is placed vertically. Nails are driven to hold it to the framework by setting them between the ungrouted tile joints. When laying out a tiled side panel, be sure to align the joints with those of the tiles on the top surface.

Caulk the rim of the tub and carefully set the tub into position. (This job will require a few extra hands, as cast-iron tubs are very heavy.) To protect yourself from mashed fingertips, set it upon 1 × 1 corner shims, which are later removed. Insert a pry bar under the lip of the tub and raise it while you

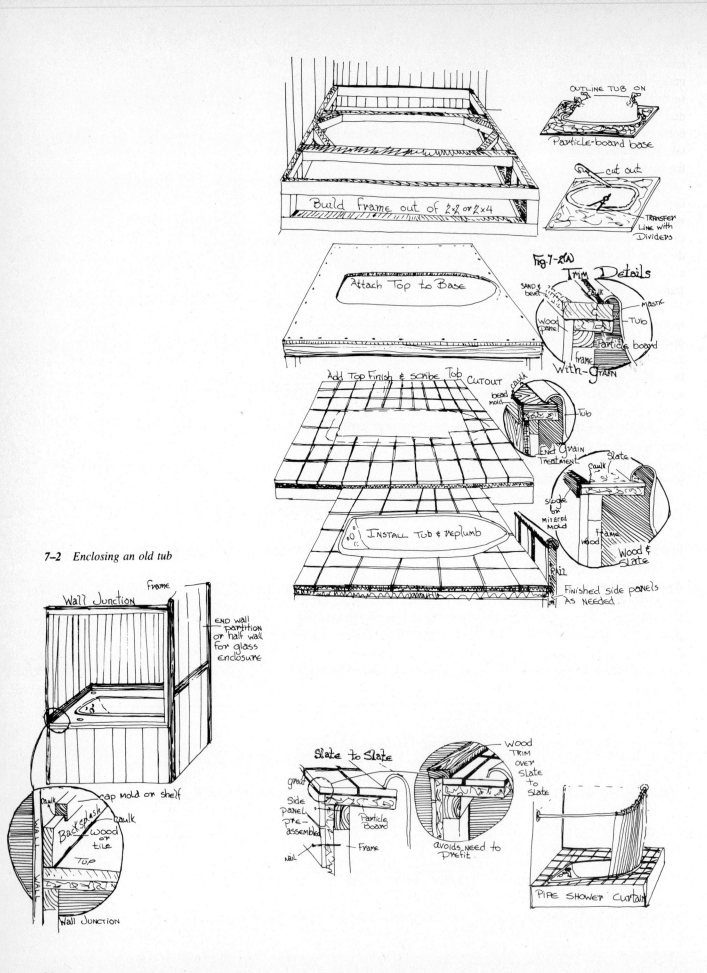

OUTLINE TUB ON
Particle-board base

cut out

TRANSFER Line with Dividers

Build Frame out of 2×2 or 2×4

Attach Top to Base

Fig. 7-2(A)

Trim Details

SAND & bevel
caulk
mastic
Wood panel
Tub
Particle board
frame
With-grain

Add Top Finish & scribe Tub CutOut

caulk
bead mold
Tub
End Grain Treatment

Slate
caulk
single or mitered mold
Frame wood
Wood & Slate

Install Tub & replumb

Rail

Finished side panels As Needed.

7–2   Enclosing an old tub

Wall Junction

frame

END wall partition or half wall for glass enclosure

cap mold or shelf

caulk
Backsplash
caulk
Wood or tile
TOP

Wall Junction

Slate to Slate

grout
Side Panel pre-assembled
nail
Particle Board
Frame

Wood TRIM over slate to slate

avoids need to prefit.

PIPE SHOWER CURTAIN

remove the temporary blocks. Be sure to insert a protective shingle or shim under the fulcrum of the pry bar itself to avoid damaging the finished tub-top surface. With your finger, smooth the caulking bead around the rim. A small drain hole can be cut in the top and fitted with a sink or shower drain that is connected to the tub drain, to carry away water that splashes onto the top when taking a shower. Reconnect the plumbing before you install the side panels in the frame.

One of the advantages of enclosing a tub is that the shower stall can be easily fitted to the enclosure. Glass doors are caulked and fitted between the end walls. A partition or half-partition wall may be needed if the tub enclosure is to fit the glass shower doors. Check on the standard measurements of glass doors before you build the enclosure. A simpler solution is to hang a shower curtain from a chromed pipe, a homemade copper-pipe unit, or even a bentwood frame.

Essex tubs were manufactured before showers became common and are lacking the shower-head connection of a standard tub faucet. The centers of the openings are also closer together than on a modern faucet unit. Consider a European-style, personal shower-massage unit, which is hand held and connects to the tub spout. If you must have a standing shower, it is a simple matter to splice into the existing tub-feed lines and add an additional set of faucets to control the shower head. (See Figure 7–4.)

Many people prefer a separate shower stall. The commercial options are either a metal enclosure, which is reminiscent of the stall around a public toilet, or a molded fiberglass unit that is functional and easy to install and can be quite elegant. It can also be featureless.

A wood shower stall can be built that is not only watertight but also a pleasant and sensual alternative. The base can be all wood or else copper sheet soldered at the corners. The copper should extend up the sides of the stall. In fact, it can be carried up to tub height. When wood is used, a coat of epoxy finish should be applied. Only dry, stable wood is suitable for the base. Joints should be sealed with silicone caulking. The base can be built perfectly level, in which case water will remain to be sponged up after the shower is done, or it can be tilted to drain toward either end. A copper base can be shimmed with shingles and the metal formed to drain to a low middle point. A fascinating alternative for the true madman is to carve the entire base out of a single slab or bole of wood. Carve with the face grain instead of into end grain, which would tend to check and be hard to seal.

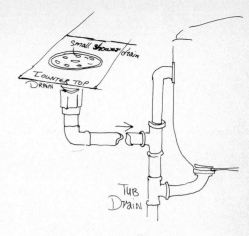

7–3 Auxiliary drain for enclosed shower/tub combination

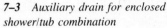

7–4 Adding shower-supply lines

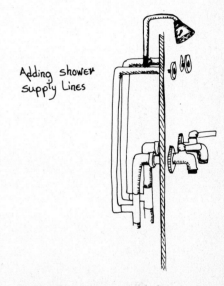

7–5 Home-built shower stall

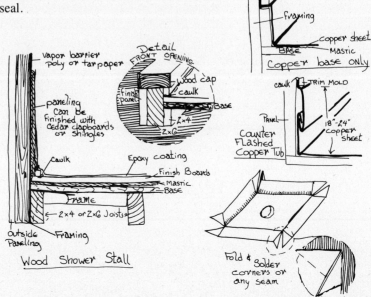

The same techniques can be used to set the lavatory sink in a countertop or base cabinet. Use a rim-mounting bowl sink. A homemade copper sink is quite simple, and even a wood sink is possible. Often, a search of antique shops or demolition yards will uncover a treasure like a marble-basin sink. A wall-mounted sink can also be paneled and enclosed into a base cabinet, either by building a cabinet under the sink, if it is a modern vitreous unit, or by fitting the boards behind the lip of an old-fashioned, cast-iron type.

Actually there is no intrinsic reason why the bathing and the excretory functions have to be carried out in the same room. A complete separation is possible: The indoor bath and outdoor toilet is the old-fashioned standard. Equally possible are a separate Saturday night bathhouse and/or sauna cabin and an indoor toilet. A simple stall shower can be used inside the house for convenience, while the outside unit can be wood heated and spring or pond fed.

7–6 *Wall-mounted and basin sink enclosures*

The Bedroom

The interior space in most houses is designed by default. The typical scheme treats a room as an empty box into which pieces of furniture are indiscriminately dumped. The greatest concentration of furnishings is found splayed against the perimeter walls. In effect, nothing happens within the room itself. People themselves are only part of the package, pieces moved through a minuet.

The bedroom is typical of this design by neglect: a box with a bed, a dresser, and a closet (more boxes, with or without covers)—a place to sleep, to dress in, and to leave. There may well be a relationship between the dull torpor many marriages slip into and the dullness of the spaces in which the nuptial rites are carried out. This drabness must be another facet of the ethos of shame, which denied the healthy pleasures of the flesh; sex wasn't supposed to be fun. The average bedroom dampens the heat of passion, extinguishes the spark of joy. The colors are somber or soporific at best, the sleep is that of weary bodies in seedy motel beds.

Well-oiled wood is the substance of exotic dreams: Faces peer from the knots, like wood nymphs, fauns, the very walls are the smooth skin of living trees. They are fluid in the glimmer of a kerosene lamp or a candle, casting angled planes of shadow on the mysterious ceiling. And in the morning the sun rises with you, smiling through the eastern windows. Plants stretch and yawn in their pots; this is the dawn of creation.

The foolishness of bedding down on an expensive and complicated web of wire springs and board and fabrics should be apparent to any thoughtful person. A built-in platform bed with a foam mattress will give a much sounder and relaxing sleep. Building in a bed runs counter to the mobility of the average family, which picks up its possessions every few years and sticks them into another box. Building in your own furniture is an investment in place as well as a way of avoiding the overblown cost of commercial furniture. The built-in bed can be incorporated into the wall as well as the floor to include a headboard, storage space, and night tables. Deep, wide drawers for linen, blanket, and pyjama storage can be built into the base of the bed itself. Compare this living and sleeping center to the conventional box-spring mattress.

7–7   *A built-in bed*

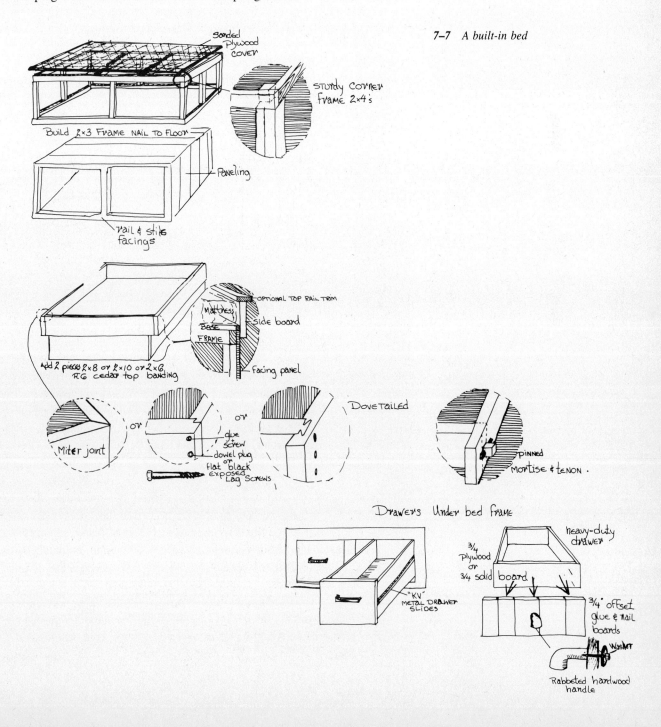

Storage Spaces:
Attic, knee wall, closets

Flexible storage space is another function of the house that must be planned. At what each square foot of floor space will cost you to build, maximum utilization is imperative. Applying this standard, closets are unaffordable, but unfortunately, they seem to be indispensable. The best compromise is to utilize for storage as much as possible of what would otherwise be dead space and then add closets as needed. The knee wall of a saltbox or gable-roofed cape is a typical example of dead space. The limitations of height are overcome by storing items on horizontal shelves or in pull-out drawers. The depth of the closets can be varied along a single wall if desired. The inaccessible recesses formed where roof meets floor are insulated and closed off from the usable part.

An attic is an unaffordable waste of space if it is used only for storage and not for living. But the area above the collar ties (on a 28-foot-wide house with a 12-12-pitch roof, this will be a triangle approximately 10 feet across the base and 5 feet to the ridge) is an excellent place to store those items that are better forgotten but somehow worth keeping. A trap door between the joists provides access. If the entire length of the ceiling is not closed in but a portion left open to the ridge, a hinged door can be built into the face of the triangular opening that is created.

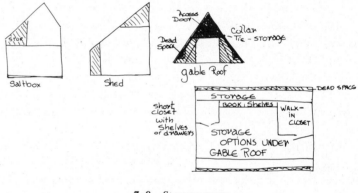

7–8 Storage areas

Closets can also fit under and over stairwells. A built-in drawer unit can replace a bureau and save floor space. The bed can be set against a partition wall that also contains a walk-in closet and perhaps ducts for pipes or chimneys. Built-in benches under window seats also allow additional storage under their movable tops.

The Cellar

The need for a full basement is questionable in a new house. The owner no longer needs a place to store coal or firewood (although this is changing). Furnaces that heat with forced hot air or hot water can be installed anywhere in a first-floor utility closet. They are clean and quiet. Refrigerators and freezers do the work of the root cellar, and the washer and dryer can be piggybacked into a single closet. But a house built in grandfather's day is more than likely equipped with a cellar, which was a vital storage space in the days before refrigeration. This space is often woefully underused today, dark and damp, a place to store things no one wants, a place to frighten children. Or else it is finished off into a workshop for the weekend handyman and a game room for the teenagers.

As people rediscover the advantages of growing their own food and heating with wood, the rationale for restoring the cellar to its original role in the household system gains credibility. If you have the space, it may as well be well used. Converting a dark and damp cellar into a game room or television den, may prove as costly, when figured on a square-foot basis, as building it from scratch, whereas subdividing a cellar into an earth-floored cold room and a utility core and workshop on a slab floor is perhaps more economical and suitable to your lifestyle.

A cold room is the old root cellar garbed in modern terminology. The freezer can be kept in this even-temperatured room where the motor will not have to work as hard to keep the contents cool. The wall that separates it from the rest of the cellar should be well insulated to help control temperature. Floor and ceiling vents made from a block louver can be installed in the wall to control natural ventilation currents. The ceiling vent is opened in the winter if additional heat is needed to prevent the room from freezing. Both vents can be opened in the summer to induce a cooling air flow. The access door should be an insulated sandwich door. Storage inside the cold room is provided by racks of wood shelves. Oenophiles will appreciate the advantages of an even and cool room temperature for storing their treasures. Bins for apples and potatoes, barrels for cider, crocks for sauerkraut and salt pork, sand-filled boxes for carrots and turnips, and rows of pickles and preserves in jars—the only modern note is sounded by the freezer humming to itself against the back wall. The ceiling between the cold room and the first floor should also be well insulated with a minimum of six inches of fiberglass. The vapor barrier should be directly under the floorboards. Homosote sheets make an inexpensive and functional ceiling and wall covering.

The cold room is installed at the opposite end of the cellar from the furnace. The rest of the cellar can be devoted to wood storage. The wood should be protected from direct contact with a dirt floor by piling it upon skids of creosoted scrap planks. Uprights made from 2 × 4s can be nailed to the floor joists and braced to these skids to help keep the firewood stacked upright. A kindling bin can be built for odd pieces too troublesome to stack. The front boards are made to remove for easy access.

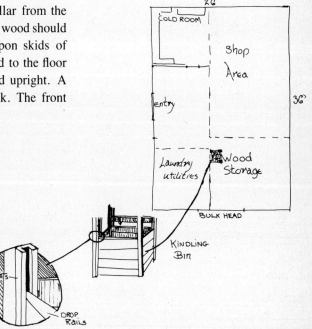

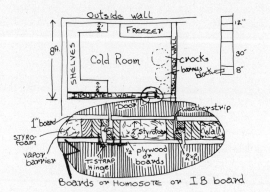

7–9   Cold room in cellar

7–10   Well-utilized cellar

A Few Pertinent Remarks on Getting in the Wood

Wood heat is the cornerstone of self-sufficient living in the forested regions of the North. Wood as a fuel suffers from the disadvantage of bulk: You need a place to store it. If the furnace is in the cellar, the ideal place to store your wood is in the cellar also. The residual heat from the furnace will help keep it dry, particularly if a floor-level duct is directed toward it. Try to avoid loading wood into the cellar during or after a rain. The wood should be as dry as possible when it is brought inside. Damp, rain-soaked wood will not dry out very quickly, and the moisture it contains will add to your mold and dry-rot problems. If you heat with an upstairs stove instead of a furnace, the cellar is still a good place to keep your wood, especially if you can avoid the need to carry up armloads of wood several times each day. The solution is to build a dumbwaiter, which can be operated from below by a rope and pulley.

The key to efficient wood heating is to minimize the number of steps between tree and stove. Set up a flow chart to analyze the path of that piece of maple, and see how many times it is actually handled before it gets burned, and where you can eliminate extra steps and handling.

If you cut your own wood rather than purchase it split and delivered, you are already several steps behind (and several dollars ahead). Getting the wood out of the woods can be a major energy expenditure. Your analysis starts at the tree. Do you block the wood to length on site, or do you cut it into the largest billets you can comfortably haul and truck it home to where it can wait further cutting at your "leisure"? Once the wood is in your yard, it is a lot closer to the stove than out in the woods. But is the time involved in rehandling each piece before it goes into the cellar balanced by the convenience of having a woodpile to work at during those odd hours before supper, a cord to split when you are feeling frustrated? If you cut your wood early in the year (March or April), it pays to take the time to buck it up to stove size in the woods. It can even be left stacked in the woods all summer long and quickly gathered in, come

7–ll A dumbwaiter for the cellar woodshed

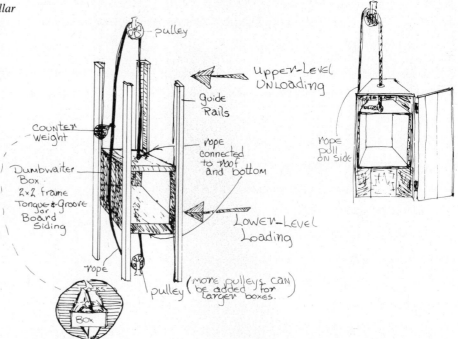

fall, although more typically, the first thought about getting in the wood generally coincides with the first frost, and the first cord actually comes in with the first snow. If at least the bulk of your wood is in the yard in wholesale form, so to speak, it can be blocked up during the winter as needed. This plan involves a lot of shoveling out, chipping away ice, burning off water before the wood thaws and is a most inefficient system. At least cover the pile and the outdoor woodstacks with a tarpaulin or a sheet of old steel roofing.

A woodshed attached to the house, with a door that you can drive up to for unloading wood and another door or hatch opening through the house wall directly behind the stove is a way to shorten the number of extra steps from cellar to stove. The ideal system would include cutting the wood to length in the spring of the year and, as the trees are felled, loading directly onto a truck or tractor-drawn wagon, unloading and stacking in the woodshed and then loading only once more, into the stove. Selecting trees of a small diameter that do not require splitting is the key to this system. Billets of wood can be stacked in the yard to be split and dried during the summer, with the addition of one more handling cycle. How well you approximate this ideal is a function of how well you can coordinate your time with the demands of your lifestyle.

Building an Attached Woodshed

If your house does not already have one, build an attached woodshed on the north wall. This location actually helps conserve wood by acting as an insulating baffle between the house and the heat-sucking north winds. There are no heat-squandering windows on the common wall.

If a shed is to be attached to an existing wall, it must be properly flashed to prevent leakage at the junction between shed roof and house wall. In new construction, the flashing is installed before the sheathing is nailed to the wall. Unfortunately, that is not possible in remodeling work. To build an attached shed, whether for wood or other storage, first determine the point where the rafters will intersect the wall and level a line for the header or ledger. There are several ways to fasten and support the rafters. Figure 7–12 details the specifics. When the header must be fastened to a beveled surface (such as clapboards and shingles), it should be aligned so as not to tilt. Use a shim to hold it plumb, if necessary.

To fit the flashing against an end wall (with horizontal siding boards), remove as many courses of siding as will be covered with flashing. Pry the nails

7–12 Headers and rafter connection to side wall for a shed

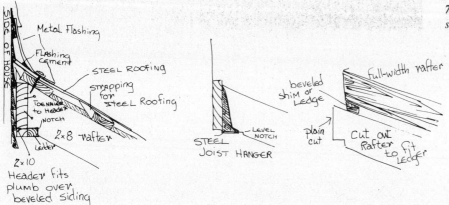

carefully from the last course and slide the flashing up between it and the substrate or studding. Renail the siding. Fold the flashing to fit the roof and fasten it securely, sealing it with a bead of flashing cement laid under its bottom edge. If the gable end of a shed must be fastened to the wall or the rafters and header must be fitted to vertical boards (this same technique is used for the addition of gabled roofs to existing walls), a chalk line is snapped at the point where the flashing will enter under the siding. Another line is marked at a point about 2 inches above the first line, and the siding is cut through on both these lines to the substrate or studding. Keep a careful eye for nails as you make the cut. Set the saw for proper depth of cut. Gently pry up the last course of sheathing above the cutout and insert the flashing well up under the gap (2 to 4 inches). When cutting through clapboards or shingles, it will not generally be necessary to cut out a section of the siding first. One or more passes of the saw blade should allow enough room to slip the flashing up under. This method works best for vertically sided walls where the flashing enters the side wall at an angle. All siding courses can be removed between the shed roof and the flashing on a horizontally sided wall and the flashing inserted under the last remaining course, if there is a good substrate to nail the flashing itself to under the siding boards.

A shed requires no more foundation than a simple concrete pier (or even a pressure-treated creosote pole) set below frost line. Sonotubes® are cylindrical cardboard tubes used to form concrete pillars and are ideal for this purpose. The tube must rest on a pad of concrete, which gives it stability and prevents it from tilting or heaving. The pad can be poured separately or simultaneously with the tube. To lay out the foundation, stretch a line between stakes to mark the outside of the shed wall. Measure out from the house wall the desired width of the shed. By using a *batter board,* it will be possible to adjust the mark and reset the strings, which can be removed while the holes are dug, either by hand or with

7–13 *Fitting flashing to the side wall*

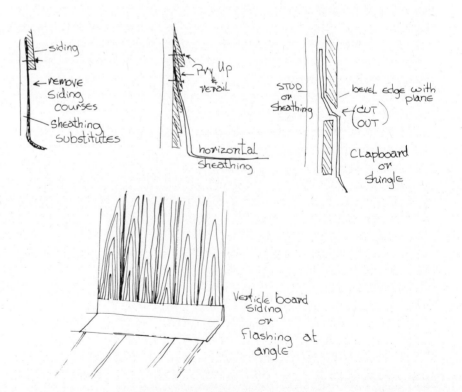

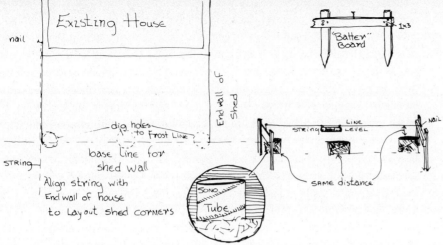

a backhoe, depending on soil type and depth of hole. (See Figure 7–14.) The line for the end wall of the shed is squared with the house by fastening a string to the far corner of the house and stretching it along the house wall, until it is aligned in the same plane as the house wall. The intersection of this string with the baseline string marks the outside corner of the shed. The top of the batter boards should be leveled and a string set to the desired height for the top of the concrete piers and leveled from one end of the line to the other with a line level, a transit level, or even a straight-edged board and a carpenter's level. (A transit level is a handy tool for the professional builder, but hardly necessary for the home builder. Essentially, its operation involves leveling the base of the telescope and then sighting to a leveling rod and reading the difference between the surface being measured and the level line set up by the scope. You can rent one for laying out foundations for houses and barns. It is particularly useful for establishing level points over uneven ground and slopes, or for drainage ditches and the like. A line level is simply a small leveling vial that hooks over a tightly stretched string, which then reads level when it is properly aligned.) The string itself need not be set to the actual height of the foundation piers; so long as the batter boards are level with respect to each other, a common distance can be taken off the string between it and the desired pier height. This allows a low string to span rough and uneven ground without having to shovel a path through the humps for it. The location of the center piers are taken off the string by measuring along its length. Mark the rough centers of the pier holes with stakes and remove the strings from the batter boards. After the holes are dug and a pad poured for the tube, the tube forms are set in the holes. The strings are reset on the batter boards. A plumb line dropped from the string will locate the centers of the tubes as necessary. Generally it is enough if the outside edges of the tubes are touching the strings and the tubes are held plumb. (The strings should always be set to allow the *centers* of the tube to align with the *centers* of the posts. Otherwise the posts will bear on the edge of a tube or the dimensions of the structure will have to shrink.)

To pour a tube and its pad simultaneously, cut the Sonotube® slightly longer than the estimated length needed. Build a frame of 1 × 6 boards about 2 feet square. Nail a 2-foot square of scrap ½-inch plywood to its top. Center and scribe the outside circumference of the Sonotube® on the plywood and cut out the hole with a sabre saw. Insert the end of the Sonotube® into the plywood flush with the bottom edge, and staple the cardboard to the plywood (small nails can be used in lieu of staples). Center the form in the hole, using pebbles under its edge, if needed, to shim it level and plumb and then backfill it with a hand shovel until it is stable. Check the alignment of the tube while you are backfilling it. A backhoe can be used once the tube is stable, so long as the fill is carefully emplaced. Drive one or two 4-foot lengths of rebar into the ground in the center of the tube. The entire pad and column are now ready to be filled with concrete.

A cement mixer or wheelbarrow can be used to fill each tube if only a few tubes must be filled. For larger jobs, such as a shed barn, use a ready-mix truck and wheelbarrow the concrete to each tube. The base form is left in the ground, and the cardboard is peeled back from the form below the ground line. Since the cardboard is spiral wound, it peels back rather easily.

An alternative is simply to use the sides of the hole itself as a form for the pad, or else a simple wood 2 × 2 form and to pour the tube after the pad has set. A length of rebar should be driven into the pad before it sets to help tie it to the tube.

The outside of each tube is marked for height and a 16d spike driven through its wall to mark the height of the pour. This is easier than trying to cut a tube to a level height. Cut a slit in the side to the level mark to allow excess concrete fluids to drain out. Use a stick as a plunger to settle the concrete while it is poured. Before it sets completely, insert a threaded ½-inch sill anchor bolt in the center, or allow the rebar to project 4 inches or so above the surface as a post anchor. If your tubes are poured to only an approximate level height with respect to each other, the posts themselves can be leveled across their tops instead.

The corner posts should be drilled to fit over the anchor pin. Drill a ⅝-inch hole for a ½-inch pin, to allow slack for adjustment. Alternatively, sills can be bolted to the threaded anchor bolts and posts and stud walls framed above. The post-and-girder system is faster and cheaper. The posts are plumbed and braced with temporary supports. A header timber or built-up beam is fastened across the tops of the posts, which should be cut to a level height. The corners are tied into the house walls. The rafters are then cut and nailed to the header and plate (or girder). The pattern for the rafter layout is made by holding the rafter piece against the plate and header at the end wall of the shed and scribing the line of intersection. Use a square to mark the plumb cut from the header first, cut that angle, and then scribe the birdsmouth over the plate and cut it. Otherwise it will be difficult to determine the proper rafter length. Strapping to carry metal roofing or decking for roll roofing is added, the roofing material is

7–15 *Forming for Sonotubes®*

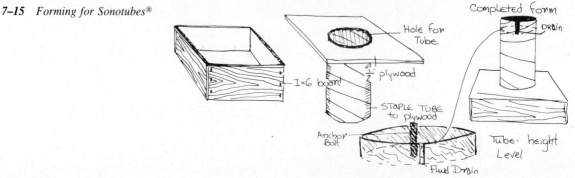

applied and flashed. Nailers are then inserted between the upright posts (or over the outside faces). Use 45-degree corner braces.

Next, frame the door(s) into the end walls. The sill can be made from a creosoted length of 2 × 4, which should be set in a crushed-stone-filled drainage trench flush with its surface. Otherwise you will always have a nailer to step over or will need to pour an additional pier to support the side of the door frame. The continuous sill member helps keep the bottom of the walls from kicking out. Sheathing boards are nailed to the frame. The structure need not be airtight (in fact, good air circulation is desirable to aid the wood in drying). Straight-edged boards will be more than sufficient. These boards should not be in direct contact with the ground, or they will rot and the shed will lift from frost action. A 2-inch separation will be enough, so long as the ground is graded to drain away from the shed. Otherwise water from the roof will tend to flow back into the shed.

Apply the roofing after the fascia trim is in place. If the roof is framed to project about 2 feet beyond the plate at the eaves, a storage area for ladders, garden hoses, planks, pipes, or extra wood will be created.

Because of the low pitch of the shed roof, the rafters and the plate girder must form a heavy-enough frame to carry a substantial snow load. Otherwise

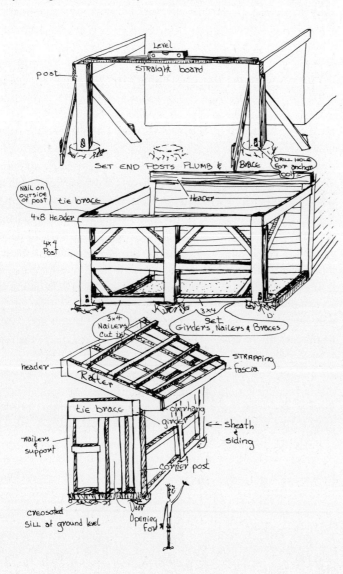

7-16 Construction details for a simple woodshed

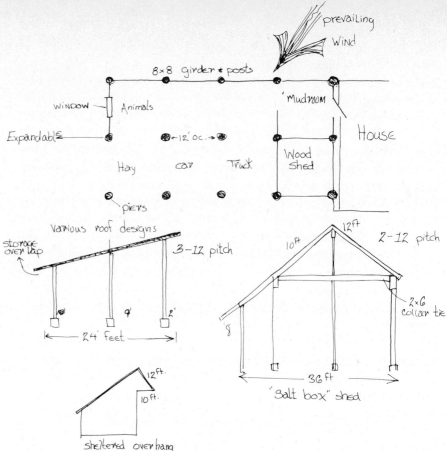

7–17 *Expandable shed barn*

the roof will have to be shoveled off during the winters. Two-by-ten rafters 16 inches on center will be heavy enough to carry a load of over 160 pounds per square foot, which should be about twice that needed to support two feet of heavy wet snow. A built-up 6 × 8 over a 10-foot span will support about 2 tons. A solid 8 × 8 will carry 3¼ tons and a built-up 6 × 10, over 3½ tons.

The basic post-and-girder shed design is infinitely expandable. The module can be repeated to suit any purpose: A hay barn, woodshed, animal or equipment barn, garage, storage shed, or any combination of the above. Widths much over 30 feet are impractical because the roof pitch becomes too flat or the front will be too high and the back too low. The pitch for a shed roof of this sort should never be less than 2-12 or much greater than 3-12. Steeper pitches will create low back walls and unusable spaces, and flatter pitches will accumulate too heavy a snow load. The length of the shed is infinite.

It is an easy structure to build, as well as inexpensive. The tolerances are not exacting, and therefore it is a good way to recycle hewn barn beams or old lumber of various thicknesses. Partitions and stall dividers are added as needed. The front can be left open or fitted with sliding or hinged doors. The open side should face away from the prevailing winds.

Porches: *Construction and repair*

An analog to the attached shed is the porch. In northern climates the enclosed porch protects the house from the direct force of the wind and shades the living rooms in summer. It can be a place to hang clothes to dry on a rainy day or to start trays of seedlings in the early spring. In southern regions, where the verandah is traditional, the porch is a barrier against the hot sun. The porch becomes an integral part of the house in the summer months. Open and screened, it will be cool and breezy, a place to sleep on sticky summer nights, to eat and gather during the days. The porch also makes an ideal makeshift winter workshop while the main living areas of the house and kitchen are being rebuilt. Heavy power tools can be set up and boards cut there, while the interior of the house is protected from burial by sawdust. If the door between house and porch is kept open, the porch will remain at a comfortable working temperature. Any heat loss is offset by stoking the stove with the cut-off board ends from the workshop.

The usefulness of a porch is counteracted to some extent by the effect it can have on the light level of the living spaces behind it. Sunlight will be indirect, the rooms will darken earlier and never quite attain the brightness of full daylight. These side effects are not altogether undesirable—the rooms may seem cooler in summer and cozier in winter. The mood can be lightened with bright ceilings.

A front porch is a place to watch the world go by, to lean back in the rocker, sipping at a cold beer, lost in the golden green light of a late summer afternoon. The world spins slowly when viewed from the porch. The static in your mind fades, replaced with the whisper of leaves and the hypnotic creak of the rocking chair.

If the old porch is at all restorable, do not let it decline further. Porch repair is the most common and also about the simplest rebuilding task you can undertake. Because they are so often exposed to water, the floorboards will most likely be rotten, in whole or part. This rot can often extend into the joists and especially the front sills. The bottoms of the roof-support posts and railings are also frequent casualties of time and hard weather. Enclosed porches do not tend to be as ravaged by the weather as an open porch because a good deal of the wind-driven rainwater and snow is kept out by their half wall, or by windows. Drainage slots built into the front wall (if it is not completely enclosed by storm windows or screens) allow any water to drain out. A porch facing into the teeth of winter winds will be protected from much of their force if covered with a poly sheet or if it has storm windows. The same winds will also drive summer rains as well as breezes over the floors. Pitching the floor toward the front edge allows it to drain. Using square-edged instead of tongue-and-groove decking will let water drain between boards rather than remaining trapped under the joints. A pitch of 1 inch over 20 feet will be sufficient. An overhanging eave will also help minimize the amount of wind-blown water entering the porch. A one-to-two-foot overhang is more than sufficient.

Rotten floor boards are cut back to where they are still solid, breaking on the nearest joist. Examine the exposed joists and sills for rot, and replace if necessary. Support the porch roof with a 4 × 4 jacking post under the header beam. Position the post to jack from sound flooring or sills, or remove flooring to insert the post between the header and the ground. The jacking post can be offset slightly since there is relatively little weight to be lifted and the danger of slippage is not as great. Porch posts that have rotted can be replaced by the same method. New joists can be scabbed alongside partially rotten members. Use joist hangers or toenailing to secure the new framing. All surfaces of new wood and the existing underpinnings should have a coat of wood preservative. The top edges of the joists can be coated with asphalt cement or covered with a strip of metal flashing. When sills are to be built up, each face of the individual plank should be coated with the preservative before they are nailed together.

Often the columns that support the porch are highly ornamental, unique, and antique. Very few lumber yards carry stock replacements. The types that are available are likely to be rather expensive. A suitable alternative, if not the original-style post, may be discovered by scouting demolition yards. If the rot is not extensive, the post can be shortened and the height of its pillow block increased. If you remove more than a few inches from the post, a prosthetic section can be fastened to the original by doweling and gluing with wood or pinning with a length of ¾-inch rebar. A circular pillow block can be cut from a plank of 2 × 12 stock and its edges shaped to the required curve with a Surform® plane and then sanded smooth.

Very often the problem with a porch is not so much rotten framing as it is unstable foundation supports. Porch sills often rest on rocks or concrete blocks, which do not extend below frost line, or on steel pipes driven into the ground. These foundations rise and fall seasonally, throwing the porch out of alignment. Jack the porch sills off their supports and replace them with permanent and stable Sonotube® piers. Concrete blocks can also be laid up under a porch to support the sills so long as the pier extends below frost. An old-time solution for porch foundations was to use a length of steel pipe and collar, which was fitted over a smaller-diameter pipe driven into the ground. As the pipe heaved, the larger pipe could slide down over the smaller one if the pin that held the two pipes together was removed. There are no advantages to this system other than making it easier to jack the porch into place each spring. It still requires seasonal adjustments. The space between the sills and the ground is generally filled in with a skirt board, which can be quite ornamental. The lattice design shown in Figure 7–18 allows the area under the porch to ventilate, which helps to protect the joists from rotting.

7–18 Porch problems

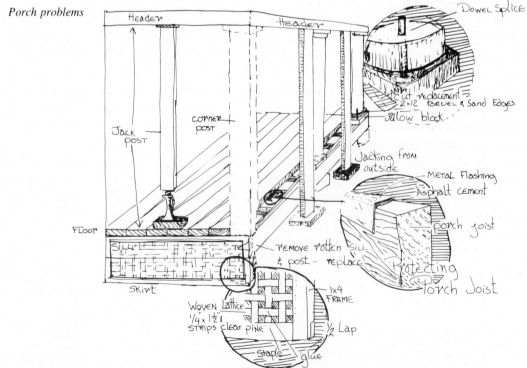

If your present house is unadorned by a porch, consider adding one. A porch is not a deck. A deck is in some ways an unroofed porch designed to allow water to run between its surfaces. Old houses and decks do not seem to go together well, at least not on their front faces. The flatness of a deck seems tacked onto an old house, it squashes the gabled façade. A deck, if used at all on an old house, is better built off the back of the house. Porch framing follows the same principles as shed frames. The concrete piers are poured to the height of the sill, which should be set to the same level as that of the house sills. A header is nailed across the house sill and rested across the porch piers and joists used to span the gap. The deck is laid over the joists.

Notice the details of porches as you drive about the countryside and keep an eye out for a pleasing design that you may wish to incorporate into your own.

The advantage of a semi-enclosed porch is that the front wall will keep out weather as well as form a convenient sitting and foot-resting place. The level wall used with square-framed posts makes it easy to fit standard screens and storm windows between the uprights. A porch with only a rail between the roof and floor deck requires custom-built screen panels, which are subject to frequent tears since they extend to the floor and the use of poly sheets in the winter. The half wall of the semi-enclosed front porch ties in very well with the rest of the house. It is not possible to use screens and storms with other than square-framed posting. Ornamental turned posts require that the porch be kept open, or that the window and frame units be supported independently of the posting, with cleats installed on floor and header, to which they can be fastened.

Take care to fit the appearance of the porch to the style of the house. Contemporary lines against a Neo-Hellenic façade can be extremely jarring. While it is not necessary to duplicate every detail of trim, the porch should approximate the feeling of those details and strive toward economy of construction without doing violence to the design.

Because of the low slope of most porch roofs (3-12 or less), metal roofing will tend to leak unless sealed between the overlapping seams. Half-lap roll roofing is preferable for an absolutely watertight deck. Shingle roofing can be

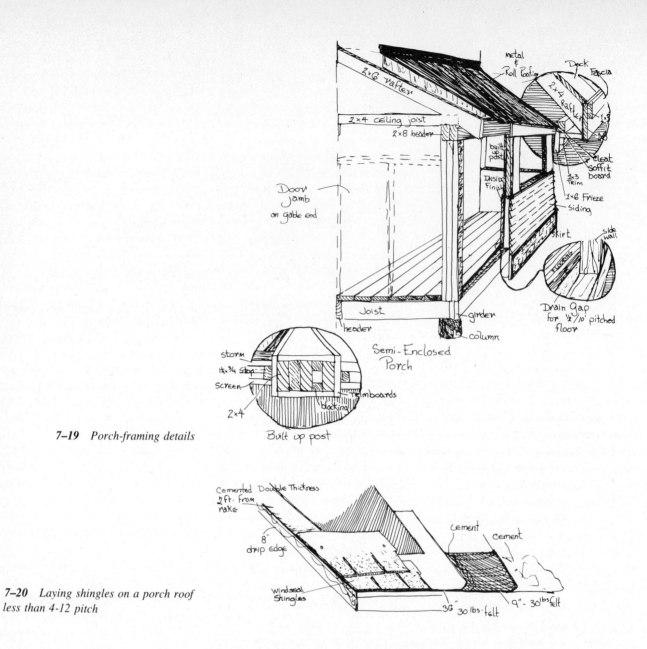

7–19 *Porch-framing details*

7–20 *Laying shingles on a porch roof less than 4-12 pitch*

used on slopes as low as 2-12 if special precautions are taken. Use a double thickness of 30-pound felt underlayment, lapped 19 inches. The layers are cemented together to a point at least 2 feet up from the eaves and in from the rakes. Use only windseal shingles.

Be sure to place the entrance to the porch in the gable wall. Otherwise a stoop will be necessary to protect the doorway from rain and snow, and that is just added trouble. The simplest stoop is framed directly over the existing roof deck, and a valley is laid and shingled as with a standard roof. A gutter hung from the eaves will also keep guests dry as they enter.

Stoops and Mudrooms

Stoops are a convenient way to shelter an entrance from the weather and protect the homeowners from an avalanche of icicles and snow, which can drop without warning from the eaves when a door is slammed or the weather thaws. If the

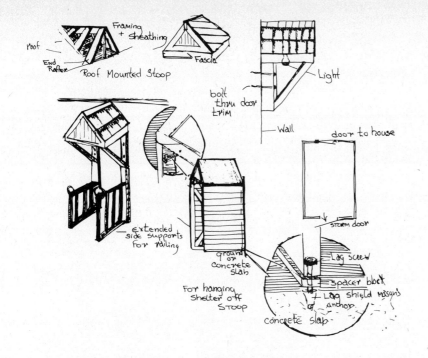

7-21 *Porch stoops*

sides are framed out, they will form a semi-enclosed space that keeps the wind from sweeping through the house every time the door is opened. If the front of the stoop can be anchored to a masonry slab or otherwise securely anchored, the stoop can be fitted with a storm door across its front for additional weather and heat-loss protection. A bench and coat pegs on the inside wall or a hook to hang snow shovels or battery-jumper cables on will be handy.

Country people hardly ever use their front doors, which seem to be a concession to architectural tradition; the life and breath of the house comes and goes by way of the back door, which is generally the kitchen door. In the city and town houses, this door is the service (delivery and servants') entrance. The front door maintains its re(moat)ness even today, being opened upon invitation only. It is not uncommon to find, in the country, the front door walled over with a poly sheet for the winter. One path to shovel is enough. Only on formal occasions is the front door ever used. A city person new to the country can be identified by the door he or she walks up to first.

A rear-door stoop is often elaborated into the mudroom, which is an air lock and transitional space between the inner and outer worlds. It provides protection from the extremes of weather as well as storage for empty jars and kettles and a place to take off and leave skis and snowshoes, hang coats, and remove barnyard boots. The more undesirable aspects of the country environment are left in the mudroom instead of being deposited throughout the house. Fire-

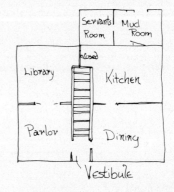

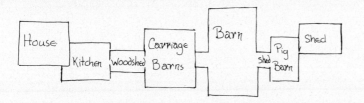

7-22 *A vestibule and the connecting buildings*

wood and garden harvests also pause there before they are worked into the processing machinery of the house. Mudrooms can vary in size from nothing more than an enclosed stoop to an entire rear porch, complete with storage cabinets, lockers, and shelves. The needs of the household will determine its size and function. On the one hand there is the front vestibule: a formalized space suitable for removing coat and overshoes—even the outermost part of the house has been drawn completely behind the house wall. The other extreme is the connecting architecture of New England—the house extends itself into the mudroom, which leads to a breezeway to the wood shed, which is continuous with the main barn and connected to other sheds and shops. The farmer could do an entire day's chores and never once step out into the foul weather.

SECTION 2 IN RELATION TO THE LARGER WORLD

There is nothing more desirable in this world than love; and nothing is better suited to cultivate love than a nature-based home.

[Ken Kern, *The Owner-Built Home*]

. . . the problem of excessive choice, the difficulty of selecting or finding constraints which arose naturally in the past and which are necessary for the creation of meaningful house form. There may lie the great lesson of vernacular building for our own day—the value of constraints to establish generalized, "loose" frameworks where the interplay of the constant and changeable aspects of man can find expression.

[Amos Rapoport, *House Form and Culture*]

Man may not be so much controlling his environment as escaping it.

[*Ibid.*]

A house is not a new car, something to be traded in every few years, a commodity bought and sold as the need or whim moves us. The current attitudes about housing unfortunately tend to ignore the basic fact that a house is part of the total environment. Its parts are built in a factory, crated, shipped, to inflict themselves, full blown, upon the landscape. A creeping drabness, a diminution of regional distinction is the result of this insensitivity to the needs of place. Like the sterile predictability of fast-food franchises, contemporary housing styles are stamped from the same mold, the face of unconscious machine intelligence, wherever they may be built. A ranch house in Vermont is about as sensible as an igloo in Texas, and yet, when a new house is built, the chances are good that it will be a ''ranch house,'' ordered out of a catalog of plans drawn up in a New York City skyscraper. Regional styles of building evolved in direct response to the needs of local climates, the materials available for building, and the cultural heritage of the builders. The modern house ignores nature, rather than cooperating with it. Like the subjugation of a captive people, great expenditures of energy and ingenious technological systems are the cost of keeping nature at bay. The inefficiency and long-term impossibility of this way of dealing with our world is becoming apparent. And it is far easier to break the spirit of a person than it is to call the tune for Mother Nature.

Insofar as a house becomes a fortress, it is also a prison. We are prisoners of our own designs, servants of our slave machines. We work to feed our furnaces, to keep our automobiles warm. The roots of all living things are to be found in the earth. So, too, the house must be rooted. Like a tree, the house root draws its strength from the soil. A house is not limited to the space enclosed within its walls but rather is the nucleus of a larger system—the land upon which it stands and is surrounded by, or the community in which it functions (com-

munity is the equivalent of land for the urban homesteader). The healthy house is built upon healthy land. It is the land that gives it meaning and dimension. The gardens provide the food, the woodlot, the heat. Water wells up from the earth; barns, sheds, and fences are the outstretched ganglia of the living house. As the house is to the family, the land is to the house.

Water Supply Systems

Water is the life blood of the household. Getting it into the house is a problem of overcoming gravity or working with it. The owner of a country home may discover that the spring that never ran dry in the living memory of man has suddenly developed asthma and emphysema, and finally, the pump, in a fit of apoplexy and burning wires, gives up the ghost.

Other than a direct municipal hookup, there are four basic systems for supplying water to the house. The simplest and most efficient is *gravity feed*. The height of a water source in relation to the house is the crucial factor in bringing water into that house. The weight and force of falling water supply the energy and are the only power required. When a source, generally a spring, is located sufficiently above the house, the water will flow through a pipe into the house. The higher the source, the greater the pressure. It's like filling a milk carton with water and punching a series of holes in it: The hardest stream of water is at the bottom.

This example points out the disadvantage of a gravity system as well. Since the pressure of the water will decrease as the water is raised within the house, a second-floor fixture may not get sufficient flow to operate. Gravity systems tend to be low pressure unless the height of the supply is great. The pressure will equal one-half pound per square inch for every foot of drop. Thus a source 40 feet above the second story of a house will provide 20 pounds of pressure, which is quite suitable. If the source were only 20 feet above the house, the pressure would drop to 10 pounds, which is too low to run a dishwasher.

The supply line for a gravity system should be of large diameter; 1¼-inch pipe should be used for runs of over 100 feet to minimize pressure losses by friction. Low-pressure (80-psi-rated) pipe will be sufficient for such a system if the pressure is less than 40 pounds. The pipe should be buried below the frost line. Where this is impractical, because of ledges or other obstructions, a layer of foam insulation and a heavy straw-and-burlap mulch covered by a foot of earth will help prevent freezing. It is common for lines to be buried quite shallowly in many old installations, especially where the runs are long. If the work had to be done by hand, that is understandable. These pipes will rarely freeze if sufficient early snow cover prevents the ground from freezing solid and there is no midwinter thaw, and most important, if the water is kept moving through the pipe at a constant trickle. A tap left open will suffice. When the house is left unoccupied, it will be necessary to install a bypass drain line on the incoming supply line. The water system is drained back to a shutoff drain and the supply left running into a foundation drain. A pint of antifreeze (Methanol alcohol type, not the "permanent" ethylene-glycol base, which might kill the bacteria in the septic tank) is dumped into the toilet bowl (after the tank has been shut off and flushed) to keep the remaining water in the toilet trap from freezing and thereby cracking the bowl.

The low-pressure problems of gravity feeds can be overcome by installing a piston pump in the cellar. These pumps are electrically powered versions of the old-fashioned (and still quite workable) hand pumps. The pump and its pressure tank will pressurize the system. A check valve (a one-way valve) should be inserted in the line before the pump to prevent the pressurized water in the distribution pipes from flowing back against the incoming gravity-feed source water.

A relative of the gravity-feed system is the artesian well, which is a well drilled through nearly impervious stratum to reach water at a point where it is actually under pressure. Thus the system is self-pressurized. If you are lucky enough to live above such a stratum, your water-supply problems will be solved.

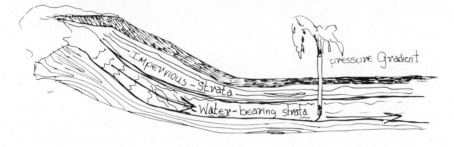

7–23   *Artesian well*

A much more typical installation is the *shallow well pump*. While the archetypical pitcher pump mentioned above has been replaced by the electric piston pump, the principles of operation are the same. The pump pulls water by suction. Its effective range is limited to a vertical lift of about 25 feet. The horizontal pull, however, is virtually unlimited, especially if the run is slightly downhill in places. A foot valve (a type of check valve with a built-in strainer) must be inserted in the source end of the line to prevent the water in it from draining back to the spring when the pump shuts off. A foot valve plugged or held open with debris or otherwise not operating will cause the pump to loose its "prime." Pumps are designed to work immersed in water and will soon heat up and wear out if pumping air alone. When a pump loses its prime, there is too much air in the line for its suction to overcome, and the water stays in the spring. Examine the foot valve first; if no water is coming into the pump and a visual inspection shows water in the spring itself, the line must be reprimed before it will operate. This means filling it with water between the foot valve and the pump to expel the air. A one-inch line 300 feet long will take 30 gallons to fill completely. To prime a system, shut off the outlet end of the pressure tank (or the main shutoff valve to the house distribution lines) and unscrew the priming plug located on top of the pump head (usually a ½-inch square plug, top dead center above the impeller housing). Use a funnel to pour water slowly into the line, allowing the air to work itself free. When the line will accept no more water, screw the plug back in loosely and turn on the pump. Air will bubble along with water from the sides of the plug. You may have to repeat this process several times (or several dozen times) until enough air is sucked from the lines to allow the water to be pulled. If the supply line has high places (for example, where it must cross a ledge or hillock) along its run, an air lock will form which prevents complete priming. This condition is indicated by a line that refuses to prime yet will accept no more water through the priming plug.

A force pump, which can be rented from the local plumbing store, is used like a bicycle-tire pump to force water from a bucket into the line under enough pressure to expel any air. The foot valve must be removed for the force pump to work. Either connect the force pump to the intake side of the pump-supply line or adapt it to fit into the priming hole. A solution to the problem of high spots, and insurance for future pump primings, is to install a tee and above-ground filling valve at the high spot. The line can be primed in both directions from this point. Of course this must be done when the line is first laid, otherwise you will have no way of knowing where such a spot might lie. When priming the line from such a valve, leave the priming plug cocked open slightly and remove the foot valve as well. If there is a check valve installed in your line before the pump itself (which is quite common on long runs), it will have to be removed before you can prime the pump. A check valve will be a solid casting inserted in the supply line directly before the pump housing with a directional arrow stamped on the case pointing in the direction of incoming water flow.

The piston pump itself is sealed with a leather cup washer, which can wear or dry out. Replacement kits, available from the manufacturer or distributor, will give new life to a pump that runs a lot but doesn't seem to draw much water. A pump is set to switch on automatically when the water pressure falls below a predetermined level and to shut off when it reaches the desired pressure. A pressure-sensing diaphragm (which looks like a flying saucer inserted in the line), is connected to a relay that controls the motor. There are adjusting screws on the relay, which can be turned to raise or lower the shutoff and starting pressures. Never raise the shutoff pressure to exceed the safe working limits of the pump and distribution pipe system or leaks will spring from joints and pipes can burst. Forty psi is more than enough pressure for any household.

Another problem that can occur with pumped water supplies is water-logging of the pressure tank (the cylindrical tank upon which the pump itself is frequently mounted). The symptom of this ailment is a constant cycling of the pump whenever the smallest amount of water is drawn. The pump will turn on as soon as any drop in pressure occurs within the system. In severe cases it will be impossible to raise the pressure much above the cut-in point no matter how long the pump runs. The tank maintains the pressure of the water in the system when the pump is not running by compressing a cushion of air above the water in the tank. This air exerts a constant pressure on the water flowing within the pipes. If the pressure tank becomes too full of water (as gradually happens over time as seals loosen and wear), there will not be enough air in the tank to exert the required pressure. The tank is said to be water-logged. The cure is to shut off the pump motor and close the main distribution shutoff valve and then drain the pressure tank. When the system is turned back on and the valves opened, the tank will automatically fill with water to the desired level.

In regions afflicted with hard (heavily mineralized) water, the entire system can eventually become coated with insoluble mineral deposits, which will cause arteriosclerosis in the system and, ultimately, pump failure. Plastic supply lines and an epoxy or glass-lined pressure tank will be a necessity. A water softener will protect these investments. In some areas, not only a water softener but various filters will be required to remove minerals in the water. Test the water before you purchase the place. Avoid the unpleasant surprise of having to add these expensive items to your system. At least taste the water to see if

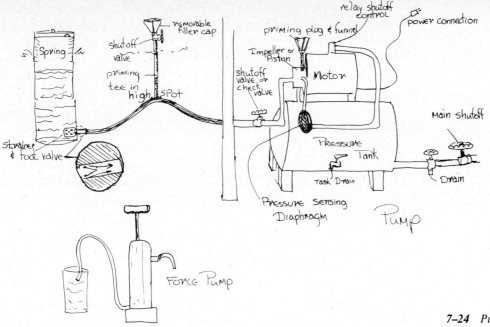

Labels in figure:
Spring
removable filler cap
shutoff valve
priming tee in high spot
Strainer & foot valve
relay shutoff control
priming plug & funnel
power connection
Impeller or Piston
shutoff valve or check valve
Motor
Main shutoff
Pressure Tank
Tank Drain
Drain
Pressure Sensing Diaphragm
Pump

Force Pump

7–24   *Pump problems and priming*

it is potable. Sulfur is detected by its bad taste and rotten-egg odor. Iron leaves brown stains on the enamel of fixtures. Cloudy or dirty water indicates a poorly constructed spring and a possible health hazard from surface-water infiltration.

A more powerful version of the shallow-well piston pump, and one that has fewer maintenance problems is the centrifugal pump, which operates by drawing the water through an *impeller* (a set of spinning blades in a sealed chamber). It is less noisy and a lot more efficient than the old piston models. The impeller blades will burn up very quickly, however, if the pump is run without water in the chamber for very long, as water flow is relied upon to cool the heat generated by friction between the closely fitted nylon blades and the chamber wall.

An improvement upon the shallow-well piston or centrifugal pump is the *jet pump,* which will bring water up from depths as low as 125 feet. It requires two pipes to operate, one for the water coming up from the well and another that returns some of the water to the well, where it is jetted through a special orifice into the upcoming pipe to create a boosting pressure. Since the pump is located within the house, it is easily serviced. Both this pump and shallow well pumps should be fitted with 100-psi-rated plastic supply pipe to handle the higher operating pressures. The jet pump uses more power than a piston pump, but it is required for any system where the source lies more than 25 feet below the house. In case of loss of prime, you will have two lines to fill. An electric or gas-operated priming pump will be needed to force the quantities of water through the lines.

If the water source lies much below 100 feet, you have no choice but to use a *submersible deep-well pump,* which can force water up from depths as great as 500 feet. Because this pump is actually at the bottom of the well on the end of a long rope, connected to plastic pipe and an electrical supply cable, pulling it up for repair and replacement is quite a task. Also the 240-v motor that runs it is connected by a buried cable to the house electrical system. This cable is about as good a ground for lightning as can be desired. The result is usually a burned-out pump motor. Lightning can actually travel underground to the pump cable and into the house, where it can do further damage. The pump power should be disconnected whenever a storm is approaching or when you leave the house vacant during thunderstorm season. A lightning arrester (which costs about $20) installed across the line, while not foolproof, is a lot better insurance than nothing. Pumps whose motors are encased in insulating oil baths also seem to be less susceptible to lightning damage. Check your homeowner's insurance policy to see if the pump is protected against lightning damage. Plastic pipe rated at 140 psi can be used down to about 250 feet. Below that, iron pipe will be necessary to withstand the pressure created by a very long column of standing water.

Water Sources: *Springs*

The source of supply for domestic water should be free from contamination. Contact the local health officer for a sampling kit (usually free) and have a batch of your water analyzed by the state health lab for possible bacterial contamination. The presence of high levels of coliform bacteria indicates a potential health hazard and a spring that might be contaminated because of improper construction.

A spring is a naturally occurring water source, a point where the water table coincides with the surface or a vein of underground seepage, or even an underground river that can be tapped. Many old springs, especially those walled by loose stone or wood, are easily contaminated by surface run-off. Drawing water from a stream is also potentially dangerous unless the drainage pattern of the stream above the house is known to be free of contaminants, which is unlikely except in the deepest boondocks. A spring must be covered to prevent leaves, dirt, surface water, and most of all, animals from getting into it. A farmer I know told me how one year his water developed a very unappetizing smell and tasted like rotten meat. He let it run, hoping it would clear, to no avail. Finally, he went out to have a look at the spring. When he lifted up the heavy lid and peered down into the gloom, he could make out the pale, bloated remains of a mouse floating upon the surface. He fished out the body and dumped a half gallon of Clorox into the water and let it run until he could smell it at the tap end. He let the water sit overnight before he ran it again.

A good spring should be built with concrete tiles and cover. Seal the tiles together with a thin mortar grout. The area surrounding the source should be excavated and, after the tiles are set at the bottom of the source, or slightly deeper, backfilled with clean, washed gravel to just below the finished grade. The spring casing should project above the grade about the height of a single tile. The gravel holds extra spring water, acting as a reservoir as well as keeping the water purified. It should be covered over with an impervious layer of clay and seeded down to prevent surface water from infiltrating the supply. Contrary to popular opinion, rainwater is not pure any more but is filled with all manner of atmospheric contaminants—the legacy of our industrial and nuclear boondoggles. Even it it were pure, surface water could wash ground-borne contaminants from animal wastes, herbicides and fertilizers into the supply. The ground covering should be graded away from the spring as well.

A pencil-thin trickle of water, if it is constant, will fill an entire pond in a few months and will more than supply the needs of a household so long as the water is not drawn from the reservoir faster than it can be replenished. Leaving the garden hose running all morning during a summer dry spell can do that surprisingly easily. Rarely is the water in a spring infinite. You will soon come to know your spring's capabilities and learn when to use it gently. Drawing your own water involves you as intimately in your life-support system as heating with wood or the sun. The vagaries of the water table are only theoretically knowable. The variables affecting the availability of water at any given point and season are incalculable. If your spring has a habit of failing, there are two possible solutions.

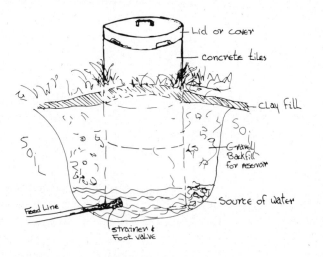

7–25 *Spring construction*

Far simpler (and cheaper) than drilling a well, is to dig a new spring. It may well be that your present spring is only tapping a vein of the major aquifer—a capillary rather than the artery. If the main source can be found and utilized, your water problems may be over. Modern technology has not been able to locate water with any more success than it has been able to predict the weather in the mountains of New England. Like the *Old Farmer's Almanac* with the weather, the dowser seems to possess an uncanny ability to find underground water. Whatever science and skeptics may say to the contrary, empirical evidence shows that dowsing works far too well to be merely coincidental. Theoretically, anyone can dowse for water, but in practice, not everyone will find it. It seems to be a matter of innate sensitivity: As some radios are more attuned than others, so it is with dowsers. As with anything bordering on the parapsychological, there are charlatans in this field. Ask around the neighborhood; chances are someone will know of a bona fide dowser of recognized repute.

I still wonder if there was an element of collusion in the fact that the backhoe contractor's uncle happened to be a dowser. But after three weeks without water, we were willing to try anything:

The old man stood wizened like last fall's fruit, clinging to the Y-shaped branch of apple wood he held tensioned between his outstretched arms. The branch seemed alive, it quivered as he slowly moved across the pasture. He seemed to be following an invisible trail, pausing to sniff the breath of moist earth. The branch dipped sharply. He moved off at an angle to his left, the branch vibrating like the wings of a honeybee as he followed a new scent, then it dipped again, harder. ''Just as I thought,'' he said, ''t'was a vein. Here's the real source, should be maybe eight or ten feet down by the feel of it.'' We marked the spot. Later, after he left, I tried holding an apple branch, cut from the old tree out back. It did seem to have a curious tension, totally unrelated to anything I felt I was doing to it. It did seem to quiver as I found myself heading in the general direction of the dowser's trail. I veered away and the branch lost its tension. I knew I hadn't changed my grip. As I turned back it suddenly slipped, dipping downward several times in rapid pulse. I was standing only a few feet from where the stake marked the dowser's spot. Of course, I told myself, I knew where the water was supposed to be and was following a subconscious track. I pulled the stake and let a friend experiment. She stopped within a few yards of the exact spot, the stick pointing straight down.

We dug for the new spring and at about four feet we struck ledge. Nothing but dry, powdery dirt. At seven feet the bucket of the hoe was still scraping along the sloping face of the ledge when the earth appeared damp. A tiny trickle was oozing from a crack in the seal of the rock face at just about eight feet down—the source for our new spring.

Supply Lines

A water-supply line should be laid without splices if at all possible. Plastic pipe is sold in rolls up to 400 feet long, which is generally longer than the average spring run. Splices are weak spots, potential trouble. A slug of water 300 feet long traveling through a pipe at about 10 mph develops considerable momentum. When a valve in the plumbing system is closed or the pump cycles, this column comes to a sudden stop, with an effect similar to a speeding auto slamming into a concrete wall. The car is ultimately compressible, water is not. The shock waves travel through the pipe, and the joints take a good deal of this force. The joints of the supply line should be sealed with double clamps (two on each side of a coupling). Tighten them as far as the screwdriver will turn. The nylon fittings will not slide on easily. Soften the pipe by immersing it in a bucket of boiling water, or persuade it by tapping it with a block of softwood and a rubber mallet. Digging up a pipe for lack of a 69¢ clamp is not a relaxing way to spend a day. Don't scrimp on clamps.

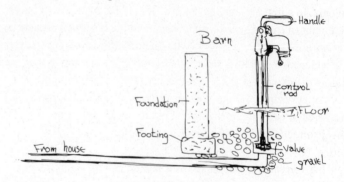

7–26   A frostless hydrant for outbuilding water supply

Occasionally it is necessary to run a line to supply water to a barn or outbuilding. A line tapped off the water supply in the cellar can be buried below frost and run to the barn. A frostless hydrant allows the water to run year round. This is a standpipe with a valve actually mounted in its base, buried below frost. The handle is connected by a rod to the actual valve. When the line is shut, the water in the pipe between valve and outlet flows out a special drain in the base of the valve itself. The standpipe should be buried in a layer of good gravel, which will absorb the water that drains from the pipe during normal use.

Access:

Driveways in mud and snow

In Vermont, in addition to the standard four seasons, we are blessed with a fifth season, which occurs sometime between winter and spring, mostly in April. Historically, the suicide rate increases dramatically during this time of year. As the warming sun causes the snow and ice to melt, the land and, more important, the dirt roads (most of Vermont is paved with dirt) thaw out. The days are still short and the sun's heat wan, the nights are frosty. Only the first few inches of the hard-frozen roadbed melt. The water from the snow soon saturates this thin layer floating on the still-frozen base, and the traffic churns it into wheel-twisting, sucking mud. The ground thaws in increments, the mud deepens, and MUD season is upon us. The alternation between cold nights and warm days is the pump that pulls up the sap into the body of the maples. It is fine weather for sugaring but terrible weather for going anywhere. The whole world is a swamp of mud. Your boots sink into the oozing, spongy ground, lying barren and sore, littered with an emerging glacial rubble of winter, the garbage, the sawdust, cinders, and an amazing amount of dog shit scattered over the stiff and gritty moraine of the snow plow. Your truck sinks to its differential in the bog of the driveway, only to freeze in solid overnight. You chip away at the locked-in tires with an ax, jacking the axles level to the road surface. Small wonder that those who can afford it go somewhere else during mud season and the rest of us wish we could.

The moral is that a house is of little comfort if you can't get to it. Most of us are forced (voluntarily or not) to live with a machine that, unlike a horse, does not travel well in mud or snow. You can't leave a car parked out in the road if you expect to find it after the plow goes by. The *driveway* should be given the same structural consideration as any other element of the house. What may seem like a fine roadway in the heat of July may be an impassable quagmire in the quicksand of April. A good driveway is built to shed water. Shallow ditches on either side channel this water away. A six-inch-deep layer of good gravel, which will not hold water and turn to mud, will keep the surface stable so long as the ground water is able to run off.

The driveway can be used as a means of secluding the house from a well-traveled road, in conjunction with a shielding line of trees. Instead of running it directly, you can change its direction with a gentle curve that will screen the house from view of the road. Be careful when cutting a driveway through the forest to leave room enough for the snowplow to bank the snow. Do not make curves too sharp—a sharp bend and a gentle rise will find cars in the snowbanks. Plan the driveway as if it were to be coated with ice at all times.

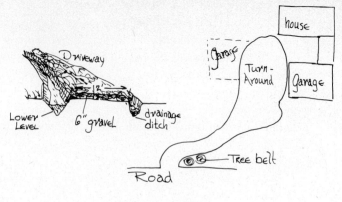

7–27 *A good driveway*

Any driveway that cannot be negotiated under icy conditions is bound to be a source of future trouble. There is nothing more frustrating than being stuck in your own yard. Allow room to turn your vehicles around, both your own and a visitor's. Avoid planting trees or ornamental shrubs where the snowplow and snowbanks will bury them, if you wish them to grow more than a few inches.

Gardens:

Siting for sun and growth

The same principle of clearance should be considered when siting any outbuilding you may have cause to build. A pleasant walk to the barn on a summer morning can be an arctic expedition through winter's snowdrifts. Build your barn down-wind of the house, so that the prevailing summer breezes will not gently waft the fragrance of the manure pile into your dining room. For this reason, and also for reasons of fire insurance, do not attach your barn to your house (an attached barn would make fire insurance prohibitively expensive or impossible to get at all).

Finally, a word should be mentioned about the siting of the garden. Most plants grow best in sunlight, but for some reason many people seem to forget this when they lay out their gardens and they end up with their corn shaded by overhanging trees or the shadow of the house. Study the path of the spring and summer sun; watch where the shadows fall. A shadow that covers a garden plot until 10 a.m. will cost you five hours of precious growing time each day. Afternoon shadows will do the same. Do not neglect drainage, either. Never site your garden at the bottom of a slope. Gardens should be oriented toward a southern

7–28 *Siting a garden*

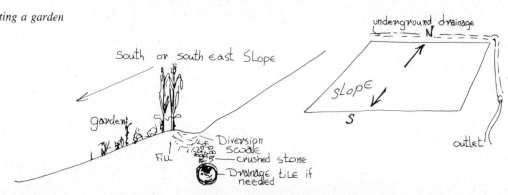

or southeastern slope for maximum sunlight, but a garden at the bottom of such a slope will be very wet to work early in the spring, will remain wet after a rain, and because cold air drains like water, will be more susceptible to early frost damage. A garden halfway up the slope will be much better so long as a swale is cut into its top edge to drain off surface waters. A subterranean drainage system similar to a leach field may be necessary where your soil overlays hardpan that prevents good drainage.

Level gardens should be sited above the low places of your land. Where gardens are sited against a south-facing building wall, consider painting that wall white or covering it with aluminum foil. The reflected sunlight will do wonders for growing tomatoes and peppers.

In the discussion of retrofitting a house for solar heating in chapter 5, the advantages of a lean-to-greenhouse were touched upon. (See Figure 5–29.) Such a structure not only can bring the outdoors in but can help significantly in heating the house. A lean-to is preferred over a free-standing greenhouse because of the ease of construction and the cost savings inherent in having the main support wall (the house wall) already built. When a lean-to is placed under the eaves, however, the snow will have to be diverted from its roof to avoid damage to the relatively fragile frame from falling ice. If the greenhouse roof runs directly into the main roof, there will not be such a problem. A saddle can be built on a higher roof if you do not have a suitable south-facing gable wall.

A greenhouse will lose more heat at night than it gains during the day unless insulated shutters are used to prevent this. Panels of styrofoam insulation, fitted to wood frames that can be fastened to the greenhouse walls on the inside, are simply and inexpensively built.

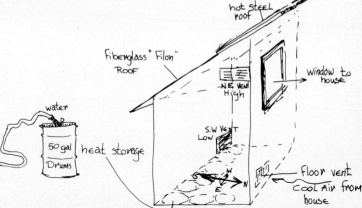

7–29 *Some greenhouse details*

"How do you like them new folks down the road?"

"Can't say. They don't neighbor none."

"City people," a neighbor once observed, "talk a lot. Give them a simple answer, they keep askin'. Like they never heard you. You nod again, ayep. They talk more at you. Got to *explain* what it is they really mean, you see. So you nod along to be neighborly. Then they get this funny look on their face all of a sudden, like they'd noticed that their fly might be down. And they've got to be running along you know. Trouble is, they don't know how to visit."

In the country you don't walk up to a neighbor's house and just right out ask to borrow something, at least not until you've lived there a few years, and borrowed a few things in the past. Your neighbor's not in business to serve you with his or her favors; there is a ritual of oblique approach that must be observed. The canons of neighborly contact are designed to allow interaction with options, to tread lightly on a person's independence while recognizing mutual dependency. The form is at least as important as the contents.

You might start off with an observation on a topic of general interest, like the weather or the state of the garden. In the course of the conversation, you kind of sidle up to what it was you might be needing . . . by the way, you wouldn't know where someone might be able to find a good skidding chain? Well, you skiddin' out logs now? No, I've got that back wall of the barn to pull in and not quite enough length on the come-along cable. That wall's a christlin' mess ain't it? I guess. Well I think I might have a chain out in the shop. You'd be welcome to. Great. Sometimes I think that goddam thing, I ought to bulldoze it over. Well, it's still worth something, I suppose. I guess. You know Old Harry never was one for cleaning out the manure pile, used to leave it settin' against the wall all year. Why I remember once . . . Like a river easing across its delta, the talk meanders on. The art of "hunkering" is vital to good neighborly relations. When you borrow equipment or time of a neighbor you are establishing an open account. In order to keep your credit rating, you must make minimum payments on the balance due. You should return the favor. When your spring runs dry and your neighbors let you draw water from theirs, along with your buckets you bring a few extra lettuces, or a crate of apples from the tree they used to pick from before you bought the place. You give their kids a ride down to school; he pulls your truck out of a snowbank. The proper forms are observed: "What do I owe you?" "Consideration, when it happens to me." "Well, thanks until better paid."

As you begin to establish your roots in a community, and its residents begin to believe you won't blow away after the first winter, they slowly open themselves up to you. Like the teasing stop-and-go dance of spring, you are joined to something that is both a support and a responsibility. Your neighbors are a precious resource, an information bank, a directory, a navigational guide, even a warehouse. There is always a family down the road who happen to have what you need that they just might be willing to part with for reasonable consideration, a tool that they don't need as much as the money they can get for it. Your neighbors will take you in so long as they do not feel threatened by you. Tread lightly, respect them; they've lived here all their lives, and sometimes that alone is enough: "I've lived and paid taxes in this town all my life and my parents and grandparents before me," is the final ground invoked and accepted without appeal. These people know a lot more than you will ever learn in your lifetime. A little humility goes a long way. Forget how smart you were in the city because in the country things are greener, especially you.

Of course it is quite possible to miss all this, to live oblivious to the culture around you, to bring the suburbs with you. As more and more people do just that, the country increasingly resembles what they left behind and soon it will be one vast hamburger-alley strip, no one will know or trust his or her neighbor, the padlock and peephole of suspicion will replace the friendly wave and open door.

In the cities, people give dinner parties. The host and hostess go to a great deal of trouble and expense to fete their guests with sensations that will bestir their taste buds. The guests stand about, comparing trophies and verbally maneuvering, eating, and leaving. Nothing really happens to fill the emptiness. After the smoke and the dishes are cleared, the hollow feeling remains. Just another party. In the country, people still give pot-luck dinners. Every guest brings part of the supper. The result is a meal that is sumptuous and full of surprises, as it represents the best energies of everyone. The sense of meeting and enjoyment is as genuine as the lonely roads that separate these people. Babysitters are not needed. The children are part of the feast, and by late evening the upstairs bedrooms are heaped with their tired but happy bodies. And there's plenty of help with the dishes.

The pot-luck party is a great way to bring together the extra hands for a rebuilding project that gets too large for your own. The host is, of course, expected to provide the beer or hard cider and some basic dish, perhaps a chili or a roast turkey, and the guests bring what they wish. Some people can be asked to cover a specific course, the salad, breads, or vegetable dishes, but rarely are there too many salads and not enough other vittles. The spirit of trusting to chance seems naturally to coordinate the meal. The work is done as part of the celebration of friendship and is only a preliminary appetite builder for what is to follow. Try to avoid passing out the beer before the work is well advanced however. The results might not shed water.

The longer you live in an area, the more familiar you become with its resources. Auctions and barn sales are a great way to combine a pleasant outing with the business of finding what you need. The problem is self-discipline. An infectious madness can cloud your mind at an auction and you awake to find your hand raised when the auctioneer says "SOLD, to the hippie in back!" And you have paid twice its worth for something you absolutely didn't need. It is easy to develop an entirely new set of needs at an auction.

One of the most valuable sources of used equipment, household furnishings, tools, and the like is the local paper. No part of the country seems to be without its *Trading Post,* a local publication that lists items for sale or barter. An advertisement detailing your wants can bring quick results. One of the greatest tragedies is to go out and pay top dollar for a new item only to see it advertised for half that price in the next week's paper. Or even worse, to see what you really could use and not have the money to buy it. For that reason, I often avoid reading these papers unless I have money to buy the specific item I'm looking for. I can't stand heartbreak. Local radio programs also sometimes run a swap or buy-and-sell feature in the early morning.

In the country, it can be harder to come by the basics of living than in the city. So little is thrown out. Here is where the urban scroungers equipped with a pickup or van are at a definite advantage over their country cousins.

Cruising city streets can be an excellent way to find furniture, appliances, used building materials, and lumber. Incredible amounts of junk turn out to be someone else' treasures. "Dumpster" trash bins on the street in front of a remodeling operation are particularly valuable lodes. Railroad yards, furniture stores, glass companies, any business that receives goods in wooden packing crates can be a source of lumber for remodeling projects. Construction sites generate huge amounts of waste. Ask a foreman for permission to scrounge.

The demolition yard is the true scavenger's heaven. Professional wrecking companies have yards where they sell salvaged materials. Wood is only one of the possibilities. Your best buys will be doors and windows, plumbing fixtures, pipes, electrical materials, and structural oddities, such as moldings, railings, ornamental cornices, stained glass, and fancy flooring. The range is from the practical to the fantastic. Visiting a salvage yard may fertilize your garden with design ideas. Unusual materials may send out thought tendrils of their own, leading you down novel paths of building. Salvage yards are a valuable primary source for the urban rebuilder, perhaps more valuable than the lumberyard or hardware store. You should know your local wrecker at least as well as your therapist.

Salvaging Your Own:
How to tear down an old building

Tearing down an old building as a source of building materials is an ambivalent undertaking. In the words of a professional wrecker/rebuilder, "Wrecking is a way of thinking, a totally different approach to building than working with new materials. After you've built with used wood for a while, new lumber begins to look raw, characterless."

There is definitely a case to be made for the joys of working with recycled materials, for the spirit of resurrection inherent in rebuilding an old house. Old wood does have character. It also has plenty of saw-blade-eating nails, and it can be multidimensional, sawn to sizes that do not fit any known modules—certainly not the sizes of your particular construction. You definitely do have to approach old wood with an entirely different mind. You must put aside the notions of regularity, straightness, and linear structure, and instead be flexible, letting the materials determine the form the building will take. The patina of old wood cannot be duplicated. But getting the wood to your building site can be a lot more trouble than you had imagined and even more than it will be worth.

Ultimately, taking down a building is simply the reverse of putting it up. This sounds a lot easier than it is. Wrecking is dirty and tiring work and can even be dangerous. While you may be able to obtain a surprising amount of usable building material from a single old structure, the energy and time it takes to tear it down, clean up the materials and the site, load it, truck it, and unload it, may be better spent earning the money to buy new wood or old wood already cleaned from someone who tears down buildings for a living. The time/money equation is the warp and woof of the tapestry upon which buildings are both built and torn down. If you have the time to do the work but not the money to buy the material, demolition may be the answer. Relieved of the strictures of economics, living on the margins of the economic mainstream, you find it possible to surrender to the creative force of entropy, to take the time to find and appreciate what a more hurried and harried person will have passed over.

When there are no payments to be met, no mortgage to service, and only a house to build, wrecking an old place is a good way to start and a good way to get the feel for the structure of buildings, of the nature and resistance of materials. Those who have only money and no time, will find themselves forced to substitute the work (and often the minds) of others for their own. The result can be a hollow parody of creativity.

The inside walls of a building to be torn down are gutted first. If they are plaster and lath, haul all the rubble to the dump before the work proceeds further. (This is a good reason to avoid tearing down a plastered building. The sheer amount of drudgery spent cleaning up after yourself can be very depressing and economically disastrous.) The wiring and plumbing are torn from the exposed walls and salvaged either for reuse or scrap value. The roofing and roof decking are stripped and the rafters taken down and the exterior siding removed. The second-floor platform and floor joists are next. Demolition can easily become an outlet for fantasies of destruction—Joshua at Jericho—as the walls are battered down, plaster and debris fleeing in spectacular and very satisfying disarray before the onslaught of the hammers of destruction. This approach is as foolish as it is tempting, no more sensible than walking into the woodlot and felling a dozen trees at once to fall into a tangled heap of tops and trunks. It may seem like a lot is getting done until the cleanup begins. Destruction must be as orderly as construction. As material is removed, it should be cleaned. The real danger is in stumbling over piles of nail-studded and splintered boards.

A large truck is a necessity. An ordinary pickup will be severely taxed if you must haul all the rubble to the dump. One full-time person will be needed just to haul away garbage. Look into renting a dump truck for the day. Figure the cost and labor involved in loading and unloading the pickup truck a dozen times against the cost of renting and loading the dump truck once. Before you sign a contract to tear down a structure, be absolutely sure as to the terms and whether you can carry them through, particularly if you must post bond or purchase the building before you can wreck it. Generally there will be a time limit for completing the work. The extent of cleanup should be specified. If the contract requires you to remove the structure completely, down to the foundation and filling in the cellar hole, consider passing it by unless you plan to subcontract out that final phase of the job to a heavy equipment operator. If you are allowed to leave the foundation walls and toss the rubble into the cellar hole, the work will be much simpler. It all depends on whether you are paying for the right to wreck the building (which is common in the country with old barns) or the owner is paying you to tear it down (which is mostly the case in the cities, with large structures).

All boards should be cleaned as you go. Since the nails have to come out sooner or later, they may as well come out as the boards are stripped from the building. One person stripping and another cleaning nails is very efficient. There is an art to pulling nails. The first step is to use the right hammer. A straight-clawed, 20-ounce, steel-shank hammer is best. The weight of the head gives you extra power and the length of the handle and its strength, leverage. A wooden-handled hammer is useless and will snap with the first tough nail. Pound nails through from the back. Bent nails can be pounded flat first and pried up again before they are driven through. A really corkscrewed nail can be cut with nipping pliers and the stub pounded out. To get added leverage for pulling stubborn nails, use a block of wood under the hammer head. This same block can be used to protect the surface of fine-grained boards from damage. Twisting the claw sideways will pull out twisted nails and even nails that have lost their head, if the claw is hammered tightly with another hammer against the nail shank. Larger spikes are pulled with a crowbar.

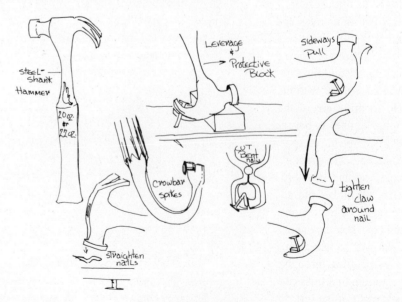

7–30 Nail pulling

Tearing down a stud-framed building is relatively simple work, and so long as cleanup proceeds in an orderly fashion, no more dangerous than putting it up. The individual framing units are light and easy to handle with a minimum of strain. The demolition of a post-and-beam framed structure is of a different order of magnitude. Because of the great weight of the timbers and the structural criticality of each member, the job demands careful attention and concentration at every step. There is a poetry to tearing down an old barn, born out of the tension between the presence of those huge beams, its vital strength, and the physics of its undertaking. There are moments when the wind falls still, the work has stopped, and those timbers stand looming in the gathering darkness, like Stonehenge in wood. You can sense the awe of the druids when their forest gods stirred.

Demolition of a barn starts at the roof. Old steel roofing is one of the most valuable salvage items you will find. So long as it has not rusted through, there is long life left in it. A brushing and a coat of roof paint are all that will be needed for its reconditioning. Sheets of steel roofing command a good price on the used-materials market and always find ready buyers. The nails cannot be pried up without crimping the steel. A block of wood inserted alongside the rib under the hammer is one solution. Another is to use nipping pliers to cut off the nail heads first. The sheets are removed and the shanks pulled free from the boards after they are taken off the roof. Start at the ridge, working from a ladder and ladder hook. Once the first sheet is off, the roof strapping provides the working ladder. On solid decks you will have to work along with the ladder until all the roofing is stripped. Shingle roofs are removed using staging brackets, as explained in chapter 3. After the deck is cleaned, the boards or nailers are removed.

Ordinary "common" rafters can be lowered singly or in pairs, if they are not hitched to a ridge pole. Heavy-timber rafters are lowered in pairs, using a pulling and a braking rope, as outlined in chapter 3. The pulling rope is hitched to the bumper of the truck, and a few turns of the braking rope are wound about a convenient girt, leaving enough slack for the truck to start the rafter moving. As the tension is transferred from pulling to braking rope, the rafter is lowered slowly to the deck or across the girts. Large buildings that are spanned by a principal-rafter truss and purlin framing system utilize the same basic rigging except that the joint between the kingpost and the girt must be cut through.

There are two radically different approaches to tearing down old timber-framed buildings. The first involves the meticulous disassembly of each timber and joint with the notion of eventual reassembly upon another site. Pegs seldom drive out of their borings easily. A heavy-duty drill and suitable bit should be used to bore through the peg. This type of work will proceed slowly. A broken beam or split joint is a catastrophe. Unless you actually do plan to reassemble the structure as it was originally, there is little reason to save the timber joints. Saw through them with a chain saw. This method results in a truncated timber but saves a great deal of time and effort and also increases the safety of the operation. New mortises and tenons will have to be cut in the timbers when they are reused, anyway. This is the second method, which is the safest way to take apart a principal-rafter truss.

Cutting through the tenon of a kingpost where it joins a girt that forms the bottom of a truss can be an unnerving experience. This timber actually holds the weight of the girt rigidly and is the central support of the entire truss. When cut, the girt will sag suddenly, deflecting as much as a foot over a 32-foot span.

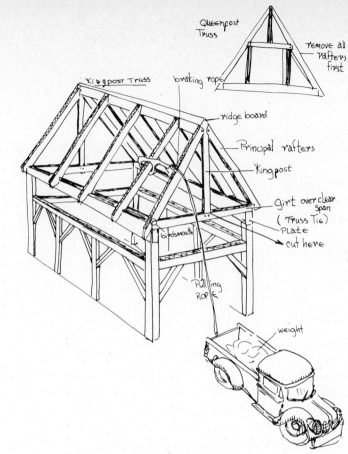

7-31 *Pulling down timber rafters*

Work from a staging tower set up below the joint. The sudden shift in the beam can easily throw you off balance if you are standing on the beam itself when cutting through the kingpost. The purlins, which join each truss and carry the common rafters, should be sawn through where they join the principal rafters and removed after the common rafters have been stripped. The rafters are dropped one pair at a time and disassembled when they are in horizontal position. It may be necessary to cut through the birdsmouth if the rafter wants to lift the plate beam itself, although that is to be avoided as you will not be able to control the rafter's descent if its legs are not hitched to the plate.

After the rafters are removed, the girts themselves can be lowered. If the entire triangular truss unit were to be removed at once, there would be the danger of the walls' collapsing outward. The girts should always be left in place until the rafters are down. Likewise, the exterior wall sheathing is also left intact until after the rafters are removed, to help brace the building. For roof-framing systems other than clear-span trusses, such as a posted girt supporting a queenpost truss, the work is not as critical. The rafters are supported and often lapped by each other over purlins. They can be removed entirely; then the purlins are cut and lowered, followed by the uprights (queenposts), and finally the girts.

Secure one end of the girt to the plate with a rope sling. Cut through the joint with your chain saw. Do it carefully to avoid cutting the rope as well. Repeat the procedure at the other end of the girt, which will now hang in a rope cradle. The hitch is loosened and the girt lowered to the floor.

The wall sheathing is stripped and the boards cleaned of nails. The corner joints at the top of the plate are sawn through to unhitch a wall section. Cut all angle braces. Hitch a rope to the center of the wall. On long walls, two ropes

7-32 *Lowering a girt*

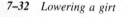
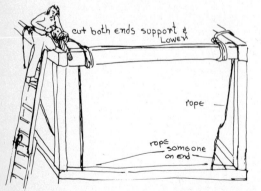

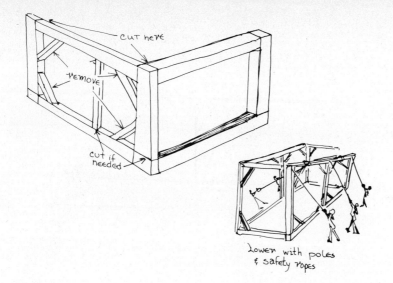

cut here

remove

cut if
needed

Lower with poles
& safety ropes

may be needed. The entire wall is pulled over at once. Sometimes it may be necessary to cut through the mortises at the bottom of the uprights or studding before the wall will move. If you do this, be sure to release the tension on the rope first. Cut carefully and stand well clear of the post, to avoid both pinching the saw bar and being struck by a post, which can kick back with lethal force. Repeat this procedure on both end walls, pulling them over onto the deck if necessary to avoid striking adjacent buildings. The last remaining side wall is pulled down and the deck cleared. Each wall should be disassembled and cleaned up before the next is brought down. Timbers break when they fall against other timbers. The deck is cleared and the flooring torn up and joists removed.

Larger barns with more than one level to the plate are framed from a basic unit called the *bent*, which is joined to the other bents by purlin-type girts and plates. These bents are disassembled much as principal-rafter trusses are. Once the rafters are removed, the purlin girts and plates are sawn through (temporarily braced if necessary) and the entire bent pulled over at once with a truck or tractor. The purlins are cut and lowered and the next bent started down.

Store salvaged timbers with care. They should never touch the ground. Instead, rest them across skids made of shorter timbers supported on concrete

7–34   *Pulling over a bent*

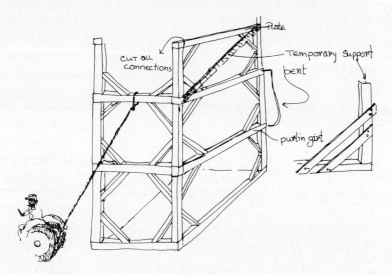

cut all
connections

Plate

Temporary support

bent

purlin girt

blocks. It is best to level these skids to prevent the beams from warping or twisting. Insert 2 × 4 stickers between each course of beams to prevent them from touching. Turn the beams so mortise pockets are not facing upward to fill with rainwater and rot. Sunlight will soon weather the beams to grey. If you don't want them to weather, cover them with a tarpaulin. The same treatment should be given to all salvaged boards. Handle weathered boards with care, as they are easily scratched. These scratches not only mar the finish but lower the resale value.

Chances are good that a demolition job will result in more lumber than you can use. This is money in the bank as long as you have a place to store the surplus. If you don't have a storage area, don't get involved in house wrecking. You will rarely sell lumber as fast as you can take it down. There is always a market for used building materials, particularly hand-hewn beams. Protect your investment by storing it properly. The pile will keep for years, as a hedge against future projects, or it can be sold off during times of tight money. You certainly won't make a fortune tearing down buildings, but it is possible to make a living at it if you do it on a regular basis and to cover your expenses and earn free building materials if you do it only occasionally. Consider hiring help to do the dirty work. This may be cheaper than doing it yourself if you have another source of income that earns you more than your help costs.

The Local Sawmill:
A source of lumber and lore

Your local sawmill is a resource not to be underestimated. Unfortunately, sawmills are no longer a common feature of the urban landscape, as all the timber lands have been paved over for shopping centers. The city dweller or suburbanite has no choice but to purchase materials from a lumberyard. The same thing is true of areas where there is no natural timber. Out on the prairies and the deserts, timber is imported. The settlers followed the Indians and built with what was available—sod and adobe. Adobe is being rediscovered as the practical material it is. So is native lumber.

Strangely enough, the politics of lumber are such that city dwellers can purchase lumber at a lower cost than their rural counterparts can. For New Englanders, that is true even when the lumber has originated in their own back yard. Native lumber is not approved for use in FHA-financed housing, which represents a large percentage of all new housing being built. The FHA doesn't actually outlaw native lumber. It simply requires that all framing lumber be stress graded. This commendable attempt to insure quality requires the presence of a federal inspector at the sawmill. Few local eastern sawmills (almost all eastern mills are ''local'') have the resources or business volume to support this program, and consequently, native lumber is shipped out to large buyers who do grade it and then dry it and sell it back to the natives at a higher price. The western lumber lobby, which represents some truly gigantic corporate interests, has a stake in seeing that this requirement is not amended to allow native lumber to undercut their lucrative New England market. Also, since places like Vermont are at the end of the transportation lines, lumber and building materials coming into the ports of Boston and New York from the West Coast must carry an additional markup when they are shipped north. The urban builder benefits not only from the volume discounts available because of high turnover at large discount building supply emporiums but also from proximity to port of arrival.

The rural builder who is not limited by the constrictions of FHA financing can benefit by using the products of his local sawmill. Lumber can be purchased from the source at a 30-to-50-percent discount. There are also other benefits beyond the purely economic that are part of patronizing your local mill.

Lumbermen are unique people. They have seen horses replaced by huge skidding machines and tree-chopping behemoths, muscle power by chain saws, the physics of ingenuity by brute mechanical force. They are as hard as a spruce knot, with a wit pungent as pine gum, and the fierce individuality and tenaciousness of the yellow birch clinging to a bitter rock ledge. Their hearts burn with the same rich heat as a block of good, hard maple. A lumberman can teach you more about wood and the grain of life than years of schooling and reading ever will.

Sitting by the stove in the machine shed on one of those brittle cold days when the motors refuse to start, when wood shatters like ice cubes if struck, one has time to dilate, to talk without shouting above the roar of the machines. The old man sharpens the teeth of the sawblade, his eyes squinting, ice blue and bright, to measure the file stroke, as keen as any micrometer. He keeps cadence with the rasp of metal on metal, the counterpoint of tobacco juice splattering on the stove grate as he tells how it was when they logged off the back of Bean Mountain the winter of '32, of the horse teams and the loads of logs they pulled, the heavy sleds crashing down the snow-packed slopes, you got to keep a sharp edge, whether it be chisel or sled runner, you can't work without a sharp edge. That's all the difference, in the edge . . .

He uses a band saw to cut his lumber instead of the more common circular saw. The blade makes a thinner cut, it figures out to about 10,000 board feet each year in sawdust alone. His lumber shows this same keen attention to detail, straight and square, planed mirror smooth, without burn or gouge. The floor of his mill is worn smooth from the grit of bark and boot and clean enough to eat off of.

There are trees that have grown by themselves at the edge of a field. Unhampered by competing trees, with no need to grow tall and straight, they send forth a wild aureole of branches, twisting and turning to follow the sun and wind. Lumbermen call these trees bullish. A log from a bull pine will be full of knots and twisted grain, its lumber difficult to saw and hard to use. There are lumbermen like these bull trees: men who shove logs through the saw, who breathe diesel fumes and drink machine-oil coffee, men who are one with the noise and tenor of their rumbling machines, who shout over their bacon and eggs to be heard above the whine of the coffee pot and the roar of the frying pan. These men fix things with a hammer. If it can't be fixed with the hammer they have, they find a bigger hammer. The lumber such a fellow produces is as novel as his politics. "Ole thick and thin," famous for his "four-dimensional" lumber, fine for a barn or sugar shed, but pretty hard to fit into a house. Caveat emptor is the rule. Know what you are buying and what you need.

The Perils and Practices of Working with Green Lumber

Occasionally a lumberman will set aside a stock of logs or boards to air dry; the larger the mill, the greater the stock he can afford to carry. More often, the smaller mill, operating on a hand-to-mouth inventory system will turn out "pond-dried" lumber, wood that was standing on its roots the day before. Other than the sheer weight of the stuff as you move it about, working with green lumber presents no special difficulties so long as a few basic principles are observed. Hemlock, of course, seems to be about half water, showering you with each hammer blow.

Plaster or sheetrock should never be fastened to green lumber. As the wood dries it will shrink away from the nails, causing them to "pop" through the joint compound and the sheetrock itself. Lumber will always shrink more across the grain than it will along its length. Thus green boards used for casing or finish paneling will develop gaps at their joints. A door jamb nailed directly to a green heavy-timber frame will open up, leaving a gap between the door and its weatherstripping as the timbers shrink. Uprights will not shrink in a critical dimension; the wall may become thinner overall, but not shorter. The weight of the wood upon itself keeps it tightly together as the plates and shoes shrink. The building will settle a half inch or so without any appreciable effect.

Nails drive more easily in green lumber but only have about 50 percent of the holding power they develop in dry wood. Galvanized nails seem to hold harder than bright steel nails, and although no concrete evidence has ever been submitted to prove this, any carpenter will swear by the shaft of his broken hammer that it is true. If the board is actually frozen, it can shatter, like ice struck with a pick, as you attempt to nail it—a good reason to avoid working with green lumber outdoors in the winter.

Green lumber should always be stored and stacked level and well stickered, preferably out of direct sunlight, or covered by a tarp, which allows the sides of the stack to ventilate. The topmost layer of boards will twist like pretzels in the oven if left unprotected. Because native woods are ungraded, there are bound to be pieces that are structurally worthless in every batch. As you sort through the pile, be wary of using any pieces with splits or large knots where they will be called upon for support. Cut them up for blocking, fillers, or jack studs under window sills. Avoid green wood for interior use until it has air dried inside the house for at least six months prior to use. Oil and water do not mix: A green board will not accept a stain or finish other than latex paint (and that poorly).

Even the best sawn rough lumber will vary enough in width and thickness to make accurate modular calculations impossible. The many small differences will compound themselves into increasingly greater inaccuracies by the time you reach the roof. It makes sense to pay the extra cent or two a board foot for planed lumber, unless you are building a very rough shed where economy is more important than accuracy or are matching existing rough-lumber studding. Planed lumber will be true in all dimensions. Its smooth surface will be easier on your marking pencil and your eyes. Be sure to measure the actual size of the lumber module. Western kiln-dried lumber of a nominal 2 × 4 size is milled to an actual size of 1½ × 3½-inches. Native air-dried lumber is milled to 1⅝ × 3⅝ inches on the theory that when it shrinks it will be about the same size as western lumber. The actual size of the lumber can vary mill to mill as much as ¼ inch. Do not take its size for granted.

When a log is sawed into lumber, a slab is cut off the round edge. These slabs are often free for the hauling or for a very slight charge at many mills. Cut up, they make excellent kindling or, if they are hardwood, fairly decent firewood. Used whole length, they make a serviceable and pleasing-to-look-at fence for gardens and small pastures. The slabs are nailed directly to fence posts driven on 8-to-10-foot centers with 8d or 16d galvanized nails. Start at the bottom rail with the thickest slabs first and allow them to thin down as you reach the top rail. A four-rail fence will keep in most animals, and a strand of barbed

wire stapled between the bottom gaps will keep in lambs and piglets as well as horses, sheep, and goats. Slabs should be nailed flat side to the post on the inside of the area to be fenced. (A horse pushing against a fence nailed to the outside of a post will eventually work it free from its nails.) The slabs need not be cut to length to fit between each post but instead are laid full length and nailed together at the overlap with protruding nails clinched over. By matching thin tapers to each other and butts to butts, you obtain a pleasing flow in the line of the fence rails. Each course should fill in the gap formed by the taper of the previous course to keep the fence rails running more or less level and evenly gapped. Where thick butts are to overlap, saw a rough half-lap into each end of the butts with your chain saw and splice together.

Such fences take considerable time to set up, but the material itself (other than fenceposts, unless you grow cedar on your land) is free. Gates are built from vertical slabs nailed over horizontal boards for lightness and strength. An entire fence can also be built using vertical slabs nailed over sapling top and bottom rails, poles, or boards.

There's more to a sawmill than just lumber. The bark left by the debarker that some mills use is excellent for a permanent mulch around foundation plantings and garden paths. The sawdust and planer shavings are much in demand as an absorbent and warm bedding for livestock. Yet none of this even matches the treasure that your local sawyer himself can be.

> The next true being of Buddha-nature that you meet may appear as a bus-driver, a doctor, a weaver, an insurance salesman, a musician, a chef, a teacher or any of the thousands of roles that are required in a complex society—the many parts of Christ's body. You will know him because the simple dance that may transpire between you, such as handing him change as you board the bus, will strengthen in you the faith in the divinity of man. It's as simple as that.
>
> [Baba Ram Dass, *Be Here Now*]

> Every man loves his native state, whether he was born there or not.
>
> [*old Vermont proverb*]

SECTION 4 **TOOLS: SOME THOUGHTS AND SOME PICTURES**

The Sanskrit root of the word "man" is related to the word for "measure." The first tool was the mind, the rational mind, which filters the seamless whole of the universe into discreet quanta of information that can be manipulated and processed. Each idea is a point along the linear projection from beginning to end. The mind's line is the arrow's flight, the rocket's terrible trajectory. The first astronauts sat huddled around the dim glow of the cave fire, chipping at flints with stone axes. Tools are the handles of the mind, the levers by which we *manipulate* reality. A tool itself, the rational mind is only a vehicle, a gate valve, which controls the flow of energy from without to within. There is a purpose that controls a tool and a mind that operates beyond our rational mind.

In the hands of a craftsman, a tool transcends the arbitrary convenience of subject and object, worker and work piece. It pierces through the linear veils into the timeless void within each form. In the hands of a fool, a tool only multiplies that sad division.

We carry within us dim and shifting intuitions of greater perfections beyond those normally seen or experienced on earth. We try to grasp them while remaining in our everyday consciousness and attribute our failure to the assumption that they must have been pure conjecture, astral fantasy, or wishful thinking and suffer for want of giving them expression in ourselves, for they are knocking at our door, offering to fertilize us with their bounty, and our feeling of slipping failure is nature's way of reminding us of the urgency of fulfilling this imperative human need.   [Pir Vilayat, *Toward the One*]

These words of the Sufi mystic, Pir Vilayat, remind us that tool implies a *telos* or purpose. A tool is used with (for) purpose. The house is a tool for living. We rebuild ourselves as much as we rebuild walls and roofs. The tools we use to accomplish this task should be selected and maintained with the same care we give to grow our gardens. There are those who find their meditations disturbed by the speed and noise of power tools, purists who eschew the smoke and roar of the chain saw for the flash and clean bite of the ax and the song of the crosscut saw. A tool is only a tool. There is a dance for chain saws as well as the hand ax.

There is nothing good or bad but thinking makes it so.
[William Shakespeare, *Hamlet,* act II, scene 2]

You can do a lot with a Skilsaw.® (The Skil Company, like the Thermos Company, has succeeded so well with its product that the brand name has become, among carpenters, the generic name.) There are miter guides, cut-off guides, rip guides, and a host of attachments to increase the accuracy and versatility of this tool. But ingenuity notwithstanding, even a skilsaw has its limits. After a while, the setup for the jigs takes longer than the work they perform. And the saw ultimately is a hand tool, limited in its accuracy by the skill of the user and the steadiness of the user's hand.

You can build an entire house with only a level, saw, square, tape measure, and chalk line. Why not? Our forefathers built theirs with only an ax. But of course they used the ax only out of necessity—it represented the upper limits of the technology available to them. If they had had the choice, how many

of them would not have used a chain saw instead? Where is the cut-off point? When does a table saw or radial arm saw become a necessity? There is no real necessity, other than that which you create for yourself. Applied to the mundane level of karmic action, this means that the attainment of accuracy will be infinitely easier, if that is your goal, and the process much faster, if that is your need, if you invest in a bench saw to do your finish work.

Accuracy with hand tools is the result of patience, self-discipline, and years of experience. The apprentice system of the Middle Ages (which still exists in some cultures today) saw to it that this skill developed at the proper pace. One must attain complete control and yet surrender entirely to the tool in order to work with it. Some of that control is built into a modern power tool like the bench saw. It compensates the user for lack of patience with its speed and machine-consciousness. Working with hand tools is meditative because there is no other way to do the job. Boredom or lack of attention is the root of poor work. A power tool frees the user from the requirement of extreme focus and concentration. Insofar as this liberates the user to focus his attention onto higher things, it is valuable. Insofar as the power tool allows its user to become another machine, it is a curse. The tool always remains neutral, it is the spirit in which it is used that invites judgment.

Following is a compendium of the basic hand and power tools a rebuilder might find useful or necessary to his task. Tools are grouped according to function. (See Figure 7–35.)

CARPENTRY TOOLS, THE BASIC HOME BUILDER'S TOOLBOX

20-ounce steel-shank, straight-clawed hammer (framing)
20-foot carpenter's sliding measuring tape, 100-foot tape
Nail apron, hammer holder
Pencils
4-foot level, 2-foot level
Framing square with rafter tables
Chalk line, string, plumb bob
Combination square
Cat's paw
Utility knife
Handsaw, 8-point crosscut, 12-point finish
Auger and bits
Pry bar
Chisel set
Block plane, jack plane, Surform® plane
Nail set
Screw drivers, Phillips and slotted head
Sledgehammer
Bevel square
Staple gun or hammer
½-inch square-drive socket set
One pair sawhorses
A good 6-foot stepladder

POWER TOOLS (HAND)

Circular saw (skilsaw) 7¼ inch with choice of blades
⅜-inch variable speed drill and wood and metal bits
Sabre saw
Power sander, orbital type
Reciprocating saw
Chain saw

POWER TOOLS, STATIONARY (BEST BOUGHT USED)

> Bench or "table" saw, 10-inch blades
> Radial arm saw (for the serious home cabinetmaker)
> 6-inch jointer-planer (for the serious home cabinetmaker)

SHEETROCKING TOOLS

> Aluminum hod
> 6-inch taping knife
> 4-foot square (also useful for marking sheathing, plywood, etc.).
> 14-inch taping paddle

PLUMBING TOOLS

> Open-end wrench set
> Vise grips
> Channel-lock pliers
> Pipe wrench, 14-inch
> Basin wrench
> Tubing cutter
> Propane torch
> Hacksaw

ELECTRICAL TOOLS

> Wire strippers
> Insulated pliers
> Screwdrivers
> ½-inch electric drill and auger bits
> Keyhole saw
> Test light

ROOFING TOOLS

> Good 28-foot wood extension ladder
> Staging planks
> Tin snips
> Staging brackets

MASON'S TOOLS

> Trowel
> Wire brush
> Joint striker
> Brick hammer
> Chisel
> Mortar hoe
> Wheelbarrow

HOUSE WRECKING TOOLS (AND REBUILDING)

> Crowbars
> Pry bar
> Come-along
> Ropes
> 6-foot crowbar
> 4-pound hammer

GENERAL

> Spade shovel, long and short handled
> Rake
> Ax, for splitting
> Splitting maul and wedges
> Pickax
> Peavy

Carpentry Tools

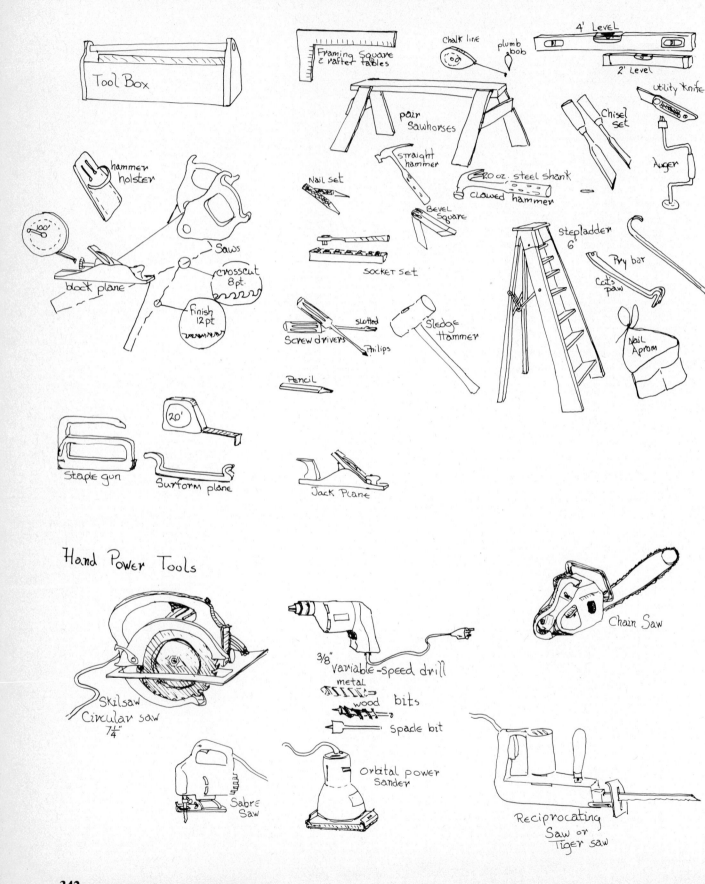

Tool Box

Framing Square & rafter tables

Chalk line

plumb bob

4' Level

2' Level

utility knife

pair Sawhorses

Chisel Set

Auger

hammer holster

straight hammer

Nail set

20 oz. steel shank

clawed hammer

Stepladder 6'

Pry bar

Cat's paw

block plane

Saws

crosscut 8 pt.

finish 12 pt

Bevel Square

socket set

Sledge Hammer

Nail Apron

Screw drivers

slotted

Philips

Pencil

Staple gun

Surform plane

Jack Plane

Jack Plane

Hand Power Tools

Chain Saw

Skilsaw Circular saw 7¼"

3/8" variable-speed drill

metal

wood bits

spade bit

Sabre Saw

Orbital power sander

Reciprocating Saw or Tiger saw

Power Tools
Stationary

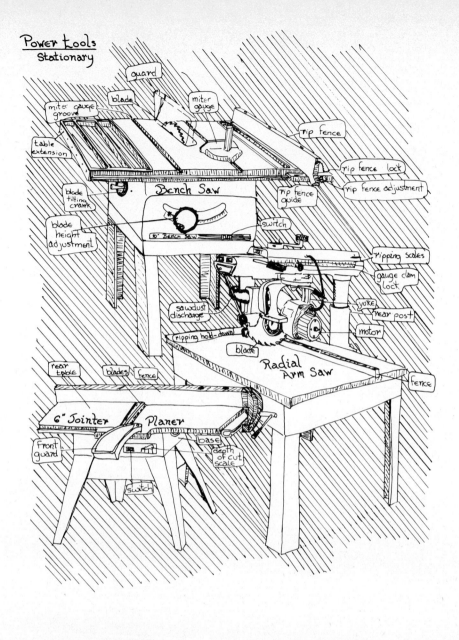

guard

blade

miter gauge

miter gauge groove

rip fence

table extension

rip fence lock

rip fence adjustment

Bench Saw

blade tilting crank

rip fence guide

blade height adjustment

switch

10" Bench Saw

ripping scales

gauge clam lock

sawdust discharge

yoke

rear post

motor

ripping hold-down

blade

Radial Arm Saw

rear table

blades

fence

fence

6" Jointer Planer

Front guard

base

depth of cut scale

switch

Sheetrocking Tools

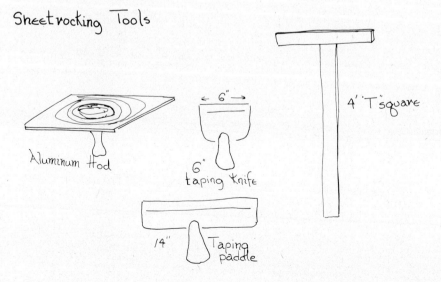

Aluminum Hod

← 6" →

6" taping knife

4' 'T' square

14" Taping paddle

Plumbing Tools

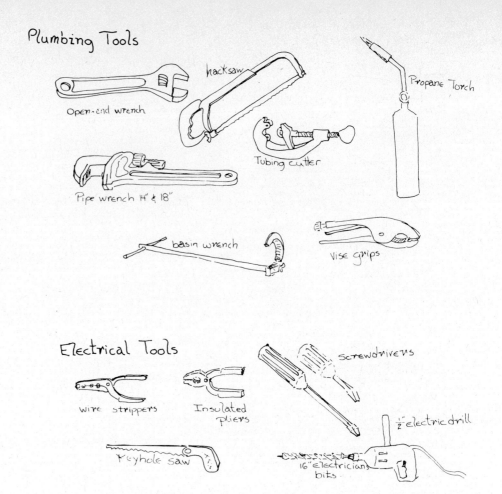

Open-end wrench

hacksaw

Propane Torch

Tubing cutter

Pipe wrench 14" & 18"

basin wrench

Vise grips

Electrical Tools

wire strippers

Insulated pliers

screwdrivers

Keyhole saw

16" electrician's bits

½" electric drill

Roofing Tools

28' Extension Ladder

staging bracket

Staging plank

Tin Snips

Mason Tools

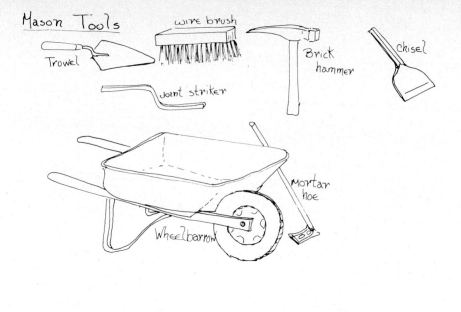

Trowel

wire brush

Joint striker

Brick hammer

chisel

Mortar hoe

Wheelbarrow

House-Wrecking tools (& rebuilding)

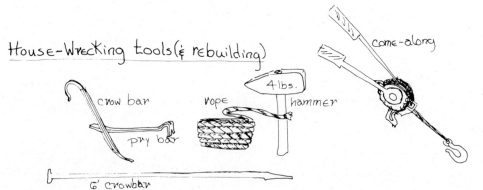

come-along

crow bar

pry bar

rope

4 lbs. hammer

6' crowbar

General

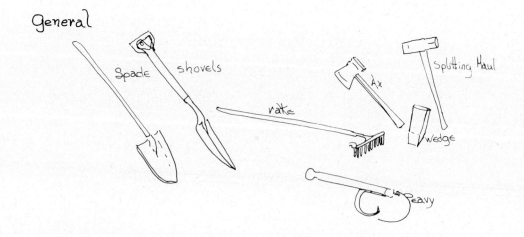

Spade

shovels

rake

Ax

Splitting Maul

wedge

Peavy

Fireside Reflections on Building Design as a Political and Moral Choice:
The house as meditation

I've often thought that if it were possible to choose another life, in another time, I would be a master builder for a medieval cathedral. In the period when the great cathedrals were built, the builders coordinated an undertaking that involved the resources and spirit of an entire community for generations. Today, there are no shared undertakings, no overarching visions. Tradition has disintegrated, like the mortar in an old chimney: The moral order has been replaced by the technical order, intuitions with institutions, beatitudes by bureaucracy. We have only the shards of personal mythologies. We build our cathedrals in our back yards and find transcendence at the hearts of our homes.

After a day of hard work, sleep is welcome, deep and dreamless. Sitting by the wood stove of a winter's evening a peace settles over me like an old quilted comforter. At this moment it seems possible to live like a pebble on a stream bottom, worn smooth and rounded by the flow, the rough edges, the bad dreams forgotten.

> I could be bounded in a nutshell
> And count myself king of infinite space.
> [William Shakespeare, *Hamlet*, act II, scene 2]

There is a danger inherent in individualism untempered by a sense of community that extends beyond itself. Individualism without responsibility or the recognition that we all live downstream from someone else is the root of the rapacity that can poison our planet. Fundamentally, the universe runs on a moral keel. If we are all one, what we do as individuals reverberates forever.

How does this relate to the rebuilder on the mundane level? What we feed our family dog each year could support a family in India; does that mean that we shouldn't keep dogs? I don't think so. But it might mean that you should think very hard about using a material like aluminum or vinyl siding to refurbish your dwelling. The products of high technology have one characteristic in common—they require a prodigious amount of energy for their production and transportation, involve the consumption of nonrenewable resources at an alarming rate, and tend to pollute the environment. These materials are also increasing in cost. In fact, there seems to be a direct relationship between the costs of a material and the damage done to the earth to produce it. Processed materials also appear to have a short useful life span. Plastics, for example, once heralded as the salvation of housing in the future, disintegrate in the light of day. Their use is confined to specialized applications, such as insulation of houses and wire.

Wood is a renewable resource. The earth gives itself to us for our use. To use it gently requires patience and skill; the result is a house that lives in harmony with its materials. Feel a piece of wood, absorb its grain and texture: It is a living material. Now meditate on a piece of vinyl or aluminum. These processed materials, like white flour, have had the life ground out of them. Because they have no soul, they give nothing back to the craftsman who uses them; without any exchange, there is no joy.

Use natural materials, native materials, wood where available, stone, brick, earth, adobe, bamboo. Use processed materials as a last resort, where nothing else will fit the function. Examine the function first and decide if it is necessary. Try to use processed materials that are low on the energy scale—asphalt shingles, steel roofing, gypsum wallboard—materials whose manufacture involves a minimal disturbance of the environment and that are ultimately bio-degradeable. Use real boards instead of textured plywood.

The choices you make affect the flow of energy. No one will manufacture what no one uses. Energy is the distillation of the blood of the earth. We are responsible to this planet; our choices should not contribute to its further hemorrhaging. This is the ethic of husbandry, diametrically opposed to the ethic of consumption; use it new, use it old, use it again, or use it up and throw it away. The payoff is actually economic as well as karmic. Natural materials are less expensive to buy and use. Like wood or solar heating, they demand an involvement with the user. They require time. The time we have bought with our energy slaves is paid for by mortgaging our future. The time we spend reestablishing the link between ourselves and our sources is energy well spent.

Because natural, unprocessed materials reverberate with life, the structures they become share this vitality. Life is not regular: Contrast the pleasing variation of board-and-batten siding with the machined simulation of Texture 1-11® plywood siding. Plywood may be justified functionally because of its strength and utility for reasons of structural support, but it can never transcend the deadening modular regularity that is its hallmark and reason for being. Use it where it is hidden and useful, not as a travesty of something it can never be. The hardboard panelings discussed earlier are another example of this alienation—like artificial Christmas trees, they are a poor substitute for the real thing. Aluminum has no place in a house. As a siding material it has no heat-retaining value other than that gained by an insert of styrofoam insulation. It is a perversion of the very function that siding should perform. Its only reason for being is to avoid maintenance and the costs of painting, for which there is no excuse in the first place. Paints create particularly vile pollution during their manufacture. Their use should be strictly limited.

The perception of built form as beautiful or satisfying seems to be proportional to the organic nature of the materials used in its construction, i.e., its ''spiritual'' content. So much of monumental modern architecture is only momentarily satisfying, a game of the architect's ego, played with fashion rather than substance. Glass and steel are the archetypes of the soulless, of the environment of alienation. The architectural mentality seeks to encase nature's bountiful breast in a stainless steel brassiere, the tract builder settles for a pasteboard takeout box.

> If a man does, in fact, have certain inborn rhythms, biological rhythms, biological needs and responses, which are unchanging, a complete relativism becomes impossible and the built environment of the past may still be valid.
>
> [Amos Rapoport, *House Form and Culture*]

The forms of the past are vessels of accumulated sensibilities derived from the constraints of environment and an appreciation for the fruitful interaction between man and nature. Linear thinking is the devil's tool, that which minces the fullness of the world into an assembly of variables, sums, additions and subtractions and solutions, which spawn further problems. Goethe said it nicely when he had Mephistopheles, that archtechnician, describe himself as ''the Spirit which always negates'' (Der Geist der stets verneint). The technician chases the horizon with computer readouts, forgetting that parallel lines meet only in infinity.

A house is a creative tension, an interface between earth and sky. It recapitulates the tree from which its bones are fashioned. A tree is the image of the cathedral, the play of light in the lofty vaulting of the leaves and the soaring trunk thrusting out of the earth, carrying the sap and spirit far above gravity's dark embrace. A house is linear only in the narrow sense that wood has a grain, a linear direction, unlike stone and formed earth, which duplicate the roundness of earth. The nature of these materials dictates the form their use creates. Building with wood is the achievement of a balance between the fastness of the earth and that which drives the tree beyond it. As the tree tires, it returns to earth, the house slowly inclines toward the horizontal. A state of pleasing decay, the slow music of return, strikes in us the chord of our own mortality.

In the words of the Prophet:

> Build of your imaginings a bower in the wilderness ere you build a house within the city walls.
>
> For even as you have home-comings in your twilight, so has the wanderer in you, the ever distant and alone.
>
> Your house is your larger body.
>
> It grows in the sun and sleeps in the stillness of night; and it is not dreamless. Does not your house dream? and dreaming, leave the city for grove or hill-top?
>
> Would that I could gather your houses into my hand, and like a sower, scatter them in forest and meadow.
>
> Would the valleys were your streets and the green paths your alleys, that you might seek one another through vineyards and come with the fragrance of earth in your garments.
>
> But these things are not yet to be.
>
> In their fear, your forefathers gathered you too near together. And that fear shall endure a little longer. A little longer shall your city walls separate your hearths from your fields.
>
> And tell me, people of Orphalese, what have you in these houses? And what is it you guard with fastened doors?
>
> Have you peace, the quiet urge that reveals your power?
>
> Have you remembrances, the glimmering arches that span the summits of the mind?
>
> Have you beauty that leads the heart from things fashioned of wood and stone to the holy mountain?
>
> Tell me, have you these in your houses?
>
> Or have you only comfort, and the lust for comfort, that stealthy thing that enters the house as a guest and then becomes a host, and then a master?
>
> Ay, and it becomes a tamer, and with hook and scourge makes puppets of your larger desires.
>
> Though its hands are silken, its heart is of iron.
>
> It lulls you to sleep only to stand by your bed and jeer at the dignity of flesh.
>
> It makes mock of your sound senses, and lays them in thistledown like fragile vessels.
>
> Verily the lust for comfort murders the passion of the soul, and then walks grinning at the funeral.
>
> But you, children of space, you restless in rest, you shall not be trapped or tamed.
>
> Your house shall be not an anchor but a mast.
>
> It shall not be a glistening film that covers a wound, but an eye lid that guards the eye.
>
> You shall not fold your wings that you may pass through doors, nor bend your heads that they strike not against a ceiling, nor fear to breathe lest a wall should crack and fall down.
>
> You shall not dwell in tombs made by the dead for the living.
>
> And though of magnificence and splendour, your house shall not hold your secret nor shelter your longing.
>
> For that which is boundless in you abides in the mansion of the sky, whose door is the morning mist, and whose windows are the songs and silences of night. [Kahlil Gibran, *The Prophet*]

BIBLIOGRAPHY

General Reading, Resources, and Ideas

Basic Building Data: 10,000 Timeless Construction Facts. Don Graf. 1949. Van Nostrand Reinhold Co., 450 W. Thirty-third St., New York, N.Y. 10001. $11.95. A smaller version of *Architectural Standards* and, despite the date of publication, very useful. Actually timeless reference source of standards and techniques on building practices, designed for the professional builder who is not an architect.

The Last Whole Earth Catalog and *The Whole Earth Epilog.* 1974. Point, Box 99554, Calif. 94109. $5 and $4, respectively. Still just about the finest general educational tools available. These catalogs are primary sources for access to information on methods, materials, and equipment.

Modern Carpentry. Willis H. Wagner. 1969. Goodheart-Wilcox Co. 123 W. Taft Dr., South Holland, Ill. 60473. $10.95. Designed as a textbook for vocational instruction, it is a wealth of clearly presented and well-illustrated information on every aspect of standard carpentry practice for residential construction. It will become your bible.

Public Works: A Handbook for Self-Reliant Living. Walter Szykitka. 1974. Links Books Div. Music Sales Corp. 33 W. Sixtieth St., New York, N.Y. 10023. $10. An encyclopedic compilation of information (most of it from government pamphlets) about almost anything a person would need to know about building his or her own life. If you could only afford to buy one book, this might be it.

Rainbook: Resources for Appropriate Technology. 1977. Schocken Books. 200 Madison Ave., New York, N.Y. 10016. $7.95. Another whole-earth-type catalog, containing a wealth of current listings in the field interspersed with well-written reviews and commentary.

The Reader's Digest Complete Do-It-Yourself Manual. 1973. Reader's Digest. Pleasantville, N.Y. 10570. $15.95. This book will pay for itself in what it saves you around the home. Handy for just about anything.

Chapter I

Don't Go Buy Appearances. George C. Hoffman. 1972. Ballantine Books. 457 Hahn Rd., Westminster, Md. 21157. $1.50. Tells you what to look for when you buy a house and how to make an accurate evaluation of its condition.

Addresses of publishers and prices are included in this bibliography for the convenience of readers who wish to order books by mail. It's a good idea to check prices before ordering, as they may change.

Finding and Buying Your Place in the Country. Les Scher. 1974. Collier Books. Order Dept., Front and Brown Sts., Riverside, N. J. 08075. $6.95. Written by a lawyer and tells you how to do exactly what the title states with a minimum of hassle and expense.

From the Ground Up. John Cole and Charles Wing, 1976. Atlantic–Little, Brown. 34 Beacon St., Boston, Mass. 02106. While primarily an excellent treatise on designing your own home, does contain much useful information.

How to Rehabilitate Abandoned Buildings. Donald R. Brann. Easi-Bild Pattern Co. Briarcliff Manor, N.Y. 10510. $3.50. A good book for the urban homesteader, as it deals with the problems of rehabilitating city buildings.

The Old House Journal. 188 Berkely Pl. Brooklyn, N.Y. 11217. $12 per year issued monthly. A magazine dedicated to "renovation and maintenance ideas for the antique house." Also provides the sources for that antique trim work or Victorian gingerbread molding.

Remodeling Old Houses (Without Destroying Their Character). George Stephen. 1972. Alfred A. Knopf. 457 Hahn Rd., Westminster, Md. 21157. $3.95. Contains excellent information on restoring city tenements and brownstones as well as wood-frame buildings.

The Restoration Manual. Orin Bullock, Jr. 1966. Silvermine Publishers. Norwalk, Conn. 06850. $12.95. A book for the restoration fanatic, devoted to ferreting out the original beauty of antique buildings and rescuing them from misuse and modernization.

Simplified Carpentry Estimating. J. Douglas Wilson and Clell M. Rogers. 1962. Simmons-Boardman Books. 30 Church St., New York, N.Y. 10007. $6.95. Shows you contractors' short cuts for figuring out how much material and how many dollars you will need to do a given job.

Chapter II

Early Domestic Architecture of Connecticut. Frederick Kelly. 1963. Dover Publications. 180 Varick St., New York, N.Y. 10014. $4. An excellent way to familiarize yourself with the basics of antique timber-framing systems, necessary to know when repairing your own.

Stone Masonry. Ken Kern, Steve Magers, Lou Penfield. 1976. Owner-Builder Publications. P.O. Box 550, Oakhurst, Calif. 93644. $6. For those who want to build a stone foundation the right way.

How to Work with Concrete and Masonry. Darrell Huff. 1976. Harper & Row, Pub. 10 E. 53 St. New York, N.Y. 10022. $3.95. If you plan to do your own concrete work when you replace the foundation, this is a good book for finding out how to work with this often intractable material. One of a series of Popular Science Skill Books, many of which are quite useful.

The Timber Framing Book. Stewart Elliot and Eugenie Wallas. 1977. Housesmith's Press. P.O. Box 416, York, Maine. 03909. $9.95. Actually tells you how to make the joints and frame a timber house from scratch. A good source book.

Chapter III

Roofing Simplified. Donald R. Brann. 1972. Easi-Bild Pattern Co. Briarcliff Manor, N.Y. 10510. $1.50. This little book does exactly what it says.

Wood Frame House Construction. L. O. Anderson. 1971. Craftsman Book Co. of America. 124 South La Brea Ave., Los Angeles, Calif. 90036. $2.75. An inexpensive and less extensive version of Wagner's magnum opus. Has particularly clear drawings and might be useful when you frame your new roof or dormer.

Chapter IV

In the Bank or Up the Chimney. U.S. Dept. of Housing and Urban Development. 1976. Chilton Book Co., Radnor, Pa. 19089. $1.95. This pamphlet is one of the best on *how* to insulate a house.

How to Do Your Own Home Insulating. L. Donald Meyers. 1978. Harper & Row, Pub. 10 E. 53 St., New York, N.Y. 10022. $3.95. Another title in the Popular Science Skill Book Series. Not only shows how to do it, but explains the theory and economics of insulation very well. Also covers caulking and weather stripping.

Low-Cost, Energy-Efficient Shelter for the Owner and Builder. Edited by Eugene Eccli. 1976. Rodale Press, Emmaus, Pa. 18049. $5.95. Both a design book and a reference book, with many good ideas for reducing the costs of heating and maintaining your home, particularly good on insulation and prevention of infiltration heat losses.

350 Ways to Save Energy (And Money) (In Your Home and Car), Spies, Konzo, Calvin, Thoms. 1974. Crown Publishers. 419 Park Ave. S., New York, N.Y. 10016. $3.95. A good book that asks some basic questions, such as, do you really need that dishwasher?

Chapter V

Section 1. Electricity
Do-It-Yourself Wiring Handbook. Sears Roebuck and Co. 50¢. A really great, clear, and concise booklet. You can wire a house using it as a guide.

Electrical Code for One and Two Family Dwellings. 1969. National Fire Protection Association. 60 Batterymarch St., Boston, Mass. 02110. $1.75. Another great bargain wiring guide.

Wiring Simplified. H. P. Richter. 1968. Park Publishing Co. P. O. Box 8527, Lake Street Station, Minneapolis, Minn. 55408. $1.25. And yet another.

Section 2. Plumbing
Audel Plumber's and Pipe Fitter's Library. 1966. Jules Oravetz, Sr. Theodore Audel Co. Div. Bobbs Merrill. 4300 W. 62nd St., Indianapolis, Ind. 46268. 3 Vols. $16. By no means exhaustive, and a little weak on modern materials, but good for cast-iron work.

Home Guide to Plumbing, Heating and Air Conditioning. George Daniels. 1973. Harper & Row, Pub. 10 E. 53 St., New York, N.Y. 10022. $3.95 Yet another Popular Science Skill Book. Good on trouble-shooting, easy to understand.

The Home Owner's Book of Plumbing and Heating. Richard Day. 1974. Bounty Books. 419 Park Ave. S., New York, N.Y. 10016. $2.98. The best book on plumbing for the homeowner.

The Practical Handbook of Plumbing and Heating. Richard Day. 1969. Arco Publishing Co. 219 Park Ave. S., New York, N.Y. 10017. $4.95. An earlier effort for a different publisher, pretty much the same stuff, good on plastic pipes.

Septic Tank Practices. Shelter Publications. Box 279, Bolinas, Calif. 94924. $2.50. All about the whys and wherefores of septic tanks.

Stop the Five Gallon Flush. Minimum Cost Housing Group. 1973. School of Architecture, McGill University. P.O. Box 6070, Montreal H3C, Canada. $2. A survey of alternatives to the conventional flush toilet and information on adapting or replacing present toilet systems.

United Stand Privy Booklet. 1972. United Stand. P.O. Box 191, Potter Valley, Calif. 95469. $2.50. How to build composting privies suitable for rural applications.

Section 3. Alternative-Energy Readings
Audel Mason's and Builder's Guide. Vols. 1 & 2. Frank D. Graham. 1924. Audel div. of Bobbs Merrill. 4300 W. 62nd St., Indianapolis, Ind. 46268. $11. The book for bricklaying techniques.

Bricklaying Simplified. Donald R. Brann. 1973. Easi-Bild Pattern Co. Briarcliff Manor, N.Y. 10510. $2.50. The prolific Mr. Brann is at it again, this time with a very clear and simplified approach to a complicated subject. A good book for beginners.

Electric Power from the Wind. Henry Clews. 1973. Solarwind Co. P.O. Box 7, East Holden, Maine 04429. $2. Read this if you're thinking about installing a wind generator. He's done it and distributes them also.

The Forgotten Art of Building a Good Fireplace.
Vrest Orton. 1969. Yankee, Inc. Dublin, N.H. 03444.
$2. This treasure of a book is based on the findings of
Count Rumford and will show you how to build a fireplace
that really works.

Heating Your Home with Wood. Neil Soderstrom.
1978. Harper & Row, Pub. 10 E. 53 St. New York, N.Y.
10022. $3.95. A very complete and up-to-date guide on
installing wood stoves and furnaces as well as combination
systems. Also includes good advice on chain saw use,
logging, and seasoning your wood. One of the best in the
Popular Science Series.

Home Guide to Solar Heating and Cooling. Jackson Hand. 1978. Harper & Row, Pub. 10 E. 53 St. New
York, N.Y. 10022. $3.95. Not only good on theory and
design information, but includes collectors' plans for
building out of everyday materials and installing them into
your home.

*Hot Water (Solar Water Heaters and Stack Coil
Heating Systems).* Scott & Chole Morgen and David &
Susan Taylor. 1974. Hot Water. 350 East Mountain Dr.,
Santa Barbara, Calif. 93108. $2. How-to-do-it plans.

*Other Homes and Garbage Designs for Self-
Sufficient Living.* Jim Leckie, Gil Masters, Harry White-
house, Lily Young. 1975. Sierra Club Books. 530 Bush
St., San Francisco, Calif. 94108. $9.95. An *engineering*
manual for alternative energy systems. Pages of formulas
and tables to help design solar, wind, and water power
systems; evaluations of site and design factors.

Solar Water Heater Plans. Steve Baer. Zome-
works Corporation. P.O. Box 712, Albuquerque, N.M.
87103. $5. Steve Baer's designs work. Adapted for the
cold and sunny regions of northern New Mexico; will be
suitable anywhere.

The Woodburner's Encyclopedia. Jay Shelton and
Andrew Shapiro. 1976. Vermont Crossroads Press.
P.O. Box 333, Waitsfield, Vt. 05673. $6.95. Compares
the different kinds of wood heaters for efficiency and
performance.

The Woodburner's Handbook. David Havens.
1973. Media House. P.O. Box 1770, Portland, Maine
04104. $3. A charming book and full of useful information.

Chapter VI

Cabinetmaking and Millwork. John L. Frier. 1967.
Charles A. Bennett Co. 809 W. Detweiller Dr., Peoria,
Ill. 61614. $16.95. It may even be worth the expense. A
big book, heavy on power tools, with a *Popular Mechanics* approach. Very complete.

The Complete Book of Woodwork. Charles H.
Hayward. 1972. Drake Publishers. 381 Park Ave. S., New
York, N.Y. 10016. $8.95. A good introduction for the
amateur cabinetmaker.

How to Do Your Own Painting and Wallpapering.
Jackson Hand. 1976. Harper & Row, Pub. 10 E. 53 St.
New York, N.Y. 10022. $3.95. If you have to paint your
house and want to know the best way to do it, this Popular
Science Skill Book will of course give you all the information
you would ever want to know. Includes material
on floor finishing.

Plastering Skill and Practice. F. Van den Branden
and Thomas L. Hartsell. 1971. American Technical Society. 848 E. 58th St., Chicago, Ill. 60637. $9.95. For
those who will settle for nothing less than the real thing,
this book will tell you how to do it.

Chapter VII

Generally Thought-Provoking Books
Handmade Houses: A Guide to the Woodbutcher's Art.
Art Boericke and Barry Shapiro. 1973. Scrimshaw Press.
149 Ninth Street, San Francisco, Calif. 94103. $12.95.
A beautiful book, with exquisite photographs of owner-
built houses. An inspiration for design, and indication of
possibilities.

The Owner-Built Home. Ken Kern. 1972. Charles
Scribner's. 597 Fifth Ave., New York 10017. $6.95. A
good idea book, with emphasis on designing to fit function,
it examines many of the preconceived notions about
building and finds them lacking.

Shelter. Shelter Publications. 1973. Mountain
Books, P.O. Box 4811, Santa Barbara, Calif. 93103. $6.
An amazing, mind-boggling look at building in a
cross-cultural context. A veritable compost heap of ideas.
It connects your own efforts with the greater patterns of
shelter-building as an archetypical human activity.

Planning and Remodeling
An Attached Solar Greenhouse. Bill Yanda. The Lightning
Tree. P.O. Box 1837, Santa Fe, N.M. 87501. $1.75.
Excellent step-by-step instructions for low-cost add-on
greenhouses, by a recognized expert in the field.

Audel Guide to Domestic Water Supply and Sewage Disposal. Edwin P. Anderson. 1960. Same address
as other Audel books. $4.50. Good on springs and wells.

Clean and Decent. Lawrence Wright. 1960. University of Toronto Press, 33 E. Tupper St., Buffalo, N.Y.
14203. $2.95. A fascinating history of the bath and toilet.
Makes interesting reading and gives useful insights into
our attitudes towards our bodily functions, sewers, and
bathing.

*DeCristoforo's Complete Book of Power Tools.
Both Stationary and Portable.* R. J. Cristoforo. 1972.
Harper and Row. Keystone Industrial Park, Scranton, Pa.
18512. $9.95. Tells you how to do just about anything
with a table and radial arm saw.

Hand Woodworking Tools. Leo P. McDonnell. 1962. Delmar Publishers. P.O. Box 5087, Albany, N.Y. 12205. $5. Very thorough.

How to Work with Tools and Wood. Robert Campbell. 1952. Pocket Books Div. of Simon and Schuster. 630 Fifth Ave., New York, N.Y. 10020. $1.25. Originally put out by Stanley Tools, it is a small basic classic.

Kitchens. The editors of *Sunset Magazine*. Lane Publishing Co. 1976. Menlo Park, Calif. 94025. $2.45. A bargain, like most Sunset books, full of good solid information and excellent photographs.

Living Lightly. Tom Bender. RAIN. 2270 N. W. Irving St., Portland, Oreg. 97210. $2. A discussion of energy flow in the home as seen in the light of appropriate technology.

The Organic Gardner. Catherine Osgood Foster. 01972. Vintage Books. Random House. 457 Hahn Rd., Westminster, Md. 21157. $2.95. One of the better and more readable books on the subject.

Planning for an Individual Water System. American Association for Vocational Instructional Materials. 1973. Engineering Center, Athens, Ga. 30602. $6.95. This is the book that tells you how to get the water from the ground to the house.

Plants, People and Environmental Quality. G. O. Robinette. 1972. Government Printing Office, Washington, D.C. 20402. $4.35. An interesting book on the relationship of people and plants, of home comfort and landscaping.

INDEX

Storm windows, 138, 139, 157, 158
Story pole, 143, 182–83
Stovepipes, 229, 230, 235–38
Stoves, wood-burning, 225–38
Straight-run stairs, 183
Strapping, 164–65, 169, 258, 267, 275
Stringers, 181–84
Strip shingles, 92, 93
Structolite, 251–52, 269
Structural evaluation, 12–26
  checklist, 12, 20
  contractors, 21–23
  exterior, 13–16
  interior, 16–18
  organizing priorities, 23–26
  property, 18–19
Structural timbers, replacement of, 68–78
Studs, 71, 173, 174, 176, 177
Styrofoam insulation, 167
Subfeed distribution, 192
Submersible deep-well pump, 319–20
Summer beam, 172
Sump pit, 44–45
Supply line, 206
Surform block plane, 248
Swale, 39

T

Tarpaper, 100–101, 103, 108–9, 166
Telephone service, 18
Temporary quarters, 31
Tenblend, 280
Termites, 15
Terne-metal roofing, 94
Thermopane windows, 138, 150, 153–54
Thimble, 235
Thomas, Wendell, 228
Three-tab shingles, 103
Thresholds, 159
Tiger saw, 129
Title insurance, 19
Toenailing, 148
Toilet drain, 17
Toilets, 212, 216–17, 294
Tongue-and-groove flooring, 271
Tongue-and groove paneling, 256–59
Tongue-and-groove siding, 146, 148
Tools, 338–45
Trading Post, 327
Transit level, 305
Trap doors, 185
Treads, stair, 181, 182
Tremco Company, 113, 137
Trim, exterior, 141
Trimmer joists, 182
Trimmers, 130
Troweling, 49

Turnbuckles, 62, 85, 86

U

UF type cable, 192, 193
Uniform National Plumbing Code, 205
Urea-formaldehyde insulation, 165, 167,
  169
Urethane:
  insulation, 167
  varnish, 292

V

Valleys, 105–6, 112
Vapor barriers, 139, 166–67, 170
Velux skylight, 127
Vent flashing, 112
Ventilation, 51, 115, 154–55
Vent stacks, 213
Vermiculite, 167
Vermont Casting Company, 241
Vermont Weatherboard, 262
Vertical-board siding, 149
V-groove siding, 146
Vinyl-asbestos flooring, 293
Vinyl-plastic gutter, 121
Vinyl siding, 140
Volts, 190
V-200 Auto-Vent, 213–14

W

Wagner, Willis, 49, 64, 125, 239–40
Wall cabinets, 281
Wallpaper, 253–54
Walls, 134–85
  doors, 157–62
  evaluation of, 17–18
  exterior siding and trim, 140–50
  foundation:
    evaluation of, 15, 16–17
    house jacking, 53–59
    leaning, 83–87
    repair of, 49–51
    replacement of, 51–53, 60–68
  functions of, 134–35
  infiltration and heat loss and, 136–40
  insulation and (*see* Insulation)
  interior finishes, 244–65
    novel, 264–65
    paint, 252–53
    plaster, 251–52
    sheetrock, 246–51
    wallpaper, 253–54
    wood paneling, 246, 254–63